NAPOLEON

AS A GENERAL

BY THE LATE

COUNT YORCK von WARTENBURG

COLONEL OF THE GENERAL STAFF OF THE PRUSSIAN ARMY

FORMING THE SEVENTH BOOK

OF

The Wolseley Series

EDITED BY

Major WALTER H. JAMES

VOL. II.

Printed and bound by Antony Rowe Ltd, Eastbourne

AUTHOR'S PREFACE

THE favourable reception given to my bold attempt to criticize Napoleon's strategical conceptions has served as a stimulus to me to complete the second part, which was indeed already far advanced despite of many difficulties which had to be encountered. I hope the reading public may give the same reception to this, the concluding portion. For the early appearance of the volume my thanks are due to Lieutenant v. Kameke, of the Emperor Alexander's Grenadier Guard Regiment, who has taken the trouble to draw the map of the Russian theatre of war.

I must repeat with regard to this part what I said with regard to the first. I have in no way tried to write an exact and complete history of the Napoleonic campaigns, but have confined myself to a consideration of the points which were necessary to form a proper judgment on the French General.

In the first volume I endeavoured to follow the course of the rising star of the General and to admire its constantly increasing brilliance. In the second I try to describe its path and show the inherent weaknesses which led to its decline from the zenith.

If in the first portion I seem to have yielded too much to the aspirations of the poet who said, "I love the man who strives beyond his might," I trust in the second I have not been oblivious of the warnings of the same writer :

> The man you choose is various and great,
> His deeds will serve you long for much reflection ;
> Yet strive to learn from his untoward fate
> He is not fitted as a model for selection.

CONTENTS

CHAPTER I.
SPAIN 1

CHAPTER II.
THE EVENTS OF RATISBON 29

CHAPTER III.
WAGRAM 60

CHAPTER IV.
THE INVASION OF RUSSIA 104

CHAPTER V.
MOSCOW 136

CHAPTER VI.
THE BERESINA 187

CHAPTER VII.
1813.
UP TO THE ARMISTICE 234

CHAPTER VIII.
DRESDEN 271

CHAPTER IX.

LEIPZIG 305

CHAPTER X.

THE CAMPAIGN IN FRANCE 370

CHAPTER XI.

THE GENERAL'S EXIT 420

INDEX 455

NAPOLEON AS A GENERAL

CHAPTER I.

SPAIN.

TILSIT had revealed to the amazed eyes of the world a height of power such as history had never seen united in the hands of any individual man since the times of Attila. All the states on the Continent were frightened and weakened, or had become humble vassals of the colossus; and he, with his hand on the map of Europe, exclaimed: "All this is mine, or will soon be mine; I can dispose of it already."[1] Russia alone seemed still to have some independence and self-assertion, but even she had been shaken by the powerful general, misled by the cunning politician, and he had only to display proper statecraft to make it his fully and permanently.

But the Emperor's thoughts were bent in another direction. It is the statesman's part to be patient, to wait for the right moment, to mature his plans and to delay action until such a moment. It is the general's never to postpone, but to take time by the forelock, because the way for him to attain his end lies in superior strength. For both statesman and general, however, it is of importance to seize the right moment; yet whilst the

[1] Lucian, Mém. iii. 113.

former employs for this mainly patience and calm calculation, the latter will succeed rather by passion and boldness. Of course the statesman cannot altogether dispense with passion nor the general with calculation; but in their actions these two feelings respectively will play a different part. The statesman will be more prone to fail through too much impatient boldness, and the general through too much cautious calculation.

Indeed at this very time the Emperor was to furnish a great example of how little his soul, striving impatiently for the empire of the world, could bear to wait for the right moment, and how little he himself justified his own dictum: " To choose the right time is the great art of man ; what is to be done in 1810 cannot be effected in 1807. Gallic nerves are not capable of submitting to this cool waiting for the right time, and yet by this capacity alone have I been so successful in all that I have done."[1] He could not look upon the conquests he had made hitherto as assured, and yet he was about to attempt new ones. With infinite cunning he laid the train for the seizure of Spain. The treaty of Fontainebleau facilitated the entry of his troops; he occupied the country and the capital. Then Bayonne gave up to him the royal family, the latter resigned their rights, and in their place he established Joseph on the throne of Spain.

But "these treaties were not confirmed by the Spanish nation";[2] it did not acknowledge the resignation of Charles and Ferdinand, but rose up unanimously against the foreign rule. Thus the Emperor was confronted by a new military task: the quelling of a general national rising in a large country, and indeed in one which, intersected as it is by irregular mountain chains, and provided with but an imperfectly developed system of roads, lent itself more readily to a successful guerilla war than any other in Europe. This was more especially the case as it was

---

[1] C. N. To Joseph. Osterode, 1st March, 1807.
[2] C. N. To Laforest. Paris, 7th November, 1810.

inhabited by a people simple in their bodily wants, but violent and easily excited, and moreover endowed with the strength afforded by separate provincial life, together with a full preservation of the feeling of unity. We will now enter upon a consideration of the manner in which the Emperor solved this problem.

His forces in the Peninsula towards the end of May, 1808, were distributed in the following way: Murat was at Madrid, invested with the chief command as the Emperor's representative; he had in and about the capital 30,000 men under Moncey; Junot with 25,000 men stood in Portugal; Bessières had 25,000 men, viz. 13,000 in Old Castile and 12,000 under Verdier in Aragon. In Catalonia there were 13,000 men under Duhesme, and finally Dupont was with 24,000 men on the Tagus in the neighbourhood of Toledo. At first the Emperor remained at Bayonne, watching thence the course of affairs on the Spanish theatre of war. He did not consider the situation in any way serious at the time, and thought he would quickly crush the rebellion, by despatching flying columns in different directions. He therefore advised his generals to resort to summary proceedings. "In this kind of war, retrograde movements are never any good. Such movements are dangerous in regular warfare; in a national rising they should never be employed."[1] Consequently he sent Moncey with 10,000 men to Valencia, Dupont with 9000 to Andalusia, and Bessières' troops to the various central towns of Old Castile and as far as Santander.

But the result was not what he had expected. Moncey failed before Valencia and fell back upon Alvacete; Dupont evacuated Cordova, after having captured that town, and retreated to Andujar; Bessières saw himself, owing to risings in Logroño, Palencia, and Valladolid, compelled to relinquish his enterprise against Santander. This last fact annoyed the Emperor; the attempt on

[1] C. N. To Bessières. Bayonne, 16th June.

Santander had been of importance in his opinion, for if any English army should land there, it might, by an advance along the Ebro, endanger the communications of his troops in Spain. In Aragon also the situation became more and more serious; there the resistance of the Spaniards found a rallying point in Saragossa and a powerful leader in Palafox. The French were compelled to bring up a siege-train, and Verdier undertook a regular siege of Saragossa with a newly-arrived corps of 6000 men, to which he added 2000 of his own men.

Now the Emperor began to examine the theatre of war more carefully, and to seek in his usual way the decisive point, where his main strength ought to be applied; columns detached in different directions no longer satisfied him now. "In civil war the most important points must be occupied; it is not enough to march in every direction."[1] And thus he fixed upon that point as the most important, to which his communications ran and whence the capital could be threatened. "If General Dupont suffered defeat, it would not be of any great consequence. It would have no other result than that of forcing him to cross the mountains again; but any defeat inflicted upon Marshal Bessières would be a thrust in the heart of the army, which would produce a sort of paralysis and be felt in its furthest extremities.... The object of all our efforts must be to hold Madrid. Everything is there. Madrid can only be threatened by the Army of Galicia."[2] "The most important point of all is the position of Marshal Bessières, as you will have seen in the note I sent you. You must do everything possible so that this corps may be forced to no retrograde movement, nor suffer any reverse. General Dupont is the next consideration. The affairs of Saragossa come next, those of Valencia only in the fourth place. This is the true state of military affairs in the kingdom."[3]

[1] C. N. Note for General Savary. Bayonne, 13th July. [2] Ibid.
[3] C. N. Note for the King of Spain. Marracq, 14th July.

Bessières was able later to drive the Spanish forces from Leon and Galicia, to the Emperor's great satisfaction, and things having thus taken a good turn on the most important point, the theatre of war to the south of the Sierra Morena assumed the first place in the Emperor's calculations. "To-day the only doubtful point is on the side of General Dupont, and here we need some success quickly,"[1] consequently he was reinforced up to 25,000 men. In spite of this, however, the Spaniards succeeded in surrounding him close to the Sierra Morena in the defile of La Carolina, and Dupont had to lay down his arms near Baylen with his whole corps.

This reverse had most important results. The first consequence was, that Madrid had to be given up, and that Napoleon became convinced that his own personal intervention at the head of the "Grand Army" was necessary, to bring about a decisive turn in the affairs of Spain. He expressed his views on the military situation in Spain, on the 5th August, in one of those "Notes," which he was fond of dictating in critical cases, both for the purpose of clearing up matters, and stating his own conviction, and also for the purpose of demonstrating the situation clearly to others. In that note he said the first thing to be done was to take up a position near Aranda on the Duero, with pickets on the Sierra de Guadarrama, whilst Bessières would keep up the communication with Junot *vid* Valladolid. Should this not be any longer possible, the French would have to concentrate near Burgos and fall back to the Ebro, and finally, if the worst came to the worst, the line Vitoria-Pampluna would have to be occupied, in order to keep open the issues from the Pyrenees for the approaching Grand Army. For the rest he exhorted his men not to lose courage immediately on account of a few unfortunate occurrences. "We must

[1] C. N. Notes on the present position of the army in Spain. Bayonne, 21st July.

not conduct the war timidly, nor suffer any massing of the enemy within two days' march of any army corps."[1] "Where is the soldier who has gone through even six months of war, who does not feel, that in such a situation one must be cautious of believing reports, which see the enemy everywhere and always through a magnifying-glass?"[2] Above all he warned his commanders not to adopt any system of cordons, which was effective against smuggling perhaps, but not against an enemy in the field; "shall we return to such nonsense after ten years' experience in war?"[3] in 1814 also we hear him reiterating the same view: "His Majesty does not approve of a line twenty leagues long; that may do very well against smuggling, but such methods have never met with any success in actual war."[4] He at once set eagerly to work to hasten the march of the Grand Army from Germany.

In the meantime the state of affairs became more and more serious on the Peninsula. In consequence of the battle of Baylen, Madrid was evacuated, as indeed the Emperor had anticipated, but the French army did not expect to be able to hold either the line of the Duero or Burgos, and it therefore fell back behind the Ebro, where it took up a position, 53,000 strong, near Miranda and Logroño, and, giving up the siege of Saragossa, fell back as far as Milagro; Duhesme also could no longer hold Catalonia, and had to withdraw all his troops to Barcelona. Still more unfavourable was Junot's position, after 14,000 English had landed in Portugal under Wellesley in the beginning of August. Junot's attack on the latter near Vimeiro failed, and his force too, cut off from its communications with Spain, had to surrender, on condition of being conveyed back to France by sea.

The retreat behind the Ebro and the purely defensive

---

[1] C. N. Note on the present situation in Spain. Rochefort.
[2] C. N. Memorandum for Berthier. St. Cloud, 16th August.
[3] C. N. Note for Berthier. St. Cloud, 16th August.
[4] C. N. To Maison. Paris, 20th January.

posture of the army aroused the Emperor's displeasure in a high degree. "It seems the army is commanded not by generals, who have had experience of war, but by post-office inspectors."[1] "These arrangements seem to be ill considered; ... this is the first time that an army has had to abandon all its offensive positions, in order to take up bad defensive positions; to pretend to choose their ground, whilst the distance of the enemy and the thousand and one various combinations possible, do not permit any chance whatever of guessing whether a battle will take place at Tudela, or between Tudela and Pampluna, or between Soria and the Ebro, or between Burgos and Miranda. ... As to the Ebro, it is less than nothing, and should only be considered as a line."[2] "The defensive position of the army of Spain is radically wrong. The position on the Ebro, and especially the important issues from the passes at Burgos, can only be held if you occupy Tudela. ... The proof of what we assert lies in the fact, that the least rumour renders the headquarters uneasy, for the army is not in a good position."[3] "It seems that in the direction of Burgos the army is without any system; ... the enemy will not march from Saragossa to Logroño if the offensive position of Tudela be occupied."[4]

According to the Emperor's plan, 16,000 men were to be at Tudela, the same number at Burgos, and the rest of the army between Logroño and Burgos; "you will understand the position of the army, ready to act on the offensive both with its right wing and its left wing."[5] But he rejected the plan of occupying Burgos only with cavalry, for "would not that be as much as telling the

[1] C. N. To Joseph. St. Cloud, 16th August.
[2] C. N. Notes on Spanish affairs. St. Cloud, 30th August.
[3] C. N. Note for Joseph, King of Spain. St. Cloud, 15th September.
[4] C. N. To Berthier. St. Cloud, 8th September.
[5] C. N. Note for Joseph, King of Spain. St. Cloud, 15th September.

enemy that we do not intend to hold the place, would it not even be as inviting them to come and take it?"¹ Still the Emperor did not wish to give any absolute orders with respect to any such measures, for "at a distance of 300 leagues and without any information as to the strength of the army, it is impossible to advise what should be done."² Finally he admonished him to obtain frequent news of the enemy, though after all the principal thing in his opinion was to adopt a posture strictly in accordance with circumstances, for after all what is heard in time of war is really of little value. "In wartime spies attach little importance to the reports they make; to rely upon them would be equivalent to risking men's lives upon very slender grounds."³

Joseph, who stood at the head of the troops in Spain, with Jourdan as his adviser, seeing himself constantly blamed by the Emperor on account of his defensive positions, now conceived the thought of collecting all his forces and advancing upon Madrid, sacrificing all his communications with France, and beating the enemy's armies wherever he might meet them. When he interpreted this monstrous plan to the Emperor, the latter only shrugged his shoulders and pointed to the difference between the deliberately bold action of a great general and the madly rash plan before him. "To change one's line of communications is the act of a genius, to lose it altogether is such a risky operation, that it renders the general, who perpetrates such an act, criminal. . . . Those who venture to advise such a measure would be the first to lose their heads, as soon as events laid bare the madness of their operations; . . . even with an army composed entirely of men like those of my own Guards, and led by the most able general, by an Alexander or Cæsar, one could not

---

[1] C. N. Note on Spanish affairs. St. Cloud, 30th August.
[2] C. N. Note for Joseph, King of Spain. St. Cloud, 15th September.
[3] Ibid.

answer for anything in the face of such stupid errors."[1] In addition he explained to him the difference which would have resulted from his remaining in Madrid with the army. "If one is in a besieged place, one has lost one's lines of communications, but not one's line of operation, because this latter runs from the glacis to the centre of the fortress;" and finally he said: "We must renounce this plan, for it is contrary to the laws of war."

Thus we see that the Emperor had to experience now, what he had already done in 1795, namely, that for the execution of the plans conceived by a genius, nay, even for their acceptance and appreciation, a mind of like gifts is necessary. Joseph and Jourdan were as little capable of doing this as Scherer and Kellermann had been; their strategical methods were different, and assuredly not superior to Napoleon's. The latter, however, was too well aware, that in order to be effectively carried out, a plan must be intellectually assimilated by the leader, to make even the attempt of interfering by definite orders from Paris, when his advice would be of no avail. He again and again explained the state of affairs and proposed such schemes as were feasible, but the rest he left to those who were on the spot, only prohibiting absolutely dangerous and false moves; for in spite of his violent temperament and his firm conviction of his own infallibility, he recognized too clearly the nature of the war, to attempt to introduce a procedure like that of the Imperial Military Council in Austria. In this respect the opinion he expressed in 1813 with regard to the Italian theatre of war is most characteristic of him: "One manœuvre which I suggest, which I do not advise, but which *I* would execute, would be. . . . I would do it myself, but I do not advise it, if you do not understand me. . . . But I do not advise this bold manœuvre, it is not my habit to do so; for one must understand and grasp all the details and measures necessary for its

---

[1] C. N. Note for the King of Spain. Chalôns sur Marne, 22nd September.

execution; as well as the end which has to be attained, and the blows which have to be struck, etc., etc."[1]

But even though Joseph was not able to coin the gold of Napoleon's advice, thus tendered, into deeds, yet that gold was not therefore wasted. On the contrary, every soldier who is desirous of improving his knowledge of strategy will always be able to turn this series of detailed and valuable notes to good account. By a careful study of the history of war, every one can now at any moment put himself in Joseph's situation, and having determined on the map his own views of the situation and the course he would adopt, the student can consult the most qualified critic by turning to Napoleon's notes, and he will thus learn a valuable lesson.

(69) In the meantime the troops intended for Spain were drawing near the frontiers of that country. The Emperor once more exhibited at Erfurt his power in all its threatening majesty, and gave evidence before the eyes of Europe of his friendly dispositions towards Russia, and then he hastened to the army, and arrived in Bayonne at 2 a.m. on the 3rd November. His army was composed as follows:—

Chief of the Staff: Berthier.

I. Corps:	Victor	. . .	29,000 men.
II. „	Bessières	. .	20,000 „
III. „	Moncey	. . .	24,000 „
IV. „	Lefebvre	. .	23,000 „
VI. „	Ney	. . .	30,000 „
VII. „	Saint-Cyr	. .	30,000 „
The Guards and Reserve Cavalry			35,000 „

The V. Corps, Mortier, 24,000 men, and the VIII. Corps, Junot, 19,000 men, did not arrive in Spain until later.

The army was disposed as follows: Lefebvre was at Bilbao, after having, on the 31st October, defeated and pursued Blake, who had advanced to attack him there;

[1] C. N. Instructions to General d'Anthouard. St. Cloud, 20th November, 11 a.m.

Victor, who thereupon had likewise advanced, was at Amurrio; Bessières at Miranda on the Ebro, with one division pushed forward as far as Pancorbo; Ney had driven the enemy from Logroño and stood there on the Ebro; Moncey was at Tafalla, observing the enemy's forces on the Aragon; Saint-Cyr, at La Junquera, on the road from Perpignan to Gerona, ready for the invasion of Catalonia and the relief of Duhesme, who with 10,000 men still held out in Barcelona. Finally the Guards and reserves were at Toulouse and Vitoria.

Opposed to them was the Spanish army, with its left wing, 32,000 men, at Valmaseda, under Blake; the latter had retreated to this place after the failure of his abovementioned attack on Lefebvre, and here La Romana had joined him with 8000 men from Santander. The centre, 25,000 men, under Castaños, was posted along the line Calahorra-Tudela; and finally the right wing, Palafox, 17,000 men, stood partly on the Aragon and partly at Saragossa. In front of Barcelona was Vives with 20,000 men; whilst behind Castaños in reserve at Burgos there were 13,000 men under Belvedere, and near Madrid further forces were in process of being collected.

The Emperor had hoped that the enemy, filled with confidence by the successes gained, would come within striking distance, when he might crush him; "the war might with one blow be brought to an end by some cleverly combined manœuvring, and for that it is not necessary that I should be present;"[1] and indeed the enemy's left wing exposed itself by its advanced and isolated position to such a blow. It was the Emperor's intention to push forward between it and the centre, and, turning it, to annihilate it; he therefore blamed Lefebvre for having repulsed this wing, before the other corps were in a position to execute this turning movement.

Still even now the extended line of the Spaniards exposed to the Emperor's eye weak points enough to

[1] C. N. To Joseph. Erfurt, 13th October.

allow him to hope to deal a decisive blow. He resolved to pierce the centre of their line by marching straight to Burgos and then attacking right and left both Blake and Castanos in the rear. Consequently Bessières received in the first place orders to advance on Burgos, whilst at the same time Lefebvre and Victor were to attack the enemy in front of them. The Spaniards had, however, on their part again resolved upon the offensive, and therefore on the 7th November the Northern wings of the two armies encountered each other at different points; the Spaniards were thrown back everywhere and retreated again to Valmaseda. The Emperor himself arrived in Vitoria on the 5th at half-past eight in the evening.

On the 8th Lefebvre and Victor advanced further in pursuit of Blake, who retreated to Nava; on the same day Bessières reached Briviesca; but his corps was handed over to Soult, he himself receiving the command of the cavalry reserve. The Emperor now issued orders that Bessières and Soult were to push forward to Burgos;. Ney and the Guards were to follow them, and Lefebvre and Victor were to continue in close pursuit of Blake, while keeping in touch with the army on the left side; Moncey was to remain on the defensive, with one division on the Aragon and the rest of his corps at Lodosa on the Ebro, and finally one of Ney's divisions, Lagrange's, at Logroño.

Thus the advance was continued on the 9th, and at 10 a.m., near Gamonal, Bessières and Soult encountered Belvedere, who had gone out from Burgos to meet the approaching French. But his hastily assembled troops were unable to resist the attacks of regular forces; they were overwhelmed and entirely dispersed, Burgos being taken and plundered. Lefebvre reached Villarcayo. In the afternoon of the same day, near Espinosa, Victor met Blake, who had taken up a good position there; he attacked him indeed with some success, but night put an end to the engagement. On the next morning it was resumed immediately day broke, and now Blake was completely routed and driven back in full flight, with most severe losses, to Reynosa. To this place Lefebvre likewise hastened from Villarcayo to join in the pursuit, whilst Soult was despatched by the Emperor from Burgos, in order to cut off Blake's retreat. The latter had at first collected his troops on the 12th at Reynosa, as well as possible, but when the appearance of Soult's cavalry made him aware of the danger to his right flank he retreated on the 13th hurriedly into the Asturias, where La Romana then collected the remains of his force, 7000 men, and took the chief command.

The Emperor had arrived in Burgos in the morning of the 11th and watched from there the success of the first half of his plan, the destruction of the enemy's left wing. In addition to having sent Soult to Reynosa, he had despatched Ney forward to Aranda, and his cavalry to Palencia, Valladolid and Madrid, in order to collect information and to discover any possible advance of further hostile corps. As nothing was heard of any such movements, he resolved that it should now be the turn of Castaños, so that the second half of his plan of campaign might be carried out.

The following arrangements were, therefore, made: Soult was to subjugate the province of Santander and to occupy the town of this name; Victor was moved up to Burgos, where the Emperor was staying with his Guards; between Burgos and Soult Lefebvre took up a position near Carrion-de-los-Condes, to act as a link and to reconnoitre in the direction of Leon and Valladolid. Thus the Emperor would keep the centre and the right wing near him, whilst the corps of the left wing were to deal the blow against Castaños. Therefore Ney, who had arrived two days before in Aranda and opened thereby the road to Bessières' cavalry over the Duero to Madrid, received orders on the 18th to march up the Duero to Soria, from which place he was to attack Castaños in the rear. Lannes, who had been entrusted with the chief command over the forces left behind in Navarre, the corps Moncey and the division Lagrange, was to attack him frontally towards Tudela; Bessières remained at Aranda.

Between the two commanders of the Spanish right wing, Castaños and Palafox, there reigned the most absolute want of agreement as to their views, and both conceived alternately the most extraordinary plans, without, however, anything being actually done. In the meantime the Emperor sent orders to Ney and Lannes to push forward against Castaños, and on the 19th the latter first obtained news of the advance of the enemy, both from the Ebro and from Soria. These reports were confirmed more and more during the next few days, and during the night of the 21st-22nd Castaños withdrew from Calahorra to Tudela. On the 22nd Ney arrived in Soria, and Lannes collected on the same day his forces near Lodosa. Thus Castaños was already seriously threatened on his flank and his position had become a very precarious one. But the Spanish leaders were unable to understand this, and, chiefly owing to the efforts of Palafox, the whole army remained stationary near Tudela in a very extended position as far as Tarazona.

At 9 a.m. on the 23rd November, Lannes, who had crossed the Ebro at Lodosa, appeared in front of the Spanish lines and made his onslaught on the isolated right wing, which consisted of the Aragonese under Palafox in a position on the heights above Tudela; this wing was pierced and driven back in disorder upon Saragossa. But whilst the left wing, posted at Tarazona, also began its retreat in consequence towards Borja, Ney's cavalry appeared from Soria; the Spanish popular levies were unfit to resist this threatening movement, they became disorganized and sought hurriedly to escape by flight towards Calatayud. Ney could undoubtedly have completely prevented this retreat, if he had without delay continued his march from Soria. But, owing either to a want of appreciation of the situation, or for other reasons, he remained stationary at Soria, both on this day and on the 24th, in spite of the most urgent representations of Jomini, his chief-of-the-staff. Thus Castaños succeeded in collecting the greater portion of his forces again at Calatayud and withdrawing afterwards to Siguenza; Palafox having meanwhile, as mentioned already, retreated to Saragossa.

If, while considering the campaign of Friedland, we were forced to come to the conclusion, that we recognized there a violation of the great strategical principles which had up to then always guided the Emperor and led to his successes, the planning of this first campaign in Spain proves that there was no general diminution of his strategical judgment and his powers of combination; indeed these are in most brilliant evidence. With the Spanish forces extended over a distance of 190 miles in wide formation and little capable of any real resistance, to pierce the centre was, on the one hand, sure to succeed most easily, and on the other hand, the danger connected with it, namely, the immediately closing up of the wings in the direction of the threatened point, was but little to be apprehended. Quite logically therefore the Emperor chose here the same strategical methods of attack with which the young General Bonaparte initiated his brilliant career, namely, piercing the enemy's centre. We shall see the same again employed in 1812 in the most magnificent and well thought-out manner, and once more in the opening of the last of all of Napoleon's campaigns.

If in this method there exists undoubtedly, as we have already pointed out, the danger of being surrounded by the two wings of the enemy, this danger can be met only by dealing the blow, which is to pierce the enemy's centre, in a specially resolute and vigorous way, and by immediately, without hesitation or loss of time, hurling the mass of the army upon the enemy's separated wings in succession. For "in the art of war, just as in mechanics, time is the great element between weight and force."[1] On this very account, however, we can say that this was the method which corresponded most to the Emperor's bold, restless and self-reliant genius. So we note here, how he carried his piercing blow at once as far as Burgos, pushing the mass of his forces thereby even beyond the separated Spanish wings to their very rear. At Burgos he stood both against Blake and also more especially against Castaños, in the same position as in 1805 against Mack and in 1806 against Brunswick.

But the result was by no means the same. It is true, under the French attacks Blake's army became disorganized, but when Soult advanced it was already on the retreat, and he could no longer get on its flank and rear, so as to cut it off altogether from its communications. Castaños was even able to withdraw a considerable portion of his army in a condition fit for further fighting, although his retreat was already most ominously endangered. In spite of the excellent initiation of the campaign, we cannot but recognize a want of energy in its conduct on the part of the Emperor. If we recall with what untiring, nay almost superhuman energy the general of Montenotte and Dego, of Castiglione and Rivoli managed to be always personally present where the decisive blow was to be struck, we must wonder why the Emperor now stopped in Burgos, leaving his subordinate officers to deal the blows that were to annihilate Blake and Castaños. Had he himself been at Soria, as he would have been in 1796, he would have moved up Ney in Castaños' rear, or had Ney known that the Emperor was personally fighting a battle at Tudela, he would undoubtedly have hurried up and Castaños would have been annihilated. We miss in the execution of the plan, that ceaseless anxiety and restlessness, that constant desire not to lose

[1] C. N. Note on the defence of Italy. Valladolid, 14th January, 1800.

a moment, which were in such a high degree this great general's characteristics. We are led to say that only nervous and excitable natures with vivid powers of imagination can achieve great results, and these were mental attributes which the youthful Bonaparte possessed in a marked degree.

The Emperor left Burgos on the 22nd November and advanced further to Aranda on the Duero, where he arrived on the 23rd. There he awaited the result of the operations directed against the right wing of the Spanish armies. On the 26th he received the news of Tudela, and though he could not be altogether satisfied with the result, yet he had gained from it room for the further prosecution of the operations. There now presented themselves, as we know the situation of affairs nowadays, two alternatives to the Emperor. He could march to Madrid, in order to gain, by the occupation of the capital, a safer footing in the country and a great success in the eyes of Europe, or he could turn against the only enemy still in the field, namely, the English army.

After the convention of Cintra, the latter, now under Moore, had started on the 27th October in several columns from Lisbon towards Spain. The head of the main column reached Salamanca on the 13th November, whilst 10,000 fresh men, just disembarked, were on the march thither from Coruña; the advance guard of this force reached Astorga on the 26th November. But the Emperor knew nothing of all this. On the contrary, he expected to see the English army move in a direct advance from Lisbon to Madrid, indeed he could have no doubt on this point, for the advance to Madrid was the only possible plan for them. But even if he had been acquainted with the true position of the English, it is scarcely to be assumed that he would have taken any other resolution. Their small numbers, 25,000 men, and the fact that their forces were not even approximately concentrated, rendered them an objective of insufficient stability. For if he had advanced from Burgos to Medina-de-Rio-seco, neither of the enemy's columns would have stood their ground before him; they would both have retreated again, the one to Coruña, the other to Lisbon. But what Napoleon wanted in the eyes of the Spanish, as well as in those of Europe, was, that every step forward should bring him some tangible success. Besides he would have resolved upon an advance to Madrid, even if he had been aware of the English positions, for in this direction there seemed to offer an opportunity for a tactical success.

The passes of the Sierra de Guadarrama were occupied by 10,000 men, and near Madrid some larger concentrations of troops were taking place. Consequently the Emperor ordered Lefebvre, advancing *viâ* Palencia, Valladolid and Segovia, to cover the march of the army on the right flank; Ney was to do the same on the left flank, by marching to Guadalaxara; and Moncey was entrusted with the investment of Saragossa. In these orders also it becomes evident how very desirable the Emperor's personal presence would have been at the various decisive points. For Ney had after his delay at Soria advanced on the 25th to Alagon, *viâ* Agreda and Mallen, and arrived there on the 28th, whilst Moncey had despatched the larger portion of his forces *viâ* Calatayud in pursuit of Castaños; these had come in touch with the latter at Borja and had already inflicted some losses on him, when they were stopped at Calatayud on the 29th in consequence of the Emperor's orders. According to the actual situation, therefore, Moncey would have been better placed for the march to Guadalaxara, and Ney for the investment of Saragossa.

On the 28th the Emperor started on his march from Aranda to Madrid. On the 29th he went into bivouac near the village of Bocequillas at the foot of the Sierra de Guadarrama. Being restless, as he often was at decisive moments, he could not sleep, and early in the morning of

Spain

the 30th he began his march for the capture of the pass of Somo-Sierra. He found it strongly occupied and the road blocked by a battery of sixteen guns, which commanded it. Whilst the French infantry advanced along the road and by the mountain slopes on its two sides, General Montbrun, rushing up the mountain road at the head of the Polish light cavalry of the Guards, threw himself upon the battery, which could only fire one volley and was then taken. The pass was open and the Spaniards fled in full rout, part through Buitrago and part towards Segovia. The Emperor himself arrived the same evening with the pursuing troops at Buitrago.

Now there was no obstacle to his further advance, and thus he reached St. Augustin on the 1st December, and at noon on the 2nd, hastening on in advance with Bessières' cavalry, he appeared on the heights of Chamartin, which command Madrid. Here negotiations were begun for the surrender of the capital, which had been prepared for a defence by its armed inhabitants and some regular troops. If those negotiations were unsuccessful, he determined to await the arrival of infantry and guns. These came up during the evening, and whilst thirty guns were placed in battery against the height of the castle of Buen-Retiro, a portion of the infantry was sent round on the right against the large cemetery, which it took, and penetrated into the first houses of the town.

At 9 a.m. on the 3rd the artillery fire began against the castle of Buen-Retiro; soon a breach was made there and the infantry rushed in and penetrated also into the town, as far as the palace of the Duke of Medina-Celi. Negotiations were again invited, for it could by no means be to the Emperor's interest to proceed to a complete capture of the capital by force of arms, and at 6 p.m. on the 4th December Madrid was surrendered. The Emperor, however, kept to his headquarters at Chamartin, the country seat of the Duke of Infantado, and only showed himself once for a short time in the capital.

In the meantime the troops, which Castaños had succeeded in withdrawing, some 8000 men, had arrived in Guadalaxara on the 2nd, 3rd and 4th. There they heard, however, that the Emperor himself was already before the walls of the capital, and turned therefore towards Cuenca. Bessières' cavalry, which had been despatched to Guadalaxara upon the news of the arrival of hostile forces at this place, consequently found there, on the 5th, only a rearguard on the point of retreating. Of the two flank corps, Ney reached Guadalaxara, and Lefebvre Segovia, on the 3rd.

The Emperor remained for the present in his central position near Madrid and took measures for securing and subduing the country around, as well as for reconnoitring towards the west, so as to discover where the English were. Soult had been ordered forward to the eastern frontier of Leon and stood on the line Sahagun-Almanza, in order to cover the district between the Duero and the sea. The troops of Junot's corps, which were entering Spain in the beginning of December, were set in motion towards Burgos, so as later on to be moved up to join the army, nearer Segovia; Junot himself assumed, *vice* Moncey, the command of the III. Corps. In addition to the latter, Mortier's corps also, which had likewise entered Spain in the beginning of the month, was employed in the siege of Saragossa, one of its divisions occupying Calatayud, so as to restore communications with the Emperor. In Catalonia, Saint-Cyr had, on the 6th December, captured Rosas, and was on the march to Barcelona.

Napoleon now ordered Victor to advance from Madrid to the Tagus to the line Toledo-Ocaña-Tarancon, as a protection towards the south, and sent the cavalry divisions of Lasalle and Milhaud on a reconnaissance towards Talavèra, for he still thought the English would come from this point. In the same direction also he sent Sebastiani's division of Lefebvre's corps, after the latter had been brought up to Madrid. Finally on the 14th December the whole of Victor's corps received orders to start for Talavera, whilst from the rear Ney was ordered up to Madrid, leaving one division behind at Guadalaxara to keep up communication with Mortier. Ney arrived in Madrid on the 14th, and the cavalry advanced as far as Almarez and Avila to reconnoitre. Thus the Emperor stood with his main army near Madrid, but with his foot already, as it were, lifted for an advance to Lisbon *viâ* Talavera. His line of communication by Aranda and Burgos north of the Sierra de Guadarrama was covered by Soult, and a new one had been opened *viâ* Guadalaxara-Calatayud south of that mountain chain. The position was thus so well calculated and secured, that it forms one of the finest strategical displays a soldier can contemplate.

Meanwhile Moore had, while concentrating at Salamanca, received news of the various defeats of the Spanish forces, and his first thought had been to withdraw to Portugal himself, while sending orders to the reinforcing column, which was coming up from Coruña, to return to that place to embark there and then to join him by landing in Portugal. But urgent requests from all sides induced him to advance against the enemy's line of communication with Burgos. He therefore started on the 11th December, with the forces assembled near Salamanca, on his march towards Valladolid, whilst the reinforcing column was to move up from Astorga through Benavente. On the road a despatch from the Emperor was intercepted in which Soult was ordered to advance against Galicia. In consequence of this Moore changed the point of junction of his two columns to Valderas and turned to the north by Tordesillas for that purpose; on the 20th Moore's whole army was collected at Mayorga.

On the receipt of the news of the advance of the English on the 16th, Soult immediately assembled his corps near Carrion-de-los-Condes. But as he had been obliged to send out some troops to a great distance, as far as the sea, he was unable to collect all his forces in time. He therefore took upon himself to order the divisions of the VIII. Corps, which stood near Burgos, to push forward to Palencia, in order to be able to bring them up on his left wing as a reinforcement, should the necessity for this arise.

Soult's reports, as well as some information gained from deserters, confirmed what letters and newspapers, which had been captured, had long led the Emperor to suspect, namely, that the English did not intend to make an advance from Lisbon, but from the north of Spain. It is true, this plan appeared somewhat incomprehensible to him and was contrary to his expectations, but he saw in it with all the greater joy a chance for a decisive blow. He immediately guessed the train of thought of the English general. "The manœuvre of the English is unusual. It is certain that they have evacuated Salamanca. . . . Everything leads me to think that they will evacuate Portugal and fix their line of operations upon El Ferrol. . . . By making this rear movement, they can hope to inflict a defeat upon Marshal Soult's corps."[1]

He therefore determined to leave half of the troops collected around Madrid behind for the preservation of the capital and to advance with the other half as quickly as possible in the direction of Medina-del-Campo and to attack the English in the rear. Accordingly Ney was set in motion from Madrid on the 20th December as an advance guard, and on the 21st the Emperor ordered half the cavalry and the Guards to follow him, while entrusting to Joseph the chief command over Victor, Lefebvre and the rest of the cavalry. The main point of the instructions, which he left him for the time of his absence, was as follows: "The only real aim of the King must be, to hold Madrid; all the rest is of little importance."[2]

[1] C. N. To Joseph. Chamartin, 22nd December. Notes.
[2] Ibid.

On the 22nd Napoleon hastened after his army. Ney alone had up to now crossed the Sierra de Guadarrama; the rest of the army the Emperor found still at the foot of this mountain chain, which, covered with slippery thin ice and deep snow, offered a formidable obstacle to their march. Impatient to conquer it quickly, he hastened in person to the head of the column, and preceding the troops on foot, he led them across the mountains the same day and spent the night himself in a peasant's hut in Espinar; but he did not reach Villacastin, which he had wished to gain that day, until the 23rd. He immediately hastened on in front to Tordesillas viâ Acevalo, and reached that town on the 25th. Here Ney had, on the preceding day, crossed the Duero, and the cavalry scouted towards Valladolid and Medina-de-Rio-seco. As to the position of the English, the Emperor knew nothing for certain. He suspected them, however, to be on the line Zamora-Benavente, but still thought he could cut them off.

Moore had in the meanwhile pushed his vanguard on the 21st forward to Sahagun, whilst Soult was concentrating near Carrion; but the mass of the English army remained stationary during the next few days, in order to await the arrival of some portions left behind, and also the trains. In the night from the 23rd to the 24th, Moore had already set himself in motion for an attack upon Soult, when he received information of the Emperor's approach and immediately prepared for a retreat. On the 24th he ordered two columns to fall back upon Valderas and Valencia-de-Don-Juan, whilst he himself with the rearguard at Sahagun veiled this retreat from Soult. On the 25th he followed to Valderas by Mayorga, and on the 26th the mass of his army crossed the Esla at Valencia and Castrogonzalo.

The Emperor had in the meantime gained more accurate information as to the direction of the English advance, and cherished now the hope of still finding them engaged with

Soult in front of Carrion, and thus being able to fall on their rear. In spite of the cold and the extraordinary exhaustion of his troops he continued without interruption his advance upon Medina-de-Rio-seco, which place he reached on the 27th, but only with his cavalry, whilst Soult also, on his side, had now set himself in motion and had taken the direction of Mansilla. Moore had reached Benavente on this day, but had left his cavalry behind on the Esla to cover his retreat, for he intended to remain near Benavente during the 28th, in order to allow his troops to close up and destroy the depôts he had established there. When therefore the Emperor continued his advance during the 28th and reached Valderas, Moore still held Benavente occupied. In the morning of the 29th, whilst Moore was evacuating this town and continuing his rear-movement to Astorga, the English cavalry, left behind as a rearguard, repulsed the attempt of that of the French to cross the Esla, and only followed the main army to La Bañeza in the evening. During the next few days the English continued their retreat *viâ* Astorga to Coruña uninterruptedly, the Emperor still pursuing them. His cavalry reached La Bañeza on the 31st December, whilst Soult, who had on the preceding day forced the passage over the Esla at Mansilla in face of the rearguard of the Spanish auxiliary corps, arrived in Leon. On the 1st January, 1809, the Emperor himself reached Astorga.

Here he became of necessity convinced, in spite of the most strenuous exertions, for his troops had covered the 214 miles from Madrid to Astorga in twelve days, notwithstanding the severe frost and snow and glair ice, that he had after all not been able to cut off the English retreat. For it had been begun early and executed rapidly, and he was forced to be content with a simple pursuit of the retreating enemy. He therefore rightly judged that now neither the object in view nor the success which could be expected were sufficiently important to require his own presence ; he consequently left the further pursuit to Soult, placed Ney in position at Astorga as a support for him, and set his guards in motion for Valladolid, where he himself arrived in the evening of the 6th January. On the 17th he left this town to return to France, and on the 23rd January he reached his own capital again.

Thus the Emperor had brought the campaign to a victorious ending; the hostile armies which had opposed him were compelled to leave the field, and only escaped being cut off and entirely annihilated by giving up their advance and beginning their retreat immediately upon the news of the Emperor's advance. This retreat was accompanied by such great losses, that it affords an instructive illustration of Napoleon's dictum : " There is a very great difference between operating with a fixed system and an organized centre, and advancing at haphazard, abandoning one's communications without possessing any organized centre of operations." [1]

Still we know well that the Emperor did not succeed in attaining the real aim of the war, namely, the conquest of Spain ; whether he considered this aim to have been reached by the expulsion of the English, must be a mere matter of conjecture. But if we consider how accustomed to success his proud, unyielding nature was at that time, we shall be inclined to assume, that here also, as everywhere else hitherto, he thought he had overcome all resistance by success in the field. History teaches us that this was not the case, and we must therefore ask ourselves, was this a fault in the general, or was the task altogether impossible with the means at his disposal ?

What he had to deal with in this case was a national rising, supported by an army, and history shows clearly, that only with such support can any national rising hope for success. " Without the assistance of a regular, well-disciplined army, national risings can always be easily

[1] C. N. To Joseph. Kaiserslautern, 24th September, 1808.

suppressed."[1] This is indeed more particularly proved by the Spanish national rising in all its phases, even though Napier's description of the innate weakness of the Spanish levies may be rejected as not impartial. Napoleon also said in speaking about Cæsar's wars: "Any nation which loses sight of the importance of a standing regular army, and trusts to risings or popular levies, must meet with the same fate as Gaul."[2] It is therefore assuredly the right thing to act as the Emperor did here, namely, to defeat in the first place the regular armies and thereby strike at the heart of the enemy's resistance.

But what then? Continue the war, as in 1805 and 1806 against Austria and Prussia, take possession of the capital, cover the whole country, and occupy every province? This the Emperor did, and in this lies the reason of his want of success. His forces suffered defeat again and again, and had to evacuate ground already conquered; and every such retreat strengthened the power and the desire of resistance of his opponent. In order to avoid this, the victor must content himself with advancing slowly and gradually, he must first make himself really master of a small portion of the country, before making a further and cautious advance; he must not so much attempt great victorious campaigns, as await the enemy's attacks, repulse them, and force him back step by step; in short, do just the very things which were distasteful to the Emperor's genius. If we wish to have an example of this sort of warfare, we may study the struggle of the German armies in 1870-71 against the French Republic.

This is also Jomini's opinion. The interesting dissertation which he puts in the Emperor's mouth, speaking in the Elysian fields before Cæsar, Alexander and Frederick, begins: "There was only the choice between two systems of carrying on the war in Spain; the first was, to proceed methodically, etc. . . . and the second, to feed the war

[1] Jomini, Précis, etc., 45.
[2] Œuvres xxxii. 18, Précis des guerres de J. César.

by the war, to march vigorously, in order to destroy all the organized masses of the enemy, while living from day to day on the provisions taken from the country round, as we did in Italy, in Austria, in Prussia. . . ."[1] Then he continues : " Inasmuch as I sacrificed 300 to 400 millions (of francs) for the commissariat of my troops, and spent two whole years in traversing Spain in arms, and then only began to speak of subjugation and organization, it is possible that the first method would have been more successful." Then, however, the Emperor continues, and we may assume it as very likely, that the great critic rightly interpreted his ideas, and that his actual train of thought was somewhat similar : " The second method had always been successful with me, it led more quickly to the destruction of the enemy's armies," . . . and therefore he comes to the following conclusion : " Thus resolved to wage a war of invasion, by following out the same combinations which had met with such success in my former campaigns, I made my preparations, so as to deal the Spaniards heavy blows with our usual impetuosity."

But in this, one thing has to be taken into consideration, and this indeed is the core of the whole matter, namely, the political end aimed at. A method of waging war such as that of the Germans in 1870-71, may indeed be success ful in inducing the enemy at last to prefer a peace, though very disadvantageous, to a continuance of the war, but it cannot result in any subjugation of the hostile nation nor in the conquest of the whole country. But the latter was the Emperor's aim ; his measures were taken with a view to this, and they were indeed suited to this purpose, only the purpose itself was, politically speaking, insane and, looking at it more closely, impossible. The German measures in 1870-71 were indeed also aimed at a definite political result, namely, to enforce peace under certain conditions, and for this they were entirely suited. But

[1] " Vie politique et militaire de Napoleon, etc.," iii. 91, 92, 93.

if the method of waging that war had had for its aim the politically impossible result of a conquest of France, it would not have been suited to its purpose. The Germans would in that case have had to march triumphantly through the whole country, and they would have failed, as the Emperor did in Spain. For the latter indeed a voluntary limitation of his political aims might have lessened the brilliance of his military success, but it could alone have led to lasting results. The great European nations of our days cannot be really conquered by others; whoever pursued such an aim would, as in the days of the great migrations of peoples, have to destroy the conquered nation entirely. Thus we see here, how the statesman Napoleon set the general an impossible task, and how the latter consequently failed, and was bound to fail on account of its inherent impossibility, in spite of his well-conceived measures for gaining his military aims, and in spite of his brilliant execution of them.

CHAPTER II.

THE EVENTS OF RATISBON.

THE Emperor's invasion of Spain had once more, as had previously been the case on the occasion of his intended invasion of England, raised the hope on the Continent of being able to put an end to his oppressive predominance. Once more it was Austria which, in spite of its former failures, felt itself strong enough to renew the struggle. But Napoleon also was not only ready to take up the gauntlet, but at the first sign he eagerly seized the opportunity of gaining new military successes, and this perhaps the more, as there had been after all, in spite of the expulsion of his opponent from Spain, none of those crushing blows dealt there, to which the world had got so accustomed from him, and he had some reason to fear that the absence of these might produce in Europe the impression of a decrease of his power. From the moment of his arrival in Paris, therefore, his whole mind was bent upon rendering any real return to pacific counsels on the part of Austria, impossible. Thus on both sides the armies were increased, some preliminary movements of troops were undertaken, and each party accused the other, while acting in the same way, of taking measures that were fatal to peace.

The Emperor had at the beginning of the year four divisions under Davout around Magdeburg, Hanover, Stettin, and in the Bayreuth district; the same marshal had also the Poles and Saxons under him; two divisions under Bernadotte were in the Hanse towns and one under Oudinot near Hanau; moreover, all the troops of the states forming the Confederation of the Rhine were at his disposal. In the beginning of March Davout received orders to concentrate his forces near Bamberg, though the Poles were to remain near Warsaw and the Saxons near Dresden, and Bernadotte was to join the latter; Oudinot was to go to Augsburg, and was to be reinforced. In addition two divisions, which were on the point of leaving Germany, were stopped and sent to Ulm, whilst two others were ordered up from France to Strasburg. Massena was to form these troops into an army corps near Ulm. Finally all the states of the Rhine Confederation received orders to mobilize their forces, and the Emperor said: "Should any extraordinary events occur, I shall be in Munich as quick as lightning."[1] On the same day he again appointed Berthier Chief of the Staff of the Grand Army, and calculated that the above-mentioned measures would be matured by the end of March, and that then there would be: 63,000 men near Bamberg, 30,000 near Ulm and 20,000 near Augsburg; moreover the Bavarians, 30,000 men, the chief command of whom was given to Lefebvre, would stand on the line Straubing-Landshut-Munich. "If the Austrians attack before the 10th April the army will concentrate behind the Lech; the right wing will occupy Augsburg, and the left wing the right bank of the Danube towards Ingolstadt and Donauwörth. Donauwörth must then be the centre of the army."[2]

On the 30th March voluminous instructions were given Berthier for the settlement of all questions concerning the army. The Emperor was of opinion that the opening of the campaign by the Austrians could scarcely be expected before the 15th April, and that therefore he ought to be ready by that date. He now sought on the map the right point for the concentration of his army and fixed upon Ratisbon as that point; "it is my intention

---

[1] C. N. To Otto. Paris, 4th March.
[2] C. N. Orders. Paris, 28th March.

to establish my headquarters at Ratisbon and to assemble my whole army there."¹ For this purpose he resolved to place Oudinot and the entire cavalry near Ratisbon, Davout near Nuremberg, Massena near Augsburg, and the Bavarians in the neighbourhood of Ratisbon, and "thus the headquarters would be in Ratisbon in the centre of 200,000 men, on the two sides of a large stream, covering the right bank of the Danube from Ratisbon as far as Passau, and they would thus be in a position secure against all apprehensions from the enemy's movements, and possess the advantage of the Danube, which would quickly convey to the army all it could stand in need of."² Thus he intended to concentrate his army as far forward as was possible, in order to be able to open the campaign in any direction required, and from the very beginning with the greatest possible gain as to space and time, and at the same time at a point where he could remain master of the Danube, for "if·one is operating in Austria, nothing can be more advantageous than to follow the Danube. For the army can thus lack neither ammunition nor provisions, and can therefore manœuvre at will."³

For the rest it is characteristic of the Emperor's strategy that he never, in any of his plans for the opening of a campaign, began by asking: "What can the enemy do?" and then developed his own course of action, but always sought on the map first for the point where he could most advantageously concentrate his army, and then only considered what the enemy could do, after he himself had taken up that position. Even as an abstract question it was distasteful to him, to shape his course by that of the enemy instead of the reverse being the case; once indeed he gave way to the vivacity of his imagination so far as to say: "One should never try to guess what

[1] C. N. Instructions for the Chief-of-the-Staff, Paris.
[2] Ibid.
[3] C. N. Note about Passau. Paris, 1st March, 1809.

the enemy can do. My intention is always the same,"[1] an expression which of course must not be taken literally, but which after all is distinct evidence of the high value he set on not allowing one's plan to mature under the influence of all the possibilities open to the enemy, but rather to frame it so correctly according to general, and, more particularly, geographical considerations, that it might be applicable whatever the enemy might do.

Thus, after having here in the first instance fixed upon Ratisbon as his point of concentration, he asked only in the second instance: "What will the enemy do, once our army is cantoned around Ratisbon?" and his own reply was: "Will he move on Cham? We shall be able to assemble all our strength against him, so as to hold him fast in the positions which we shall have reconnoitred on the Regen. Will he move on Nuremberg? He will in that case be cut off from Bohemia. Will he move on Bamberg? He will be cut off there too. Finally, will he resolve to march towards Dresden? In this case we shall enter Bohemia and pursue him into Germany. Will he operate against the Tyrol and at the same time break out from Bohemia? In this case he will undoubtedly reach Innsbruck; but the ten or twelve regiments which he would have in Innsbruck could not take up a position near the issues from Bohemia, and these troops would only learn the defeat of their army in Bohemia by our appearance at Salzburg."

"Finally, if it should appear as if the enemy intended to take our extreme right or left wing as the goal of his operations, we shall have to choose the central line by a retreat to the Lech, while holding Augsburg occupied, so as to be certain of being able to make use of this town at any moment."[2]

We note therefore here, how the Emperor settled upon one thing as independent of all the enemy's measures,

---

[1] C. N. To Soult. Osterode, 5th March, 1807, 4 p.m.
[2] C. N. Orders for the Chief-of-the-Staff. Paris, 30th March.

The Events of Ratisbon

namely, the concentration of his whole army on one single line of operations; but was compelled to leave the manner of employing this mass at first an open question. In this respect of course the enemy's measures would decide matters. For "one ought not to calculate as an abstract question, what one is going to do, this must depend on what the enemy does or is going to do."[1] According to the direction in which the Austrians were going to advance, he intended, should they invade Franconia, to fall upon their left flank, or should they invade Saxony, to fall upon their rear, or should they advance from Bohemia against the Danube, to oppose them frontally on the Regen, or finally, should they choose a concentric offensive simultaneously from Bohemia and the Tyrol, to throw himself, taking advantage of his central position, first with all his might upon the Bohemian army, and then attack the army from the Tyrol *viâ* Salzburg in its right flank.

The Austrians had in the meantime assembled their main army in Western Bohemia, one corps being despatched south of the Danube, to the Traun and the Enns; but later a change occurred in their strategical views, and the main body was now to be concentrated on the south of the Danube. The movements in this respect began on the 20th March. On the 8th April two army corps, 49,000 men, were at Pilsen and Budweis in Bohemia; and on the Inn the main army, 126,000 men, under the Archduke Charles, in six corps from Schärding as far as Braunau.

During this change of front on the part of the Austrians, however, the necessary movements for the proposed concentration at Ratisbon took place on the part of the French, and on the 8th April the head of Davout's corps stood at Ratisbon, the rest of his forces being still behind at Bayreuth and Erlangen. His headquarters were at Nuremberg, and the Bavarians on the line

[1] C. N. To Joseph. Kaiserslautern, 24th September, 1808.
VOL. II. D

Straubing-Landshut-Munich; Oudinot was in the neighbourhood of Augsburg, Massena beyond Ulm. The immediate superintendence of these movements lay in the hands of Berthier, who had been in Strasburg since the beginning of April.

The army destined for the impending campaign was, to begin with, composed as follows, though we must remark that in the course of the campaign several alterations took place :—

The Emperor.
Chief of the Staff: Berthier.

	Inf. Divs.	*Light Cavalry.*	
III. Corps Davout :	Morand	Montbrun	
	Friant		
	Gudin		
	St. Hilaire		
	Res. Div. Demont		66,000 men.
IV. Corps Massena :	Claparède	Marulaz	
	Legrand		
	Carra St. Cyr		
	Molitor		40,000 men.
Oudinot's Corps :	Tharreau		
	Boudet	Colbert	14,000 men.
Lefebvre's Corps : (Bavarians)	Crown Prince		
	Deroy		
	Wrede		32,000 men.
Vandamme's Corps : (Würtembergers)			13,000 men.
Bessières' Cavalry Reserve :	Heavy Division	Nansouty	
	Cuirassier „	St. Sulpice	
	„ „	Espagne	11,000 men

In the evening of the 9th April the Austrian declaration of war was handed to the Bavarian troops, and on the next day the Inn was crossed at Schärding, Mühlheim and Braunau; but the army remained close to the river. On this day the French troops stood in the following positions: Lefebvre had the Crown Prince's division at Munich, with Deroy at Freising and Wrede at Straubing; Massena stood around Ulm; Oudinot around Augsburg; Vandamme near Elwangen; Davout had Morand near Pielenhofen on the Lower Naab, with Friant near Amberg, Gudin near Neumarkt; whilst at Ratisbon stood

THE EVENTS OF RATISBON 35

St. Hilaire and the cavalry division of Nansouty; Montbrun was at Nittenau.

From the attitude of the Austrian ambassador in Paris, and from intercepted despatches, the Emperor had come to the conclusion that the enemy would shortly open the campaign, and he therefore hastened to telegraph to Berthier at noon on the 10th: "I believe the Emperor of Austria will attack without delay. I desire you to go to Augsburg and to carry out the instructions I gave you; and, should the enemy have attacked before the 15th, you must concentrate the troops at Augsburg and Donauwörth, and everything must be ready for marching. Send my Guards and my horses to Stuttgart."

This despatch arrived in Strasburg at noon on the 13th, but the Chief-of-the-Staff was no longer there.

Berthier, informed on the 11th of the crossing of the Inn by the Austrians, had, in accordance with the Emperor's earlier instructions, handed the chief command of all the troops on the right bank of the Danube to Massena, and of those on the left bank to Davout, and instructed the former to concentrate on the Lech, the latter towards Ingolstadt. Up to that time, therefore, he had adhered to the rules of Napoleonic strategy; it was only the rush of events and the reports, as usual contradictory, which created in Berthier's mind that indecision and confusion of his strategical views, that vague halting between several resolutions, and the mistakes which resulted, which proved what a great difference there was between the Chief-of-the-Staff and his master. Jomini is of opinion that the former "had failed to grasp the very first principles of strategy in his twenty campaigns";[1] and as an explanation of this fact we may weigh Willisen's remarks as to the acquisition of the art of war: "It is true, war can only be learned by experience; but what are we to understand by 'experience'? Who will gain experience, the man who has been present during this

[1] Jomini, "Vie de Napoleon," iii. 160.

or that event, but has never thought in the least about it, either before or after it or while it took place, or the man who may possibly not have had any personal experience whatever of such matters, but who studies a great number of wars, and who has always and everywhere examined the causes of the results and learnt from them that certain results always recur, if they had been preceded by the same causes, and who thus has come at last to formulate views and to deduce general principles? Has not the latter 'experience' and the former none? Shall I not by such experience alone learn to know war, whilst by the other I shall remain altogether ignorant of it?"[1]

At midnight on the 11th-12th April, Berthier left Strasburg, in order to go to Donauwörth, after having communicated to the Emperor the measures taken by him up to then. That day the Austrians had been content with bringing their last troops across the Inn, their army being otherwise stationary. The two corps from Bohemia had likewise begun their advance and reached the Naab; at Hirschau they came in contact with Friant's troops and forced them back to Amberg. On the French side Davout was still advancing to Ratisbon and the rest were in their former positions.

The Chief-of-the-Staff of the French Army hastened on the 12th through Baden and Würtemberg, in order to betake himself to the theatre of events in Bavaria. At 7 a.m. on the 13th he was at Gmünd, and communicated from there with Davout in answer to reports received on his way from that marshal. But now his views began to be confused; his letter conveyed the idea that he really would like to see Davout concentrated near Ratisbon, and that he only adhered to the concentration further to the rear, because he thought Ratisbon was already evacuated. About 8 p.m. Berthier arrived at Donauwörth, by which time his plans had suffered a complete change. Davout was to carry out the originally intended concen-

[1] "Theorie des grossen Krieges," i. 8.

tration near Ratisbon, and consequently St. Hilaire and the cavalry, of whose continued presence near that town the Chief-of-the-Staff was now aware, were to remain there. Oudinot was likewise to advance thither, and Lefebvre, who had retreated from the line of the Isar, was to occupy Landshut and Straubing again. " It seems, the enemy is manœuvring towards our wings. His Majesty desires to concentrate his troops in Ratisbon. He even intends to establish his headquarters there, in order to manœuvre from there against the enemy."[1] This was the result of the clear and definite instructions of Napoleon. Was it indeed possible to misunderstand him, when he wrote on the 28th March: " If the Austrians attack before the 10th April, the army must concentrate behind the Lech, holding Augsburg with its right wing, and the right bank of the Danube towards Ingolstadt and Donauwörth with its left wing;"[2] and two days later: " What could the enemy, ready as he is, attempt to-day against our army? He would have to march from Pilsen to Ratisbon *via* Waldmünchen and Cham. From Pilsen to Ratisbon is five days' march. Should this be the case the Bavarian division in Straubing would fall back upon Ingolstadt. The Bavarian division in Landshut would do the same ; the Duke of Auerstädt's corps would go to Ingolstadt and Donauwörth, and in that case the headquarters would have to be moved to Donauwörth."[3] It was the ever-present principle of uniting the army before a meeting with the enemy could take place. Hence, if the enemy's offensive began before the Emperor's army was ready, this retreat to the Lech ; otherwise a concentration at Ratisbon, so as not to lose ground unnecessarily. But in spite of his work for many years under the personal guidance of the Emperor, this axiom was not clearly recognized by the Chief-of-

---

[1] C. N. Berthier to Davout. Donauwörth, 13th April, 8.30 p.m.
[2] C. N. Orders, Paris.
[3] C. N. Instructions for the Chief-of-the-Staff, Paris.

the-Staff. He had not yet gained that "experience" as pointed out by Willisen, to such an extent but that the changing difficulties of an individual case led him to forget that great principle, although he had himself acknowledged on the 13th that Napoleon's anticipation had been verified; "the enemy, Sire, has anticipated us, by unexpectedly crossing the Inn." [1]

The position of the opposing armies was, on the evening of the 13th, as follows: The Austrians had reached the line Eggenfelden-Alt-Oetting with their main forces; their two Bohemian corps were on the Naab between Wernburg and Naabburg. Of the French there lay at Ratisbon part of Davout's corps (St. Hilaire) and the cavalry of Nansouty; Morand, Gudin and Demont at Ingolstadt; Friant at Neumarkt; of the troops south of the Danube Lefebvre stood on the Abens and Isar, Massena in extended formation around Augsburg, Oudinot at Augsburg, and Vandamme at Rain.

In the morning of the 14th Berthier seemed, it is true, again to look with much more favour upon the concentration of the whole army on the Lech, at least this is the impression conveyed by a letter to Massena. But as a matter of fact Davout was again instructed to take up his position at Ratisbon, though this marshal drew attention to the danger and inadvisability of this movement, and pointed out that Ingolstadt was the Emperor's choice. Thus on this day the idea of concentrating the French army was given up, whilst the Austrians advanced to the line Ganghofen-Neumarkt-Ober Bergkirchen.

During the 15th nothing was changed in the general situation on the French side, though Berthier's orders became more and more hesitating and contradictory. The Austrian main body reached the Vils and the two Bohemian corps were near Schwandorf and Schwarzenfeld. On the following day Berthier arrived in Augsburg at 6 a.m., and here the above mentioned despatch from the

[1] C. N. Berthier to Napoleon, Donauwörth.

Emperor was handed to him, which differed entirely from all that the Chief-of-the-Staff had ordered hitherto, for it said, as we know : " If the enemy has attacked before the 15th, you must concentrate the troops about Augsburg and Donauwörth." A letter of the same date is couched in no less definite terms : " The Duke of Auerstädt must have his headquarters at Nuremberg. Inform him that everything points to the fact, that the Austrians will take the initiative in the attack, and that if they attack before the 15th, all the forces are to retreat to the Lech."[1] Yet on this very day the two French wings completed their separation, Davout beginning his march for the purpose of concentrating his whole corps at Ratisbon, and Berthier doing nothing to change this movement, which he had ordered.

On the 16th the Archduke Charles advanced towards the Isar, drove the division of Deroy from Landshut and thus forced the passage there ; his right wing was at Ohn, and the vanguard of his left near Moosburg. Deroy fell back before him upon Siegenburg. The Crown Prince's division also left the passage of the Isar at Freising free and retreated to Pfaffenhofen. Wrede stood at Abensburg. Thus the French army formed two bodies, at Ratisbon and at Augsburg, separated by an interval of seventy-six miles, and in the gap between them there stood only Lefebvre, isolated and not concentrated, in face of the advancing enemy, who was ready, with united forces, to take the offensive on the morning of the 17th from the Isar. But the Emperor now rejoined his army.

On the 12th April at 8 o'clock p.m. he had received by telegraph the news of the passage of the Inn, as well as the declaration of war on the part of Austria, and on the 13th he left Paris at 4 a.m., to hasten to the theatre of war. After a short stay, first in Strasburg, where he heard that the Austrians had, on the 12th, not yet advanced beyond Mühldorf, and then in Kehl, where

[1] C. N. To Berthier. Paris, noon.

he inspected the fortifications in course of construction, he went to Durlach, rested there two hours, and then hastened on to Ludwigsburg *viâ* Stuttgart, and arrived there at 3 a.m. on the 16th. Here he received a letter from Berthier, dated the 13th, evening, with a report of the measures ordered at that time, namely, the despatch of Oudinot forward to Ratisbon, and of Lefebvre back again to Straubing and Landshut.

The Emperor was quite taken aback: " You do not inform me what has rendered necessary such an extraordinary measure, which weakens and divides my troops. . . . I cannot quite grasp the meaning of your letter of the evening of the 13th yet, and I should have preferred to see my army concentrated between Ingolstadt and Augsburg, the Bavarians in the first line, with the Duke of Danzig in his old position, until we know what the enemy is going to do. . . . Everything would be excellent if the Duke of Auerstädt had been at Ingolstadt, and the Duke of Rivoli with the Würtembergers and Oudinot's corps at Augsburg . . . so that just the opposite of what you have done should have been done."[1] The Emperor informed Massena that he had given Oudinot counter-orders, and then, after a short rest, he hastened forward, on the one hand rendered uneasy by the knowledge he had gained of the position of his army, and on the other hand reassured by a report just received, that the Austrians had, on the 14th, not yet advanced much beyond the Inn.

By nightfall he reached Dillingen, spoke a few encouraging words to the King of Bavaria, and then reached Donauwörth on the 17th at 4 a.m. Here he had hoped to find Berthier and to be enlightened by him as to the situation of his army, but he was still in Augsburg, and the Emperor only gradually found out the position of his various corps, and therewith the full danger of his situation. At 10 o'clock he wrote to Davout and ordered him to come up to Ingolstadt *viâ* Neustadt; Lefebvre

---

[1] C. N. To Berthier. Ludwigsburg, 16th April.

would cover this flank movement. But even in that march, necessitated though it was by circumstances and caution, his military instinct, ever thinking of the offensive, did not quite reject the possibility of an attack upon the enemy. Davout was to march not on the safe left bank of the Danube, but on the right, " and should you during this abrupt movement, unexpected by the enemy, see an opportunity of attacking the column from Landshut, in case the latter has started, it will be a favourable chance to do so ; but do not go more than half a day's march out of your way to provoke it." [1] Then Lefebvre received corresponding orders to cover and support Davout's movement, and Wrede was, as an additional safeguard, immediately informed of the resolutions taken.

But it was not long before the thought of an offensive became the only paramount one, and the cautious rearward concentration of the army towards Ingolstadt gave place to a forward concentration against the enemy. About noon Berthier arrived at the Emperor's quarters, and we may reasonably suspect that he brought news of the enemy's very slow advance, and this news now induced Napoleon to send orders to Massena to begin his forward march early the next morning from Augsburg along the Ingolstadt road. " Your march is intended to connect you with that of the army, in order to catch the enemy in the act, and to destroy his columns."

Whilst thus Davout was to come up by a flank movement along the enemy's front, the right wing of the army, under Massena, was to advance either to effect a quicker junction with the left wing, or even to be ready to act on the enemy's flank or in his rear. " To-morrow will be a day of preparation, spent in drawing closer together, and I expect to be able by Wednesday to manœuvre according to circumstances against the columns [2] which may have advanced via Landshut or from any other direction."

[1] C. N. Donauwörth, 1 p.m.
[2] C. N. To Davout. Donauwörth, 17th April, 6 p.m.

Another despatch to this effect was sent to Davout, informing him of Massena's forward movement to Pfaffenhofen *viâ* Aichach ordered for the 18th, whilst Berthier sent the corresponding order to the latter marshal. Thus on the 17th the situation on the French side had entirely changed by the evening, as compared with the morning of the same day. At the same time the Austrians occupied a line in advance of Landshut extending as far as Hohenthann and Weihmichel, with their right wing at Essenbach and their left at Moosburg; the Bohemian corps being near Nittenau and Schwandorf.

During the night of the 17th-18th news arrived at the Emperor's quarters as to the points reached by the Austrian columns, and he became of opinion that the Archduke purposed to throw himself upon Davout, isolated at Ratisbon. At 4 a.m. therefore orders were sent to Lefebvre, in accordance with his former instructions, to fall upon the Austrian left flank as they advanced, so as to relieve Davout. Massena was most urgently enjoined to advance as quickly as possible to Pfaffenhofen, in order to be able to take part in the fighting which was to be expected; "your movement is so very important, that it is possible I may myself join your corps."[1] The Emperor calculated that the Archduke would attack Davout on the 19th with 80,000 men. The latter might of course meet that attack successfully with his 60,000 men alone, but if Massena's main body were to advance over the Ilm on the morning of that day, the enemy would be lost; "everything leads me therefore to suppose, that between the 18th, 19th and 20th all the affairs of Germany will be settled;"[2] and with his own hand the Emperor added: "Activity, activity, speed! I trust to you," and then he betook himself to Ingolstadt.

From this place he again opened communications with Davout by despatching an officer to him. This marshal

[1] C. N. To Massena. Donauwörth, 18th April.   [2] Ibid.

The Events of Ratisbon 43

led on this day all the forces he had collected at Ratisbon—Morand, Gudin, St Hilaire, and the cavalry corps of St. Sulpice and Montbrun—over to the right bank, and only waited for the arrival of Friant, to commence his departure. Of the Bavarians Lefebvre had Wrede at Siegenburg and the other two divisions at Neustadt; the divisions of Demont and Nansouty were at Vohburg, and Vandamme reached Ingolstadt; Massena had employed the preceding day, as well as the 18th, in assembling his forces, which now stood beyond Augsburg on the road to Pfaffenhofen, their advance guard, under Oudinot, being near Aichach. The Archduke had, to begin with, set his army in motion towards Rottenburg (72) and Pfeffenhausen, but when the presence of Davout at Ratisbon, which he had hitherto doubted, was confirmed, he collected the greater portion of his army, 66,000 men, near Rohr, posted 35,000 men to cover his flank near Ludmannsdorf and Pfeffenhausen; whilst one corps, 25,000 men, remained behind at Moosburg.

During the night before the 19th, Friant also joined Davout, and the latter immediately began his departure in three columns by Abach, Teugen and Saalhaupt, after having occupied the bridge of Ratisbon with one regiment. Montbrun, marching through Dinzling, covered his left flank. From the Imperial headquarters at Ingolstadt orders were issued to Massena during the night, instructing him to hold his forces in readiness to act either on the left towards Abensberg in the direction of Davout, or on the right towards Landshut in the enemy's rear, for as yet the situation was not sufficiently clear to decide which to do. At 3 a.m. Lefebvre then received orders to remain in any circumstances in a defensive position near Abensberg, against a possible attack, until the approach of Davout, who was soon to be expected, and of whose departure from Ratisbon the Emperor was now aware. But he waited in vain during the forenoon of the 19th for the sound of the cannon of the suspected attack of the Austrians upon Davout's march; there was nothing to be heard, only a report came in from Massena, that the advance of the right wing, under Oudinot, had met about 4000 men near Pfaffenhofen early in the morning; as a matter of fact, it was only an insignificant detachment sent forward, but which offered a most resolute resistance.

Thereupon the Emperor wrote about noon to Massena: "All this must be cleared up to-day; and time is precious. You must hold Oudinot's corps in readiness, and place your own four divisions in position around Pfaffenhofen, in the three directions of Neustadt, Freising and Au, so that, according to circumstances, one of them may lead the way and guide the other columns to the point to which they may have to march. It is all a matter of hours only." [1] Thus the situation was as yet unchanged; as yet he did not know whether he would have to order Massena up to his own position, or throw him on the enemy's rear. In order to be ready for either event, Oudinot was to order one of his divisions to Freising, and the other to Au; "from Freising and Au, I shall, according to the news which will come in to-day, set you in motion towards Landshut, and in that case Prince Charles will have lost his line of operations, and his screen, the Isar, and might be attacked on his left wing." [2] At 1 o'clock, at the moment of mounting his horse, the Emperor, however, altered his orders so far as to send the division of Oudinot's corps, not to Au, but to Neustadt, thereby accentuating his idea of its twofold employment; then he rode forward towards the Abens.

In the meantime, the heads of Davout's columns had reached at 11 o'clock the brook of Feking, when they learned of the enemy's approach. For the Archduke had ordered his army on this day to advance upon Ratisbon in three columns, and his left column, set in motion towards Abach, 18,000 men, now met Davout's

[1] C. N. To Massena. Ingolstadt, 19th April, noon.   [2] Ibid.

THE EVENTS OF RATISBON 45

troops near Hausen. The latter made his rear divisions wheel up, whilst the leading ones and his transport trains continued their march, and then proceeded to attack; he forced the enemy to retreat through Hausen and inflicted heavy losses upon him. None of the Archduke's other troops had taken part in the fighting; they reached Dinzling and Eggmühl; only 10,000 men being placed in readiness at Grub to support the left column.

Before Lefebvre's front, also, an engagement took place. This marshal was advancing *viâ* Abensberg, in conformity with the Emperor's orders, and met near Offenstetten a detachment sent forward from Rohr to cover the Austrians' left flank, and repulsed it; the Crown Prince's and Deroy's divisions took up a position near Abensberg; Wrede was checked near Siegenburg by considerable hostile forces, for the Archduke had started upon his march towards Ratisbon with only 66,000 men, little more than half his army, while employing the rest in the direction of the Abens. Massena stood in the evening of this day near Pfaffenhofen. Of the Austrian corps operating to the north of the Danube, the one arrived at Stadtamhof, situated on the left bank of the Danube opposite Ratisbon, and the other at Amberg.

The Emperor having during the afternoon ridden along the line of the Abens and then visited the Bavarians at Abensberg, established his headquarters for the night in Vohburg. He had been personally present on the theatre of events only sixty hours, and how marvellously the situation of affairs had already altered in his favour! When he (71) arrived in Donauwörth early in the morning of the 17th, his army, divided in two, had stood at Ratisbon and Augsburg, whilst the enemy stood united at Landshut on the left bank of the Isar. From Landshut to Ratisbon is thirty-four miles, as the crow flies; from Landshut to Neustadt twenty-six and a half, and to Augsburg sixty-two, from Augsburg to Ratisbon seventy-six miles. The Austrian army was thus in a position to attack Davout and also Lefebvre, advancing right against the middle of the exposed centre of the French line and rend it asunder, three days before there could be any possibility of Massena's coming up. Less advantage of time and space had been sufficient for Napoleon to defeat Beaulieu and Colli, Wurmser and Quosdanovich, Alvintzy and Davidovich, in detail. But the Archduke did not utilize the occasion with the resolution of Napoleon, whilst the latter knew how to deal with the unfavourable situation, which was not of his making, in such a manner, that by the evening of the 19th he had collected between Neustadt, Offenstetten and Siegenburg: Vandamme, Lefebvre, Morand's and Gudin's divisions of Davout's corps and the cavalry corps of Nansouty and St. Sulpice, in all 60,000 men. Davout himself, with Friant, St. Hilaire and Montbrun's cavalry, lay near Teugen, and Massena was at Pfaffenhofen. Thus the centre had been considerably strengthened by the moving up *en masse* of the left wing, and the right wing had also been brought within twenty-four miles of it.

Facing the French, the Archduke stood with his right wing, 38,000 men, near Eggmühl-Dinzling; with his centre, 28,000 men, near Hausen-Grub, and with his left wing, 35,000 men, in the neighbourhood of the Abens about Siegenburg; one corps, 25,000 men, being on the left flank near Mainburg. He had therefore, since his start from Landshut, extended his front to a length of twenty-four miles (as the crow flies). The greater portion of his forces, pushed forward in a northerly direction, had no longer any enemy in front of them, but exposed their left flank to the Emperor's main body, which was near Abensberg. This main body was for the present only opposed by inferior numbers, and if the Austrians, before accepting battle, wished to concentrate again, the French right wing, under Massena, would in the same time be able to come up to take part in the battle, for it stood only at a distance of fourteen miles from the left wing of the Austrians at Mainburg.

The Events of Ratisbon

The Emperor's strategic conception had been forced to adapt itself rapidly to the situation of affairs, changing as it changed. First the rear concentration of the whole army towards Ingolstadt; then the forward movement of the right wing to meet the left, which latter had to fall back; and finally the complete offensive with the right wing against the enemy's line of operations. This latter resolution became matured in the night before the 20th. At midnight Massena was instructed to despatch his forces in both directions, towards Abensberg and Landshut; he himself was to push forward to Moosburg *viâ* Freising, leaving only Oudinot for the support of the left wing. Finally at 6.30 a.m. the plan was fully matured, Vandamme received orders to advance *viâ* Siegenburg, while Massena, advancing along the Isar, was to throw himself upon the enemy's line of retreat, and if possible to penetrate as far as Landshut.

Then the Emperor rode forward to Abensberg and observed the enemy from there. He was resolved to attack with the utmost determination whatever forces he might have in front of him, with Vandamme, Lefebvre and Lannes, having placed Morand, Gudin and Nansouty under the command of the latter marshal, who had during the night arrived from Spain. Davout was to keep the enemy in front of him engaged. Napoleon looked with confidence upon his situation; "all this morning's reports agree that the enemy is retreating in all haste."[1] How very useful, nay, necessary, such a confidence in himself, such a complete assurance of victory, is in a general, even though it be excessive, we have emphasized before. Indeed the Emperor was fond of impressing upon his subordinates that they should not have too favourable an opinion of the enemy; "in war one sees one's own difficulties and does not take the enemy's into consideration; one must have confidence in oneself."[2]

(73)

---
[1] C. N. To Massena. Vohburg, 20th April, 6.30 a.m.
[2] C. N. To Eugène. . Burghausen, 30th April, 1809.

This is just that special gift of nature which is one of the primary conditions of existence for a military genius. It, on the one hand, permits things to be seen clearly and distinctly as they are in reality, and yet, on the other hand, does not exclude that play of imagination with which the remotest consequences and possibilities that result from the nature of a situation are immediately recognized with prophetic certainty. A gift akin to that which constitutes a great poet: the recognition of a truth above that of mere matters of fact. Thus Goethe said his works "were as a rule conceived from the immediate contemplation of some particular object . . . but they all agreed in this, that the poet, while contemplating some particular, external, and often trivial circumstance, has before his mind's eye some inner and more lofty view."[1] As a matter of fact the Emperor was in error when he imagined in the early morning of the 20th the enemy already " retreating in all haste "; but in a higher sense he was right after all, for all moral power of resistance was already undermined in his enemy; only the external circumstance of an attack was wanting, and on the evening of the 20th his prophecy of the morning had come true.

Napoleon himself described this mental capacity; he first points to the necessity of always seeing things clearly and correctly. "The first quality of a general is to have a cool head, which receives correct impressions of things, which never becomes heated, nor allows itself to be blinded or dazed by good or bad reports;"[2] and on another occasion he said: "A general's mind must in respect of lucidity and clearness resemble the lens of a telescope and never create any mirage."[3] He then went on to emphasize how greatness of mind alone made

[1] Notes to some poems, in Goethe's journey in the Hartz in winter.
[2] Œuvres xxxii. 231. Précis des guerres de F. ii.
[3] O'Méara, N. en exil, ii. 251.

the general: "Marshal Saxe was a mere general, he had no mind," and the same want he ascribed to Wellington.[1] Of course, where this breadth and flexibility of mind are present, there is also the danger ever present, that, more particularly in success, this power of imagination may become too great and interfere with that first and no less necessary quality, clearness of the mind. Indeed we know it was to this danger that Napoleon's genius, destroying itself, succumbed. His contemporaries marvelled at this process, but to us, who can nowadays examine his life more minutely, it appears easy of explanation, nay, almost obvious. "Although he was the most matter-of-fact man probably that ever existed, yet I have never known anyone who allowed himself more easily to be carried away by the charms of imagination; in many circumstances wishing and believing was for him one and the same thing."[2] We shall see before long how the Emperor, during those eventful days in June, 1815, continued, after Ligny, to persist most obstinately in believing that the Prussians were for the time being incapable of hurting him, and that he would have only Wellington to deal with. This was not merely an error in connection with that one individual event, but an error in what he himself called the divine side of the art of war, namely, in a correct appreciation of the opposing general's moral force and the opposing army's condition. But the general who no longer knew how to see the situation clearly with his mental eye, had, when Bülow's appearance at Chapelle-Saint-Lambert at 1 o'clock forced him at last to see with his bodily eye that his obstinately-persisted-in conviction was an error, to pay with his own complete downfall for the fact that his wishes had become a reality to his mind, unhinged by his hitherto boundless success.

Whoever reflects upon this and considers the dangers

[1] Naturally; Wellington beat him.—ED.
[2] Bourrienne, Mém. iv. 120.

which a want of balance in these qualities must entail, will be compelled to remember, before taking upon himself the responsibility of a great command, Napoleon's dry admonition: " War is a serious game, in which one can ruin one's reputation and one's country; a man of any sense will examine himself and ascertain whether he is born for the trade or not." [1]

In accordance with the Emperor's resolve the French therefore proceeded about 8 o'clock to the attack on the Abens. The Emperor himself, with the Crown Prince's and Deroy's divisions, advanced towards Offenstetten; Lannes towards Pattendorf, Wrede by Biburg, and Vandamme *viâ* Siegenburg; everywhere the enemy was forced back and commenced a general retreat to Rottenburg and Pfeffenhausen, continuing it the same evening towards Landshut. Davout, in order to keep the enemy occupied according to the Emperor's instructions, likewise attacked about 11 o'clock and forced the enemy's vanguard back towards the Laber. The Archduke on his side did nothing decisive; with one half of his forces he remained stationary on the Laber, in the neighbourhood of Leyerndorf; the other half he sent forward to Ratisbon, which town was surrendered in the evening by the French garrison. On the other hand an assault upon Stadtamhof, north of the Danube, was unsuccessful, and the division which had undertaken that assault, one of the two Bohemian ones, started on its march to Hemau, in accordance with an order which directed these two corps to advance *viâ* Beilngries to Eichstädt. The other corps had reached Neumarkt.

Thus on this day the Austrian line had been pierced by the forward movement, directed by the Emperor personally from the centre, and the whole left wing, 60,000 men, thrown back upon Landshut, was separated from the Archduke. The latter stood isolated with his 66,000 men, for his line of retreat over the Isar was so

[1] C. N. To Eugène. Burghausen, 30th April, 1809.

THE EVENTS OF RATISBON   51

much threatened by the advancing Emperor and by
Massena, that he would have to give it up. Indeed only
the fortunate circumstance of the surrender of Ratisbon
in the evening of the 20th, offered him the possibility of
opening for himself a new line of operations across the
Danube and a communication with the Bohemian corps,
and even these latter were then marching in a direction
very dangerous for them.

The columns led forward by the Emperor himself had
reached the Great Laber; Lannes was in the neighbourhood of Pattendorf, Lefebvre near Pfeffenhausen, and
behind him Vandamme and Demont. Davout had,
generally speaking, remained in his position near Tengen.
Massena reached Freising, and Oudinot stood halfway
between the latter and the Emperor, in the neighbourhood
of Nandlstadt.

Napoleon spent the night in Rohr; he was of opinion
that after that day's defeat, which he went so far as to call a
second Jena, the Archduke would without delay retreat to
Straubing. Lefebvre was to pursue him with the divisions
of Demont and Deroy, supported if necessary by Davout.
The latter, with Oudinot as a reserve, was then immediately
to turn to Ratisbon and drive the two Austrian corps
north of the Danube into Bohemia, whilst the Emperor
himself with Lannes, Vandamme and Wrede would
advance towards Landshut and pursue the enemy's left
wing, which he considered the main mass, Massena at the
same time blocking its retreat to the Isar.

The Austrians had continued their retreat to Landshut
uninterruptedly, not without some disorder and confusion
in their columns, and in the morning of the 21st the
masses of their infantry were just crowding through this
town, whilst their cavalry showed front to protect the
crossing, when, about 9 o'clock, the Emperor appeared on
the heights near Altdorf. He placed Nansouty and the
Bavarian cavalry under the chief command of Bessières,
and the latter threw the enemy's cavalry into the Isar

valley. The infantry, however, still defended the bridge of Landshut, but about noon Morand's troops captured it by a resolute assault. At 1 o'clock Landshut and large numbers of prisoners were in the hands of the French. Massena had started early in the morning and marched on the left bank of the Isar to Moosburg. Here the bridge, still watched by an Austrian detachment, was in flames; but Massena's advance, under Claparède, succeeded in forcing a passage, and Massena then continued his march on the right bank towards Landshut, where he however did not arrive until the afternoon, too late to cut off the retreat of the Austrians. These had retreated through Geisenhausen and reached Neumarkt during the night.

(74) Davout advanced towards Dinzling and Leyerndorf, the enemy retreating before him behind the Laber and then occupying the road to Ratisbon, whilst holding Eggmühl. In the evening the Austrian divisions stood at Laichling, Sanding, Alt Egglofsheim and Gebelkofen, with Davout's two divisions opposite them in front of Dinzling, and Lefebvre near Schierhng. The two Austrian corps to the north of the Danube, which had been set in motion towards Beilngries, were now countermanded, and consequently the one returned to Ratisbon from Hemau during the night before the 22nd, and the other arrived in Hemau.

Between the two wings of the French army, under the Emperor and Davout, there still stood the Crown Prince's division near Rottenburg, and Tharreau's near Nandlstadt; Boudet had been sent back to Ingolstadt, in order to secure the rear against the two Northern Austrian corps.

The Emperor, who had made his entry into Landshut at 5 o'clock in the afternoon, now began more and more to be convinced that Davout after all had more in front of him than "a mere screen of three infantry regiments";[1] but still expected that his own advance would induce the part of the Austrian army facing Davout to fall

[1] C. N. To Davout. Rohr, 21st April, 5 a.m.

back. In any case he ordered Vandamme, **Lannes** and
St. Sulpice's cavalry to start for Ergoltsbach, in order to
support Davout, if necessary. But reports which came
in immediately afterwards represented the enemy to be
in such force there, that the Emperor was even led to
believe the Bohemian corps had arrived south of the
Danube, for he had now heard of the surrender of
Ratisbon. Consequently he resolved at 3 a.m. to
send only Bessières with the divisions of Molitor and
Wrede and the cavalry of Marulaz in further pursuit of
the Austrian left wing towards the Inn, and to start
himself for Eggmühl, where he intended to arrive at noon,
calculating that he would be able to attack the enemy
with effect about 3 p.m. "I am determined to destroy
Prince Charles' army to-day or at the latest to-morrow."[1]
Vandamme in front, followed by Lannes, whom St.
Sulpice also was ordered to join, was to advance early in
the morning on the high-road *via* Ergoltsbach
to Eggmühl, whilst Massena had orders to collect his
corps and Espagne's cuirassiers at Ergolding and to follow
the others.

We have here again the resolute prosecution of the advantage to be derived from interior lines, brought about by
penetrating the enemy's strategical front, a position which
would enable the Emperor, after having first overwhelmed
the enemy's left wing, to defeat his right wing also.
Such a position permits a general, employing the same
troops first against the one and then against the other
body of the enemy, the two being separated, to outnumber either of them, if only this employment of his
forces is carried out with rapidity and determination. The
Emperor himself undoubtedly felt that it is just in such
manœuvres that the possession of these high mental
qualities alone can give the victory, and therefore we can
understand why he later referred with more pride to these

[1] C. N. To Davout. Landshut, 22nd April 2.30 a.m. Postscript.
4 o'clock.

April days near Ratisbon than to any other of his successes; "the most successful manœuvres I ever carried out, and upon which I congratulate myself most, took place at Eckmühl, and were infinitely superior to those of Marengo and other campaigns before or since."[1] " The battle of Abensberg, the manœuvres of Landshut, and the battle of Eckmühl were the most brilliant and most able of Napoleon's operations."[2]

It is the suddenness of the resolutions taken and the limited time at command, which make of this campaign such a striking contrast with that of 1805. In the latter case there was a most methodical execution of a plan, sketched out in a definite form and strictly adhered to, whilst in what took place round Ratisbon we see constantly changing situations and a constant birth of new resolutions. " In warfare, plans are conceived in face of the enemy. One always has the previous night to prepare oneself,"[3] thus he admonished his brother in 1808, when the latter seemed to succumb under the pressure of his precarious position in Spain. And therefore 1809, that campaign of impromptu resolutions, is no less instructive for us than 1805 was as a striking instance of the logical development throughout the campaign of the one idea contained in the first plan.

The Emperor's activity was tremendous in these days; ever in motion, ever present at the critical point, scarcely allowing himself a few moments for sleep or food, he seems to us almost superior to the conditions of physical existence, and is an example of how a strong will and great mental excitement conquer the inertness of the body " Work is my element, for work I was born and created. I have found the limits of my legs, I have found the limits of my eyes, but I have never been able to find the limits of my power at work;"[4] and of these days Berthier writes:

[1] O'Méara, N. en exil, ii. 226.
[2] Œuvres xxxi. 285. Notes on the Ste. Hélène MSS., etc.
[3] C. N. To Joseph. Kaiserslautern, 24th September.
[4] Mémorial de Ste. Hélène, vi. 272.

"His Majesty is in good health, and is, as usual, equal to his mental labours and able to bear all physical fatigue."[1]

While the Emperor had resolved on the 22nd to overwhelm the Archduke with the mass of his army, the latter also thought of offensive operations for the same day, for he had been reinforced at Regensburg by one of the corps which had hitherto operated on the north of the Danube; he intended to direct his forward movement on Abach and Peising, still, however, holding Eggmühl, and starting at noon. But just as the Austrians were about to move, Vandamme, with the Emperor's advance guard, appeared on the Landshut road, and, at 1.30, forced the enemy's vanguard back upon Eggmühl. The Emperor himself with Lannes came up very soon after and watched the Austrian movements from the heights above Lindach. Then he ordered Vandamme to capture Eggmühl, and Lannes to advance over the Laber on his right, so as to turn the enemy. Simultaneously with this advance and the assault upon Eggmühl, Davout also proceeded to attack in the direction of Lower Laichling. After a resolute resistance the enemy was thrown back upon Sanding. Lannes had crossed the Laber near the Stangl-mill and near Rocking, and at 3.30 the French were advancing along the whole line and the Austrians were in full retreat upon Alt Egglofsheim.

About 7 o'clock the Emperor deployed his army in a line with Hagelstadt and sent the cavalry divisions of Nansouty and St. Sulpice in pursuit of the enemy along the high-road and parallel with it. These overthrew the Austrian cavalry, which opposed them in small bodies, and pursued them hotly as far as Köfering, where their further pursuit was arrested by the infantry. The Emperor, surrounded by his marshals, had personally ridden forward in order to watch this cavalry fight, and it is said that Lannes, under the influence of its fortunate issue, gave him the advice to

(75)

[1] C. N. To Eugène. Ratisbon, 24th April.

follow up without delay with his whole army and to pursue the Austrians uninterruptedly as far as the Danube and to Ratisbon. But the other corps-leaders pleaded the great exhaustion of the troops and the approach of night, and the Emperor, yielding to these representations, called a halt. The cavalry remained in front of Köfering and the infantry on the line Alt Egglofsheim-Thalmassing.

It is true, men who had marched sixteen to nineteen miles between 3 a.m. and 1 p.m., and then pushed forward another five miles, fighting hard by 8 p.m., must have been very fatigued, and their order must have been considerably loosened. Still the Emperor's decision surprises us, who have so often seen him achieve the greatest results by his contempt for any such obstacles. "Genius consists in acting despite all obstacles, and finding few impossibilities, or none."[1] This was the Emperor's opinion, and the very opinion his greatest critic puts in his mouth in the situation which we are at present considering, is no less characteristic of the energy of his strategy: "Had I pursued in the manner the Prussians did after Waterloo, the enemy's army, forced back on the Danube, would have been in the greatest embarrassment."[2] The halt at Alt Egglofsheim is a strange feature in Napoleon's strategy, one of those rare instances where the Emperor, with respect to victory and pursuit, is not a worthy example for us.

The Archduke collected his troops immediately in advance of Ratisbon near Burgweinting and Upper Isling, and sent orders to the one corps still on the north of the Danube at Hemau, to make for Ratisbon; he then took advantage of the night, to throw a pontoon bridge across the river, in addition to the existing stone bridge at Ratisbon. On the southern portion of the theatre of war the Austrian left wing had on this day, continuing its retreat, crossed the Inn near Neu Oetting; of

---

[1] Mém. de Ste. Hél. vi. 210.
[2] Jomini, Vie de N. iii. 175.

Bessières' corps Wrede reached Neumarkt, and Molitor Vilsbiburg.

It is of course a rash proceeding, while sitting at one's desk, to accuse the Emperor of a want of energy; still, if we place the situation clearly before us and examine what consequences might have resulted from this failure to remain in close contact with the Austrians, we may venture to formulate such an accusation, particularly as it is implied in Jomini's criticism, mentioned above. We saw, and shall see still further in the subsequent course of affairs, that the Archduke, forced back upon Ratisbon in the evening of the 22nd, utilized the night to retreat behind the Danube, leaving only some cavalry to oppose the foe the next morning on the right bank. Thus, being in safety on the left bank, he effected a junction with the as yet unbeaten corps marching up from Hemau, and on the 25th April he again stood with his forces reorganized, and mustering 80,000 to 90,000 men in position near Cham. Are we not necessarily, in view of this fact, reminded of the Allies, who though beaten on the 26th August, 1813, at Dresden, yet annihilated Vandamme on the 30th at Kulm, and further of Blücher, who though beaten at Ligny on the 16th June, 1815, reappeared on the morning of the 18th at Wavre with 90,000 men, ready to fight or march as required? In both cases the Emperor had, just as here at Ratisbon, gained the advantage of operating on interior lines, but to follow this advantage up properly it is necessary that the one opponent should, beyond the region of doubt, be *hors de combat* before the main attack upon the other is made in full strength, as Napoleon had done in such a magnificent manner in April, 1796.

But in this case on the 22nd April, just as later on the 28th August and still more on the 17th June, he returned from one of his two interior lines of operation before the enemy, manœuvring there and already defeated, was entirely destroyed by an immediate and relentless pursuit, and thus the latter had leisure to rest and recover, and was, after a short interval, ready for further operations. In 1813 this proceeding entailed a partial defeat for the general. In 1815 it entailed his entire overthrow, for the separated opponents effected a junction on the battle-field. In 1809 circumstances were less favourable for the Austrians, for whilst the Emperor pushed forward on the south of the Danube towards the capital, the Archduke likewise hastened thither by the northern bank. Thus the latter stood on the flank of the French with a strong, reorganized army, a threatening position, and the final result of the Emperor's operations was in no way to be compared with that which he attained after Marengo, after Ulm, and after Jena. We are fairly well enlightened as to the physical and moral conditions which affected the Emperor in June, 1815, and interfered with his operations. In a less degree this is also the case with respect to the same situation in 1813, but as to the 22nd April, 1809, we are altogether unable to account for it; our information is too scanty This abandonment of operations on one of the interior lines, before the effect was complete, an obvious strategical error, must therefore remain for the present a mystery. Still we may look upon it as a significant symptom, as the first link in the chain of future failure.

The opening of the campaign of 1809 is more particularly interesting on account of the rare spectacle of operations badly begun and then quickly altered for the better and carried to a successful issue. This spectacle is rare in the annals of war, for only a very capable general can furnish it, and if such a one stands at the head of the army, the operations will, as a matter of fact, not be begun badly. Yet we can observe the great effect due to a single individual in strategy when in such a situation the commander-in-chief is changed in time. If we examine the course of conduct at the Prussian Headquarters in 1806 or the French in 1870, we shall see a position becoming day by day more unfavourable, a deterioration ever increasing and feeding on itself, like some spreading ulcer. In spite of this, however, we cannot disguise our belief that during the whole course of that process some means of escape still offered themselves; and it will scarcely be denied that, had a gifted general suddenly assumed the chief command over the army in question, on one of those days in October, 1806, or in August, 1870, a considerable change in the course of affairs would have been visible.

Such examples show, indeed, how eminently the whole fate of armies and, through them, of whole states depends on the command of those armies, and more particularly on the individual in whom that command is centred, and history furnishes but very isolated instances of such individuals fulfilling all the conditions required of them in the highest degree; "the causes of that admiration for great generals which history cherishes, and which is so often criticized by narrow hearts and heads, lie in the fact that such leaders must have a combination of the qualities which in other men are most readily admired even when present singly. Head and heart, natural gifts and acquired knowledge, mind and character, coolness and fire, calm and activity, hardness and gentleness, caution and boldness. But if all these have to be united to produce a really great general, what wonder that the latter are so rare, and that, when one appears, contemporaries and posterity alike pay homage to him!"[1] We may indeed appeal to Napoleon himself, for he said: "The art of war is the most difficult of all arts; therefore military glory is universally considered the highest, and the services of warriors are rewarded by any sensible government in a splendid manner and above all other services; a general must have intellect, and what is more rare still, a strong character."[2]

[1] Willisen, Theorie des grossen Krieges, i. 185.
[2] Gouvion St. Cyr, Mém. iii. 48.

CHAPTER III.

WAGRAM.

(76) THE Emperor had spent the night of the 22nd April in the castle of Alt Egglofsheim; he had given up the immediate pursuit of the enemy, and thus he could expect nothing else, but that they would take advantage of the night to place the Danube between themselves and the victor. The few camp-fires which were to be seen in the plain served to confirm this view. As therefore the Archduke had for the present removed himself out of reach of any fresh blows, the Emperor fixed his eyes upon that part of the country where the shortest road would most speedily lead him to the enemy's capital, namely, that which crossed the Inn at Braunau. We know that Bessières stood already in that direction, hitherto, it is true, not so much as the vanguard of the advance upon Vienna, as for the purpose of pursuing and keeping engaged the left Austrian wing, separated from the main body. He now received orders to cross the Inn, whilst for his support Lefebvre, Vandamme, Oudinot and the division St. Hilaire were set in motion as quickly as possible. The same direction was assigned to the Guards, 15,000 men, who were marching up *viâ* Augsburg. Massena, together with Espagne's cuirassiers, received orders to push forward to Straubing, seize any bridge which might have been thrown across there, and to reconnoitre as far as possible along both banks of the Danube. The Emperor himself intended, with Davout,

WAGRAM

Lannes and the cavalry corps of Nansouty, St. Sulpice and Montbrun, to advance to Ratisbon.

At 8 a.m. on the 23rd the cavalry appeared in front of this town and drove the Austrian cavalry back into it. But, although the Emperor brought a considerable number of field guns against it, it remained in the hands of the Austrians, whose departure across the Danube was, however, owing to the effects of the French fire, attended with very heavy losses. It was not until 6 p.m. that the infantry, under Lannes' personal leadership, succeeded, after several vain attempts, in entering by a house near the Straubing gate, which had been demolished by the artillery fire. At 7 o'clock the town was in the hands of the French. But the Austrian rearguard still held the stone bridge; the pontoon bridge was destroyed, but the former was not evacuated until midnight, when the rearguard followed the army, marching away towards Nittenau.

On the 23rd also the left Austrian wing, now 30,000 strong, under the command of General Hiller, had ceased to retreat, and resumed its march towards the west, so as to relieve the Archduke; and Hiller, recrossing the Inn, defeated Wrede's advanced troops at Erharding. On the same day Bessières received the Emperor's orders to advance, while his troops were still in the positions taken up the preceding day. Massena arrived at Straubing, where he found the bridge destroyed.

The Emperor, very tired, established his headquarters in the evening at the Carthusian convent of Prüll. He sent orders to Massena to continue his advance towards Passau, and to assume the chief command over Bessières also, until his own arrival on the Inn. With the possession of Ratisbon the Emperor had on the one hand secured his rear during his further advance upon Vienna against any threatening movement on the part of the Archduke, and on the other hand it was now certain that the latter had retreated towards the Böhmer Wald and was for the present beyond reach. The Emperor therefore resolved to start without delay upon his march to the capital with the mass of his forces, for the shortest road thither was now open to him, and he hoped to arrive there before the Austrians.

It is, of course, generally the enemy's army which ought to be the main objective of the operations, and not any geographical point, however important, and we have already remarked that the fact of letting the enemy escape, appears to us an error on the part of the Emperor; but now that this had been permitted, the advance upon Vienna must be considered as the only correct course. It was now too late to follow the Archduke beyond the Danube, for he could easily find shelter behind the Böhmer Wald, in the defiles of which he could oppose to the advance of the French a resistance which would have taken much time to overcome, and if he finally retreated upon Vienna, would certainly arrive there before the Emperor. Thus by the left bank there was neither a tactical nor a moral success to be expected. But if the Emperor on the other hand marched along the southern bank of the Danube to Vienna direct, he would have the advantage of the shorter road and arrive there before the Archduke, thus gaining the moral success of the capture of the capital. If the Archduke were to leave his position on the Emperor's flank, and cross the Danube in his rear, Napoleon would still have an opportunity for a tactical success. Thus on the morning of the 23rd, after the enemy had been allowed to escape in the evening of the 22nd, the adoption of Vienna as the objective was certainly strategically the best course.

But in any case Ratisbon had to be held securely, and the Archduke constantly watched. This task was entrusted to Davout, and he assembled for the purpose on the 24th the divisions of Morand, Friant and Gudin at Stadtamhof, with the cavalry of Montbrun in advance at Regenstauf. Ratisbon itself was to be occupied by the division Dupas advancing from the rear, and there also the Emperor established his headquarters. Lannes received the chief command over Oudinot (with Tharreau and the cavalry of Colbert) and St. Hilaire, who were, as we know, together with Lefebvre and Vandamme on the march to Landshut. From this town Lefebvre was to turn towards Salzburg, and secure the right flank of the general advance. Massena crossed the Isar at Plattling on the 24th, whilst behind him Boudet occupied Straubing. Hiller, continuing his advance, begun on the preceding day, met Wrede at Stätten and forced him back behind the Rott, where he effected a junction with Molitor; both then withdrew to Aich, whilst Hiller remained at Neumarkt.

On the 25th we find, in continuation of the movement, Davout at Regenstauf, Bessières at Vilsbiburg, Massena was crossing the Lower Vils, Lannes and Lefebvre were in the neighbourhood of Landshut, and Vandamme near Eggmühl. As regards the enemy, the Archduke assembled on this day his army in the position of Cham; Hiller, who received orders to fall back, arrived at Neu-Oetting. In addition the Emperor had ordered Bernadotte to come up as quickly as possible from Saxony, in order to relieve Davout at Ratisbon and set him free for the further advance to Vienna. Meanwhile news came in of the renewed advance of Hiller, and consequently Massena received instructions to try to get on the flank of this column, if the general situation permitted it. In the meantime the Emperor "would not leave Ratisbon until he was sure that the left bank of the Danube was clear."[1] During the night a report came in from Davout, announcing that the Archduke was leaving Cham for Passau, but the Emperor did not credit it, and proposed to the former to push to Bruck, where he would receive news about the Archduke, as Massena's reports did not render any such movement probable.

At 8 a.m. the Emperor started from Ratisbon and

[1] C. N. To the King of Wurtemberg. 25th April.

arrived about noon at Landshut, where he collected Vandamme, Demont (who thus again left Lefebvre's corps), and the cavalry divisions of Nansouty and St. Sulpice. Lannes arrived in Neumarkt and effected there a junction with Bessières. As regards the enemy, Hiller proceeded to Burghausen. Lefebvre was on the march to Wasserburg with his two divisions. Of Massena the Emperor had no news. This marshal reached Passau on that day, and seized there, as well as at Schärding, the bridges over the Inn. The Archduke still lay at Cham; Davout, advancing in accordance with the Emperor's orders, encountered him with his vanguard at Bruck, whilst the mass of this French corps was at Regenstauf and Kürn.

From this date the French army moved rapidly and directly on towards Vienna, as in 1805. On the 27th their centre, Bessières and Lannes, crossed the Inn at Neu-Oetting and Mühldorf, and the Emperor also arrived at the latter place during the evening. The troops which had been assembled as a reserve at Landshut marched to Neumarkt, and Vandamme only to Vilsbiburg. On the left wing Massena collected his forces at Schärding, with orders to call up Boudet also to him. On the right wing Lefebvre reached Wasserburg. Hiller fell back upon Altheim. To the north of the Danube Davout stood at Regenstauf and Rittenau, the Archduke still remaining at Cham.

On the 28th the Emperor arrived at Burghausen at noon, but the destruction of the bridges along the Salzach caused a stoppage of the troops of Lannes and Bessières at this river. The Emperor therefore decided to broaden his front, and ordered Vandamme to Braunau, and Wrede to Tittmoning; the latter thus left Bessières' command. Hiller, retreating further, arrived at Ried; Lefebvre reached Trostburg; Massena remained stationary and Boudet joined the latter. On this day the Archduke also commenced his retreat to Budweis.

The 29th was spent in repairing the bridges over the Salzach, and at last Lannes could cross at Burghausen in the afternoon of the 30th, and on the 1st May we find the army in the following positions: Massena at Siegharding, Lannes at Ried, and Vandamme at Altheim; Bessières was reconnoitring in the direction of Linz and Lambach, Lefebvre was at Salzburg and Wrede at Strasswalchen. On the north of the Danube Davout was marching to Passau, whilst the Archduke, continuing his retreat, was between Klattau and Strakonitz, and Hiller arrived at Wels. The Emperor went to Braunau, and from there urged Massena and Davout to advance as rapidly as possible. The former was to reach Linz with all speed and seize the bridge over the Traun, and the latter was to march up quickly to Passau. This place was now to become the centre of the further operations against Vienna, and consequently the Emperor issued minute instructions for its fortification and armament: "It is there, in case of a retreat, that I intend to cross the Inn, and I purpose to manœuvre constantly round Passau, in case of a retrograde movement of my army. Braunau, Schärding and Burghausen are of no importance to me."[1] Finally the army in Italy under Eugène received orders to attempt to come up by Bruck through Styria. On the evening of the 1st May the Emperor left Braunau and arrived at Ried late in the night.

On the 2nd Massena and Lannes, in consequence of the orders received, continued their forward movement with all speed, and their vanguard repulsed some Austrian troops at Efferding and Wels after a determined resistance. In the main the two marshals reached the places assigned to them. Massena, now again joined by Marulaz, had Hiller in front of him at Linz. Bessières also reached Wels, Wrede arrived at Vöcklabruck, and Lefebvre was further back at Salzburg. Davout reached Passau and the Emperor Lambach at noon.

[1] C. N. To Berthier. Braunau, 1st May.

At 3 a.m. Hiller evacuated Linz and took up a position at Ebelsberg for the defence of the passage over the Traun. Here Massena engaged him about 10 o'clock. Klein München was stormed, and Coehorn, with his brigade of Claparède's division, which was in advance, reached the long Traun bridge at the same time as the retreating Austrians, and a furious fight took place, attended by heavy losses. Coehorn, however, drove the enemy back and entered Ebelsberg along with them.

Whilst Massena placed a strong battery in position to play upon the commanding situation of the castle hill, the rest of Claparède's division crossed the bridge and advanced to Ebelsberg to the support of Coehorn, and the whole town, as well as the castle hill, were captured. Towards 3 o'clock, it is true, Hiller drove the French back again into the lower part of Ebelsberg, but now the division of Legrand arrived, and succeeded, in conjunction with Claparède's, though with heavy losses, in taking the castle and driving Hiller from his position. Bessières, who had come up in the morning with some cavalry along the left bank of the Traun, took charge of the pursuit.

The Emperor had arrived at Wels at noon, and despatched thither as soon as he heard the sound of cannon from Ebelsberg, Nansouty and Molitor along the right bank of the Traun. He also went in the same direction and arrived at Massena's quarters at nightfall. Here he was in time to witness the heavy losses, which the bold undertaking of storming the defile of Ebelsberg frontally with the enemy in a strong position behind it, entailed. He, it is true, drew Coehorn's attention to the fact, that by going less hastily to the work this loss might have been considerably lessened, "still Coehorn had commended himself to his mind as a man of great value."[1] The Emperor did not indeed demand a bloodless success, he simply demanded

[1] Savary, Mém. iv. 160.

success. Even if it were now and then gained by greater sacrifices than would have been necessary if more prudent counsels had prevailed, he still rightly rated enterprise, resolution and energy in his subordinate officers, higher than ability, and preferred to suffer the losses which the former qualities sometimes entailed, rather than there should be any shrinking on account of a too clear perception of the attendant dangers; "true wisdom for a general lies in energetic resolves."[1] Pelet replies very justly to those who wanted to blame Massena on account of this attack: "In accordance with the principles of warfare, he had only to look to the exact execution of the orders received and to the enemy in front of him. Any support from Lambach was more hinted at than actually promised to him."[2] He had indeed been told of probable support on the part of Lannes from Lambach, in case the enemy should make a stand at Ebelsberg, but on the 3rd Lannes was marching towards Steyer, and the roars of the guns at Ebelsberg did not induce him to leave that road.

But one thing must astonish us, namely, to note how, after all, the conduct of the whole affair on that day was somewhat beyond the Emperor's control. If he really did not wish for a frontal attack upon Ebelsberg, "that celebrated position, the only one on the Traun to be dreaded,"[3] he ought to have said so definitely to Massena, and not simply have urged him on to a more rapid advance. Furthermore he ought to have taken care to be informed in time whether Hiller was likely to make a stand there. For this his own place ought possibly to have been with Massena's column, and finally he should, if this was the case, have seen that Lannes really moved up, so as to turn the position. But here also his increasing indifference to the conduct of affairs became evident. Important questions became gradually matters of detail

[1] Précis des guerres de F. ii. Œuvres xxxii. 263.
[2] Mém. sur la guerre de 1809, ii. 205.
[3] C. N. To Lannes. Enns, 4th May.

for him, which were not specially his domain and which his subordinate officers were left to see to. But this duty was naturally not always performed by the latter to the advantage of the whole. The danger, therefore, increased more and more, that some operation, left as a detail to some subordinate officer, might be of such importance that the whole enterprise would fail on account of its insuccess. On the Katzbach, at Grossbeeren and at Dennewitz this danger became a reality.

During the next few days the bridge which had been destroyed at Enns caused Massena some delay, whilst Lannes was advancing to Amstetten by St. Peter. On the 7th May we find the Imperial headquarters, which had left Enns at noon, at the monastery of Mölk, where Lannes and Bessières also were. The former had now the chief command over the corps of Oudinot (divisions of Tharreau and Claparède and Colbert's light cavalry) and the divisions St. Hilaire and Demont. Bessières was put over Espagne and the light cavalry division Montbrun, which had now come up. - Massena (divisions Legrand, Carra St. Cyr, Molitor, Boudet and the light cavalry of Marulaz) arrived with his van at Amstetten; Nansouty and St. Sulpice were behind him, and the Guards stood at Strengberg. Lefebvre, joined again by Wrede from Lambach, was to secure Salzburg as a point of support, and then proceed to the conquest of the Tyrol. Davout had been at Linz since the 5th, where Vandamme also had been left behind and placed under his orders. Bernadotte, with 22,000 men, had reached the neighbourhood of Roetz. Hiller, who had during these days retreated *viâ* Strengberg, Kemelbach and Mölk, now stood at Mautern, whither the Archduke also started on the 7th from Budweis and reached Schweinitz.

From Mölk the Emperor despatched one of Lannes' aides-de-camp with a few men across the Danube, to bring in some prisoners from a hostile detachment, observed on the other side of the river. The information gained in this manner made him aware of Hiller's presence at Mautern and of the Archduke's march on that place. Thereupon the Emperor sent Lannes on the 8th after Bessières, who had proceeded further in advance towards Mautern. The former was to seize the bridge there and to guard by its destruction against any flank attack on the part of the enemy. But during the evening a report reached him that the enemy had themselves destroyed their bridge, and he immediately sent orders to Lannes to start for Vienna at 2 o'clock the next morning. Bessières and then Massena were to follow him. During the night of the 9th, the Emperor left St. Pölten, whither he had removed his headquarters in the evening of the 8th, and hastened to the head of Lannes' corps, with which he arrived before Vienna at 10 a.m. Massena reached Purkersdorf; Davout, having started from Linz, stood at Enns, Pöchlarn and St. Pölten, and Vandamme was at Linz. Hiller was at Stein; the Archduke at Zwettel. Vienna had a garrison of about 25,000 men, half militia. The Emperor remarked: "The inhabitants are armed, and seem to have a desire to defend themselves. We shall see whether this will be a repetition of Madrid."[1]

It was soon seen that the capital of Austria, like that of Spain, was by no means ready to open its gates to the conqueror without resistance. It is true the extensive suburbs, surrounded by tenaille ramparts of feeble profile, were evacuated, but the inner town, with its bastioned enclosure, revetted ditches and covered ways, was to be defended at the approach of the enemy. Whilst Lannes occupied the suburbs, the Emperor, who had established his headquarters in the château of Schönbrunn, tried negotiation, but without success. He therefore ordered, in the afternoon of the 11th, Carra St. Cyr and Boudet to take up a position on the heath of Simmering. He himself reconnoitred, in company with Massena, the canal of the Danube along the Prater, and had a

[1] C. N. To Davout. St. Pölten, 9th May, 6 p.m.

bridge thrown across during the night, opposite the Lusthaus. At the same time the town was bombarded with howitzers from 9 p.m. At 9 o'clock in the morning of the 12th Massena, advancing from the Prater, took possession of the Leopoldstadt, and now Vienna was evacuated by its defenders, who destroyed the Tabor bridge. On the same day Hiller took up a position on the Bisam hill, and the Archduke reached the neighbourhood of Meissau. Of the French there stood along the Danube: Davout at Pöchlarn, Mölk and St. Pölten; Vandamme still held Linz, and Bernadotte was at Passau, where soon afterwards the division of Dupas, left behind there, was placed under his orders.

On the morning of the next day, the 13th May, the 600 men left behind to garrison the inner town surrendered, as they had been ordered, and the Emperor was completely master of the capital. The most urgent question of the moment was the passage of the Danube. The course of the river had been reconnoitred since the 11th, and three points had been fixed upon, Fischamend, Kaiser-Ebersdorf and Nussdorf, of which, however, the first, as being too distant, was not further considered. At the other two points bridges were to be thrown across, above Vienna by Lannes and below Vienna by Massena, and it was determined to use the one which was ready first. This was not the case with the bridge at Nussdorf, for the first 500 men, who were sent to the northern bank as a protection of the work, were discovered and taken prisoners by the Austrians. Thus the other place of crossing became all the more important, and Massena pushed on the work there during the next few days with unremitting zeal, collecting and preparing the materials for the construction of the bridge. In the meantime the Archduke had marched up, and on the 16th, having effected a junction with Hiller, he took up a position between Korneuburg, Enzersfeld, Great-Ebersdorf and Strebersdorf. One of his corps had received orders to make a dash from Budweis to Linz, and Vandamme was attacked there in the afternoon of the 17th; but the Austrians were soon repulsed with the aid of Bernadotte, who had marched to this point. The Emperor felt no uneasiness about this attack upon his lines of communication, of which he was informed on the 18th; his attention was now exclusively turned to the construction of the Danube bridge. But the latter was delayed from day to day. On the 15th he fixed the commencement of the passage for the 17th, and on the 17th for the 18th or 19th; but it was not until the afternoon of this latter day that the final orders could be issued for the army to cross the river on the 20th. In the meantime Davout had been moved up closer to Vienna; he stood now at St. Pölten, Sieghartskirchen, and with his van in the capital. During this time Eugène, marching up from Italy with his army of 57,000 men, had reached Villach, and his opponent, Archduke John, retreated before him with his 45,000 men to Völkermarkt.

Soon after noon on the 19th the Emperor arrived in Kaiser-Ebersdorf. Already on the evening of the 18th some 800 men had crossed to the Lobau and had driven out the Austrian outposts stationed there. The Emperor now ordered the whole division of Molitor to cross, and at 5 o'clock the construction of the bridge was taken in hand. In the meantime the Emperor issued orders to all the corps of his army; Bessieres was to bring up the divisions of Espagne, St. Sulpice and Nansouty to Kaiser-Ebersdorf at 5, 6 and 8 o'clock in the morning, and hold them in readiness to cross; in addition he was to bring up to the same spot as early as possible the light cavalry of Colbert and Marulaz and a division just formed under Lasalle. Massena's whole corps was to be ready for crossing the stream by daybreak, and Lannes at 9 o'clock; Davout was to move up to Vienna and throw a bridge across at Nussdorf. Bernadotte received instructions to push forward towards Bohemia, either in

(77)

(76)

the direction of Budweis or of Zwettel, in order to keep the enemy from making attempts against the part of the Danube between Krems and Vienna, but Linz was to remain covered, and Enns was to be occupied by Vandamme.

(77) In the morning of the 20th the whole division of Molitor stood in the Lobau. At noon the bridges over the two arms of the Danube, which were to be crossed first, were completed, and about 3 o'clock, under the eyes of the Emperor himself, who had gone to the Lobau, the bridging of the last arm of the Danube, which separated the Lobau from the mainland (that of Gross-Enzersdorf), was begun, in the angle near Asparn House. About 6 o'clock this also was finished and Molitor crossed first, followed by Lasalle and Marulaz, the latter two being sent forward towards Asparn and Essling to reconnoitre. During the night Boudet also crossed over the bridges, though not without difficulty, for the waters of the Danube were rising, and the material, hurriedly collected and not fitting everywhere, showed itself constantly deficient, and rendered continual repairs necessary. On the Lobau fifty-four guns were at the same time placed in battery to protect the bridges, and on the left bank the construction of a bridge-head was begun.

At midnight the Emperor, who received most contradictory reports from the cavalry in advance as to the enemy, sent Massena forward to examine the situation of affairs, and the latter reported that the enemy's army was standing ready on the Russbach. The Archduke had actually formed the plan of allowing the French army to cross, and then giving battle, and he was during the night occupied with placing his corps in position along the line Strebersdorf—Gerasdorf—Deutsch-Wagram. With the break of day the Emperor mounted his horse; accompanied by Berthier, Massena and Lannes, he wished to ride forward to the edge of the heights near Asparn, but was prevented by the Austrian cavalry scouting close up to the Danube.

He ordered the latter to be driven off by Espagne's cuirassiers, who had just crossed; then he reconnoitred the ground, and remarked to Massena: "It is my purpose to refuse my left wing and attack by pushing forward my right."[1] Thus, leaning on the Danube with his left wing, he intended to wheel the right against the Austrian front.

But the Archduke also set himself in motion. His army moved off at noon and marched to the attack in five columns viâ Stadlau, Kagrau and Breitenlee on Asparn, viâ Aderklaa to Essling, and the fifth, which was to make the turning movement, on Gross-Enzersdorf, the cavalry advancing between Raasdorf and Breitenlee by Neu-Wirthshaus. At this moment the Emperor had only three infantry divisions on the northern bank of the Danube. Molitor behind Asparn, this village being only feebly occupied; Legrand behind him on the left, and Boudet behind Essling; in front of these villages stood Lasalle and Espagne.

It is difficult to account for the Emperor's proceedings, more especially as he had personally reconnoitred the ground. A glance at the map will teach us that a strong and early occupation of Asparn and Essling, so as to put them in a state of defence, was most urgently necessary. For by those measures a spacious and safe bridge-head would have been created, which would have ensured the undisturbed free passage of the whole army to the northern bank. On the other hand, if the enemy occupied those villages and the ridge joining them, the French army, surrounded and forced back against the Danube, would be in a most unfavourable tactical position, and could scarcely hope to gain sufficient space to deploy in the face of a strong enemy. Must we assume that the Emperor, spoiled by success and sovereign power, here too contented himself with giving the order, the only one which Pelet mentions, namely, "to cross the Danube and to march against the enemy,"[2] and then left all the details

[1] Pelet, Mém. sur la guerre de 1809, iii. 283.   [2] Ibid.

of execution to his subordinate officers? In that case we
can certainly not wonder that 1809 was the last campaign
which ended successfully for him.

It seems almost as if the Emperor's gifts as a leader had
taken that direction which he mentioned as characteristic
of Massena: "He was resolute, brave, intrepid, full of
ambition and self-interest; his most prominent feature
was obstinacy . . . he conceived his plans for an attack
in a very indifferent manner . . . but with the first sound
of the cannon, in the midst of bullets and dangers, his mind
became clear and strong. If he was beaten, he began
again, just as if he had been victorious."[1] This want of
definition in the plan of attack is evident here, as previously it might have been noticed at Heilsburg. But the
first sound of the cannon, the beginning of the battle,
immediately awakened the whole energy of the general
struggling for victory. That obstinacy, which, though
beaten, yet does not submit to play the part of the
vanquished. For Napoleon, though defeated at Asparn,
displayed it, even as he had already displayed it after the
indecisive battle of Eylau. We know of Massena, that he
was in the highest degree addicted to sexual indulgence
and to luxury, and we can imagine that his military
talents were obscured by these, until the first cannon
shot set him free. May not indeed a similar process
have now taken place in the Emperor? He also was
now the slave of sensual pleasures, and if not of the greed
for pecuniary riches, yet of the greed for boundless power.
Thus we may well believe that for him, too, imminent
danger, and the excitement of battle itself, were needed to
rouse him to a full exercise of his magnificent military
talents. Indeed his retinue noticed that he was less
eager than usual in his preparations for battle, and said:
"The Emperor has for a long time been tired of war, as
much so as our young conscripts; he only continues waging

---

[1] Mém. Camp. d'Italie, Œuvres xxix. 129.

it from a sense of duty and against his will;"[1] and we hear that "it was not in his army, particularly during the campaigns after Austerlitz, that most admiration, respect and attachment to him were expressed. He had, so to speak, a slovenly manner of carrying on the war. He neglected much, risked much, and sacrificed everything to his personal success. Ever trusting more and more to his good fortune and the terror of his presence, he only occupied himself with hiding his mistakes, his defeats, his losses by decisive blows, dealt by his own hands; ever resolved to deny or conceal anything that could damage his personal reputation."[2]

And yet we must not forget, in venturing to apply such criticisms to the Emperor's strategy, that as yet those two principal qualifications of a general, namely, an all-embracing eye and energetic resolution, were still undiminished in him. Our strictures do not really apply to the military genius of the Emperor himself, but to the organization of his staff. This did not prove itself competent to bear its share of the burden of details and their execution, leaving to the general only the responsibility for the conduct of the war as a whole, which he alone was able to bear. We shall see that in 1812, when the immense extension of the operations caused this want to be especially felt, the Emperor exclaimed angrily: "The general staff is organized in such a manner, that it cannot be relied upon in anything."[3] The more the armies increase in size the more this becomes necessary. If in a modern commander the same breadth of vision were combined with the same contempt for details, a carefully drilled staff would be at his command to render the latter innocuous and the successful development of the former possible.

About 1 o'clock, then, Massena's troops, in position on

[1] Pelet, Mém. sur la guerre de 1809, ii. 304.
[2] Mme. de Rémusat, Mém. ii. 208.
[3] C. N. To Berthier. Vilna, 2nd July.

the slightly rising ground south of Asparn, saw the heads of the Austrian columns appearing upon the ridge near the village, and they soon captured this feebly occupied point. Molitor was immediately sent forward to recapture it, and indeed seized Asparn, but when he wanted to advance beyond it, he observed about 2 o'clock the dense masses of the Austrians lying between Hirsch stetten and Neu-Wirthshaus. These soon commenced their attack upon Asparn, and Massena, who assumed in person the command of Molitor's troops, had to confine himself to an obstinate defence of the village, around which, for the rest of that day, a struggle raged, which was attended by heavy losses on both sides. Whilst the Archduke's right wing was thus attacking Asparn, his left advanced towards Essling, outflanking it. In the gap between these two villages the Emperor had stationed the cavalry divisions of Lasalle and Espagne, united under Bessières' command, for Legrand's infantry, the only division still at his disposal, was to remain for the present behind Asparn, as a reserve. When Gross-Enzersdorf was evacuated before the advancing Austrians, and these commenced their attack upon Essling, defended by Lannes with Boudet's division, the Emperor commanded Bessières to throw himself upon the enemy's artillery, which was concentrated in the centre and enfiladed Essling and Asparn. Bessières charged, and the Austrian batteries had to limber up and fall back, but the fire of the infantry behind them repulsed the cavalry attack along the whole line.

At 5 o'clock therefore the issue of the battle depended on the possession of Essling and Asparn. The former village was still completely in possession of the French, and the latter had been repeatedly taken and lost again by both sides and was filled with combatants from the two armies. Legrand also was involved in this struggle, and, when towards evening the Archduke made a last attempt to capture Asparn, he was replaced as a reserve by Carra St.

Cyr's division, which had just come up. But these troops were the last which could for the time reinforce the French ranks, for at 3 o'clock the large bridge over the Danube gave way under the pressure of rafts, tree trunks and other heavy masses borne down upon it by the rising waters. In spite of incessant labours this happened again and again up to midnight, so that during the whole time the passage of the troops was interrupted. With the fall of night the struggle around Essling ceased without the French losing that village, and Asparn also remained half in their possession, but the struggle only ceased entirely in the middle of the night. The remarkable aptitude of the French soldiers for the defence of villages, well known in the annals of war, was brilliantly proved at the most decisive moment.

Thus both armies rested during the night in close proximity to each other. The Emperor, who had been looking on near the brick field at Essling, went into bivouac in the evening close to the Gross-Enzersdorf arm of the river on the northern bank, and hurried on, with the greatest zeal, the passage of fresh forces. So early as 9 p.m. he sent a most urgent request to Davout: "You must send us your whole park and as much ammunition as possible. Send as many troops here as you can, only keeping sufficient to guard Vienna. Send us provisions also."[1] By the morning the following corps could be moved up to the battle-field : St. Hilaire, who was placed in position to the left of Essling, still occupied by Boudet; Oudinot, who was stationed on the left rear of St. Hilaire; besides Nansouty, a portion of the Guards and Demont, who were placed as a reserve, in front of the bridge.

On the left wing Massena had occupied Asparn with Legrand's division, Carra St. Cyr being behind that village. Molitor, who had suffered heavily, had been withdrawn and placed in rear near the river.

It was on this wing that the struggle first recom-

[1] C. N. Bivouac on the Danube.

menced. As early as 2 a.m. the Austrians made a fresh attempt to capture Asparn, but Massena brought up Carra St. Cyr, and not only repulsed the enemy's attack, but succeeded in taking possession of the whole locality. Against Essling also the attack had soon after this been renewed, and the Austrians penetrated partly into the village. But Boudet held out in a few specially strong buildings, and here too the attack was soon repulsed.

With the commencement of the firing the Emperor had mounted his horse and ridden forward. He thought himself now strong enough to assume the offensive, more especially as he expected in addition the immediate arrival of Davout. His decisive attack was to be directed to the enemy's centre, and he therefore sent a message to Lannes to say "that he was going to advance between Asparn and Essling, so as to pierce the Archduke's centre."[1] He himself took up his station again by the brick-kiln of Essling.

Massena had already begun to follow up his advantage beyond Asparn, when the Emperor was informed about 7 a.m. that Davout was commencing to cross to the Lobau; he therefore resolved to begin his decisive thrust. Massena received orders to hold Asparn and Essling, where Boudet still was, whilst Lannes was to proceed to the attack with Oudinot, St. Hilaire and Bessières. The Emperor himself pointed out to him with his finger the spot between the enemy's cavalry and the left of the three columns directed towards Asparn, that is about in the direction of Breitenlee, the point where he desired to see the blow delivered. Lannes set himself in motion; the Austrian line fell back before his onslaught, and Bessières now advanced vigorously through the gaps in the infantry. The Archduke himself hastened up to meet the threatening danger with his reserves, and a momentary pause occurred, for the French columns also were shaken. In this situation the Emperor received, at about 8 o'clock, news that the large bridge over the main

---

[1] Pelet, Mém. sur la guerre de 1809, iii. 32.

stream had again given way, and that therefore he could not expect either the arrival of Davout within a short time, or any fresh supplies of ammunition, which was beginning to give out. Some heavy vessels floated down the Danube by the Austrians had effected this.

The Emperor now ordered the attack to be at once suspended and the retirement to the line Asparn—Essling to be begun without delay. The enemy, however, soon became aware of this and began to pursue along the whole line. The violent struggle about the possession of Asparn and Essling recommenced. The former village was again repeatedly taken and retaken, but remained finally in the hands of the French, whilst the Austrians penetrated into Essling, where Boudet saw himself confined to the large massive granary, which made an excellent *réduit*. At the same time the Austrian army pushed forward in the centre, in the space between the two villages. To this threatened piercing of his line of battle the Emperor opposed some hastily collected artillery, as well as Bessières' cavalry, and succeeded in checking the Austrians. At 1 o'clock the fighting was, generally speaking, at an end, only the artillery fire continued for a time, a sure sign of complete exhaustion. On the right French wing alone Essling was altogether lost by a renewed attack, but was retaken about 3 o'clock by the Young Guard, brought up from the reserve.

But before the advance of the Austrian wings, which threatened to envelop it, the French army, exhausted, and suffering from a want of ammunition, especially as regards its artillery, was no longer able to stand, and gradually retreated upon the bridge, though still holding Asparn and Essling. The Emperor had become convinced that he must give up the hope of holding a position in advance of the bridge and was resolved to retreat to the Lobau. He went himself on to the island, in order to examine its capacity for defence, but soon saw that any speedy reconstruction of the bridge, to allow the rest of the army to come up, was out of the question. He then returned to the bridge-head, near the Asparn House, and sent for Massena. The latter, still occupied with the defence of Asparn, arrived soon after 7 o'clock, and now the Emperor invited his officers to give him their opinion as to the situation. They all proposed the evacuation of the Lobau and the retreat to the right bank of the Danube. The Emperor, having listened in silence, said: "But, gentlemen, this is equivalent to giving me the advice to go to Strasburg; if I retreat over the Danube, I shall have to evacuate Vienna, because the enemy will cross behind me, and then we shall possibly be forced to retreat as far as Strasburg. In the position in which I am at present, the only defence I have against him is the possibility of crossing over to the left bank of the river, if he cross to the right bank; so that I could manœuvre around Vienna, which is now my capital and centre of my resources. If I now recross the Danube, and the Archduke, say, should proceed to cross it at Linz, I should have to march to Linz; whilst in the position in which I am now, I should, if he commenced that movement, cross and follow him, until he turned to face me. It is impossible that I could go to a distance from Vienna without risking the loss of 20,000 men, of whom 10,000 will resume their place at the front before a month is gone by."[1] No one answered, indeed it was impossible to refute the concise strategical reasoning. Thus it was decided to hold the Lobau as a powerful bridge-head strongly garrisoned, and to repeat, after more mature and careful preparation, the passage of the Danube, which had been too hastily and carelessly undertaken. The chief command on the Lobau the Emperor entrusted to Massena, then he betook himself diagonally across the island to the main stream, and arrived soon after midnight at the destroyed bridge. Impressed by this sight he ordered Massena to be instructed to destroy the

[1] Savary, Mém. iv. 128.

bridge over the most northern arm in the morning and to send the material to the main stream, and as the restoration of the large bridge would take time, he was to take measures at the Lobau for a vigorous defence. Then he crossed, about 1 o'clock, with Berthier and Savary to Kaiser-Ebersdorf.

In accordance with the resolution taken, the Emperor's energies during the next few days were absorbed in two directions, namely, massing the army by moving up reinforcements, and careful preparations for constructing the bridge.

With respect to the former the Emperor had, at 12.30 p.m., during the battle of the 22nd, already instructed Davout to write to Bernadotte to be very careful not to penetrate too far into Bohemia. On the 24th the latter was further informed that he would have to keep a watch on Linz, and might possibly be recalled to Vienna. Vandamme received orders to come up to St. Pölten, and Davout, whose last troops would thereby be set free, was to collect all his forces near Vienna. On the Lobau Massena's corps alone remained behind; all the other troops were withdrawn to the right bank, and thus there stood near Vienna and Kaiser-Ebersdorf the Guards, Davout and Oudinot corps, hitherto Lannes', the latter having died on the 31st May of a wound received at Essling. The entire cavalry, drawn up in a huge crescent, covered the army towards the south and the east, the light divisions standing near Wiener-Neustadt, Bruck-on-the-Leitha and Hainburg, and the heavy divisions in second line near Fischamend and in front of Laxenburg.

For the present the Emperor's headquarters remained at Kaiser-Ebersdorf. Here he received on the 27th news that Eugène had arrived at Bruck, in Styria. Thus communication was established with the Army of Italy and a considerable reinforcement thereby obtained. The Archduke John, who had fallen back to Graz, now retreated into Hungary towards Körmend. In addition

(76)

Marmont's corps, 10,000 men, was approaching from Dalmatia, but had as yet only reached Fiume. Thus having secured his right wing on the side of Styria, the Emperor now gave up the cavalry positions at Hainburg and Wiener-Neustadt, and further secured himself by a stronger and more advanced position in Hungary itself. Gudin and Lasalle were watching Pressburg, which was occupied in force by the Austrians, in order to oppose any attempt at crossing there, and in addition a mixed division, consisting chiefly of cavalry with a little infantry, was pushed forward to Oedenburg.

The more the army thus increased in numbers near Vienna, the less anxiety did the Emperor feel for his lines of communication, and the more urgently did he order all the forces still in the rear to close up. Vandamme was moved up to Sieghartskirchen and Bernadotte to St. Pölten; the latter being replaced at Linz by Lefebvre, with the Crown Prince's and Wrede's divisions. For the subjugation of the Tyrol had become only of secondary importance, now that the approach of a hostile army from Italy through that country was no longer possible. The Emperor remained too faithful to his guiding principle of not attending to anything of secondary importance, when making sure of the main point, to allow Lefebvre's corps any longer to occupy itself in subjugating a country whose fate would in any case be decided by the issue of the war as a whole. It was on the Danube, near Vienna, that this would be decided, therefore nothing could be more important than to concentrate there all his forces, in accordance with the rule so often enunciated by him: "The first principle of war is, that no battle should be fought except with all the troops which can possibly be collected on the field of operations."[1] Therefore he felt no uneasiness on hearing that Deroy, who had remained alone in the Tyrol, was driven out of it.

[1] Mém. de Ste. Hel. Précis des Guerres de Fred. II., iv. 284.

WAGRAM

Napoleon's army consisted on the 1st June of:—
Guards, 11,000 men; Massena, 30,000 men; Davout, 35,000 men; Oudinot, 24,000 men; Eugène, 56,000 men; Marmont, 10,000 men; Bernadotte, 24,000 men; Vandamme, 16,000 men; Lefebvre, 22,000 men; Cavalry Reserve, Bessières, 13,000 men.

The Emperor, having received a report that the Archduke John appeared to be marching to Raab, ordered Eugène, who had at first concentrated his army at Wiener-Neustadt, to advance to Oedenburg. From there he was to march against the Archduke John and drive him back into Hungary. The Emperor did not really believe in this march to Raab, but thought the Archduke intended probably first to wait at Körmend to see what steps would be taken against him. He therefore advised Eugène to proceed to Güns, and from there, according to the news he received, to Sarvar or by Steinamanger to Körmend. He watched Eugène's further movements attentively from Schönbrunn, where he had again established his headquarters. He assisted him, it is true, with his advice; but did not, in spite of his great and conscious military superiority over his step-son, give him any binding instructions as to the manner in which he was to carry out his commission; for he was at too great a distance, and, as we have seen in Spain, he did not interfere with details in such cases. Only one thing he urged upon him: "Above all things see that you march in a collected and united body,"[1] and the next day he gave him a lecture on his late operations in Italy, about which he said: "In your pursuit of Prince John from the Tagliamento you did not march in sufficiently close order, you might have met with disasters."[2] In addition he advised him to keep an advance-guard of one division of infantry with a dozen guns and a good deal of cavalry one hour's march in front of his army, and to be carefully on the watch, for the Austrians,

---
[1] C. N. Schönbrunn, 6th June, 9 a.m.
[2] C. N. Schönbrunn, 7th June, 2.30 a.m.

manœuvring in their own country, might easily appear where least expected. But if the Archduke should await him in a well-prepared position, he was to consider carefully where and how to attack him, for "a forward movement without thorough combination may succeed, if the enemy are on the retreat, but it never succeeds if they are in a good position and determined to defend themselves; in this case only a system or combination can win a battle."[1] The Archduke left Körmend on the 7th and marched *viâ* Hidvég, Vásarhely and Pápa to Raab, and took up a position near this latter town, then fortified. Here Eugène met him on the 13th, attacked him on the 14th, and defeated him, whereupon the Austrians fell back upon Komorn.

Whilst thus the position of the army near Vienna was being rendered secure by moving up reinforcements and forcing back the enemy's troops wherever they showed themselves, the preparations for the main enterprise, viz. the crossing of the Danube, were set about with all energy and pushed on to the utmost. On the 23rd May, the great bridge over the Danube, only just restored, had been destroyed again, and after the bridges leading from the Lobau to the mainland had been removed about 3 o'clock in the afternoon of that day, the French army which had fought at Aspern found itself shut in on the Lobau and hampered by the care of about 20,000 wounded. On the 24th the great bridge was restored again; immediately the wounded were conveyed back, and on the 25th the troops began to follow them also.

Now for the first time the rich treasures in material which the arsenal at Vienna contained were brought into use, and the bridge over the main stream was protected by a line of piles, which were at the same time arranged as a foot-bridge for the infantry. On the 10th June the Emperor gave orders for the construction of six rowing

---

[1] C. N. Schönbrunn, 7th June, 2.30 a.m.

gunboats and a floating battery, so as to have complete command of the river and to be able to frustrate more easily all attempts on the bridge. He had remained in Kaiser-Ebersdorf up to the 4th and visited the Lobau daily during this period, so as to superintend the works there, afterwards moving his headquarters back to Schönbrunn.

He now intended to cross the arm bounding the eastern front of the Lobau, in order to turn the enemy completely by this movement, and then wheel to the left and attack their left flank. The Austrians, who had fallen back to the line Deutsch-Wagram—Markgrafneusiedl, now held the front from Asparn to Essling with one corps and were throwing up fortifications there. For the execution of his plan the Emperor had to secure two things; first, the possibility of issuing from the Lobau with a broad front, entailing the construction of numerous bridges, and secondly, the full command of the Lobau and from it of the plain of Gross-Enzersdorf, in order to have his masses ready there for debouching. For this latter purpose numerous infantry positions were established on the island, and 113 guns placed in position on it, of which 80 were to command the plain of Gross-Enzersdorf and prevent any preparations of the enemy there, 18 were to be kept in reserve and 15 were to defend the northern front. A few days later 12 more guns were added to the above 80.

Then the Emperor determined to secure the Hansel-Grund, in order to make from there a turning movement into the plain of Enzersdorf,[1] and also to have in case of need a fresh line of retreat thither, and thence to the Lobau. For this end a bridge was to be constructed from that island to the Hansel-Grund at the junction of the arm enclosing the Lobau with the Danube; besides which three bridges were to be thrown across from the Hansel-Grund over the small arm separating the latter from the plain of Enzersdorf. For the main crossing the material for five

---
[1] Gross-Enzersdorf.

bridges was collected in the canal behind the "île Alexandre"; and a complete pontoon bridge was constructed, so as to be put across the river in one piece. The inner channel also of the Lobau was bridged over in four places; the place where the bridge had formerly stood at the Aspern House was also to be used again, and a bridge was to be thrown over to the "île du moulin." Thus the Emperor would possess five bridges at the main point of crossing, which would permit of an almost simultaneous advance of his whole army; whilst on his right flank the bridge from the Hansel-Grund, and on his left flank that of the Aspern House and that of the "île du moulin" would afford lines of retreat in case of necessity.

Since his return to Schönbrunn the Emperor had for some time ceased to inspect the works on the Lobau personally, for fear of drawing the enemy's attention too much to that point; on the 18th June, however, he reconnoitred the river course along the eastern front of the Lobau in person, and revisited the place during the next two days. The preparations for the crossing were, it is true, completed as a whole, but the Emperor still delayed the operation a little, so as to give time to make sure of all details, and especially to bring up a plentiful supply of ammunition for the artillery, for this arm was, by its fire from the Lobau, to ensure the passage of the river. At 5 p.m. on the 30th June, Massena threw a pontoon bridge across at the old place near Aspern House, moved Legrand's division across and drove in the Austrian outposts, after which a trestle bridge was constructed at the same place. The weak resistance offered by the Austrians, and the few troops observed here, did not fail to excite the Emperor's extreme astonishment, because he saw from this, that even if he had merely repeated his former operation at the same spot, he would probably have succeeded. In the morning of the 2nd July the "île du moulin" was captured from the enemy, connected with the Lobau by a pontoon bridge, and also occupied by Massena's troops. The Emperor himself had in the afternoon of the 1st left Schönbrunn again, and pitched his tents on the Lobau to the left of the issue from the bridges. Here he sketched, at 11 o'clock at night on the 2nd, his "Orders for the Passage of the Danube," divided into five heads. In them it was laid down, that on the 4th Oudinot was to cross to the Hansel-Grund, and then take up his position in the plain of Gross-Enzersdorf, with one division at the Ufer Haus[1] and one at Mühlleuten. As soon as the artillery-fire was heard, the five bridges at the "île Alexandre" were to be thrown across, and then the passage was to begin at once; Massena and Davout in the van, Bernadotte, the Guards, Marmont and Eugène in the second line, and Bessières with the heavy cavalry in the third line. The Emperor himself would be present on the "île Alexandre."

At this time the French army consisted of the following troops:—

The Guards at Vienna.

Massena's Corps :
Infantry Divisions.
Legrand,
Carra St. Cyr,
Molitor,
Boudet,

in the northern part of the Lobau ; for the battle he was to take command of the light cavalry division Lasalle, stationed at Raab.

Oudinot's Corps :
Infantry Divisions.
Tharreau,
Claparède,
Grandjean,

in the southern part of the Lobau.

Infantry Divisions.
Davout's Corps : Morand's at Klosterneuburg,
Friant's at Kaiser-Ebersdorf,
Gudin's at Deutsch-Altenburg,
Puthod's at Kittsee ;

---

[1] Called Maison blanche by the French —ED.

for the battle he was to have under his orders the following cavalry: Montbrun's light cavalry division, 3200 men, stationed at Acs, and Pully's dragoon division, 1500 men from the Italian army. Eugène with

      Macdonald's Corps,
      Grenier's Corps,
      Baraguey d'Hilliers' Corps,

was stationed around Raab; but the division, 8000 men, under the command of Baraguey d'Hilliers, remained behind, opposite Pressburg.

       Infantry Divisions.
Marmont's Corps : Montrichard,
       Clausel,

near Gleisdorf and Graz.

       Infantry Divisions.
Lefebvre's Corps : Crown Prince,
       Wrede,
       Deroy,

near Linz; of these Wrede's alone, 7000 men, would take part in the battle.

Vandamme : near Sieghartskirchen,

would not take part in the battle, but was to occupy Vienna, replacing the Guards there.

Bernadotte : Saxons,
      Dupas' division,

near St. Pölten.

      Cavalry Reserve.
Bessières : Cuirassier division, Nansouty,
      Cuirassier division, St. Sulpice,
      Cuirassier division, Arrighi,

in the neighbourhood of Kaiser-Ebersdorf and Vienna. Thus there would be engaged at Wagram 202,000 men.

In the morning of the 3rd the Emperor betook himself to the "île du moulin," whence he examined the ground towards Essling; he ordered some works to be thrown up to strengthen the position, and then returned to his bivouac, where he issued, about noon, his orders regulating the passage of his whole army to the Lobau. On the

WAGRAM

evening of the same day at 8.30 the Guards were to cross, followed by Bernadotte at 11.30; and on the 4th Bessières was to cross at 4 p.m., Davout at 8 p.m., and lastly Eugène at daybreak on the 5th. Marmont and Wrede were to pass the river as soon as they came up; Montbrun and Lasalle, as well as the waggons of the ambulance corps and the commissariat, were to make the passage during the hours of the night. With the break of day on the 5th the Emperor wished to stand ready on the plain of Gross-Enzersdorf for the general attack.

At 10 o'clock in the evening of the 4th accordingly the actual operation of crossing the river was begun, in the face of a strong wind and heavy downpour of rain, by Oudinot passing over to the Hansel-Grund, and thence debouching into the plain of Gross-Enzersdorf by three bridges, taking up his position at Mühlleuten. Immediately afterwards the construction of the bridges was begun, whilst Gross-Enzersdorf was being bombarded. At 2 a.m. four bridges were ready and the troops began to cross. The Emperor, who had been present everywhere during the construction of the bridges, encouraging the men, now retired to rest for a short time, and meanwhile the troops took up their order of battle in the plain of Enzersdorf. By 4.30 Massena stood in a line with the northern end of the "île Alexandre," his left wing resting on the Danube. Legrand's division, which had, for the purpose of deceiving the enemy, remained in front of the bridges near the Aspern House, now left that place in order to join its own corps. Davout crossed on the bridge of rafts, took up his position with his right wing near Wittau, and finally at 8 o'clock Oudinot moved in between Davout and Massena.

The Archduke Charles, rendered uneasy by the crossing of Legrand's division, had on the 1st moved forward towards the line Aspern—Essling—Gross-Enzersdorf, and had sent one corps to Wittau; but on the 3rd he withdrew it again, and stood now, as before, on the Bisam hill and behind the Russbach, with one corps on the line Asparn—Essling—Gross-Enzersdorf, which had been strengthened by some earthworks.

About 10 o'clock the Emperor pushed his first troops into the line Gross-Enzersdorf—Rutzendorf, Bernadotte moving into the same between Oudinot and Davout; Lasalle was on the left of the line. Montbrun was sent forward towards Schönfeld, as the Archduke might possibly come up from there. At noon the second line also was formed by Eugène and the Guards, and the third by Bessières. Almost the whole army having thus been deployed, the Emperor set it in motion forwards at 12.30 by a flank movement to the left. Massena advanced by Gross-Enzersdorf, which was evacuated, towards Neu-Wirthshaus, and Davout in the direction of Markgrafneusiedl. Whilst the army was thus deploying, Eugène also was moved forward into the first line and took his position at 2.30 p.m. between Bernadotte and Oudinot. In this formation the advance was continued, whilst the Austrian corps, which up to now had alone been facing the French at this point, retreated from the line Gross-Enzersdorf—Essling—Asparn to Stammersdorf.

About 6 p.m. Massena stood on the line Breitenlee—Kagran—Asparn; Bernadotte at Aderklaa; Eugène was facing the portion of the Russbach from between Deutsch-Wagram and Parbasdorf, and Oudinot the part between Parbasdorf and Markgrafneusiedl. Davout was near Glinzendorf, and from there along the Russbach through Leopoldsdorf stood the cavalry divisions of Montbrun, Grouchy (from the army of Italy) and Pully. Behind the centre of this position the Emperor had the Guards at Raasdorf, and further in the rear, Bessières; Marmont was still near the bridges, and Wrede also was in the rear. As regards the Austrians, the Archduke Charles had on his right wing three corps at Stammersdorf, Long-Enzersdorf and Hagenbrunn respectively; in the centre the Grenadiers near Gerasdorf, as well as a reserve;

on his left wing three corps behind the Russbach in the line Deutsch-Wagram—Markgrafneusiedl. In all they numbered 128,000 men. The Emperor had been astonished that the enemy had not offered any resistance whatever to his operation of crossing, and he knew nothing definite as to their position and intentions. But at 4 o'clock he received news that the Archduke John had not as yet joined the main army from Pressburg, and that on this day he would therefore only have before him the forces under the immediate command of Archduke Charles. He consequently determined to attack the latter at once and drive him from his strong position behind the Russbach, thus preventing any junction of the two archdukes on the following day.

He therefore purposed to employ the mass of his army in overwhelming the enemy's left wing, separating it thus from the rest of the army, by making a dash on Deutsch-Wagram, the point where the Austrian left wing joined their centre, whilst meanwhile his own left wing, under Massena, would hold the centre and the right wing of the enemy's extensive formation in check. We see in this the characteristic feature of the Emperor's battles, namely, that he always chose the point of attack after a general consideration of the whole situation, and on strategical grounds, heedless of any tactical difficulties which this point might possibly present. In this respect the battles of Frederick's day differed from his. Frederick always decided upon the point of attack from a tactical standpoint exclusively, and was indeed compelled to do this, considering the character of his army, the close formation of which did not allow it to be broken by unfavourable ground, if it was to remain a fit instrument for victory. But Napoleon's battles prove, that for an army of more modern organization there are, properly speaking, no tactical difficulties which cannot be conquered, and thus the results of his battles were so very decisive, just because he always attacked where the attack was strategically most effective, without paying much attention to tactical requirements. But on this point his long and increasing success exercised a fatal influence on the Emperor's mind. Whilst he too began by choosing the point of attack in accordance with strategical considerations, but yet always tried to make careful use of all the tactical advantages which offered, he became in the subsequent course of his wars more and more indifferent to the latter, and finally directed his attacks in the plains of Russia in the most inconsiderate manner, neglecting all and every tactical precaution, heedless of the amount of his losses. He reached, it is true, his strategical goal, Moscow, but was tactically too much weakened to be able to hold it.

About 7 o'clock the Emperor gave the order to begin the attack. Eugène was to capture the ridge between Deutsch-Wagram and Parbasdorf, whilst Bernadotte was to advance on his left towards the former, and Oudinot on his right towards the latter of these two villages. Eugène ordered one of his divisions to cross the Russbach and attack the Austrian position, Oudinot, advancing at the same time towards Parbasdorf, was unable to capture this place; but to the left of Eugène the Saxons penetrated into Deutsch-Wagram. The Archduke, becoming aware of his danger, ordered up fresh troops from Parbasdorf as well as from his right wing, and led them against Eugène's division, which had crossed the Russbach. This division was thrown back, and the remainder of the Army of Italy, which had moved into line to its support, was likewise repulsed by the reserves, which the Archduke continued to order up from both his wings, and had to fall back again behind the brook. Bernadotte also saw himself forced to evacuate Deutsch-Wagram again at nightfall, and even to give up Aderklaa. Thus the Emperor's attack on the Archduke had failed along the whole line of the Russbach, and his corps resumed during the night of the 5th in the positions south of that stream which they had occupied in the afternoon.

The Emperor had been a witness of the attack of Eugène's first division and its failure; he saw that there was nothing further to be done before the next morning; but he intended to command success then, by employing all his forces. Massena was therefore instructed to move more to the right by Breitenlee towards the centre of the army, and to send one division to Asparn. Davout was to effect a similar movement to the left by Glinzendorf. Most of the corps-leaders were assembled near the small watch-fire of the Emperor the same night, on the road half-way between Grosshof and Raasdorf, and he held a consultation with them as to the probable movements on the morrow. The rest of the night the Emperor spent near the fire, obtaining, however, little sleep. With the grey of the morning of the 6th July he was up, and ordered the corps in front of the line of the Russbach to remain for the present in their positions, until he should give orders for a general attack on it. But the enemy anticipated him.

(80)

For the Archduke also had decided to assume the offensive, and had for this purpose set his right in motion towards Asparn, still resting it on the Danube; one corps remained behind on the Bisam hill, and one marched towards Breitenlee. In the centre the Grenadiers were to advance towards Süssenbrunn. On his left wing the reserve corps received orders to march to the west of Aderklaa, and the next corps to march against this village itself; the corps on the left of the latter was to maintain itself behind the Russbach until the two former had advanced beyond Aderklaa, then it was to cross the brook and attack the enemy's front. The left wing corps was to keep the right French wing occupied.

The last-named corps appeared at 4 o'clock in the morning, issuing from Markgrafneusiedl, in front of Glinzendorf. and encountered here Davout, who was executing his movement to join the centre of the army, as he had been ordered to do. He was at first repulsed, and the

Emperor, in the belief that the Archduke John had arrived, and that this was a general attack to turn his right wing, hurried himself to Davout's support with the Guards, Nansouty and Arrighi. But before the interference of these troops became necessary, Davout gained the upper hand over his opponents, and began gradually to force them back again behind the Russbach. The battle stood thus, when the Emperor received ominous news from the other wing of his army.

There Massena had begun his movement by Breitenlee, to join on to the army, and had thus arrived in front of Aderklaa, which had been occupied by the Austrian corps, sent forward for the purpose. Whilst the division of Carra St. Cyr endeavoured vainly to seize this village, the right corps of the Austrians penetrated unchecked to Massena's rear along the Danube, drove Boudet, who was to hold Asparn, back in rout, and reached the head of the bridge where the first crossing had taken place. It then executed a flank movement to the left, formed front to the north-east and advanced towards Breitenlee, whither at the same time the other corps of the Austrian right wing was marching through Leopoldau, whilst the Grenadiers were advancing towards Süssenbrunn. In vain Massena opposed Legrand and Molitor to this turning attack with superior forces; both were completely repulsed and the Austrian line continued its advance unchecked. It is true, Bernadotte now appeared on the scene to the right of Massena and turned towards Aderklaa, which had been recaptured from the division Carra St. Cyr, after a brief tenure, by the Austrian grenadiers, but Bernadotte's attack was unsuccessful and his troops fell back in disorder. The Austrian line had now, at 10 o'clock, enveloped the Emperor's almost annihilated left wing, moving from Neu-Wirthshaus by Breitenlee, Süssenbrunn as far as Aderklaa, when Napoleon himself appeared on the scene.

He had left Davout, whom he still designed should reach

Markgrafneusiedl, and had ridden first to Oudinot and then to Eugène. Pointing to the heights from Parbasdorf to Deutsch-Wagram, as the point they must endeavour to capture, he instructed them to feel always to their left in the movement, so as to get closer to the centre of the army; the order for the decisive attack he would, however, specially send them by-and-by. Then he hurried to Massena, followed by the Guards and Nansouty, whom he transferred from the right wing to the centre again. Here he witnessed the woful spectacle of the annihilation of his whole left wing. He immediately ordered Massena to withdraw his disorganized troops to Asparn and to protect the Lobau bridges, and then applied himself to devise measures to meet the threatening attack of the Austrians, who were advancing victoriously and making a turning movement along the whole line from Neu-Wirthshaus by Breitenlee, Süssenbrunn and Aderklaa as far as Deutsch-Wagram. He first ordered Bessières to oppose them with all the cavalry held in readiness near Raasdorf, viz. that of the Guards and Nansouty, but in vain. At the same time he instructed Lauriston to bring up the whole artillery of the Guards, 60 guns, and this tremendous battery, soon reinforced to about 100 guns, succeeded at last in checking the advance of the Austrians. The Emperor thus gained time to bring up some infantry, viz., the corps of Macdonald from the Army of Italy, which, wheeling to the left, came up to the south-east of Süssenbrunn, immediately followed by the Guards.

Thus about 11 o'clock he had succeeded in showing front on this wing to the Archduke's flank attack, averting the most imminent danger for the moment. The Emperor now remained here with Macdonald's troops, keeping a sharp look-out upon the tower of Markgrafneusiedl and the smoke, which marked Davout's advance in that direction. For from the beginning of the day he had looked for the decision there; indeed in the morning he had said to one of his aides-de-camp that "it is there the battle must be won."[1]

At noon he perceived that Davout was pushing forward by Markgrafneusiedl; at this time also he had Macdonald's whole corps, as well as Bessières', with the cavalry of the Guards and Nansouty and also the division of Wrede in readiness, and he now gave the order for the advance of these troops towards Süssenbrunn, sending at the same time orders to Oudinot and Eugène to proceed to the attack. Therefore Macdonald, flanked on his right by the cavalry of the Guards and on his left by Nansouty and followed by Wrede, pushed forward towards Süssenbrunn, whilst Davout, accompanied by the cavalry divisions of Grouchy, Pully, Montbrun and Arrighi, moving from Markgrafneusiedl, and Oudinot, executing a flank movement with a half-turn to the left from Parbasdorf, forced the Austrians along the Russbach back upon Deutsch-Wagram, Eugène meanwhile advancing on the village itself.

It was 1 o'clock. Before Macdonald's attack Breitenlee and Aderklaa were evacuated, but Süssenbrunn held out, and the French troops, now in the middle of the enemy's lines, had a hard fight, the attempts of the cavalry to relieve them being unsuccessful. In the meantime, however, Eugène had pushed forward to Deutsch-Wagram and had captured that village. Thereupon the Emperor ordered Grenier's division of the Army of Italy to advance from Deutsch-Wagram on the left flank of the Austrian right wing, and Wrede to reinforce Macdonald at the same time. In face of the advance of this mass the enemy now evacuated their position at Süssenbrunn and fell back upon Gerasdorf. Macdonald, Wrede and Eugène followed them closely, drove them out of that place as well, and made a halt in the afternoon near the Brünn road. On the Russbach likewise fortune had about the same time, viz. 2 o'clock, declared in favour of the

[1] Eugène, Mém. vi. 8.

French. Oudinot, having pushed forward by Parbasdorf, and Davout, coming from Markgrafneusiedl, drove the enemy from the whole of the ground north-east of the Russbach, and then made a halt on the upper part of its course, in the line Deutsch-Wagram—Helma-Hof—Bockflüss. The general retreat of the Austrians now relieved Massena also, and we find him in the evening at Leopoldau.

The Emperor bivouacked between Raasdorf and Aderklaa, where he still had, intact, the Guards and Marmont's corps. Suddenly, however, a panic broke out in the ranks of the French army, caused by the appearance of a few patrols from Archduke John's army. Thousands fled in wild rout towards the Danube; the leaders saw this with consternation, and were forced to say to themselves: "Panics are sad evidence of the moral state of an army. They have occurred sometimes in the French armies, but never in their halcyon days. The armies of Austerlitz and Jena were never guilty of them. Panics are always a proof of a serious laxity in discipline, of a want of confidence, and the decay of military virtues."[1] Indeed the effects of Napoleon's principles already showed themselves in the army. These men, accustomed to look upon plunder and luxuries and freedom from the fetters of discipline as their rights which they had won by great hardships and hard fighting, had become morally incapable of bearing up against any reverses of fate. If this army, used to victory, was for once reduced to retreat, if it had to bear hunger, cold, or privations of any kind, instead of finding a rich country to loot, it would become disorganized. Of this fact the panic of that day was a sure forerunner.

In the evening the Archduke collected his corps on the Brünn road and the Bisam hill, only the corps of the extreme left wing had fallen back upon Wolkersdorf. As the Austrians had begun their retreat without their

[1] Marmont, Mém. iii. 241.

columns having really been defeated, and had thus evacuated the battle-field rather than been driven from it, they still were sufficiently capable of resistance to prevent any actual pursuit. Moreover the Emperor did not wish to renew the attack seriously, considering his own heavy losses and his by no means decisive success during the day just past. Therefore the two armies lay close together from the evening of the 6th, nor could the Emperor gain any certainty as to the direction in which the enemy intended to retreat, whether *viâ* Wolkersdorf to the road to Brünn, or *viâ* Korneuburg to the road to Znaym. This uncertainty was not cleared up even on the morning of the 7th, though he now was inclined to the opinion that the Archduke intended to retreat to Brünn.

On this day therefore the Guards, Davout, and Marmont were moved forward to Wolkersdorf, where the Emperor also established his headquarters. Massena advanced to Jedlersee, from which place he was to reopen direct communication with Vienna. Oudinot lay at Deutsch-Wagram, and Eugène further back on the Brünn road near the Post-rendezvous. The Archduke had, however, as a matter of fact, withdrawn all his corps in the direction of Korneuburg to the Znaym road; only one of them fell back upon Brünn. At 11 p.m. Massena received orders to occupy Stockerau; Davout was to push forward beyond Wolkersdorf; and Marmont, with the Bavarians and Montbrun under his orders, was instructed to march towards Nikolsburg as the advance-guard of the entire army. In the course of the 8th, however, the situation became clearer; Marmont, who had reached Wülfersdorf at noon, learnt there that the Austrians, who had retreated on the Brünn road, had turned thence to Laa; he followed them in this direction and reached Mistelbach; Davout arrived at Wülfersdorf. Massena, whose leading division, Legrand's, had reached Stockerau, convinced himself that a good part of the enemy's army must have retreated *viâ* Korneuburg and Stockerau. Reporting this, he received orders to push on towards Znaym. Consequently the division of Legrand encountered on the 9th the Archduke's rearguard near Hollabrunn, but could not overcome its resistance. Marmont reached Laa, without, however, being able to lead his exhausted troops across the Thaya the same day. His report to Davout that he was in no need of his support induced the latter to continue his march to Nikolsburg, where his cavalry arrived during the evening. On the 10th, Massena, who had now been joined by the division of Carra St. Cyr, tried again to advance to Hollabrunn, and this time the position was evacuated, but the enemy immediately took up a fresh one behind it at Schöngrabern, by the defence of which another day was gained. In the meantime Marmont, marching from Laa, arrived in front of Znaym, and observing that he stood there in the face of the main mass of the Austrian army, which was concentrating at this town, he took up a defensive position near Teschwitz, which he held until the evening against repeated attacks. Davout arrived at Nikolsburg.

The Emperor had for the moment remained in Wolkersdorf; but when the news of the Austrians' retreat to Znaym became more and more confirmed, he sent, at 8.30 a.m. on the 10th, orders to Davout to move to that place to Marmont's support; he himself subsequently left Wolkersdorf. On the Marchfeld he had left Eugène to hold off the Archduke John and to protect Vienna; Vandamme and the Saxons joined Eugène. The corps of Bernadotte had on the 9th been broken up by the Emperor, as he was dissatisfied with its leader. Having arrived in Wülfersdorf, he ordered Nansouty and the cavalry of the Guards to advance to Laa; the infantry of the Guards and Oudinot were to follow them; he himself arrived in Laa during the evening.

On the 11th the Austrian army stood in readiness to

resume its retreat in safety, holding Znaym and defending the bridge over the Thaya. It had already repulsed a forward movement on the part of Massena, when the Emperor joined him about noon, whilst Marmont waited for Davout's arrival. From the height near Teschwitz Napoleon saw that the Austrians stood in a good position with their army, while he knew that Davout and Oudinot could not come up in full force before the early hours of the next day. As he was consequently unable to force the enemy to give battle at once, the latter could, by continuing their retreat into Bohemia, compel him to open a new campaign in that country. His heavy losses at Wagram and the partial success gained in that battle probably rendered the Emperor, at that time in indifferent health, disinclined to enter upon any new ventures. Hence, taking up the proposals for negotiations, which had been made to Marmont on the preceding day, the Emperor concluded on the morning of the 12th July an armistice, which practically brought the war to a close, and on the 15th November he returned to his own capital, for the last time as a victor.

If we consider Wagram from a tactical standpoint, we find that the Archduke's proceedings offer a good example of the modern method of attack by a concentric turning movement, such as was employed more particularly in the later stages of the war of 1870-71, for example at Orleans and Le Mans; a method favoured on the one hand on account of the heavy losses which in our days a frontal attack entails, and on the other on account of the great results which the success of a complete turning attack promises. Of course such an attack is accompanied by a continuous and far-reaching extension of one's line and a consequent loss of depth of the same, and the Emperor furnished here an example of how a capable general with a good army may meet such tactics successfully, by keeping his own forces, as compared with the enemy's far extended line, in a close and deep formation.

He may thus either attack the centre of the enemy's too much attenuated lines, as Napoleon did here, sending forward Eugène against Deutsch-Wagram; or form a defensive flank against one of the turning wings, whilst the other is crushed by superior forces, as Napoleon did here with Macdonald on the one and Davout and Oudinot on the other side.

But Wagram is more important for us in another respect. As was the case at Ratisbon, so here the enemy was not annihilated, but soon after the battle was again ready for further operations.

It is true, after Wagram, the crowning of the tactical success by an annihilation of the enemy could have been attained only with difficulty and much danger, still formerly Napoleon would not have rested until he had reached that consummation, and would rather have risked all the success he had already gained, than have been content with a result which left his enemy still capable of resistance and ready for further fighting. He was no longer true to himself, and was therefore wrong, however much any other general would have been justified, in resting content with what had been gained on the evening of Wagram. The Archduke Charles, for example, was quite right to give up the battle, even before it was finally and definitely decided, for he had no wish to subjugate the whole world, he wished only to ensure the existence of his country, and this was done by withdrawing his army while still capable of further operations. If indeed he had risked everything to gain a complete success he might have lost all. The case had been exactly the same after Ratisbon, where he did not attempt the risky flank advance from Cham across the Danube against the enemy's line of operations, which a Napoleon would assuredly have attempted.

It was indeed the difference in the high political aims which again affected the method of waging war. Napoleon, aiming at the empire of the world, had gained nothing, so long as he had any opponent left capable of resisting him. Frederick and Charles, content in their capacity as generals to save their country, had reached their aim when they kept the field and were capable of continuing the struggle. The former policy, in its very nature purely offensive, must exact from the general a readiness to risk everything over again at any moment. For there is no limit to it. The latter policy, in its nature defensive, may sometimes fail to gain a possible success by a reluctance to proceed to military extremes, preferring not to risk the entire destruction of the army, indispensable for the attainment of its strictly limited aims. And I do believe that, for these reasons only, Frederick's methods of warfare bear a different stamp from Napoleon's. Napoleon, dreaming of the empire of the world, would in 1740 and 1757 have pursued the same strategy as in 1805 and 1806; and on the other hand, Frederick, trying to found a state, would have acted in 1809 exactly as the Archduke Charles did. Still we must carefully note that this strategy is only justified from the highest political standpoint. He who has no such exalted position, but only stands as a general at the head of the army, having to consider nothing but how he may gain the victory, and that a complete one, will always fight to the last, so as to gain it, and risk everything for this object. The flank movement from Cham will be expected from him, nor will he ever be pardoned for the withdrawal from Wagram before the decision; he will take Napoleon naturally as his model, just because he, as a soldier, forgot that his throne imposed higher duties upon him.

The conclusion of the armistice indeed confirms our opinion that the Emperor, at variance with himself, did not aim here at the supreme consummation, viz. an utter annihilation of the enemy. What had he after all attained? His opponent still kept the field, beaten, it is true, and retreating, but capable of further operations. A success with which *he* may be content who wishes to attain by a war only a definitely limited political goal, and desires, as a matter of fact, to negotiate, but should not satisfy *him* who hitherto had known no other peace negotiations but those which he dictated absolutely to defenceless opponents. If he was unwilling now to venture new battles, or take upon himself the entanglements of new campaigns, his later history proved that it was not the deliberate self-restraint of a statesman. No, it seems as if lassitude and a decrease of his moral, and possibly also his physical strength were the real reason; confirming what he had said of himself in 1805 : " A man has his day in war as in other things ; I myself shall be good for it another six years, after that even I shall have to stop."[1]

The Emperor's strategy, thus in the absence of that incurrence of extreme risks, approached that kind of strategy which we recognize as in harmony with definite and more closely limited statesmanlike aims, and therefore as correct in such cases. At this juncture he expressed an opinion, which, emanating from a Frederick or an Archduke Charles, would have only been logical, but which for a Napoleon marked a departure from his own guiding military principles, and which therefore in his case must be considered illogical. This was as follows: "Battles must only be fought if one can reckon upon seventy chances in a hundred in one's own favour; nay, one should only fight a battle when there is no hope of one's luck changing, for in its very nature the result of a battle is always doubtful."[2] And this was written by the man who has been called the "Emperor of Battles," whose entire strategy always aimed, with good reason, at a decision by battle, and expected everything from battles. Therefore, however brilliant the campaign of 1809 may appear, when carefully studied by us, we must still say that the Emperor was untrue to himself in it.

[1] Constant, Mém. v. 63.
[2] C. N. To Clarke. Schönbrunn, 21st August, 1809.

CHAPTER IV

THE INVASION OF RUSSIA.

(82) THE Emperor had seen his eagles soaring victorious over all the battle-fields of Europe; now he purposed to use this continent as a jumper does from a spring-board, receiving from it the impetus which would enable him to make his leap. He purposed to throw himself upon Asia with all the forces of Europe, just as Attila of old had thrown himself upon Europe with all the forces of Asia. That dream of a march like Alexander's, which Acre had formerly interrupted, had arisen again in him with new strength. It had indeed probably long been in his mind, for even in 1808, a short time before his invasion of Spain, he had sent word to his librarian: "The Emperor would likewise wish M. Barbier to occupy himself, in conjunction with one of our best geographers, with the task of collecting memoirs about the campaigns which have taken place on the Euphrates and against the Parthians, beginning with that of Crassus up to the eighth century, and including those of Antonius, Trajan, Julian, etc.; he is to mark upon maps of suitable size the route which each army followed, together with the ancient and modern names of the countries and principal towns, and add notes on the geographical features and historical descriptions of each enterprise, taking these from the original authors." [1]

It was not the political aim of overthrowing his great enemy, England, by the conquest of India, that led him on.

[1] C. N. To Barbier. Bayonne, 17th July.

THE INVASION OF RUSSIA

For this aim he would have been more certain to attain by an alliance with Russia, which alone can fulfil the mission of expelling its rival, the native of a distant country, from Asia, its own home; no, it was the invincible impulse of the conqueror. Already, when as First Consul he had only just come into power, he addressed the army thus: "Soldiers! It is no longer your frontiers which need defending; it is into the enemy's country that you will have to carry the war."[1] In vain therefore was the touching warning in 1809, which the dying Lannes, already beyond all earthly things, addressed to him whom he no longer considered his master: "You have now committed a great mistake, and although it has robbed you of your best friend, it will not change you; your ambition is insatiable; it will destroy you; you sacrifice without scruple, without necessity, the men who serve you most faithfully, and when they die, you do not regret them. You have nothing but sycophants around you; I see not one friend who dares tell you the truth. You will be betrayed, you will be forsaken; hasten to finish this war, it is the universal wish. You will never be more powerful, but you may be much more beloved."[2]

And now, having arrived at the summit of his power, the Emperor replied to those who, apprehensive as to their own future, asked him anxiously about the real goal of his thoughts: "You wish to know whither we are going, where I shall plant the new pillars of Hercules. We shall make an end of Europe, and then throw ourselves like robbers upon those robbers, inferior to ourselves in daring, who have made themselves masters of India; we shall conquer that country;"[3] and the minority in France, who had begun to watch the career of this marvellous meteor as sober critics, and to forecast the

[1] C. N. To the French soldiers. Paris, 25th December, 1799.
[2] Constant, Mém. iv. 148.
[3] Gohier, Mém. ii. 108.

future, trembled at these words; "the unfortunate man will destroy himself; he will destroy us, he will destroy all," cried Regnault de St. Jean d'Angely on hearing the above words, and Decrès, one of his most faithful followers, exclaimed soon after Wagram: "The Emperor is mad, altogether mad, and will overthrow us all beyond retrieving; all this will end in a fearful cataclysm."[1]

But he himself was unshaken in his belief in his star. "I feel myself impelled towards a goal with which I am unacquainted; when I shall have reached it, when I shall be no longer needed for it, an atom will suffice to throw me down, but until that moment all human efforts will be powerless against me."[2] In this conviction he absolutely rejected every warning, as being only calculated to disturb uselessly the course of his fatalistic resolutions. When Davout sent him on the 28th November, 1811, ominous news as to the mood of Germany, he wrote to him these memorable words: "I beg of you not to transmit any such fanciful vapourings to me again. My time is too precious to be spent in the consideration of such nonsense. . . . All this is only calculated to make me lose my time and to sully my imagination with senseless pictures and suppositions."[3]

Thus the events of 1812 were approaching. Their development bears the stamp of the inevitableness of the final collision, which was as sharply defined in Napoleon's mind, as it was wanting in actual fact; "he felt himself drawn towards them naturally by his love of battles and their excitement,"[4] as he confessed to one of his intimates. So early as the 4th August, 1810, a letter to the King of Saxony showed how zealously the Emperor was studying the scene of the next war, on which he had resolved. On

[1] Marmont, Mém. iii. 337.
[2] Ségur, Hist. de N. et de la Grande Armée de 1812, i. 66.
[3] C. N. Paris, 2nd December, 1811.
[4] Jomini, Précis politique et militaire des campagnes de 1812 à 1815, i. 29. (My acquaintance with this posthumous and not yet published work of the great theorist I owe to the kindness of the Privy Councillor Baron Jomini.)

THE INVASION OF RUSSIA 107

the 10th December followed that celebrated message to the Senate, which extended the frontier of France, with one stroke of the pen, as far as Lübeck, and on the 28th February, 1811, a letter to the Emperor Alexander destroyed the last illusions which might possibly still have existed.

Thus the question of the formation and composition of the new Grand Army became even more urgent, and the Emperor began to devote himself to it more exclusively. To begin with, only so-called corps of observation of the Elbe, the Rhine and Italy were formed, which, however, were, as a matter of fact, whole armies, and on the 23rd June, 1811, the Emperor estimated the entire forces, ready in Germany, at 204,000 men. His care for the mobilization of this army extended to the most minute details, and on this occasion he displayed the whole range of his marvellous gifts with respect to organization, a quality which was innate in him in the same measure as his military genius, and which, combined with this latter, presents to us that characteristic spectacle of a closely calculating, mathematical mind, united with boundless powers of imagination, of which the annals of history furnish us with no second example.

In addition to his assiduous care in the composition and equipment of the army, the Emperor was closely engaged in collecting information about the country he was about to attack. "I request M. Barbier," he ordered his private secretary to write, "to send me for His Majesty a few good works, most suitable for studying the nature of the soil of Russia, and especially of Lithuania, with respect to its marshes, rivers, forests, roads, etc." His Majesty also desires to obtain whatever works treat most minutely, in French, of Charles XIIth's campaign in Poland and Russia."[1] "The Emperor requires a history of Courland, as well as all that can be obtained as to the history, geography and topography

[1] C. N. Paris, 19th December, 1811.

of Riga, Livonia, etc."[1] By the month of March the Emperor calculated upon having 300,000 men under arms in Germany, and at the end of the year 1811 he exclaimed triumphantly: "You see that I have never made greater preparations."[2]

The result of these preparations was the massing of the following army, whose distribution was fixed on the 3rd March :—

THE EMPEROR.

	Chief of the Staff: Berthier.	4,000 men.
Guards:	Old Guard: Lefebvre. Young Guard: Mortier. Cavalry: Bessières.	47,000 men.
I. Corps: Davout:	*Inf. Divisions.* Morand Friant Gudin Dessaix Compans	72,000 men.
II. Corps: Oudinot:	Legrand Verdier Swiss: Merle	37,000 men.
III. Corps: Ney:	Ledru Razout Würtembergers: Crown Prince of Würtemberg	39,000 men.
IV. Corps: Eugène:	Italians: Lechi Delzons Broussier Italians: Pino	45,000 men.
V. Corps: Poniatowski:	Poles: Zajonczek „ Dombrovski „ Kniazewicz	36,000 men.
VI. Corps: Gouvion St. Cyr:	Bavarians: Deroy „ Wrede	25,000 men.
VII. Corps: Reynier:	Saxons: Lecoq „ Funck	17,000 men.
VIII. Corps: Vandamme:	Hessians: Tharreau Westphalians: Ochs	18,000 men.

[1] C. N. Paris, 7th January, 1812.
[2] C. N. To Davout. Paris, 30th December.

The Invasion of Russia

X. Corps: Macdonald:	Germans		
	and Poles: Grandjean		
	Prussian Auxiliary Corps: Grawert		32,000 men.
Austrian Auxiliary Corps:	Schwarzenberg		
	Trautenberg		
	Bianchi		
	Siegenthal		
	Frimont		30,000 men.

Cavalry Reserve.
Murat

1. Cavalry Corps:			Nansouty	12,000 men.
2.	,,		Montbrun	10,000 men.
3.	,,		Grouchy	10,000 men.
4.	,,	Saxons and Poles:	Latour-Maubourg	8,000 men.

                442,000 men.

The IXth Corps, Victor:	Partouneaux	
	Germans: Daendels	
	Germans and Poles: Girard	33,000 men,

was to follow later on.

The first few months of the year 1812 then witnessed the march of all these troops through Germany eastward to the Vistula, and on the 9th May, while his corps were beginning to arrive on this river, the Emperor himself left St. Cloud and reached Dresden at 11 p.m. on the 16th. The more the great concentration of his army advanced, the more anxious did he become to regulate the great question of the commissariat, since he was well aware of the fact that the main difficulty of this campaign would be to feed the army in such a country. "The result of all my movements will be to concentrate 400,000 men upon one point, and in such a case nothing can be expected from the country itself, we shall have to carry everything with us."[1] "The whole army will ultimately be assembled on one and the same field; every corps, in close contact with the one next to it, will soon have exhausted the resources of the country;"[2] and consequently the Emperor's mind was most occupied with

---
[1] C. N. To Davout. Dresden, 26th May.
[2] C. N. To Eugène. Dresden, 26th May.

the question of the organization of the columns and the construction of suitable transport waggons.

In Dresden he once more enjoyed the pomp of power to the full; almost all the reigning princes of Europe assembled there around him, and he let them feel his superiority with all the haughtiness of his hard nature, not free from vanity. "All ye," exclaimed a spectator of these scenes, "who wish to gain a correct idea of the supremacy which the Emperor exerted in Europe, and wish to appreciate all the degrees of terror which had seized upon almost all its rulers, go in spirit to Dresden and look there upon this arrogant prince at the summit of his glory, yet so near his fall."[1]

At 3 a.m. on the 28th May the Emperor left Dresden and arrived in Posen on the 31st. His army stood now in a large crescent along the whole course of the Vistula in the following order:—The Prussian contingent at Königsberg, Davout at Elbing and Marienburg, Oudinot at Marienwerder, Ney at Thorn, Eugène and St. Cyr at Plock, Poniatowski at Warsaw, Vandamme at Gora Kalvaria, Reynier on the left bank of the Vistula opposite Novo-Alexandria, and lastly Schwarzenberg at Lemberg. From this disposition the enemy could not as yet guess definitely in what direction the Emperor intended to deal his principal blow. For he could with equal facility march with his left wing from the Lower Vistula to Kovno, or with his right either from Warsaw to Grodno, or even viâ Lublin into Volhynia. This uncertainty was intended to lead the Russians to divide their forces.

This object was indeed gained. In the middle of May we see on the Russian side two armies, of which the first, Barclay's, 127,000 men, lay in extended order from Schavli through Vilna as far as Prushany. The second army, Bagration, 66,000 men, stood in Volhynia, in the neighbourhood of Lutsk. Thus the Russian forces were posted in two main groups, separated by the marshy

[1] De Pradt, Ambassade 52.

lands on the Upper Pripet; a separation which may indeed be considered a result of the Emperor's position, threatening as it did the southern as well as the northern Russian theatre of war. But afterwards, when the French, in their further advance towards the Niemen, moved their masses more in a northerly direction, the Russians also proceeded to take some counter measures by reinforcing their right wing, and thus we find that at the commencement of operations they stood in the following order :—The first army, Barclay, of the above-mentioned strength, round Vilna, with its right wing near Rossieny, and its left near Lida; the second army, Bagration, 48,000 men, stood around Volkovisk; and the third army, 43,000 men, near Lutsk, in Volhynia, extending from Staro-Konstantinov as far as Kovel, though as yet only in process of mobilization.

This order was, it is true, known to the Emperor in its main outlines, nor had the reinforcement of the Russian right wing, by the moving up of troops thither, remained unknown to him. But he was unaware of the fact that Bagration had been replaced in Volhynia by a third army under Tormassov, and had already effected a junction with Barclay, though he suspected him to be on the march from Volhynia *viâ* Brest-Litovsk, for the purpose of effecting that junction. His plan, which the great critic Smitt called "one of the finest and best thought-out that he ever conceived," [1] was now to pierce the Russian line, which was too much extended, by pushing forward with the main mass of his army *viâ* Kovno to Vilna, "which will be the first objective of the campaign." [2] This movement he intended to conduct personally, and to collect for it the Guards, Davout, Oudinot, Ney, and the cavalry divisions of Nansouty and Montbrun. Eugène, who, in addition to his own corps, had St. Cyr and the cavalry of Grouchy under his command, was moved up to Rastenburg, and

[1] Fur näheren Aufklärung über den krieg von 1812, 376.
[2] C. N. To Jérôme. Thorn, 5th June.

was to advance from there to Seïny by Suvalki, so that he might, being in support on the Emperor's right rear, either fall on the flank of any possible Russian offensive operations by Olita or Grodno, or, on the other hand, widen more and more, during the continued advance, the gap between Barclay and Bagration.

Jérôme's army was to form a second support still further to the right rear, at Warsaw and on the Narev. It was composed of Poniatowski's, Reynier's, and Vandamme's corps, and the cavalry of Latour-Maubourg. Its part would be to lead the Russians by every possible means to believe that it had orders to advance to Lublin for the purpose of joining Schwarzenberg and penetrate into Volhynia, and thus distract their attention from the northern portion of the theatre of war, where the actual attack would take place. But should the Russians themselves assume the offensive towards Ostrolenka, Scherotsk, or straight to Warsaw, Jerôme was to keep on the defensive opposite them on the Narev or near Warsaw. Then Eugène would fall upon their flank, whilst Jérôme's position would secure his lines of communication, with his base at Thorn, and the Emperor, coming down from Vilna, would in that case fall upon the Russians' rear and cut them off completely. "Whilst the enemy would thus engage in operations which could lead to nothing, since after all they would find the Vistula before them, they would have lost many marches, and the left wing of our army, having crossed the Niemen, would appear on their flank and rear before they could return."[3] "The most important thing is that the right wing should not engage superior forces, and should manœuvre in one mass from position to position; even if the larger part of the Russian army took part in the flank attack, nothing could happen to my right wing, since it could always take refuge in the entrenched camp of Modlin or on the left bank of the

[1] C. N. To Berthier. Danzig, 11th June.

THE INVASION OF RUSSIA

Vistula. But the instant such a movement was decided upon on the part of the Russians, I would fall upon their flank and rear with my whole army."[1] The extreme wings of the entire army were to be covered by two corps sent out in front, namely, on the left by Macdonald, who was to push forward to Rossieny, and on the right by Schwarzenberg towards Lublin. We see thus that the whole operation consisted in refusing the right wing, which was echelonned back, whilst the left wing, reinforced and pushed on in advance, would pierce the enemy's right wing, and then manœuvre against the lines of communication of their centre and left wing. "The march of my army will be a movement which I shall execute with my left wing, whilst continually refusing my right wing."[2] The whole arrangement may very well be called a strategical Leuthen, an idea which Ségur also points out. "It was the same manœuvre, lasting several days and on a front of eighty leagues, which Frederick II. often employed on a space of two leagues and which only took a few hours."[3] Such was the grand outline of that magnificent plan, the careful preparation of which reminds us of the Emperor's own words: "In this trade and on such a great theatre of action success may only be gained by a well conceived plan, in which all the component parts are in full harmony."[4]

However, the march upon Vilna was only regarded by the Emperor as a strategical penetration of the Russian line after a more definite knowledge of their dispositions. At first he intended to use his advanced left wing for the strategical turning of the enemy's right wing; and he thus alludes to the movement: "I shall, by turning their right wing, have gained twelve or fifteen days' march upon them in the direction of St.

[1] C. N. To Berthier. Danzig, 11th June.
[2] C. N. To Eugène. Danzig, 10th June.
[3] Hist. de N., etc., i. 161.
[4] C. N. To Jérôme. Thorn, 5th June.

Petersburg; I shall be on their right flank."[1] We see thus in this plan of campaign the two strategical principles illustrated one after the other, which ruled all the Emperor's openings of offensive campaigns. First the strategical turning of one of the enemy's wings (1800, 1805, 1806, 1807, 1813), and secondly strategical penetration (1796, 1808, 1809, 1815). But he moved with the mass of his army collected upon one line of operations. This simple thought, carried out logically, gave to his successes their certainty and magnitude Still, in view of the ever-increasing size of Napoleon's armies, and especially of the increase in numbers, which has since then taken place to such an enormous extent, the question may be raised, whether the undoubted advantages of the command being in one hand only, and of the constant possibility of bringing the whole mass at once to bear, in view of any eventuality, however unexpected—whether these advantages, I say, which the operation on one single line offered to the armies of 1805 and 1806, did after all still exist for the armies of 1812, and still more for those of 1870. We only wish to raise the question here; the course of this campaign, and afterwards of that of 1813, will furnish us with reasons and opportunities for finding an answer to it.

During the first half of June the Emperor ordered his corps to advance from the Lower Vistula to the Niemen, and sent Eugène forward to East Prussia, whilst he himself visited the important places of this province, reviewed the troops everywhere, and personally urged on and encouraged them all. Then in the evening of the 21st he established his headquarters in Vilkovischki, and during the night of the 22nd went into bivouac near the farm of Naugardischki. At 2 a.m. on the 23rd he mounted his horse and rode forward to the Niemen in the direction of Kovno. He minutely reconnoitred this river, wrapped in the cloak of a Polish Uhlan, attended only by his General of Engineers, Haxo, and recognized that the

---

[1] C. N. To Jérôme. Thorn, 5th June.

THE INVASION OF RUSSIA 115

most favourable point of crossing was the bend of the river, which formed a sharp southerly curve immediately to the south-east of Kovno. Then, having returned to his bivouac, he issued his orders for the regulation of the passage of the Niemen. The various corps that were to make the crossing stood at present in the following positions:—The Guards at Naugardischki, Davout beyond Pilviski at the outskirts of the forest, Ney beyond Mariampol, Oudinot at Pilviski, Eugène with his corps one day's march behind Kalvaria, St. Cyr at Czymochen, Murat with the cavalry divisions of Nansouty and Montbrun facing Kovno, and Grouchy before Pilona. Of the rest of the army Macdonald was at Tilsit, Jérôme had his headquarters at Schtschutschin, where Poniatowski also was, Vandamme lay at Novgorod, Latour-Maubourg at Augustovo, Reynier in the neighbourhood of Novo—Minsk, and lastly, Schwarzenberg two days' march to the south of Syedletz. At 9 p.m. the Emperor again went to the river, and at 10 o'clock the construction of the bridges began; two hours later three bridges were ready and Davout commenced the passage. At noon on the 24th Kovno was occupied, and in the evening the Emperor established his headquarters there; he had taken his first step on Russian soil.

Now that actual operations had begun without the Russians having anticipated the Emperor by taking the offensive against his right wing, a movement hitherto still considered possible by him, the part that wing was to play was no longer to be an absolutely defensive one. It was on the contrary now to advance to Grodno, in order to follow on Bagration's heels, as soon as the latter, separated from Barclay by the Emperor's continued forward movement, should fall back, and was to force him on to the Emperor's army, where he would be crushed by the latter's superior numbers. This Napoleon had planned since the beginning of June in case the Russians should remain stationary; indeed on the 15th he had written to Jérôme: "As soon as I shall have crossed the

Niemen, I shall perhaps resolve to march upon Vilna, thereby offering my flank to Bagration's army. It will therefore be necessary that you should follow him closely, so that you may be able to take part in the movement which I shall execute against this army. Should I succeed in separating it from the rest of the Russian troops and be able to fall upon its right flank, you must be in a position to attack it simultaneously with myself;"[1] and on the 21st he wrote: "It is very likely that I shall give you orders to march with your whole army to Grodno. . . . You will then be in touch with the army, so that we may always attack in mass, and we shall then operate against General Bagration according to the position he may hold."[2]

(83) On the two next days, the 25th and the 26th, the army completed its passage of the Niemen, whilst the Emperor himself remained at Kovno, with the Guards. Davout was at Rumschischki, Murat with Nansouty and Montbrun at Shishmory. "Before we take one step forward, we must know more about how things stand . . . at the present moment we cannot think of marching to Vilna; in order to supervise such an extensive movement, the Emperor will go there in person; besides, our left flank must first be fully secured."[3] This latter was effected by moving Oudinot forward to Yanov across the Vilia. So far the Emperor had been cautious, for the army was not as yet fully concentrated and ready for operations on the right bank of the Niemen, and faithful to the procedure he had constantly adhered to up to now, he warned Davout: "The army must first be massed, and we must not march against an undivided army as we would march against a beaten army."[4]

On the 26th, however, he ordered Murat, the Guards and Davout to begin their march to Vilna, and on the

[1] C. N. Königsberg.   [2] C. N. Gumbinnen.
[3] C. N. To Berthier. Kovno, 25th June.
[4] C. N. To Davout. Kovno, 26th June, 3 a.m.

THE INVASION OF RUSSIA

28th he himself reached this town with his troops, having driven some weak detachments of the enemy out of it. Ney meanwhile advanced along the right bank of the Vilia in the same direction by Mieschagola; whilst Oudinot, turning through Schati against the right wing of the Russians, drove their rearguard out of Vilkomir on the same d the 28th. Macdonald, who had crossed the Niemen at Tilsit, was to march up from Rossieny, to assist in the movement against this enemy; he reached Tauroggen on the 28th. Eugène had assembled his corps on the left bank of the Niemen, opposite Pilona; Jérôme was on the march to Grodno, whither the Emperor urged him to hasten with all speed. He himself was with Poniatowski and Vandamme at Augustovo; Latour-Maubourg had already arrived in front of Grodno, Reynier lay at Sambrov, and Schwarzenberg at Syedletz. The Russians had begun their retreat in face of the Emperor's advance; and on the day when the latter reached Vilna, Barclay stood near Nyementshin; his right wing had fallen back before Oudinot to Perkale, and his left wing stood near Oshmiana, having retreated from Lida. Bagration was still at Volkovisk. Thus Barclay retreated, generally speaking, in the direction of Sventsiani, and Bagration also had just received orders to fall back upon that place.

For a time the Emperor was not quite clear as to the object of these movements; he formed therefore two columns at Vilna on the 29th; one under Murat (Friant, Gudin, Nansouty and Montbrun) was sent forward towards Nyementshin, and the other under Davout (the remaining three divisions of his corps) towards Michalishki and Oshmiana. Thus splitting the head of his main body in two, the Emperor hoped not only to receive sufficient news about the direction of the enemy's marches, but also to keep the parts of the Russian line, torn asunder by his advance upon Vilna, effectively separated. By this means the movement of Barclay's left wing corps was discovered, and the Emperor, considering this to indicate the march of Bagration's army towards Sventsiani, ordered on the 1st July Davout, to whom he also entrusted the corps of Grouchy, which had in the meantime come up, to push forward *via* Oshmiana on the flank of Bagration, who was, he thought, closely pursued by Jérôme.

Meanwhile Eugène also had on the 29th and 30th crossed the Niemen at Pilona, and on the 1st July was at Kronyay. Jérôme, who had reached Grodno on the preceding day, collected there on the 1st and 2nd Poniatowski, Vandamme and Latour-Maubourg, whilst Reynier arrived at Sokoli, and Schwarzenberg stood on the left bank of the Bug opposite Drogitshin. At Grodno Jérôme had encountered only a body of Cossacks, which immediately fell back upon Lida. Bagration stood on the 1st July at Slonim, and on the same day Barclay reached Sventsiani; his right corps was at Soloki, and his left, recognizing the danger it was in of being cut off by Davout's advance, made some forced marches and reached Svir on the 1st July.

While the Russians were thus retreating in haste to the Dwina towards Drissa, and Bagration was already in imminent danger of being cut off by Davout and caught between the latter and Jérôme, the various portions of the French main army reached the following points on the 1st July:—Murat Nyementshin, Davout Oshmiana and Michalishki, Ney Glinzishki, and Oudinot Vilkomir; the Guards remained at Vilna, and Macdonald reached Rossieny. The Emperor was as yet confident that Bagration could still be arrested and attacked while on the march, and that at best he might, by making a detour by Minsk, reach the Dwina in safety. Indeed, it was only the next day that he comprehended that the troops observed near Oshmiana were not Bagration's, but Barclay's left wing, and had to confess that he knew nothing of the former. Eugène also was now urged to come up to Vilna to assist in the manœuvre against

Bagration, and was reprimanded for having remained inactive at Pilona for two days before beginning the passage of the river.

The interest of the moment was concentrated upon Bagration, for it was now only possible to march after Barclay, who was in full retreat. But there was still some hope of cutting off Bagration and annihilating his 50,000 to 60,000 men. This was again one of those cases in which one cannot but feel, as we have already pointed out at the opening of the campaign in Spain and on the occasion of Ebelsberg, that the general of 1796 would, irrespective of fatigues and great distances, have hastened to join Davout, examined the situation of affairs personally, and discussed it verbally with him, making himself sure that he could act in accordance with the circumstances, i.e. in this instance that he could vigorously take the offensive. He would then have hurried without a respite to Jérôme, having urged him meanwhile to advance with all speed; he would have led his army forward in person, and thus have ensured success as far as lay in his power. Such would have been the conduct of General Bonaparte, and, as we now know, success, thus eagerly pursued, would have been attained. But the Emperor remained quietly at Vilna, sent orders and wrote, and—Bagration escaped.

Already his personal capacity for resisting the effects of exertion and fatigue, and his insensibility to the influences of weather, had sunk very low. The first days of July brought an extraordinary wave of heat with them; many officers and men succumbed to it, and just as in Egypt, the fields of Russia saw many a soldier of the French army preferring suicide to continued hardships. But unlike Egypt, the unfavourable climate affected here the commander-in-chief as well. The Emperor also suffered from this extraordinary excess of heat; his body no longer showed that extreme thinness which bore witness to his nervous energy during his youth, but an unhealthy corpulence, and urinary disorders began to appear and to interfere with his activity.

All the more should he have exercised the greatest care in his choice of those to whom he now left the execution of his great plans with less restriction than of old. But by putting the incapable and sensual Jérôme at the head of three army corps, simply because he was his brother, he himself rendered the success of a plan which depended on energy, enterprise and capacity most doubtful. Must he not have had a very low opinion of the military capacity of the man to whom he sent the following :—" His Majesty is in no way surprised that you should not understand that instructions given from a distance of a hundred leagues may allow of different interpretations, which events must decide"?[1] Formerly he had not taken any such princely relationship into account when filling up important commands; " I feel that in the army there are no princes. There are men, officers, colonels, generals, and there is the commander-in-chief, who must be more capable than all the others and stand far above them."[2] Now he had changed in this respect also, and when a short time afterwards he saw the necessity of placing his brother, in spite of his royal title, under the command of the experienced Davout, it was too late, and the badly conducted operation had already failed.

On the 3rd July the Emperor learnt from the news which had meanwhile come in, that Bagration had crossed the Niemen on the 30th June at Mosti; he judged he was that day at Lida retreating to Molodetshno viâ Voloshin; and he expected Jérôme would follow him towards Minsk. The latter had, however, remained stationary at Grodno, giving his troops time to close up, and occupying himself with the commissariat; he was therefore still at this place on the 3rd July. Schwarzenberg crossed the Bug on this day and took post at

---

[1] C. N. To Berthier. Vilna, 11th July.
[2] C. N. To Soult. Milan, 8th June, 1805.

Drogitshin, and Reynier was at Bialostok. Davout awaited at Oshmiana the approach of Bagration, in order to fall upon him and check his march. The latter had, however, by no means advanced as far as the Emperor supposed, and on that day had got no further than Novogrudok. Of the Emperor's main army, Murat had reached Sventsiani and was there in touch with the enemy's rearguard; whilst Barclay arrived at Davgelishki, having his right and left corps respectively at Rimshani and Posstavi. The Guards were still at Vilna; Eugène with the IV. Corps was moved up to Novoyay-Troki, and arrived there on the next day; St. Cyr followed him and was near Shishmory. On the left stood Ney at Maliati; Oudinot at Avanta; and finally Macdonald was still at Rossieny, with orders to march up to Ponyayvesh.

The Emperor now purposed to make a short halt with his centre and left wing, and only to prosecute the operation with his right wing against Bagration. But already the difficulties of campaigning in Russia had become apparent, for Ney had not been able to transport his artillery to Maliati. The cavalry especially suffered; "We lose so many horses in this country, that we shall have much difficulty, even with the full resources of France and Germany, in keeping the present complement of the regiments mounted."[1] The commissariat came to a standstill, for the great line of supply,Vilkovischki-Kovno, very soon became unfit for use, and the men, left to themselves, turned to the means long habitual to them, viz. pillaging; "Already a want of provisions made itself felt; the army lived on the resources of the country, and these resources, in themselves scanty, were still more so before the harvest; already the men indulged in insubordination and plunder."[2] As there were no rich towns in this part of the country able to furnish sufficient supplies within a short radius, the numbers of stragglers and

[1] C. N. To Clarke. Vilna, 8th July.
[2] Fézensac, Souvenirs, milit. 224.

plunderers, roaming about singly, increased to an enormous extent. St. Cyr says bluntly of the advance of his corps from the Niemen to the Dwina, that he left daily so many men behind him, that they amounted in numbers to a full battalion; and scarcely had the frontier been crossed, than the Emperor saw himself forced to issue strict orders against pillage.

It was thus to the Upper Niemen that the Emperor's attention was mainly directed; he first sent, on the 4th, a division of the Guards after Davout as a reinforcement (on the other hand, Davout's division under Morand, which had gone to Michalishki, had joined Murat); then he ordered Berthier to write a sharp letter to Jérôme, urging him forward on Bagration's track, for he had remained immovable at Grodno, entirely failing to appreciate the circumstances. "All my manœuvres have miscarried, and the finest opportunity ever offered in war has been missed, by this extraordinary disregard of the first principles of warfare."[1] Finally he issued, on the following day, an order which convinced the King of Westphalia most unmistakably of the Emperor's dissatisfaction, inasmuch as it placed him and his whole army under the chief command of Marshal Davout. Subsequently too he reprimanded his brother very severely: "Since you had no knowledge of what forces Bagration had left behind in Volhynia, since you were ignorant of how many divisions he had with him, since you did not even start at all in pursuit of him, and he could effect his retreat as quietly as if he had had no one behind him, and since all this is directly in opposition to the usual practice in war, it is not at all astonishing that things should be in the state they are."[2]

As a matter of fact, indeed, Jérôme had only ordered Latour-Maubourg's cavalry to start from Grodno on the 4th, and this latter reached Novogrudok on the 8th, whilst

[1] C. N. To Berthier. Vilna, 5th July.
[2] C. N. To Berthier. Vilna, 14th July.

THE INVASION OF RUSSIA 123

Poniatowski and the VIII. Corps did not leave Grodno until 2 a.m. on the 6th, and arrived at Lebeda on the 8th. Davout had in the meantime marched forward by Voloshin, reaching Minsk on the 8th; on this same day Bagration was at Nesvish. Again and again the Emperor urged Jérôme on, and disregarded all the objections and excuses of the corps-leaders; "Cousin," he wrote to Berthier, "tell Prince Poniatowski that you have laid his letter before the Emperor, and that His Majesty was very annoyed to see that he speaks of pay and food, when it is a question of pursuing the enemy."[1]

Thus the march was continued, and Jérôme's two corps reached Novogrudok on the 11th, and Nesvish on the 14th. Now Davout also had halted, afraid of meeting Bagration, whose force he over-estimated at 60,000 men, before the arrival of Jérôme; thus he was still at Minsk on the 12th, whilst Bagration, who had left Nesvish two days before, arrived at Slutsk on the 13th. It will thus be seen that he had already escaped the danger of being surrounded, and Berthier was right when he wrote to Jérôme: "The two or three days which your Majesty's troops have lost may save Bagration;"[2] though the latter, of course, was not yet certain of being able to effect a junction with Barclay.

The two other corps belonging to Jérôme's army had meanwhile followed more slowly in the right rear, directing at the same time their attention to their right flank, towards the Russian army assembling in Volhynia. Schwarzenberg was now at Prushany and Reynier at Slonim. From the main army also the Emperor had detached some troops, in readiness to support the operation against Bagration, which had now become his principal object. He moved Eugène behind Davout; that commander left Novoyay—Troki on the 7th, and stood on the 8th with the IV. Corps at Bolschiya—Soletshniki; St. Cyr had since the 6th been at Ganushishki.

[1] C. N. Vilna, 9th July. [2] C. N. Vilna, 7th July.

But Eugène was not only posted at Soletshniki[3] in support of Davout, but also in view of the further advance of the whole army. It was indeed now the Emperor's plan to engage Barclay, who was retreating to the Dwina and concentrating his army on the 11th in the fortified camp of Drissa on the left bank of that river, frontally with Murat, Ney and Oudinot, whilst Eugène and Jérôme also, as soon as the latter was ready, were to turn his right by Polotsk and Vitebsk, thus cutting him off from his communications with St. Petersburg and Moscow. In this manner the Emperor hoped to bring matters to an important issue; "instead of a little war of rear-guard engagements and harassing, this will lead to great flank movements."[1] However, the Emperor did not wish to leave Vilna before the affair with Bagration had taken a definite turn, and consequently the main operation was postponed, for "it is not my desire that such a great affair should be begun in my absence."[2]

The forward movements progressed, therefore, but slowly for the present, and on the 14th July the position on the whole theatre of war was as follows:—Murat, having advanced at the head of the main army by Midzy, had afterwards turned to the right in the direction of Drissa, and lay at Samoshyay, with the cavalry divisions of Nansouty and Montbrun pushed forward towards Tsheres and Druya. On this day Barclay left the camp of Drissa and took up a position near this place, but on the right bank of the Dwina. Ney had been closing up to Murat at Drisviaty. Oudinot, having arrived in front of Dunaburg, started on this day on his march up the Dwina towards Murat. Macdonald, marching forward towards Ponyayvesh, had reached Smilgi. He was now to consider himself as a flank corps sent forward, and " the first task of your corps is to cover the Niemen, so that the navigation on it may in no way be interfered with; its second task will be to hold the garrison of Riga in check, and its third

[1] C. N. To Berthier, 6th July.   [2] Ibid.
[3] Bolschiya-Soletshniki

THE INVASION OF RUSSIA 125

to cross the Dwina between Riga and Dunaburg, so as to harass the enemy, its fourth to occupy Courland and to keep that province clear, since it contains so many supplies for the army, and finally as soon as the right moment has come, to cross the Dwina, invest Riga, order up the siege train and commence the siege of this place, the possession of which is of importance to us, in order to secure our winter quarters and to give us a point of support on this great river."[1] Thus the left wing was pushed forward, and had partly already reached the Dwina, a manœuvre intended to threaten the enemy's right wing. On the other hand, Eugène's corps was as yet only at Smorgonj, St. Cyr at Vilna, the Young Guard at Kobilnik, the Old Guard at Vilna, and the Emperor himself still at his ease at the same place.

The operations of the right wing had brought Jerôme on the 14th to Nesvish, with the cavalry of Latour-Maubourg in advance at Romanovo; Schwarzenberg was still at Prushany, and Reynier at Stolovitshi. Bagration started on this day on his retreat from Slutsk to Bobruisk, whilst Davout had left Minsk the day before and was marching towards Mohilev. In the meantime Tormassov had completely mobilized his army and now lay in readiness near Lutsk, with the intention of beginning within the next few days an advance into Poland on the communications of the French army. The Emperor had his attention now drawn to him, and ordered Jérôme on the 11th July to send Reynier back to cover Poland.

At this juncture therefore the Emperor's first operation must already be considered to have failed. The useless stay of Jérôme at Grodno and of Davout at Minsk rendered any surrounding of Bagration out of the question, and moreover Tormassov's advance would soon draw further forces away from the French right wing in his direction and thus contribute to Bagration's relief. The question now was, what was the chance of success of the

[1] C. N. To Berthier. Vilna, 9th July.

other part of Napoleon's plan, namely, the operation against Barclay?

With the 9th July the Emperor had almost entirely lost all hopes of cutting off Bagration, for he perceived that the latter was retreating towards Bobruisk. Eugène, who was at first to have advanced to Oshmiana in support of that operation, was now ordered to move in the direction of Dokshizi, whence he was to proceed, according to circumstances, either to Polotsk or Vitebsk. The Emperor himself intended to follow Eugène with the Guards and then to push forward with these three corps to Vitebsk, whilst Murat, with his troops (the two cavalry corps and Davout's three divisions), and with the corps of Ney and Oudinot (whose dash to capture Dunaburg the Emperor had disapproved of, as it separated him from the army: "You have interfered greatly with the Emperor's plans by your movement against Dunaburg"[1]) was to keep Barclay engaged at Drissa and to follow closely upon his heels, as soon as the latter saw himself by the Emperor's advance compelled to retreat towards St. Petersburg. Meanwhile Davout was to force Bagration across the Dnieper, thus securing the line of the Dwina and keeping the two Russian armies still separate.

It is, however, noteworthy, that there was no longer any talk of the plan of the 6th July, or of the "great flank movements." The Emperor seemed already to have given up all hopes of arresting Barclay at Drissa, of turning him, and forcing him to a battle in which he would be crushed. He thought now that he would do enough if he compelled him to retreat to St. Petersburg. "The Emperor does not intend to attack the enemy either in their entrenched camp at Dunaburg or in their entrenched camp at Drissa; he intends to turn their positions, render them untenable and attack the enemy on the march."[2] It is true, there was still some

---

[1] C. N. To Oudinot. Vilna, 16th July.
[2] C. N. To Berthier. Vilna, 15th July.

THE INVASION OF RUSSIA 127

hope that Barclay might be induced to attack Murat, if he saw him alone in front of him. "The Emperor expects to cross the Dwina between Disna and Vitebsk, and thus to induce the enemy to enter upon one of the two following operations, either to evacuate their entrenched camp at Drissa, in order to cover St. Petersburg, or to break out from Drissa in order to fall upon the army corps in front of them ; in this latter case a battle would be fought." [1] Of course, for the Emperor, having crossed the Dwina, would not fail to advance along it against Barclay's left flank.

At 11.30 p.m. on the 16th the Emperor left Vilna and arrived in Sventsiani at 10 a.m. on the 17th. At the moment of starting from Vilna he had been informed that the enemy had made a dash across the Dwina in the morning of the 15th, and had attacked a part of Montbrun's cavalry. Since it was not unlikely that this movement might be the forerunner of a general offensive on the part of Barclay, which indeed, as we have seen, had been already contemplated, he sent orders to the army to make no further advance for the present. Having arrived in Sventsiani, some additional information proved that this was not the case, and therefore the advance was continued. The Emperor also proceeded forward in the evening, and reached Glubokoyay in the morning of the 18th. At this place he now had his Guards, and two marches behind them St. Cyr; on their right, at Dolginov, Eugène with his corps ; Murat and Ney were on the march to Disna, the former's cavalry divisions, Nansouty and Montbrun, were in the neighbourhood of Disna and Polotsk, whilst Grouchy was reconnoitring near Bobr, towards Orsha. Oudinot, marching up the Dwina, was approaching Drissa.

In Glubokoyay the Emperor received various reports, which raised his suspicions of Barclay's departure for Polotsk, and during the night confirmatory news came

[1] C. N. To Berthier. Vilna, 16th July.

in from his cavalry. "It seems really as if the Russians had evacuated their entrenched camp of Drissa and were in full retreat to Polotsk."[1] Generally speaking, all the reports of the reconnoitring detachments had to be sent to the Emperor in the original. "The Emperor reads these volumes of reports and draws from them the information, in accordance with which he directs the movements of his troops. . . . In warfare valuable knowledge is often gained even from very contradictory reports."[2] Barclay had, as a matter of fact, started upon his reported march, and was that day at Polotsk, leaving his right wing behind at Drissa to cover the road to St. Petersburg.

Now the Emperor urged Eugène to advance with all speed towards Kamenj, in the direction of Vitebsk, whilst proceeding to bring his left wing up the Dwina in the same direction. Davout was to take up a position at Mohilev and thence open communications with Eugene, and might also draw in Jérôme's army to him. The latter, hurt by being placed under the marshal's orders, had resigned his command, and Poniatowski was at the head of the force consisting of Latour-Maubourg's cavalry and the V. and VIII. Corps. Thus all the corps of Napoleon's main army advanced in close order towards Bieshenkovitshi, the point of crossing the Dwina. The Emperor was moreover aware that Barclay had also left Polotsk and was retreating up the Dwina, and he intended, should the latter march towards Vitebsk, either to attack him or to await his attack, if he himself should cross the Dwina, for he took even this latter contingency into account. "It is impossible to predict, whether the enemy will march towards Bieshenkovitshi, or turn at once towards Vitebsk."[3]

In consequence of these movements the following was the situation on the 24th July. The Emperor had left

[1] C. N. To Eugène. Glubokoyay, 19th July, 3 a.m.
[2] C. N. Berthier to Jérôme. Vilna, 7th July.
[3] C. N. To Eugène. Glubokoyay, 21st July, 1 p.m.

Glubokoyay in the evening of the 22nd, had spent the forenoon of the 23rd in Ushatsh, and starting from there at 5 o'clock in the afternoon arrived in Kamenj during the night of the 23rd. The next day, the 24th, Murat, having marched by Disna and Ulla, reached Bieshenkovitshi. Nansouty and Montbrun had preceded him, and Ney had followed him closely; these therefore also were at the same place. From the west Eugène had marched up to the same town by Kamenj and Botsheïkovo, and after him the Guards from Glubokoyay, likewise by Kamenj. St. Cyr was at Ushatsh, and Oudinot stood near Disna to observe the Russian right flank corps. Barclay had, as we mentioned above, left this at Drissa when he withdrew from that town, and while he himself arrived at Vitebsk on the 23rd, it marched down the Dwina, with the intention of crossing this river and attacking the hostile corps opposite. Accordingly we find on this day, the 24th, Barclay at Vitebsk on both sides of the river, and his right wing at Pridruisk. Macdonald's corps, which was on the Emperor's extreme flank, had arrived at Jacobstadt as early as the 21st. The Prussian contingent had advanced to Riga and driven a division, which opposed them at Bauskay, back into that town. Thus the mass of the French army stood ready at Bieshenkovitshi for the passage of the Dwina and the advance to Vitebsk. "It is of importance for us to march quickly, so as to seize this town, and let the army have a few days' rest. But the passage of the river at Bieshenkovitshi must be first accomplished, for it alone will hasten the enemy's movements."[1]

If we now turn to the southern portion of the theatre of war, we find there that Davout had arrived at Mohilev on the 20th, Grouchy at Kochanovo connecting him with the main army. Bagration left on the same day Bobruisk, which he had reached on the 18th. He marched in two columns, the first of which arrived before Mohilev on the 23rd, where it found Davout in a strong

[1] C. N. To Eugène. Kamenj, 24th July, 9 a.m.

position, and was repulsed when it attacked him. Thereupon Bagration, seeing this road blocked, marched back on the 24th to Stary—Bichov, in order to reach Smolensk from there, by Mstislavl, avoiding Davout, and thus effect a junction with Barclay. Davout was in Mohilev on the 24th, Poniatowski was at Krupki with the VIII. Corps, the V. at Igumen, and Latour-Maubourg was reconnoitring near Bobruisk.

On the extreme right wing matters had changed owing to Tormassov's advance. The latter left Lutsk on the 17th, and the heads of his columns appeared on the 24th at Pinsk, Yanov and Brest-Litovsk, driving some Saxon outposts from these places. As we know, Reynier had received orders from the Emperor to see to the defence of Poland against Tormassov, and had therefore fallen back on the 14th from Stolovitshi by Slonim to Kobrin. On the 24th he was at Chomsk. Schwarzenberg stood on the same day at Slonim on his march towards Nesvish.

The Emperor had on the 24th hurried up in person to the main body of his army at Bieshenkovitshi, and found, on arriving there, Eugène busy throwing a bridge across, whilst some cavalry had already forded the river in order to observe Barclay's rearguard stationed not far from there at Kovalovshtshina. He joined this cavalry and pushed forward about a mile with it, thus convincing himself that the mass of the enemy had already gone beyond the point of his advance and was at Vitebsk, and that therefore all hopes had to be abandoned of making a flank attack upon their column on the march. Only the hope remained, of forcing the hostile army to accept battle at Vitebsk. On the 25th, in the morning—for the Emperor had remained in Bieshenkovitshi—he ordered Nansouty, with Murat in chief command, forward along the left bank of the Dwina towards Vitebsk, whilst Montbrun was to execute the same movement along the other bank. At Ostrovno Murat met with an advanced detachment, attacked it, but was only able to drive it back after the arrival of an infantry division from Eugène's corps.

The Emperor having remained behind at Bieshenkovitshi, was of opinion, that "from the reports which we gather from the prisoners, the enemy await us at Vitebsk."[1] In hopes of fighting a battle there, he ordered Murat not to press the enemy too much, lest they should fall back too soon, for he was compelled to confess that he was not in a position to force them to the battle he longed for so eagerly. "The enemy either wish to fight or they do not. If they wish to fight it will be very lucky for us. They might be deterred, however, by the non-arrival of one or two of their corps; it is therefore no disadvantage to us, if we allow them time for concentration, otherwise they might find reasons for not fighting."[2] On the 26th Murat continued his advance, and the Russians, though slightly reinforced since the preceding day, had to fall back again. They tried to make a stand at Komari, but the Emperor himself appeared at the head of his troops and forced them back still further. In the evening the Russians were close before Vitebsk and the Emperor pitched his camp near Kukovitshi.

On the next day he resumed his advance to Vitebsk, and soon met Barclay's whole army, which had taken up a position to the south of that town, behind the Lutshessa, and seemed prepared to accept battle. The Emperor forced their advanced posts back behind that brook and formed his army up on its left bank in sight of the Russian host. However, he did not commence the attack upon Barclay on that day, as he had not yet all his forces with him, and besides he thought that the Russian General, if he once determined to fight, would be found on the same spot the next day.

As a matter of fact the latter had intended to fight

[1] C. N. To Berthier. Bieshenkovitshi, 25th July.
[2] C. N. To Eugène. Bieshenkovitshi, 26th July, 4 a.m.

the day before, for he had ordered Bagration to march up to meet him through Orsha, and he now saw that he could not retreat any further, without exposing his subordinate officer to the danger of encountering unsupported the enemy's main army. But during the night of the 26th news came in from Bagration that he had not been able to get through at Mohilev and was now seeking to join him at Smolensk by Mstislavl. With this news there was an end of the necessity for meeting the Emperor with inferior forces, and thus at the moment when Napoleon was joyfully interpreting Barclay's taking post behind the Lutshessa as a determination to offer battle, this position was in reality only the outward sign of a plan which the Russian commander-in-chief had already given up. Thus the day passed, the armies standing inactive opposite each other; and in the evening Barclay evacuated his position and drew off during the night in three columns in the direction of Studnia and Poretshyay.

In the morning of the 28th July the Emperor saw no forces in front of him, and all trace of the retreating enemy was lost. He might have fallen back upon Smolensk, or have turned aside at Surash and fallen back behind the Dwina. The Emperor himself went to Vitebsk and ordered Murat forward along the road, which, leading thence eastward, branches off at Gaponova and runs in the one direction to Surash and in the other *vid* Poretshyay to Smolensk. As the Russian rearguard was also retreating along this road, Murat came in touch with it. It retreated slowly, and Murat stood in the evening at Gaponova at the fork of the road with Eugène and the Guards close behind him. The Emperor himself had also moved by this route and established his headquarters in a château not far from it; Ney alone had advanced on the shortest road to Smolensk by Rudnia. As yet no certainty had been gained as to the real direction of the enemy's retreat.

The next day also passed without any better result, and, whilst Barclay's columns reached Rudnia and Poretshyay, followed on this latter line by Murat, Eugène proceeded to Surash, and the Emperor returned with his Guards to Vitebsk. He had to confess to himself that his manœuvre against Barclay had come to an unsuccessful end. "The enemy is on all sides in full retreat. I have pushed forward as far as Surash in pursuit, but as they have separated and taken different roads, it is impossible to reach them. The general opinion is that they are falling back upon Smolensk in order to cover that town."[1]

When on the 20th September, 1792, the Prussian army stood ready to attack in front of Kellermann's forces, sure of numerical superiority and in the most favourable strategical position, fate offered it one of those moments, such as few campaigns afford, which, resolutely taken advantage of, not only lead to a great victory, but are bound to bring about a far-reaching change in the history of nations. Military criticism rightly condemns the general, who, incapable of using such a favourable moment, only indulged in the artillery duel of Valmy. But what must we say when we see Napoleon at Vitebsk commit the same error, the leader who owed his successes hitherto to nothing so much as his bold seizure of such moments, now the embodied antithesis of want of resolution and cautious hesitation? Yet we have seen him at Ratisbon, hesitating and delaying to take full advantage of the favourable moment, and thus we have to confess that it was the very root of his strength which was beginning to wither. Vitebsk again shows that it was becoming a rotten reed to lean upon. At Ratisbon this diminution in the Emperor's energy occurred after the victory, and thus the latter at least was safe, though it had not all the results it might have had. But

[1] C. N. To Murat. Vitebsk, 29th July.

here he was hesitating before the battle, at the moment when it was of the utmost importance that a battle should be fought before the opportunity had passed, an opportunity which would possibly, as at Valmy, never occur again. It was not seized, and consequently the whole campaign remained fruitless.

The Emperor had opened the operations by crossing the Niemen with 363,000 men on a front of seventy-two miles, at Kovno, Pilona and Grodno. Now he stood with 229,000 men on a front of 135 miles from Polotsk by Vitebsk to Mohilev. Thus the advance from the Niemen to the Dwina, 214 miles in five weeks, had cost him a third of his strength, and the advantage which the method of opening the campaign chosen by him was to have given him, namely, the maintenance of his own close order and the separation of the enemy, had vanished. The junction of Barclay and Bagration could no longer be prevented. The advance of the left wing marching *viâ* Kovno, combined with keeping Eugène and Jérôme in reserve supporting each other, was to have resulted in a situation which, while keeping Barclay and Bagration separated, was to permit the Emperor to fall on the flank of the one and of the other successively. But first the hope of turning and annihilating Bagration vanished; then that of keeping him separated from Barclay, and finally, when nothing remained but the hope of beating Barclay in a frontal battle, this chance also was allowed to slip. The operations against Bagration had failed, because the Emperor no longer possessed sufficient physical energy to conduct matters personally at all the most important points in his former indefatigable manner. The operations against Barclay failed because he no longer possessed that mental energy which formerly had led him to recognize with lightning rapidity the decisive moment.

Here his principle, which he formerly obeyed with such brilliant success, was verified: " Fortune is a woman;

The Invasion of Russia

if you let her slip one day, do not expect to find her again the next." On the 27th July she offered herself to him at Vitebsk, he rejected her, and on the 28th she was no longer to be found. The one general, exhausted by over-indulgence in self-confidence, was as little able at Vitebsk to engender success, though Fortune offered him her favours, as was the other, also suffering from his want of resolution, at Valmy. The consequence was the same in both cases—a barren result.

CHAPTER V.

MOSCOW.

(84) ON arrival at Vitebsk a short time of rest was given to the French army; "It is the Emperor's intention, unless forced by the enemy to make differ grant seven or eight days' rest to the army, so as to be able to establish the magazines."[1] We have already noted how very rapidly its effective strength had diminished during the few weeks which the campaign had so far lasted, and this proves the necessity of the resolution the Emperor had taken. Indeed he never entertained in earnest the faulty plan ascribed to him later by various critics, namely, to halt here on the Dwina and the Dnieper, and to leave the real decision to a campaign in 1813, abandoning that of 1812, as being unsuccessful. This possibility only flashed transiently across his fertile powers of imagination, which were always accustomed to view a situation from all sides and in all aspects.

What indeed would have been the use of giving the Russians time to collect all their forces and to strengthen all their important places, of raising their courage by adopting such a cautious defensive attitude, and of awakening from its admiring obedience, by an inaction which would seem dictated by apprehension, that Europe which he had accustomed to such decisive blows? He could still hope to attain a great success by a battle, and thereby bring the whole war to a victorious termination.

[1] C. N. To Berthier. Vitebsk, 29th July.

At Vitebsk itself the Emperor retained only his Guards; the other corps took up during the next few days the following positions: Eugène stood at Yanovitshi and Surash; Nansouty aud Montbrun were pushed forward to Poretshyay and Rudnia; Ney went to Lyosno; of the three divisions of Davout, which were again to join their proper corps, Morand and Friant remained near Vitebsk, whilst Gudin was moved forward on the right to Pavlovitshi, so as to establish communication with Davout. St. Cyr remained behind at Bieshenkovitshi.

We will, now for the present leave the centre resting and look after the wings, which were still in motion. Davout had, as we know, repulsed Bagration's attack near Mohilev on the 23rd. He then remained at this town until the 28th, on which day he started, moving up the Dnieper on its right bank, so as to get nearer the centre, and finally, on the 2nd August, took up his position at Dubrovna. Grouchy, who had gone to Babinovitshi, linked him to the main army. The V. Corps arrived at Mohilev on the 28th July, and the VIII. on the 27th at Orsha. Both corps remained stationary near that town, the command of the latter corps passing to Junot. Latour-Maubourg alone still continued his movement; having reached Mohilev on the 5th August, he advanced further towards Rogatshov, where he halted on the 9th, reconnoitring on the right rear towards the Beresina and the Pripet. Davout had scarcely started on his march up the Dnieper, when he received orders from the Emperor to continue the movement to Orsha, so as to come in touch with the army.

On the extreme right wing there reigned more activity. (85) Reynier had after his first engagement with Tormassov on the 24th advanced to Antopol; but there he heard that the post which he had established at Kobrin, to hold that place, had been surprised on the 27th, surrounded and destroyed; he therefore retreated to Slonim. Here

Schwarzenberg arrived on the 3rd August to reinforce him. This general had halted at Nesvish on receiving news of Tormassov's advance, but when Reynier's requests for support became more and more pressing, fell back to join him.

This movement met with the Emperor's approval, when he heard of it, although he had only a very poor opinion of the strength and quality of Tormassov's army. "It is difficult to understand why the enemy should employ seasoned troops for a minor operation, when it would have been of such great advantage to him to reinforce Bagration, who allowed himself to be beaten at Mohilev by the Prince of Eckmühl. It is therefore more likely that the divisions in question are only composed of third battalions, as well as those under the orders of General Essen, and consequently both those divisions probably consist only of 8000—9000 men, inferior troops."[1]

There is no doubt but that Tormassov's army would have been of greater use if combined with Bagration's; but formerly the Emperor did not take so long to convince himself of a faulty separation of the forces of his enemies. Thus, whilst his opinion of Tormassov's troops shows here, on the one hand, with what careless contempt he now underrated the value of those who intended to offer resistance to him, in spite of reports and the facts of the case, on the other the conclusions upon which he founded that opinion furnish striking evidence that he was now blind even to the enemy's mistakes, as he no longer argued from facts, but from his own views, which he conceived at haphazard.

Soon after this the Emperor placed Reynier under Schwarzenberg's orders, and instructed the latter "to march against Tormassov and Kamenski and give battle; in fact to follow them wherever they went, until he had made an end of them."[2] Schwarzenberg, there-

[1] C. N. Berthier to Schwarzenberg. Vitebsk, 31st July, 10 a.m.
[2] C. N. To Berthier. Vitebsk, 2nd August.

fore, advanced on the 10th by Kossovo to Prushany and drove back a Russian detachment there, which retreated to Gorodetshna, on the road to Kobrin, whither Tormassov also, who, on the enemy's approach, had collected his forces at Chomsk, led his army. On the 12th August Schwarzenberg attacked Tormassov's position at Gorodetshna; but Reynier's flank attack upon the left wing of the latter was unsuccessful, and not till the evening did he succeed in crossing at one spot the marsh, which covered the front of the Russians. However, darkness was already coming on, and during the night Tormassov retreated to Kobrin.

On the left wing of the French, also, an engagement took place at this time. We left Oudinot at Disna on the march up the Dwina, still engaged in covering the left flank of the army against the Russian right wing; the Emperor had then instructed him as follows: "If circumstances permit you to take up your headquarters in Polotsk, so that this may be your base, it will be very advantageous to do so, for it is likely that a strong advance guard sent forward from Polotsk towards Shebesh would cause Wittgenstein[1] to evacuate Drissa and Druya." [2] Accordingly Oudinot crossed the Dwina at Polotsk on the 26th. The Emperor kept continually urging him on to victorious action, representing to him, as was his custom, the enemy to be fought with there, as little to be feared; indeed he considered it an absolute principle in war, "that if one is forced to speak of one's own strength, one must exaggerate it and represent it as formidable, by doubling or trebling its numbers, but that, in speaking of the enemy, one must diminish their strength by half or a third; . . . that it is characteristic of the human mind, to believe the smaller number must in the long run be beaten by the greater. . . . But if the commander-in-chief is incautious enough to allow his own views to spread,

(84)

---

[1] This general commanded Barclay's right wing corps.
[2] C. N. To Oudinot. Ushatsh, 23rd July.

and to assume himself exaggerated estimates of the enemy's strength, it will give rise to the disadvantage, that every cavalry colonel who reconnoitres sees an army, and every captain of light infantry whole battalions. . . . It has ever been the habit of great generals to palm off their own troops to the enemy as very numerous, and to allow their own armies to consider the enemy as inferior to them. . . . I always exaggerated my forces during my campaigns in Italy, where I had only a handful of men. This device served my purpose and did not detract from my glory."[1] His views on the subject always remained the same. Even in 1814, when the Emperor's numerical inferiority must have been perfectly patent to his enemies, he wrote: "The newspapers are edited most stupidly. Is it right to publish at present, that I have but few troops, that I only won a victory by surprising the enemy, and that they are three to one? You must indeed have lost your heads in Paris, to say such things, whilst I publish everywhere, that I have 300,000 men, when the enemy believes it, and we have to repeat it, until we are tired of doing so. . . . One of the first principles of war is to exaggerate one's own forces, and not to minimize them."[2] In the case here before us, he certainly showed again that facts were disregarded by him in the most reckless manner; "since Wittgenstein has only 10,000 men, infantry, he (Oudinot), being ready for battle, may march against him."[3] But Wittgenstein had 28,000 men at his disposal, and was a particularly enterprising general, whilst the French general's strength had sunk to 23,000 men.

In accordance with the Emperor's instructions, Oudinot now started on his march to Shebesh, and reached Kliastitsi in the morning of the 30th. Wittgenstein had, as we know, conceived the plan of crossing to the left bank of the Dwina at Druya and attacking the enemy's

[1] C. N. To Clarke. Schönbrunn, 10th October, 1780.
[2] C. N. To Savary. Castle of Surville, 19th February.
[3] C. N. To Berthier. Bieshenkovitshi, 26th July.

corps in the rear. But on his arrival at Pridruisk he heard, that on the one hand the French were threatening to push forward from Disna, and that on the other Macdonald was getting ready to cross the Dwina at Jacobstadt; he therefore determined to fall back upon Shebesh. On the road to this place he heard of Oudinot's advance, and that this general was already nearer Shebesh than he was himself; he therefore resolved to attack him, in order to clear his way. Consequently his vanguard met on the 30th Oudinot's vanguard, occupying a position near Kliastitsi. In the course of the engagement the remainder of the troops on both sides came up, and the encounter was indecisive. On the next day, however, Wittgenstein succeeded by a determined attack in forcing Oudinot from his position, and the latter fell back behind the Drissa to Boyartshtshino. Wittgenstein sent his vanguard in close pursuit of the retreating enemy; but it was met by Oudinot on the 1st August beyond the Drissa and driven back across the river with heavy losses. When, however, Oudinot sent a division forward over the Drissa, in order to follow up his success, it met with the same fate from the Russians. Thereupon Oudinot began his retreat on the 2nd to Polotsk, which he re-entered on the 3rd, and Wittgenstein remained behind the Drissa at Sokolishtshi.

When the Emperor received the news of Oudinot's retreat to the Dwina, he ordered St. Cyr, on the 4th, to march from Bieshenkovitshi to Polotsk, so as to enable that marshal to resume the offensive. For the rest he reprimanded him for having fallen back so far; "this rather frivolous manner of acting endangers the general operations, as it may induce the Emperor to make wrong movements, and if we were not much superior to the enemy in numbers, the retrograde movement of the II. Corps upon Polotsk would be a real mistake. . . . War is a matter of impression, and what he ought to have done was to keep up the impression, which was in his favour, after the great advantage which he had gained;"[1] just as later, in March, 1813, he said when Eugène retreated too prematurely to the Elbe: "You have thereby given up an attitude, in the maintenance of which lies the art of war."[2] Thus he always showed great anxiety to create, by an attitude seemingly offensive, an impression which would puzzle the enemy, if he were forced to remain on the defensive. But the fact that he alludes to the "great advantages" which Oudinot had gained, shows how the marshals in their accounts of battles evidently copied their master, for Kliastitsi had assuredly not been a "great advantage." On the 7th August St. Cyr arrived at Polotsk, and Oudinot then immediately resumed his advance, whilst Wittgenstein had meanwhile taken up a position at Rossiza. Upon the news of Oudinot's approach he started to meet him, and defeated his vanguard on the 11th August at Svolna, whereupon Oudinot again fell back upon Polotsk, which place he reached on the 16th.

(85) During these events Macdonald, having first begun the construction of a bridge at Jacobstadt, had then gone to Dunaburg, which the Russians evacuated; he arrived on the 5th August and remained there, whilst the Prussian contingent continued to besiege Riga vigorously.

(84) This was the state of affairs on his right and left on the 13th August, the day on which the Emperor again left Vitebsk. He immediately occupied himself with the question of continuing to advance against the enemy, now concentrated at Smolensk, and had resolved, generally speaking, to start from Vitebsk towards the right in the direction of Davout and to cross the Dnieper simultaneously with the latter, thus turning the enemy's left wing, cutting them off from Moscow, and preparing for them the same

---

[1] C. N. To Berthier. Vitebsk, 7th August.
[2] C. N. Trianon, 9th March.

MOSCOW

fate as that of Mack and Brunswick. But even whilst he was thinking over this plan, Barclay anticipated him. The latter had reached Smolensk on the 1st August with 78,000 men, and had there been joined by Bagration with 43,000 men; their junction was thus effected. A forward policy now found favour in the Russian camp; they imagined the Emperor to be in a very extended formation, and hoped to break through it with their own concentrated masses.

For this purpose Barclay started on the 7th and advanced in three columns in the general direction of Rudnia, reaching on that day Verchovyay, Debritsi and Katinj. The next day he continued his advance and the vanguard of his centre column routed at Inkovo some French cavalry, belonging to Montbrun's corps. Barclay, however, apprehending an offensive movement on the part of the Emperor from Poretshyay on his right flank, now turned aside from his direct line of advance, more to the right, and marched to Vidra and the inn of Stobna; but his left column, under Bagration, remained at Katinj. The movement towards the Poretshyay road was continued on the 9th, and on that day Barclay's right and centre columns reached Moshtshinki, and Bagration Vidra.

The skirmish at Inkovo had attracted the Emperor's attention to the enemy's movement, and he had immediately given orders for the three divisions of Davout, Ney and Eugène to concentrate at Lyosno, in order to oppose their supposed advance. And when, through Barclay's wheeling to the right, the forces in the Emperor's front disappeared, and no further advance of the enemy was noticeable, he thought Inkovo had only been an outpost skirmish, occasioned by some needless forward movements of his own cavalry; still, as he had ordered his forces to start, he wished now to remain in motion and begin his operation against Smolensk. "I intend to march to Smolensk to see whether the enemy means to wait for us, a thing which is very probable, since the junction with

Bagration has been effected, and they have nothing much else to expect."[1] He therefore instructed Davout, to make every preparation at Rosasna for the construction of four bridges, so that these bridges might be thrown across during the night of the 13th. As the Russians still failed to resume their advance on the 10th, the Emperor concluded thus: "The news which reaches me is to the effect that the enemy have completely withdrawn; we have reconnoitred for several leagues and found no trace of them."[2] He therefore ordered Nansouty, Montbrun, the Guards, Ney, the three divisions of Davout's corps and Eugène, to advance together to Rosasna, where they were to arrive on the 13th. Davout was likewise to proceed thither, and bring Grouchy with him; his former divisions would then again come under his command, and thus the massed army would, in the evening of the 13th, stand at that point, ready to cross. Davout was to move the two corps of Poniatowski and Junot forward to Romanovo, whilst finally Latour-Maubourg was to cover the right flank at Mstislavl and Mohilev.

Whilst the French army was thus marching upwards the Dnieper, Barclay for a time remained stationary, expecting an attack from the direction of Poretshyay, and Bagration had even retreated as far as Smolensk. On the 13th, however, Barclay resolved, since nothing was to be seen of the enemy, to resume his advance towards Rudnia, and got as far as Schilomez, Bagration being still at Smolensk. But on the same day the Emperor left Vitebsk before daybreak and joined the columns, which were just arriving at the Dnieper; he confidently expected a decisive battle. "Everything leads me to anticipate that a great battle will be fought at Smolensk."[3] On his arrival at Rosasna, he found there two bridges, which had been thrown across during the

---

[1] C. N. To Murat. Vitebsk, 9th August.
[2] C. N. To Davout. Vitebsk, 10th August, afternoon.
[3] C. N. To Davout. Vitebsk, 12th August, 5 p.m.

afternoon, completed, and Grouchy, followed by Friant, Gudin and Morand, crossed the river. A third bridge had been constructed at Chomino, and there Murat crossed with Nansouty and Montbrun, followed by Ney. Eugène and the Guards were at Ljubavitshi and Babinovitshi on their march to Rosasna, where they crossed the river on the 14th. Davout was at this place on the left bank of the Dnieper. Poniatowski reached Romanovo, having left behind in Mohilev Dombrovski with 6000 men, as a garrison to cover Minsk. Junot also was at Romanovo close behind Poniatowski, and Latour-Maubourg at Rogatshov.

Thus on the 14th August the Emperor stood with 185,000 men on the left bank of the Dnieper, ready to advance along the great road to Smolensk; he hoped to capture this town in Barclay's rear, thus becoming master of the latter's communications with Moscow. He then intended to march against him, defeat him and force him northwards; once again one of those great and simple turning movements with his whole force, calculated to beat the enemy, after first cutting them off from any possibility of a retreat to their base, so that the loss of the battle meant annihilation for them. Thus had he acted at Marengo, at Ulm, and at Jena, thus had he even in 1809 forced the Archduke Charles at Ratisbon across the Danube. It had ever been the key-stone of his strategy, and therefore he rightly reckoned the manœuvre of Smolensk among the finest of his career "Napoleon executed at that time that splendid operation, which is a pendant to that of Landshut in 1809; he screened his line behind the forest of Bieski, turned the left wing of the Russian army, crossed the Borysthenes and advanced to Smolensk, where he arrived four-and-twenty hours before the Russian army, which fell back in all haste."[1]

This change of front is one of the most characteristic features of Napoleon's strategy and one of the highest

[1] Œuvres xxxi. Dixhuit, Notes, etc., 456.

efforts of his genius. The whole army is massed together at the point where a river is to be crossed, the movement being executed with the utmost celerity and concealed from the enemy by some natural obstacle or by a screen of troops. Thus had he in 1796 by marching along behind the Po, towards Piacenza, gained the passage by a surprise, whilst his army seemed still to be threatening Beaulieu's front at Valenza. Thus also did he effect the great and rapid massing of his army on the Lobau in 1809, and thus in this present campaign the concentration at Bieshenkovitshi, and now that at Rosasna, moving his army behind the river to the east and its marshy forests, while screening its movements in addition by some cavalry at Rudnia from Barclay. Thus also we shall see him conceiving the plan, in 1813, of moving his army forward to Havelberg, behind the Thuringer-Wald and the Elbe, so as to cross at that place and put himself on the enemy's right flank. Indeed in August he concentrated his army at Stolpen, with the intention of breaking out with his whole massed strength at Pirna over the Elbe into Schwarzenberg's rear. The most characteristic feature of this operation is this, that he always, before crossing a river, selected his new line of operations, thus already commencing the turning movement against the enemy, concentrating his troops on the hither side and then forcing his way in a close mass through the obstacle.

Accordingly on the morning of the 14th Murat advanced along the road to Smolensk with the cavalry divisions of Nansouty, Montbrun and Grouchy, followed by Ney, then by Davout, then by the Guards, and finally by Eugène. On the right Poniatowski marched *viâ* Trojany—Tolstiki, and behind him, Junot, likewise in the direction of Smolensk. In the afternoon Murat encountered at **Krasni** a division of Bagration's corps, left behind there to cover the left bank of the Dnieper. Ney's vanguard, which came up soon afterwards, captured the place, and the Russian division fell back along the

Smolensk road, repulsing the continually renewed attacks of Murat's cavalry, though not without heavy losses; in the evening it reached Koritnia. The Emperor established his bivouac at Boyarintsovo, behind Krasni. Will he be successful with his advance upon Smolensk and be able to capture the passage over the Dnieper by a surprise? " The opinions of the prisoners disagree. Some say the enemy's army is in full force at Smolensk; others, that only a part of it is there." [1]

On the 15th the army continued its advance and its leading columns reached Lubnia, whilst its rear columns were at Siniaki, behind Krasni The Russian division above mentioned had retreated to Smolensk. The Emperor spent the night at the post-house of Koritnia. Barclay had in the meantime, on the 14th, advanced to Volokovaya, and Bagration reached Katinj, having orders to push forward to Nadva. But while the latter was, on the 15th, on his march to this place, he received the news of the attack upon the division which he had left behind at Krasni, on the other bank of the Dnieper, and began at once to recognize the danger threatening Smolensk. He immediately sent one of his corps back to this town for its defence and withdrew the rest of his troops again to Katinj. There he was informed that the whole French army was on the march to Smolensk along the left bank of the Dnieper; he therefore demolished the bridge and hastened to Smolensk on the morning of the 16th. Barclay also, having halted on the 15th, being now informed of the state of affairs, started on the 16th on his return to the same town.

In the early morning of this day Murat and Ney arrived in front of Smolensk; the Emperor also came up immediately afterwards and ordered the attack upon the town to be begun. The latter, without being an actual fortress, possessed within its suburbs a brick enceinte

---

[1] C. N. To Murat. Bivouac of Boyarintsovo, between Krasny and Siniaki, 15th August.

eighteen feet thick, with dry ditches and covered ways. An opening in the enceinte was protected by a large earthwork, which served also, in a certain sense, as a citadel. Against this the first attack was directed, after the division sent back the day before by Bagration, as well as the one which had been pursued from Krasny, and which up till now had formed the sole defence of the position of Smolensk, had been thrown back into the suburbs. The attack was unsuccessful, and at 10 o'clock Bagration arrived at Smolensk, while the other corps of the French army were also coming up one by one.

Bagration threw some reinforcements into Smolensk, and by the aid of its fortifications, imperfect though they were, the town was held the whole day. In the evening Barclay's army also appeared, and took up its position by the side of Bagration's on the heights of the right bank of the Dnieper. On the other bank the Emperor's troops invested the town of Smolensk in a large semi-circle; to the left Ney, in the centre Davout, then Poniatowski; and on the right wing Murat, resting upon the river. This formation was completed during the night and on the morning of the 17th. The Guards stood behind the centre in reserve at Ivanovskoyay on the road to Mstislavl, and there the Emperor's quarters also were established. Junot was still in the rear at Tolstiki,[1] and Eugène at Liady, covering the rear of the army against a possible forward movement across the Dnieper.

The Emperor's first and most important plan of operation had failed, this could no longer be denied; knowing the Russians to be absent from Smolensk and on the forward march against Rudnia or Poretshyay, it had been his plan to turn them on the right and appear before Smolensk unexpectedly, to capture this town by assault and thus to gain the road to Moscow in the rear of the Russian army. "Had the French army taken Smolensk by surprise, it would have crossed the Borysthenes there and have attacked the Russian army, in its disorganized and

[1] Trojany—Tolstiki

divided condition, from the rear."[1] The reasons why Napoleon's plan failed were that Bagration sent troops in time for the defence of Smolensk, and that this town with its works was after all capable of resisting a *coup de main*. It cannot be said that this ill-success was due to any mistake on the part of the French leader; it happened here, as it often happens in war, that the suppositions upon which the plan was based did not come true and the enemy's measures counteracted his own. In such cases it becomes a merit in a great commander, to adapt his resolutions rapidly to the new conditions, to make the best of the changed circumstances, and thereby to reach the goal aimed at, in spite of all.

We have seen in Napoleon's career, for example in the campaign of Arcola, such a failure in his first plan of operations, followed immediately by his adapting his further plans to the new conditions; we have seen how he thus, in spite of the first failure, gained the victory ultimately. Here we shall see the opposite; we shall see how he adhered obstinately to his first plan of capturing Smolensk, and thus failed in the principal object, which was to have been gained thereby, namely, winning the Russian line of retreat to Moscow, though he might still have hoped to gain that object, by a quick change of purpose, by the choice of another point for crossing the Dnieper, a little above the town, say at Dresna, where Junot was to cross on the 19th. And the conviction is forced upon us, that his great genius was, it is true, still at its former strength with regard to its intellectual sharpness and clearness in the perception of strategical situations, but that the freshness and vivacity of his conception and also his energy had diminished. The fact that Barclay retreated, without having been beaten, is a proof that the latter quality is more important in warfare than mere sharpness of intellect.

In this very campaign indeed, at Glubokoyay, the

[1] Œuvres xxxi. Dixhuit, notes, etc., 456.

Emperor had once again taken the opportunity to say how necessary for a perfect general the equilibrium is between insight and strength of character, and the simile of a sailing vessel, which he chose as an illustration, assigned the greater moment to the latter quality; "the sails are the insight, character is the draught; if this latter is deep, and the canvas scanty, the vessel will be slow of motion, but it will resist the force of the waves; but if the canvas is abundant and the masts high and the draught great, the vessel may travel fast in fine weather, but it will sink in the first storm. In order to make a prosperous voyage, the draught and the spread of canvas must be in accurate proportion."[1] It seems to us, that Napoleon's vessel in Russia showed a tremendous area of sail, offering a broad surface to the wind, but insufficient ballast to resist the storm.

The night before the 17th Barclay ordered the defenders of Smolensk to be relieved by a fresh corps, for that town had to be held, without fail, until his retreat upon the road to Moscow was ensured. At 4 o'clock in the morning Bagration then began to depart, and took up his position behind the brook of Kolodnia, so as to cover the Moscow road; Barclay still remained near Smolensk. The Emperor had cherished, during the whole forenoon, the hope that the Russians would make a sortie from Smolensk and fight a battle in front of the town, a mistake which can, in that position, scarcely be excused. He consequently remained inactive, awaiting events. At last, recognizing his error about 2 p.m., he began his attack; he indeed succeeded in partially capturing the suburbs, but the fight for the covered way and the enceinte continued unabated until late in the evening, without the French, who suffered heavy loss, being able to storm the position. About 9 o'clock the fighting ceased. The Russians, to whom Barclay had, during the combat, sent a division as a reinforcement, succeeded in holding

[1] Gouvion St. Cyr, Mém. iii. 49.

Smolensk and thus attaining their object, viz. a safe retreat for the army. During the night they evacuated the town, moved to the right bank of the Dnieper and destroyed the bridges.

The Emperor's army remained encamped in the same position as the day before, in a semi-circle round the town; at 10 p.m. Junot came up, and took up his position behind Poniatowski, whilst Eugène reached Koritnia. With daybreak, on the 18th the French entered the town, now abandoned and still burning; the Emperor also soon arrived and ordered Ney to cross over to the right bank. Barclay, however, already in the act of retreating, as soon as he perceived this, sent some troops back. These threw the few French who had crossed, back again over the river, and then occupied as a rearguard the part of the town situated on the right bank, called the St. Petersburg suburb. During the day they succeeded in preventing Ney's passage at this point, and at 6 p.m., when the French were beginning to force the passage, the Russian rearguard set the suburb on fire, and in the night proceeded to follow their army. Of this latter, Barclay had remained behind on the St. Petersburg road, engaged in observation, and in the evening he started on his retreat in order to reach, by a detour *viâ* Sikolina, Prudishtsha, and *viâ* Korochotkino, Gorbunovo, Shukowa, the road to Moscow at the point where it crossed the Dnieper at Solovyova. Bagration had marched back along the same road as far as Sloboda-Puyevo.

On the 19th, during the early hours of the morning, Ney crossed the Dnieper on some bridges, which had meanwhile been completed, and Murat did the same by a ford; at the same time Junot marched up the stream, in order to construct another bridge in the neighbourhood of Dresna. The Emperor now sent Grouchy forward in the direction of Duchovshtshina, and Nansouty and Montbrun under Murat along the Moscow road, to make sure of the enemy's retreat. Ney advanced to Gorbunovo and met there Barclay's rearguard, which offered resistance for a short time; then the Emperor, having himself come up, ordered Ney to wheel to the right, so as to gain the road to Moscow. Here Barclay had sent back a division to cover his retreat, and this had taken up a position behind the Kolodnia. Ney attacked it, but was only able to force it back a little way with hard fighting and heavy losses on both sides, although one of the divisions of Davout, who had crossed the Dnieper after him and had taken up a position behind him on the Moscow road, came up also; for Barclay was likewise reinforcing his division, on whose steadiness the safety of his line of retreat depended.

In the meantime Junot had crossed the Dnieper in obedience to his orders, but had then taken up a retired position and remained immovable in it during the whole day, in spite of Murat's urgent personal requests, though his mere advance must have brought him on to the Russian line of communications, the road to Moscow, to the rear of the division defending it, the very thing which had been the object of his crossing the Dnieper at this spot. His incomprehensible behaviour can probably only be explained by the fact that some premonitory symptoms of that mental derangement showed themselves, which, caused by sensual excesses, brought about his death a year later. Eugène crossed the Dnieper at Smolensk and took post on the St. Petersburg road; the Guards, to which the division lately attached to Davout now returned, remained in Smolensk, and Poniatowski was still on the left bank of the Dnieper.

Early in the morning of the 20th Barclay continued his retrograde movement and crossed the Dnieper on this day at Solovyova, and the next day the Usha at Usvyatye. But here he determined to make a stand and to accept battle; he consequently remained stationary at Usvyatye, behind the river, and ordered Bagration on the 23rd to join him there, though the latter had fallen back as far as Dorogobush. The Emperor in the meantime caused Murat to follow the enemy along the Moscow road, and this marshal came on the 23rd, at 11 a.m., on the Usha, upon the Russian position at Usvyatye, followed closely by Davout. Ney reached Sloboda—Puyevo; Junot was still at the farm of Shenkowa, near the place where he had crossed the Dnieper; Eugène, set in motion on the same day towards Duchovshtshina, where Grouchy had arrived also, reached Pomogailova; the Emperor was as yet in Smolensk with the Guards; Poniatowski, who had started the day before, had taken the direction by Byelkino towards the road to Dorogobush—Yelnya, and Latour-Maubourg was at Mstislavl, in the right rear.

During the night before the 24th the Emperor received Murat's report to the effect that the enemy had been discovered in position behind the Usha and was apparently prepared to make a stand there. He thereupon instructed Eugène and Poniatowski to close up to the army for the expected battle; Latour-Maubourg also was to hasten his approach; Junot and the Young Guard had, on the 24th, already been ordered to advance on the Moscow road; the Old Guard was to follow early in the morning of the 25th. The Emperor himself left Smolensk at midnight before the 25th.

But meanwhile Barclay had again given up his intention, and reached Dorogobush on the 24th, having evacuated the position of Usvyatye during the night of the 23rd. Continuing his retreat during the next few days, he arrived on the 27th at Viasma, but here also he considered the opportunity of making a stand unfavourable, and having set fire to this town, he proceeded further back, until he at last showed front, on the 29th, at Zarevo—Saimishtshe, where he determined to accept battle with the Emperor. But on this day Kutusov, now entrusted with the chief command, joined the army.

We have seen that the Emperor left Smolensk in the hope of fighting a battle on the 25th at Usvyatye. But when he reached his leading columns on this day, he became once more aware of the fact that the enemy had not made a stand, and he was therefore again reduced to follow in their tracks. This he did; the main column, Murat, Davout, Ney, the Guards and Junot, advanced on the high road to Moscow, on its left marched Grouchy and Eugène, who crossed the Dnieper at Molodilova, whilst on their right Poniatowski advanced by Volotshok and Bykova on the left bank of the Vosma. The Emperor spent the night from the 25th to the 26th in an old castle, situated in front of Dorogobush, on the right side of the road. In the course of the 26th he visited the town itself, but left it again at 11 p.m.; he reached Slavkovo on the 27th, was on the 28th in the château of Rybka, and arrived on the morning of the 29th in front of Viasma.

(85) At the moment of the departure of the French army from Smolensk, the absolute impossibility of the success of the whole enterprise planned by the Emperor revealed itself. He had thought to bring about a complete subjugation of Russia, an actual conquest of that country, by a rapid campaign into its centre and by a few military successes. But here again, as in Spain, the political aim was unattainable by the mere action of the general, even though he were successful in a military sense. The Spaniards, like the Russians, had been at a greater distance from the centre of civilization than the other nations of Europe; but their religion and national self-esteem had remained the stronger, the less they felt indebted to foreign civilization. In Spain the country, by its natural features, facilitated the resistance of small bodies against a more numerous enemy. In Russia the enormous extent of the country facilitated the escape of the weaker defenders from the stronger assailant. In both countries the struggle, which had become a national war, adapted itself insensibly to the nature of the ground; it became in Spain a guerilla warfare and in Russia a system of evasion, thus prolonging indefinitely the period of resistance, until finally

the assailant, being exhausted, was no longer the stronger.

Consequently the goal, which the statesman Napoleon had set before the general Napoleon, became more and more remote, and only two courses remained. The general had either to renounce his task as impossible, or to pursue it obstinately, and in the latter case he was sure to fail and involve the statesman in his fall. In Spain the general had, it is true, renounced the solution of his task, as far as he personally was concerned, but had left its prosecution to his subordinate officers. In Russia, where he had staked his whole strength and his whole supremacy, he could not do this, and, having arrived at Smolensk, he had to decide between remaining there and continuing his advance to the enemy's capital.

Strategically speaking, he could have stopped at Smolensk; he would then, if he stationed his forces so as to be ready for a rapid concentration, and covered his wings by keeping the lines of the Dwina and Dnieper strongly occupied, have been in a similar position to that of 1805 in Moravia before the battle of Austerlitz, or of 1807 in Poland before the battle of Eylau; he could, as he did then, have awaited the enemy's approach, marched quickly against them and fought the decisive battle. But in that case he would have failed, in the eyes of Europe, in his enterprise; as a general he would thereby have acknowledged that he had not been able to reach the goal desired by the statesman, for he could never have thus compelled Russia to submit to his will; but such a confession would be sure to have had an incalculable indirect effect upon conquered Europe. And more than this, in a mere military sense such a course of action might have brought about his ruin, for the Russians would have had time to utilize all the resources of their large country, to bring up the inexhaustible masses of their human material, to equip and organize them, and since in that case the resumption of the struggle would have lain in their hands, for they would assuredly not in their then mood have repeated the mistake of Austerlitz, viz. a premature advance, the Emperor would probably have been, strategically speaking, even then in an unfavourable position. We must therefore decide, that to stop at Smolensk would have been unwise in the general.

And what, on the other hand, did the advance to Moscow promise? It might lead to a complete success, either if the general could conclude peace, or, in case this did not happen, if he was strong enough to maintain himself there. Peace he did not find there, and the fact that he hoped for it, must, as matters stood, be considered as a deliberate piece of self-deception. Of course it is more easy for us now to recognize this than it was at that time, but from genius we expect that its vision should be wider and keener than that of ordinary mortals. What indeed constitutes its greatness is, that genius, by its full recognition of the highest mental motives and material facts, forecasts the future, whilst the mass of humanity recognizes events only after they have taken shape, and is only able subsequently to explain the causes of them.

But was the general strong enough now in a military sense to maintain himself in Moscow? He was not. To extend a line of operations far into an enemy's country is ever accompanied by the risk of being cut off from the base and sources of supply. This danger may be met in two ways, either by directly protecting the lines of communication by means of special flanking corps, or by such an indisputable superiority of the main army over the opponent, that, if the latter proceeds to cut it off, it can turn against him, and when he has thus in turn been cut off, fall upon and annihilate him.

Thus we saw, that in 1805 and 1806, the superiority of the Emperor's main army, advancing in suitable order, insured him against the danger of being strategically cut off, and that afterwards, when his first successes were followed by a forward movement into the most distant portions of the enemy's country, he had, in view of his very extended line of communications, to take immediate steps for its protection. Thus we saw him during his stay in Moravia (vide vol. i. pp. 250 to 252) in 1805, covering his line of communications, extending for over 420 miles from the Rhine, by flanking corps, placed in such positions, that he was always able to concentrate his forces fully and in good time at any point, thus ever ensuring his superiority of numbers. In the same way his formation in 1807 (see vol. i. pp. 337 to 345) was such, that he was again fully able to concentrate his forces, while securely covering the flanks of his line of communications, which, reckoning only from the Elbe, extended over 380 miles.

But with these two dispositions, patterns of correct strategy, the one resulting from the march upon Moscow forms a startling contrast. If we examine the situation, as it took shape on the arrival of the French army in Moscow, we shall note the following:—

The Emperor crossed the Niemen along the line Kovno —Grodno with 363,000 men;

He reached Vitebsk with 229,000 men;

He began operations against Smolensk with 185,000 men;

He left that town with 156,000 men;

He arrived before Borodino with 134,000 men;

He reached Moscow, the end of a line of communications, extending 550 miles, with 95,000 men.

It is thus evident, that if any threatening movement against this line of communication, or any interruption of it should compel him to face about and march to its protection, he could not arrive at any point of it with sufficient forces to ensure a tactical victory.

And how about the immediate protection of this line? It was threatened on the right by 64,000 of the enemy.

who, under Tshitshagov and Tormassov, lay at Ostrog—Lutsk; against these it was to be protected by 34,000 men under Schwarzenberg at Tortshin. Thus it was threatened by an almost two-fold superiority of numbers at a distance of about 240 miles from a point on the line of communication, some 420 miles distant from Moscow. On its left it was threatened by Wittgenstein, who was posted at Sokolishtshi behind the Drissa on the Polotsk road; he had, it is true, at present only 20,000 men under him, but was, during the stay of the French army at Moscow, reinforced to double that number. He was to be kept in check by St. Cyr, posted with 28,000 men beyond Polotsk near Gamselyeva, and this force was, at a time when Wittgenstein was being reinforced, reduced to 17,000 men fit for fighting. Thus here also was a superior force 100 miles from Borissov, a point on Napoleon's line of communications distant 380 miles from Moscow. Neither in 1805 nor in 1807 did the Emperor leave such strong hostile bodies so far in his rear.

It was therefore impossible to secure the Emperor's line of communication, either by the tactical superiority of the main army, or by the immediate protection of adequate flanking forces; nor was there any possibility of a concentration of the entire French forces in time on any threatened point. The general's error lay in this, that he should not have allowed his line of communications to be threatened so far in his rear by the smaller armies of the enemy, as he was unable to face about and defeat them with superior forces; he should not have attempted to reach his final goal with such inferior numbers, while exposing his communications by such a distant advance.

It is indeed with gratification that we recognize, that the military destruction of the general in Russia had become inevitable if the enemy acted even partially as they ought. We say, with gratification, for the above proves that the situation was brought about by the nature of the situation created by the man himself, and not by the action of climatic or other external and accidental circumstances. The insane idea of the statesman had placed the general at Smolensk, in a position in which a victory was no longer possible; if he remained there, he acknowledged himself beaten; if he advanced to Moscow, he courted defeat.

It is true Kutusov had, on assuming command, determined to fight the battle, longed for, nay, almost demanded by his country in defence of Moscow; he did not, however, consider the position of Zarevo — Saimishtshe suitable, and therefore on the 31st August led his troops for the present back to Yavashkovo. On this day the Emperor arrived at Velitshevo from Viasma with the main column; his last corps, Junot, reached Viasma; Eugène was at Pokrov, Poniatowski at Sloboda. During the 1st and 2nd September Kutusov continued his retreat on the road to Moshaïsk, but on the 3rd he reached the position selected beforehand, on the heights on the right bank of the Kalatsha opposite Borodino, and here he determined to place his army in position and to accept battle. (84)

The Emperor had reached Gshatsk on the 1st September, and the news which came in there convinced him that the enemy was at last willing to fight, and he therefore remained for the present in this town, giving orders to all his corps to close up, so as to be able to have his whole army disposable for the expected battle. Murat advanced only a short distance beyond Gshatsk; Davout and Ney remained close to it; on its left lay Eugène at Pavlovo, on its right Poniatowski at Budayevo, and thus the army remained stationary during the 2nd; Junot was still in the rear at Tyayplucha. On this day the Emperor gave orders to prepare for him by 10 o'clock in the evening an accurate estimate of the strength of each army corps, so that he might know the force with which he could go into battle. "These estimates are also to contain lists of the men sent to a distance, who would not be present here for the battle, if it took place to-morrow, but who could be brought up, if it took place in two or three days; mention should also be made of the points where they are, and of the means necessary to assemble them. These estimates are to be drawn up with the greatest care, for upon them my resolution will depend. They must contain in the first place all the men who are present at roll call, and in the second place all those who could be present for the battle. You will likewise add, that I desire to know the number of horses which have lost their shoes, and the time necessary to shoe the cavalry and get them fit for battle."[1] The result was, that 128,000 men were on the spot, and 6000 could come up within five days.

With a view to the preparations for battle, the Emperor remained at the same place on the 3rd also, while Junot was ordered to close up. On the 4th the army resumed its march, and in the afternoon Murat encountered the Russian rearguard at Gridnyeva; it defended itself until nightfall and then fell back upon the convent of Kolotskoyay. The Emperor had pitched his tent for the night near the post-house of Gridnyeva. On the 5th Murat again came upon the Russians in their position at Kolotskoyay, which position they evacuated, since Eugène, having advanced *via* Lussotsk, threatened to turn it. The Russian rearguard joined the army in the position at Borodino, and about 2 o'clock Murat arrived in front of it, whilst Eugène approached from Bolshije and Poniatowski through Yelnya.

(86)   Now the Emperor gave orders to carry the villages of Fomkina, Alexinki, Doronino and Shivardino, as well as the redoubt thrown up near this last place, inasmuch as these, forming an advanced position of the Russians, were an obstacle to the further advance of the army along the great road, on its right flank. Fomkina was occupied

[1] C. N. To Berthier. Gshatsk, 2nd September.

without much resistance by Murat, who crossed the Kalatsha there; Davout followed at once, and whilst these two captured Alexinki and deployed their lines against the right flank of the Russian position, Poniatowski advanced from Yelnya, captured Doronino and threatened the left flank. A violent struggle began for the possession of the entrenchment of Shivardino, until at last, about 10 p.m., the Russians, relinquishing this advanced post, retreated into their main position and left the hotly contested entrenchment in the hands of the assailants. The Emperor pitched his tent to the left of the road to Moscow, at Valuyeva, in the midst of his guards, Eugène being in front of these. Ney was in the rear of Davout and Junot at Gshatsk.

After a short rest the Emperor mounted his horse soon after 2 a.m., and, accompanied by Caulaincourt and Rapp, reconnoitred the enemy's position. This lay with its right wing on the Moskva at Goroshkova, and extended thence, on the right bank of the Kalatsha, and covered by this river, as far as Gorki, and from this place its left wing extended through Semionovskaya to Utitsi. The left flank, no longer covered by the course of the Kalatsha and exposed to the danger of being turned on the side of the road leading up from Yelnya, was put in a better state of defence by the erection of breastworks. In the centre also, at Gorki, a large earthwork had been thrown up, though of course these works were of no great strength, considering the limited time and the sandy nature of the soil. In this space Kutusov had assembled 120,000 men, of whom, however, 17,000 were militia and irregulars. Once more, in the afternoon, the Emperor rode along the enemy's front, and noted with satisfaction that the Russians meant this time to make a stand.

His army had fallen in with the first break of day, and taken up the following formation. On the right wing, on the road from Yelnya, stood Poniatowski; next him, in front of the earthwork of Shivardino, Davout with the divisions of Friant, Dessaix and Compans; behind him the Guards; beyond the village and as far as the Kalatsha was Morand. The latter, as well as Gérard,[1] who was with Eugène's corps beyond the Kalatsha between Valuyeva and Borodino, were put for the battle under the chief command of Eugène, under whom Grouchy also was placed, and the Prince moved Morand by the morning of the 7th closer up to him on the left bank of the Kalatsha. A little to the left rear of Davout's position, near Alexinki, stood Ney, and behind the latter Junot came up at nightfall. To the right rear of Davout were the cavalry corps of Nansouty, Montbrun, and Latour-Maubourg. The latter had joined the army again from Mstislavl *via* Yelnya.

The Emperor, having returned to his tent, issued during the evening his orders for the opening of the morrow's attack. It was to be commenced by a heavy artillery fire; 62 guns of Davout's corps and the Guards, and 40 of Ney's corps were to attack the batteries at Semionovskaya, whilst the remainder of the artillery of the Guard was to hold itself in readiness. At the same time Poniatowski was to turn the enemy's left wing. Compans was to attack the entrenchments at Semionovskaya, and the Emperor sent for him and gave him his instructions personally. Eugène had already in the morning received orders to throw three bridges during the night over the Kalatsha; as soon as the attack began on the right wing he was to advance, occupy Borodino, cross the Kalatsha and attack the enemy's right wing with the IV. Corps, whilst Morand and Gérard advanced towards the centre for the assault on the entrenchment of Gorki. Then the Emperor lay down, but the excitement of the impending decisive battle allowed him but little rest; he soon rose again, sent for Berthier, and worked with him until about 5.30; then he mounted his horse and rode forward to the entrenchment of Shivardino,

[1] The Division had formerly been under Gudin; the latter had been mortally wounded on the 19th August.

which had been carried the day before. Here he dismounted, and took his position a little in front of it, on the left, nor did he quit it during the whole day. He was at this time suffering from a severe cold, which rendered talking difficult for him, and which two days later deprived him altogether of his voice.

Having arrived here about 6 o'clock, he immediately ordered the artillery fire to begin. During its continuation Poniatowski and Compans set themselves in motion for their appointed tasks, Dessaix following the latter on his right rear as a support. Compans threw himself upon the earthworks, and Ney also assisted from the left in the violent struggle which now ensued. At 7.30 the French succeeded in entering them, but a vigorous counter attack of the Russians drove them out again, with heavy losses on both sides. In the meantime the Emperor, anxious lest the Russian should fall upon the flank of Davout's divisions, by penetrating between them and Poniatowski, had sent orders to Junot to leave his position behind Ney and Davout and to move to the front on the latter's right wing, for this spot was only covered by Murat's cavalry divisions. Junot started this movement immediately after 8 o'clock, but he had scarcely proceeded along behind Ney's corps, when the Russian counter attack was delivered and he received orders to enter the first line of battle between Ney and Davout. He massed his troops here, but the Russian advance did not penetrate as far as his front. Ney and Davout advanced again about 9 o'clock, Murat supporting the movement by leading up Latour-Maubourg on Davout's right, whilst Montbrun was placed in readiness behind Ney. Thus the struggle for the entrenchments near Semionovskaya began again in the centre, the French line on the wings advancing also.

Poniatowski had during the above-mentioned fighting started upon his turning movement against the enemy's left wing, and was now in possession of Utitsi. But his corps, reduced to 10,000 men, could not overcome the

(87)

resistance offered to his further advance on the part of the Russians, who at once formed a fresh front on their flank with increased numbers, and here, therefore, the battle
(86) came to a standstill. Eugène had also begun the fight immediately after the cannonade in the centre had reached his ears. He advanced, to begin with, towards Borodino, an hour later he had occupied that place and thrown back its defenders behind the Kalatsha. Following up his advantage, he was in turn driven from the right bank of the Kalatsha and forced to fall back again to that village with heavy loss. Eugène now prepared once more to cross that brook with his whole army corps under the cover of his artillery posted at Borodino, leaving only Delzons behind
(87) to hold Borodino itself. About 8 o'clock Eugène proceeded to the assault of the entrenchment of Gorki.[1] Morand, who had crossed the Kalatsha first, commenced this attack; he advanced quickly and captured the work, but some Russian reinforcements which had been brought up drove him out again completely, taking a large number of his men prisoners in the entrenchment itself. Eugène ordered Morand's retreat to be covered by the divisions of Gérard and Broussier, who had in the meantime crossed to the right bank of the Kalatsha and of whom the former marched into position on the right and the latter on the left of Morand, and proceeded to bring his artillery to bear on the entrenchment. Such was the situation at 9 o'clock along the whole front of battle.
(88) In the centre Ney and Davout, who had now also been reinforced by Friant, kept in reserve up to now, succeeded, after an hour's obstinate fighting, in capturing the entrenchments of Semionovskaya, and soon afterwards the village itself. Latour-Maubourg also assisted in this by a determined attack from the right; but the Russians, only retreating very slightly, soon made a vigorous stand. Their right wing still held the great earthwork to the north of Semionovskaya firmly, and the assailants, exhausted by their very heavy losses, were unable to advance

[1] Large entrenchment to southwest of Gorki.

any further. Semionøvskaya and the entrenchments there remained, it is true, in the hands of the French, but their isolated and weak attacks beyond these were repulsed, and from noon the fighting here was more and more limited to an artillery duel.

Eugène was just on the point of commencing a new assault upon the great earthwork of Gorki, when he suddenly received news that large numbers of hostile cavalry had appeared beyond the Kalatsha on Delzon's left flank. Alarmed for his rear, he postponed for the present his attack upon the earthwork and himself led back Lecchi's division across the Kalatsha. The enemy's cavalry division, which had been sent forward on the flank of the French, had, however, found the ground so unfavourable for a rapid and effective flank attack, that it only drove back the weak French cavalry which opposed it, and did not attempt anything against Delzon's troops, which were concentrating around Borodino. Eugène therefore saw that nothing serious was to be apprehended, and returned to the right bank of the Kalatsha.

The assault upon the entrenchment was now begun, Montbrun's cavalry, which had moved in from the right for this purpose, between Eugène's troops and Ney, assisting in it. Whilst Gérard, Morand and Broussier advanced frontally, Montbrun attacked the Russian troops on the left of the entrenchment, drove them back, gained the rear of the work and penetrated to its gorge. It is true the French horsemen were soon driven out again and thrown back with heavy loss, but in the meantime Eugène's regiments had reached the entrenchment, closing in on it from all sides; they scaled it and all its defenders were slaughtered. It was now 3 o'clock.

Meanwhile Junot, who had hitherto acted as a reserve to Ney's and Davout's corps, which once more went forward, had received orders to form up on the latter's right wing, in order, by pushing forward between it and the V. Corps against the enemy's left wing, to support

Poniatowski's attack upon the latter. Junot commenced this movement at 1 o'clock and deployed his lines in the appointed direction against the enemy, but was only able to make very slight progress, owing to the fact that Poniatowski was still in the rear at Utitsi, and who did not come up until 5 o'clock, when both pushed forward against the extreme left wing of the Russians. The latter were forced back, but formed again further back on the line of heights to the east of Semionovskaya. It was now 6 o'clock, and the battle at this part of the field was at an end.

In the centre and on the French left wing nothing had been done since 3 p.m., beyond a general cannonade, the artillery being very numerous on both sides. On one side and the other the losses had been so enormous that complete exhaustion ensued. The French no longer tried to leave the entrenched position which they had captured, in order to proceed to the decisive attack upon the second Russian position; and the Russians did not venture to take the offensive from that position, in order to recapture their entrenchments. About 6 o'clock the cannonade ceased along the whole line.

During the entire course of the battle the Emperor had not left his place, although both Eugène's difficulties and those of Ney and Davout really demanded the general's eye and his personal intervention. It was 4 o'clock before he mounted and rode forward to Ney and Murat, but he was now of course only in time to witness with his own eyes the cessation of the combat, a fact which the diminution of the cannonade since 3 o'clock had already sufficiently announced. Three hours later he returned; "contrary to his usual demeanour, his face was heated, his hair in disorder and his whole air one of fatigue."[1]

Thus the battle of Borodino was on the whole a purely frontal battle, in which the French line, somewhat superior in numbers, but above all tactically very superior, brought

[1] Bausset, Mém. ii. 110.

Moscow

greater weight to bear and consequently forced the Russian line back. But as the latter was partly drawn up in entrenched positions and defended itself very obstinately, and was, moreover, not very inferior in numbers, this forcing back was only effected with most heavy losses, both to the defenders and the assailants, and after the first position of the Russians had been captured by the French, the effect of their tactical and numerical superiority was exhausted. The French army lost 28,000 men, and the Russian 40,000 men, a fact which easily explains the complete exhaustion and inactivity on both sides after the third hour of the afternoon.

But, as must always be the case in a purely frontal forcing back of an enemy, no decisive result had been gained by it; such a result can only be attained where turning corps advance during the frontal attack on the enemy's flanks and his line of retreat, or where, after the frontal attack, fresh reserves are thrown upon the exhausted and shaken line of the enemy. Borodino, however, does not show anything of this kind. It is true there is some trace of a turning movement to be detected in Poniatowski's advance, but this movement in insufficient strength was easily rendered ineffective by the enemy's forming front on his flank, and exhibits neither in its conception nor in its execution the stamp of a decisive blow. In the same fashion the Emperor had attacked at Smolensk, neglecting to deliver the decisive blow by a turning movement across the Dnieper above that town.

Nor was any fresh reserve thrown upon the much depleted Russian front. It is true the Emperor had such a reserve at hand, viz. the Guards, but, contrary to his custom hitherto, he did not employ it to change the rearward movement of the enemy, still holding on to the position, into a disordered flight. Was it his fear of weakening himself too much, and arriving at Moscow with too slender forces, that prevented him doing this? So far no such apprehension was noticeable during his advance, nor had it induced him to save as much as possible the numerical strength of his forces by a more severe discipline or a more anxious care for their supplies. He had pushed forward heedlessly and with a contempt for human life. Is it likely that this anxiety came suddenly upon him during the battle, just when contempt for human lives becomes a duty in a general; and when no afterthought should interfere with a reckless employment of all the forces at his disposal, so as to gain the victory, which will compensate for all? If he then really said, "And should a second battle become necessary to-morrow, wherewith shall I fight it?"[1] we can quote his own words, namely, that "generals who save up troops for the day after a battle are always beaten."[2]

He did save up the 19,000 men of his Guards and after all reached Moscow too weak to keep himself there. Their employment, even had it entailed the loss of one-third of their numbers, might possibly have given him a complete victory over the Russian army and thereby ensured peace at Moscow. The great art in the conduct of a battle lies in attacking the opponent on his weakest part, his flanks and rear, and not in husbanding, but rather in the opportune employment of a reserve. Of these great principles the Emperor to our astonishment does not show one trace here. Must we here too look to his physical condition as accounting for this remarkable fact? It is undoubtedly true that he only left the place he had taken up when the fight was already on the point of ceasing everywhere, and that he was up till then too far distant to observe any decisive changes in it. "Nowadays the commander-in-chief must daily be present within the zone of artillery fire, often within range of grape, and in all battles within range of musketry, so as to be able to reconnoitre, observe and give orders; the range of sight is not sufficiently

[1] Ségur, Hist. de N. et de la Grande armee en 1812, i. 369.
[2] Marmont, Mém. ix. 143.

extensive for generals to remain outside the range of musket balls."[1]

Kutusov, leaving a rearguard on the battle-field, set off on the morning of the 8th and led his army back to Moshaïsk. The Emperor united all the cavalry divisions under Murat's commands, and added to these, as a support, the infantry division of Dufour.[2] This vanguard was to occupy Moshaïsk on the same day. But Murat was unable, in face of the resistance offered by the Russian rearguard in that town, to reach his appointed goal. The Emperor did not, on this day either, quit his place near the entrenchment of Shivardino, where his tents had been pitched the evening before; he " seemed overwhelmed by fatigue; from time to time he clasped his hands violently over his crossed knees, and I heard him frequently repeat, with a sort of convulsive movement : " Moscow, Moscow ! "[3] At 1 o'clock he mounted his horse and rode over the battle-field, on which the army was still standing, Davout and the Guards alone having followed in rear of Murat. A brief alarm proved that the French did not after all feel quite safe in their part as victors in the face of the retreating enemy.

On the 9th the Russian army fell back upon Semnina; the Emperor followed as far as Moshaïsk, where he assembled Murat, Davout and the Guards; Ney was behind, and Poniatowski and Eugène diverged to the right and left of the road to Moscow in the directions of Vereya and Rusa. Junot still remained on the battle-field. During the next few days Kutusov continued his retreat slowly towards Moscow, and the French army followed as slowly, being occupied in restoring their equipment and internal organization, and in drawing in supplies from all sides.

[1] Précis des guerres de Jules César, Œuvres xxxii. 105.
[2] In consequence of the losses at Borodino, Dufour had replaced Friant, Friederichs Dessaix, and Lahoussaye Grouchy.
[3] Constant, Mém. v. 84.

The Emperor remained at Moshaïsk until the 12th September. He could no longer conceal from himself the truth which became more and more evident, that the strength of his army would not suffice to hold the goal, Moscow, when it was reached, and he therefore showed the greatest ardour in moving up from the rear all the forces in any way disposable. "Cousin," he wrote to Berthier, "I have sent you various orders, to concentrate the whole of my infantry and cavalry at Smolensk. I believe I have not forgotten anything. . . . If I should by any chance have forgotten anything and left any divisions or battalions behind, send me a list of them again."[1]

(89) Thus there was to be a strong reserve collected at Smolensk, whilst the corps of Victor, which had crossed the Niemen, as a reinforcement, on the 4th September, was on its march to this town, and arrived there by the 27th of that month. In case of necessity it was to be moved up to Moscow. "It is likewise necessary that the Duke of Belluno should hold himself ready with his entire army corps to proceed from Smolensk to Moscow, in order to reinforce our army in the same measure as the enemy will reinforce his."[2] The Emperor hoped that the capture of Moscow would induce the enemy to divert his attention from the very exposed flanks of the French line of communications and mass all his forces round Moscow. "Now the enemy finding his heart threatened, only seeks to guard that heart, and thinks no longer of the extremities."[3] This indeed was the hope which had led him to Moscow, but the proposed thrust at the enemy's heart was destined not to find its way home, whilst the extremities were to develop an activity fraught with ruin to him.

(84) Thus during the days between the 9th and the 13th the Emperor's army proceeded slowly towards the enemy's

---

[1] C. N. Moshaïsk, 11th September.
[2] C. N. To Berthier, Moshaïsk, 11th September.
[3] C. N. To Murat, Moshaïsk, 10th September.

capital. He himself left Moshaïsk in the afternoon of the 12th and established his headquarters at Petelina and the next day at Borrisovka. Kutusov now stood close before the gates of Moscow at Troïts—Koye—Fili. Early on the morning of the 14th the Russian army started upon its march through the capital, and about 5 p.m. the last troops evacuated the town, and the army, taking the road to Kolomna, reached Panki. This retreat of the army and the evacuation of the capital were accompanied by a wholesale flight of the inhabitants of Moscow, and in the most distant suburbs columns of smoke began already to rise. The commander of the Russian rearguard had made an arrangement with Sebastiani, who was at the head of the French vanguard, in accordance with which the evacuation of Moscow was to be undisturbed by the French, and the latter were not to enter until two hours after the departure of the Russians. This was to guarantee the safety of the Russian retreat, whilst it at the same time afforded the advantage to the French of occupying Moscow without fighting, and experience hitherto had shown that fighting among the wooden houses of a Russian town meant its being burnt down and lost.

Murat therefore did not enter the suburb of Dorogomilov until after 2 o'clock with his cavalry. About 3 o'clock he crossed the Moskva and made his entry into the abandoned capital. In the meantime the Emperor also had arrived before the town, but did not enter it; from the top of the "Mount of Salutation" (Gora Poklonaya) he caught his first glimpse of it; "he had put on a brown frieze coat over his uniform and his features exhibited indubitable joy and satisfaction;"[1] then he went to the barrier of Dorogomilov and awaited there the approach of his various corps. The Guards alone were sent into Moscow with instructions to occupy the Kremlin.

[1] v. Guretzky-Cornitz: Geschichte des 1. Brandenburgischen Uhlanen-Regiments (Kaiser von Russland), No. 3, 84.

Eugène, having come up by Svenigorod and Tatarovo, stopped before the barrier of Pressnenski. Poniatowski formed up to the south of the town, and Davout and Ney to the west of it; Junot had remained behind to garrison Moshaïsk. In the evening Murat placed his outposts near Korotsharovo. The Emperor took up his quarters towards evening in one of the first houses on the right, in the suburb of Dorogomilov.

During that night fires broke out in various places in Moscow. At 6 a.m. the next morning the Emperor entered the Kremlin. But the conflagrations, purposely fed and spread by the Russians, began to gain ground more and more, and by daybreak on the 16th the entire town was in flames. Soon after noon even the Kremlin began to be unbearable; and the Emperor saw himself, to his regret, forced to leave it and to take up his quarters in the castle of Petrovski outside the town. On the morning of the 18th, when the conflagration of the town had, as a whole, come to an end, after having laid nine-tenths of Moscow in ashes, the Emperor returned to the Kremlin.

Meanwhile Kutusov's army had left Panki on the 16th and had at first retreated further on the road to Kolomna. But in the evening of the 16th it was resolved to abandon that direction and to turn to the west, so as to be in better communication with the rich southern provinces and the stores collected at Kaluga. The Russians, therefore marched along behind the Pachra, and on the 18th reached Podolsk, on the road from Moscow to Sherpuchov. Murat, to whom Poniatowski's corps, as well as the divisions of Claparède[1] and Dufour had been attached, had scoured the whole district to the east of the capital, after his march through Moscow, and had thus discovered the retreat of the Russians along the road to Kolomna. After having granted his cavalry a few absolutely necessary days of rest, he pursued the Russians, on the 21st, in the presumed

[1] Of the Guards.

direction of their retreat, being misled by some Cossacks left behind on this road.

On the 22nd September Murat was at Bronnitsi. But in the meantime the Emperor had received reports which revealed to him a movement of the enemy towards the road to Tula, and on the 21st he sent Bessières, with Lahoussaye and Friederichs under his command, to Podolsk. " These troops will form a corps of observation, which will collect information as to the enemy's march and cover the road to Podolsk, until Prince Poniatowski with the vanguard has again gone in pursuit of the enemy." [1] Poniatowski received instructions to move up to Podolsk, whilst Murat was still engaged in reconnoitring along the road to Kolomna, so as to discover whether the whole Russian army had really marched away to the left. This became a certainty on the 23rd, and consequently he too arrived on the 25th at Podolsk, which Poniatowski had reached the day before. Bessières was on the Kaluga road, on the Desna. Kutusov also, having continued his march to the south round Moscow, was now on the Kaluga road, near Krasnaya—Pachra, behind the Pachra.

During this time the Emperor had become more and more aware of the insecurity of his position, and had vainly hoped for overtures on the part of the Russians which might have rendered it possible to begin negotiations and thus bring to an end this war, which was beginning to assume an ominous aspect for him. But nothing of the kind happened, and on the 20th September he conquered his pride so far as to write a letter to the Emperor Alexander, which was to create the opportunity so eagerly longed for. On the 5th October he sent his aide-de-camp, Lauriston, for the same purpose to Kutusov's headquarters, and the latter promised to lay his offers before the Emperor Alexander.

In the meantime the above-mentioned troops, sent forward on the roads to Tula and Kaluga, had fur-

[1] C. N. To Berthier. Moscow, 21st September.

nished to the Emperor, on the 26th September, the certainty that Kutusov had left the road leading to Riazan, had marched round Moscow on the south and stood now on the road to Kaluga, with all the great resources of the rich south in his rear. Thus he saw himself confronted by a new situation of affairs. And one more circumstance must be mentioned to complete our knowledge of that situation. The preliminary terms of peace between Russia and Turkey, which had been signed at Bucharest on the 28th May, had been confirmed by the Sultan, and thus the Russian army in Moldavia under Tshitshagov, which had up to now opposed the Turks, was free to take part in the operations against the French.

It left Bucharest on the 31st July, and on the 20th September Tshitshagov united his 34,000 men at Ostrog—Lutsk to Tormassov's 30,000. It is true Kutusov had at first wished to order up these reinforcements to join himself at Moscow, and thus the Emperor's assumption, that "the enemy finding his heart threatened, only aims at guarding that heart, and thinks no longer of the extremities," was not without some justification. But there came different instructions from St. Petersburg, and consequently the further anticipation of the Emperor, namely, that Kutusov wished by his march to Kaluga to meet his approaching reinforcements half-way, which he actually did, was opposed to his first surmise.

Kutusov had indeed commenced that retrograde movement on the 26th, closely followed by Murat, who was, according to the Emperor's instructions, constantly endeavouring to turn his right flank. Murat pressed Kutusov vigorously, and on the 4th October we find the latter behind the Nara, in a position chosen beforehand and strengthened by earthworks. His rearguard occupied Tarutino. Murat was in touch with him at Vyankovo, and Bessières, following close behind Murat, had halted on the Pachra. During this time the

Moscow

Emperor had assigned to his troops in and around Moscow more extensive quarters to recuperate in. Davout occupied the southern parts of the town of Moscow, and Eugène the northern, at the same time holding Dmitrov, while Ney assembled his corps at Bogorodsk. But the Emperor had already come to the conclusion that the Russians would not make peace, and that he would be compelled to quit Moscow. Before we, however, enter upon a consideration of the strategical conception on which he intended to base this important retrograde movement, we will describe shortly how the situation in his rear had changed at this date, the 4th October.

We left Macdonald at Dunaburg with his Prussian auxiliary corps in observation before Riga. At first everything had been quiet on this wing; then, however, a corps of 10,000 men under Steinheil from Revel arrived in Riga, on the 22nd September. The Russians now assumed the offensive against the Prussian corps of observation, but were in the end driven back again into Riga. Thereupon Steinheil started to join Wittgenstein. We left this latter general on the 16th August, at the moment when Oudinot had relinquished his advance against him and had fallen back upon Polotsk. Wittgenstein pursued and attacked him there on the 17th, but on the next day the French, now under the chief command of St.-Cyr, for Oudinot had been wounded, took the offensive with both their corps. Wittgenstein was beaten and fell back on the 22nd behind the Drissa. Here he remained stationary and awaited the approach of reinforcements, which were gradually coming up. St.-Cyr also remained in his position, his vanguard being in touch with that of the Russians at Byelaya. Thus the two faced each other, but the Russians were constantly increasing in strength, whilst their enemy was constantly decreasing from want of provisions and sickness. The former soon numbered 40,000, the latter only 17,000 men.

In the southern portion of the theatre of war Tshitshagov having, as we said, joined forces with Tormassov's army, had advanced with 64,000 men against Schwarzenberg, and the latter, whose two corps now numbered only 34,000 men, kept constantly retreating before him; he crossed the Bug at Vlodava, and on the 4th October, having fallen back again behind the Bug, lay at Brest—Litovsk behind the Muchavyes. Between St.-Cyr and Schwarzenberg, on the main line of the Emperor's communications at Smolensk, Victor had been posted since the 27th September; his corps, with those which had been left behind there to garrison this great depôt, numbered 37,000 men.

Let us now once more survey the Emperor's scene of operations as a whole, with a view to comparing it with others. We find the following:—The entire triangle, which his formation now represents, lay approximately between the towns of Riga, Moscow and Brest—Litovsk; its left side, Riga to Moscow, was 520 miles long, its right side, Brest to Moscow, 617 miles, and its base, Riga to Brest, 360 miles : the diagonal of this triangle, or in other words the length of Napoleon's line of rear communications from Moscow to the Niemen, measured 550 miles. To hold this stretch of country, the Emperor had: at Moscow, 95,000 men, at Moshaïsk 5000, at Smolensk 37,000, on his left wing from Dunaburg to Riga 25,000, at Polotsk 17,000, on his right wing at Brest 34,000 men. Let us compare these figures with those of the greatest campaign of more modern times.

When the Germans had, in 1870, reached their main goal, Paris, and thought, by investing it and reducing it, to force the enemy to conclude peace, in the same way as Napoleon had hoped to do by capturing and then holding Moscow, their position in the middle of November was the following. The ground covered by the Germans lay within the points Sedan, Chartres, Dijon, Strasburg, which enclose a quadrilateral figure in the form of a trapeze, its northern faces, Chartres to Sedan, and Chartres to Dijon, being about 190 miles long, and its southern, Strasburg to Sedan, and Strasburg to Dijon, about 170 miles. The length of the communications of the army from Paris to the Prussian frontier may be taken as 210 miles. On this extent of country the Germans had: in front of Paris, 171,000 men; behind these at Sezanne, 21,000; on their left wing along the line Houdan—Chartres—Toury, 55,000; along the line Fontainebleau—Sens—Chatillon, 65,000; at Dijon, 20,000; before Belfort, 25,000; on their right wing from Reims to Rethel, 42,000; and lastly near Metz and before Thionville, 26,000 men. In other words, the Emperor after $3\frac{1}{2}$ months held with 213,000 men an area of 97,000 square miles, and the Germans after $3\frac{1}{2}$ months with 425,000 men an area of 29,000 square miles. On crossing the frontier, the operations had been opened by the Emperor Napoleon with 442,000 men and by the Germans with 372,000 men.

From this we gather not only that the organization of the German army was superior to that of Napoleon's, but also that the former alone was adequate to the object in view. It reduced by the good organization of its commissariat and transport arrangements the casualties which every advancing army suffers through battles and sickness, from the mere fact of its movement, to a minimum, and by judiciously replacing the losses sustained, it made it possible to reach the goal in sufficient force. The German commander expressed it thus: " The military capabilities of the actively engaged parts of an army are to a large extent dependent on the manner in which their communications are regulated, their various needs of provisions and ammunition supplied, their sick and wounded cared for, and the losses in men, horses and war material made good. It is only a far-sighted administration of these important branches of the service and the fullest devotion of all the persons engaged in them, which can maintain the troops, in spite of all the chances of war, in the necessary readiness for battle."[1] These arrangements had been brought to the highest pitch of perfection by the German staff, indeed to a higher degree than in any war before, and therefore we find even on the 1st March, 1871, on French soil a German active army of 464,221 men, infantry, and 55,562 cavalry, behind which 105,272 infantry and 5681 cavalry held the communications, and it had in Germany in reserve 204,972 men at its disposal, whilst Napoleon left, on the 5th December, 1812, the weak remnants of his army in the act of evacuating Russian soil, since it had become impossible to carry on the war any longer with them. The Germans could hope to hold out near Paris until the enemy was forced to sue for peace; they risked doing so, and met with well-merited success. Napoleon could not risk remaining stationary near Moscow, he did so longer than he ought to have done, and deservedly met with his ruin. Does it not, in the face of these facts and the infatuation of the Emperor, look as if he were passing sentence on himself when he said at St. Helena, speaking of madness: "What more especially characterizes it, is the disparity between intentions and the means of realizing them."[2] We are the slaves of material conditions, and if it is the characteristic sign of genius not to allow itself to be crushed by them, it is the sign of madness not in any way to recognize them.

Accordingly we must pass the following judgment. The changed conditions which the French Revolution introduced into the art of war, as compared with those of the 18th century, were fully recognized by Napoleon and carried into effect in his strategy. But with the subsequent changes created by Napoleon's strategy itself, in its prosecution of the principle of the employment of masses and of great national wars, Napoleon's army

---

[1] The Franco-German War of 1870-71. Edited by the department of military history of the great General Staff.
[2] Mémorial de Ste. Hél. ii. 372.

Moscow

organization did not keep pace; for organization is the work of peace. It is only the Prussian army which has fully learnt the lesson of the conditions created by Napoleon's strategy, and their effect on the constitution of armies. It has adopted "the formation in peace time of a numerous war reserve, the axiom of modern army organization,"[1] founded on universal military service, thorough preparation in time of peace for mobilization, strict regulation of the system of commissariat and transport service, with complete utilization of the progress of modern science, and lastly the General Staff. In the modern acceptation of the term, it is true, Napoleon laid the foundation of it, but as he kept the conduct and arrangements of operations in all their details exclusively in his own hands, his Staff, having only to express and formulate his ideas, had but little influence upon the success or failure of the operations; the great military names in Napoleon's army were not responsible for either. But the increase of the armies of modern times and the complicated development of military science seems to render it almost impossible for any one individual, in our time, to keep everything in his hands in the way Napoleon did. Here also, as in so many other branches of modern life, the increase in the amount of work to be done must be met by a division of labour. His masterful nature was of course averse to any such arrangement, associated as it would have been with a division of responsibility and glory, but 1812 and 1813 furnish good grounds for doubting whether the moment had not then already come, when even his great genius was no longer equal unaided to the burden of material difficulties caused by the maintenance of his system of conducting affairs.

Napoleon was the first to change the method of wars conducted by cabinets with mercenary armies, to that of national wars decided by masses. This was due to his

[1] Goltz, Rosbach und Jena, 154.

correct recognition and utilization of the state of affairs brought about by the Revolution; but he, the man of unconditioned, absolute power, did not carry his principles to their extreme logical conclusions; it has been left for our times to so develop them. It is indeed the Prussian army which may claim to have produced the men who laid the foundations of the organization and asserted the principles on which modern masses are moved. Thus our strategy seems to us to base itself in the same logical and comprehensive manner on the conditions that were the outcome of the Napoleonic epoch, as his strategy based itself on the conditions resulting from the epoch of the Revolution. Our strategy has therefore, like his, become the ideal one for our times.

Napoleon's way of leading masses corresponded to the organization of the armies of the Revolution, but the constitution of those masses did not keep pace in its development with that of strategy, and the armies themselves became finally an invincible obstacle to its employment. It seems as if the history of war at the end of Napoleon's campaigns had wished to furnish us with an example of how these three systems worked in practice, and prove by the issue their respective superiority to each other. We find at Belle-Alliance, how the English army, which as to composition and tactics was still modelled on the lines of the 18th century, held out bravely, it is true, against Napoleon's army of conscripts, but yet would undoubtedly have succumbed at the end of the day, had not the Prussian army, recruited by compulsory military service, come up and delivered the decisive blow.[1]

Thus the Emperor saw himself in the beginning of October confronted by the necessity of evacuating Moscow and beginning his retreat, though we are unable to fix the exact point of time when this resolve was finally matured. Perhaps the mission of Lauriston[2] marks

[1] The English army in 1815 was tactically as superior to those of Europe as the Prussian was to the Austrian in 1866.—ED.

[2] Lauriston was sent as a peace emissary to Kutusov on 5 Oct.

the exact moment when the Emperor's thoughts about the retreat took the form in which he placed them before us. These thoughts were as follows :[1]—

"(1.) Since the enemy is proceeding to the Kiev road, their purpose admits of no doubt; they expect reinforcements from the Moldavian army. To march against them would mean manœuvring in the direction of the reinforcements and remaining during the winter in cantonments, without any point of support, with our right and left wing in hazardous positions, whilst the enemy would have his flanks and rear secured. Moscow, abandoned by its inhabitants and burnt down, is no longer of any use to us; this town can no longer harbour our wounded and sick; if the resources there are once exhausted, it can furnish no fresh ones, nor does it lend us any aid in bringing the country into order.

"(2.) Any movement on Kaluga would only become excusable if undertaken with a view of retreating, after reaching that town, to Smolensk.

"(3.) If the army is to retreat to Smolensk, would there be any sense in seeking the enemy out and exposing ourselves to the danger of losing a few thousand men on a march which would look like a retreat, and in the face of an army well acquainted with the country and possessing many secret agents and a numerous light cavalry? Although the French army is victorious, yet such a movement would set it at a disadvantage, since a rearguard loses men daily, whilst a vanguard gains in numbers. Moreover a rearguard is intended to evacuate a battlefield daily and loses its wounded stragglers and camp followers.

"(4.) To these considerations we must add the following also, namely, that it is probable the enemy would fortify themselves in some strong position, and, the heads of the reinforcing columns having already come up, would dispute the ground and cause us a loss of some 3000 to 4000 in wounded; this would look very much like a defeat. A

[1] C. N. Notes. Moscow (without any date).

retrograde movement over a hundred leagues burdened with wounded, and harassed by encounters, which the enemy would take care to represent as victories, would give him, though beaten, the advantage in public opinion.

"(5.) If we wish to retreat, in order to go into winter quarters in Poland, would it be advisable to retreat direct along the road by which we came? We should not have the enemy harassing us; we know the road well, and it is shorter by five days' march; we can go as fast as we like, we might even meet half-way our supplies coming from Smolensk. However, the army could easily carry flour for a fortnight, and we could reach Smolensk without being obliged to forage. We could even stop at Viasma as long as we liked, we could there procure provisions and fodder, by spreading out to the right and the left.

"We are conquerors, our organization is perfect, and if we had to do some fighting and had wounded with us, we should be in the same position as when we came, with respect to the wounded, for the advance guard had some then. It is true, difficulties may arise as to fodder, but we could procure that within two or three leagues, so that this would not be a serious difficulty.

"(1.) There can be no doubt, but that if Smolensk and Vitebsk were districts like Königsberg and Elbing, the first plan would be the most sensible one, namely, to proceed to a good country, go into winter quarters there and recruit the army.

"(2.) In the above-named case, however, we cannot conceal the fact from ourselves, that the war would be much protracted, but it would be still more protracted if we chose such inhospitable districts as Smolensk and Vitebsk, which offer such scant resources, and where the situation would be so little suited for a stay of eight months in winter quarters.

"What ought to be done:
"(I.) What results are to be attained? (i.) To quarter the Emperor as near as possible to France, and to reassure the country that the Emperor, during his stay in winter quarters, will be in the midst of a friendly nation. (ii.) To allow the army to be in cantonments in a friendly country and to bring it nearer to its supplies of clothing and equipment. (iii.) To proceed to a position which would, by threatening St. Petersburg, support the negotiations for peace carried on by the Emperor. (iv.) To keep our military reputation at the height to which this victorious campaign has raised it.

"(II.) Undoubtedly a manœuvre which would combine the above four conditions would be perfect."

And then he proceeds to explain what the manœuvre is which would fulfil all these requirements. Victor, starting on the first day of the operations, was to advance to Velikye Luki, and arrive there on the tenth day of the operations; there he was to be joined by St.-Cyr and one of Macdonald's brigades. The Emperor would leave Moscow on the first day of operations, march by Voskresensk, Volokolamsk, Subtsov and Bieloi to Velish, and arrive at the last point with the head of his columns on the tenth, and with the rear on the thirteenth or fourteenth day of the operations. Ney and Junot were to retreat by Viasma to Smolensk. Thus he calculated, that on the twelfth day of the operations Victor would stand with 60,000 to 70,000 men at Velikye Luki, he himself with 40,000 at Velish, Murat and Davout on the march thither from Bieloi, and Ney with 15,000 men at Smolensk. This would, he thought, be equivalent to a gain of six days on the enemy; "the enemy's army could not enter Moscow before the sixth day of operations," and if they then followed him he would be able to accept battle at Velish with superior numbers, for under these circumstances the enemy would increase their distance from their reinforcements. "If then St. Petersburg is thus threatened we may surely assume that the enemy will conclude peace, and if the movements of the enemy render any advance on our part inadvisable, we shall remain at Velikye Luki."

We cannot but acknowledge that this whole plan has something forced about it, something like the exactitude of a war game on a map. Undoubtedly the beginning of the movement, by which it was proved that no advance against Kutusov was feasible, cannot but be approved. Indeed the situation had become such, that a retreat upon his own reinforcements alone offered any possibility of escape. As to the suggested offensive posture at Velish and Velikye Luki, we can scarcely consider it as possible of execution, and indeed it was not executed. Why should the enemy enter Moscow on the sixth day of operations, considering that they could immediately prosecute their movements against the French lines of communications, towards Viasma or indeed towards Smolensk, and their march to the left, to the road of Kaluga, was open to this interpretation and not merely to that of going to meet the army from Moldavia? In this case they would be at Viasma on the sixth day or at Smolensk on the twelfth, nor would they have thereby increased their distance from the reinforcements, which they possibly expected from Kiev.

Still the Emperor would at Velish and Velikye Luki have gained the advantage of being reinforced by Victor and St.-Cyr, and of being able to change his communications to Vilna by Polotsk and Glubokoyay; though this would not have availed him much. If Kutusov went to Smolensk, the Emperor could not have taken the offensive against him from Velish, to drive him thence, for the same reasons as he had been unable to act from Moscow against Kutusov at Tarutino. And lastly, if the Emperor thought that he would be threatening St. Petersburg by his position at Velikye Luki, he cannot have had any serious faith in this conjecture. We can only threaten a point which we can, if necessary, capture. But experience had just taught him how much too weak he was on his arrival at Moscow, and now he dreamt of making with this weakened army a fresh advance to the other capital, 230 miles distant! What would his army have amounted to on its arrival at St. Petersburg? If the actual capture of Moscow had not induced the Russians to make peace, this entirely imaginary menacing of St. Petersburg, from such a distance and by an army which had just retreated 230 miles from Moscow to Velish, would assuredly not have any such result. We must say, the whole plan was a mere display of obstinacy in a man who was well aware that he must without delay retreat by the most direct road, if he wished to escape at all.

The Emperor soon gave this plan up and considered only his retrograde movement to Smolensk, which he, however, intended to initiate by a forward move against Kaluga, so as to deceive the enemy as to his intentions, by appearing to reassume the offensive. On the 9th October he informed Maret, "that it was possible his Majesty might, towards the month of November, go into winter quarters between the Borysthenes and the Dwina, so as to be nearer to his reinforcements, give his army some rest, and be able to attend with greater ease to various other affairs." [1]

In the meantime Kutusov had remained inactive in his position behind the Nara while Murat was in observation in front of him at Vyankovo. The former, who hád reached Moscow with 70,000 men, was now reinforced up to 110,000 men by various detachments, which had come up meanwhile, and had been incorporated in his army. As every single day that Napoleon tarried in Moscow could only be of advantage to the Russians, Kutusov had taken care, without, however, being in any way definite, to foster as much as possible the Emperor's delusion that he might still succeed in opening up negotiations.

[1] C. N. Maret to Otto. Vilna, 26th October.

But a fortnight after Lauriston's mission, this deception could not be expected to last much longer, and as the Emperor's retreat, and with it the renewal of hostilities, would undoubtedly soon commence, it was decided at the Russian headquarters to begin these by an unexpected move against Murat.

Thus Murat found himself in the morning of the 18th October unexpectedly attacked on his left flank by very superior forces; he was completely defeated and had to fall back to Voronovo with heavy loss. Kutusov remained at Tarutino, but an advance guard pursued the enemy as far as Vyankovo. At noon on the 18th the Emperor was just reviewing Ney's corps, which had been moved up again from Bogorodsk—Moscow, when he received the news of the Russian advance and the defeat Murat had suffered. Immediately the whole army received orders to assemble outside Moscow on the road in front of the Kaluga barrier. This was done in the evening of the 18th and during the night, and by early dawn on the 19th Eugène, Ney, Davout and the Guards were drawn up there in readiness for the start. Mortier, with Delaborde's division of the Young Guard, remained behind to garrison the Kremlin. The Emperor himself left Moscow on the morning of the 19th.

CHAPTER VI.

THE BERESINA.

WHEN General Bonaparte wrote his celebrated letter to the Archduke Charles on the 31st March, 1797, from Klagenfurt, offering to entertain negotiations for peace, he was moved by exactly the same feeling as that which actuated him now, on the 20th September, 1812, in his letter to the Emperor Alexander; namely, by the conviction that his strategical operations had led him to a point where the strength of his army began to be insufficient for their continuation. In the former case he was successful; he had not yet advanced too far, he had only reached the limit where things were beginning to look ominous for him; his army still retained strength sufficient for the offensive, and was still superior to the enemy; nor had the latter, by the loss of half his country and his capital, been placed in a position where he had scarcely anything further to lose, and might regain everything. If the enemy had not yielded, it would, in the former case, still have been possible for General Bonaparte to arrest his own steps in time, for he was under no obligation in the eyes of Europe to subjugate the whole of Austria. But the Emperor Napoleon could not stop, as we have before mentioned, till Russia was entirely conquered.

When, on the 19th June, 1807, the Emperor's vanguard arrived at Tilsit, on the frontiers of Russia, and he there accepted readily the proposals of peace from a completely beaten and retreating enemy, it was because he felt he had reached the point where his strategical power had come to an end, and from which, if he continued his operations, it would diminish and his army would, even if its further advance were victorious, become of necessity exhausted. Here again he was able to arrest his steps, for the general had already solved the problem which the statesman had set before him, viz. the subjugation of the Prussian monarchy, though this task was considerably more comprehensive than that which Bonaparte the general had had to accomplish. Moreover he stood there in his full strength as a victor. In 1807 the Emperor still possessed a sufficiently balanced mind to recognize the fact that the forces were fairly even, and to pause on the threshold of a fresh task, viz. the subjugation of the Russian empire, for the execution of which in a military sense he no longer possessed the means. But in 1812 this last task was demanded of the general; and now when the most reckless squandering of the means at his disposal, and the want of any means of thoroughly replacing them, had brought about the same conditions, the general saw himself at the extreme limit of his capabilities, he again resorted to his old device of negotiating.

But now the enemy, who was not, as in 1797 and 1807, threatened by forces still only on the frontiers, and able by some slight sacrifices to avert great misfortunes, but had already made all possible sacrifices and had gained the conviction that the Emperor no longer possessed a full superiority; this enemy, I say, did not yield, and thus the general's task became impossible of fulfilment; it failed, as it was bound to fail. On the 31st March, 1797, the General Bonaparte had still some offensive strength, and if the Austrians had not yielded then, he would certainly have continued his advance, and undoubtedly at first with further success. On the 19th June, 1807, the Emperor was no longer capable of a continued offensive, but he was still strong enough to remain on the line reached, and we know, that if the

Russians had not yielded, he was determined to remain on the defensive along the Niemen. On the 20th September, 1812, he no longer possessed strength enough for either offensive or defensive operations at the point reached. Nothing remained for him but to retreat, and when he did begin to retire, events proved that even for this his army had become too weak.

So on the morning of the 19th October the army (90) began its retreat; Eugène in front, then Ney, the Guards and Davout. The head got as far as Vatutinki, and the Emperor took up his quarters at Troïtskoye. On the 20th the march was continued and the army crossed the Pachra; after this, however, Eugène turned westward towards Oshigovo on the road to Borovsk; Ney advanced as far as the Motsha and resumed touch with Murat, who had remained near Voronovo, and who now had to part with Poniatowski, the latter being ordered to follow in Eugène's traces. The Emperor remained at Troïtskoye, sending orders to Mortier to evacuate Moscow on the 22nd or 23rd and to fall back upon Moshaïsk; the Guards and Davout were at Vatutinki. The days were sunny and mild, though the lateness of the season betrayed itself in the coldness of the nights.

All that was said afterwards by the Emperor and his blindly devoted partisans about the cold coming on unexpectedly early and with exceptional severity, and this being the real cause of the disastrous issue of this retreat from Russia, is untrue. As a matter of fact the cold came on later that year, and was less persistent, than is usual in that country, nor was the degree which it reached anything surprising in those latitudes. "Whilst ordinarily it is not at all an unusual occurrence in Moscow to have the roads fit for sledges towards the end of October, the weather had favoured* the French army extremely, inasmuch as the first frost only occurred on the 27th October, and withal the weather remained clear and fine. On the 1st November, however, the thermometer sank to eight degrees below freezing point, and on the 4th the first snow fell."¹ "We have not as much bad weather as we might have had reason to expect at this season."² Until the 4th November the weather remained generally dry, but in no way unusually cold, only on this latter day Bausset notes: "New moon during the night, difference of thirteen degrees in the temperature, first snow;"³ and Gourgand writes: "Until the 6th November, that is during sixteen or seventeen days, the weather has been beautiful and the frost has been much less severe than it was during a few months of our campaigns in Prussia and Poland, and even in Spain."⁴ Fézensac also adds this testimony: "During the march on the following day the weather suddenly changed and became very cold;"⁵ and finally the Emperor himself acknowledged in his notorious 29th bulletin: "Until the 6th November the weather was excellent."⁶

On the 21st October the Guards and Davout, whom Friederichs and Dufour had joined again, followed Eugène's line of march. The latter reached Nary Fominskiya, and was ordered to advance further to Borovsk. Ney and Murat remained behind the Motsha, and the division of Morand formed the rearguard at Desna. The Emperor, having spent some time, for the purpose of issuing his orders, first in Krasnaya-Pachra and then at the château of Saltikov, took up his quarters for the night in the castle of Ignatievo. It will be noted that he now ordered his army to start upon a march to the right with Borovsk as its goal, for thus he hoped, while deceiving Kutusov, to approach his line of retreat. Murat was to join this movement the following day, Morand was to follow like-

---

¹ v. Guretzky-Cornitz, Geschichte des 1. Brandenburgischen Uhlanen-Regiment, &c., 103.
² C. N. Eugène to the Vice-Queen. Fominskiya, 23rd October.
³ Mém. ii. 148.
⁴ N. et la Grande Armée en Russie ou Examen critique de l'ouvrage de M. le Cte. Ph. de Ségur, 344.
⁵ Souvenirs mil. 288.
⁶ C. N. Molodeshno, 3rd December.

wise, and Ney, to whom Claparède also was attached, was in the first place, by remaining stationary behind the Motsha, to screen this departure and then start stealthily at 1 a.m. on the 23rd and follow as a rearguard. Mortier received orders to march to Vereya, instead of to Moshaïsk; he was to reach the former place on the 25th, and thus form the link between the army and Junot and the high road from Moscow.

At 7 a.m. on the 22nd the Emperor ordered Eugène to send Poniatowski immediately to occupy Vereya; "the occupation of Vereya is the great thing to be done to-day." Eugène himself started from Fominskiya[2] about noon, and took up a position to the south of the Nara, while sending Delzons forward to reconnoitre; the latter got as far as Borovsk. About 1 o'clock the Emperor with the Guards and Davout · reached Fominskiya, whither Murat and Morand were also marching; Ney remaining stationary as ordered. During the night of the 22nd, at 2 a.m., Mortier at last left the Kremlin. Some attempts to blow up the various palaces forming it were only partially successful, but they furnish in their mania for useless destruction a sad example of the gloomy spirit which had now obtained a hold upon the Emperor, and which was unworthy of his great intelligence. "Besides, this order, as senseless as it was barbarous, was a mistake; Napoleon could not, it is true, mean to return again to the Kremlin, but even if this had been the case, the Russians would not have defended it, whilst it could have been used as a citadel by his army, or in case of need a refuge for the division which would occupy the capital."[1] The great Emperor, who had already sacrificed so many and so much to his aims, had here an ominous resemblance to those mad Dynamitards of our days, whose attacks, when directed against persons, had at least a purpose, though a criminal one, but who afterwards gave vent to their mania for destruction in the senseless wrecking of public buildings,

[1] Jomini, Précis pol. et mil. des Camp. de 1812 à 15, i. 162.

[2] Nary Fominskiya

or with those Communists, who, seeing their defeat inevitable and imminent, sought in their desire for revenge to leave Paris a heap of ruins. The Emperor's lot had been cast in such circumstances that he never had self-command forced upon him, and he never recognized any necessity for controlling himself, for his own good. And thus it came to pass that he, although not cruel by nature, allowed himself to be led away to outbursts of savage fury, of destruction or brutal rage, wherever he met with insuperable resistance or whenever his expectations were disappointed. Even at his entry into Moscow, angered at the sight of the flames which threatened to snatch the hoped-for prey from his grasp, he is said to have broken out into the following words, addressed to his Guards: "Go and plunder and cut down all you meet in the streets, spare none; these barbarians are not fit to live."[1] On the 19th Brumaire, which first gave the whole sovereign power into his hands, he cried out frantically to the Grenadiers, who were bursting into the Orangery of St. Cloud: "And if any resistance be offered, kill, kill, kill!" words which Lucian calls "as senseless as they were cruel and useless."[2]

In the meantime Kutusov remained in his position. When he heard that the French had shown themselves at Fominskiya he sent some troops thither to drive them out, for he thought they were only a small force detached in that direction. The Russians started on the morning of the 22nd, but soon discovered that it was the main body of the enemy, which seemed to be concentrating at Fominskiya. They therefore halted at Aristovo and reported the fact. In consequence of this, a force of Cossacks was sent forward to Maloyaroslavets, and in the evening the whole Russian army started on its march thither. On the same day the French army continued its march in the direction of Kaluga; Eugène left his position at 2 a.m. and advanced a little beyond

[1] F. v. D N. in Dresden, ii. 68.   [2] Lucien, Mém. i. 365.

The Beresina

Borovsk, having had the 3rd cavalry corps attached to his division. Delzons, in advance of Eugène, reached Maloyaroslavets in the evening, drove some Cossacks thence, occupied the place, and worked during the night restoring the bridge over the Lusha. Davout, Murat and the Guards followed Eugène on the road from Fominskiya to Borovsk, the heads of their columns reaching this latter place. Poniatowski had been at Vereya since the day before. Ney had started about midnight and was on the march to Fominskiya.

At 9 a.m. the Emperor left Fominskiya and hurried forward as far as Borovsk at a gallop; he still imagined Kutusov to be in his former position, and uncertain as to the real object of the present direction taken by the French army. "Some reports lead me to believe that the enemy is still in his old position to-day, in his entrenched camp at the confluence of the Istia with the Nara."[1] He moreover thought the enemy would look upon the movement through Fominskiya as intended to turn and attack their left wing, and that they had sent out for its protection the corps which we mentioned above as having arrived at Aristovo. Only the occupation of Maloyaroslavets would render it clear to them, that "instead of turning their position in order to attack them, we are marching straight to Kaluga."[2] Should the enemy, on realizing this, advance to attack, the Emperor would consider Vereya as his base, "we shall there show front to the enemy from where General Delzons lies as far as Fominskiya."[3] Had he, on the other hand, succeeded in reaching Kaluga, the Emperor would have changed his line *via* Yelnya to Smolensk and continued his retreat in that direction. "The army will proceed to Kaluga and direct its operations from there on Yelnya."[4] "Should the enemy think of covering Kaluga,

---

[1] C. N. To Eugène. Borovsk, 23rd October, 7.30 p.m. [2] The same.
[3] C. N. Berthier to Junot. Fominskiya, 23rd October, 5 a.m.
[4] C. N. Berthier to Eugène. Borovsk, 24th October, 3.30 a.m.

the Emperor will fight a battle."[1] To ensure his communications in accordance with these views, orders were forwarded to Junot, to send all the troops which he had ready for marching at Moshaïsk, to Vereya; to Victor, to come up to Yelnya with whatever forces he had at his disposal at Smolensk. During the 24th the Emperor intended only to concentrate, to make sure of the crossing of the Lusha and of the road to Kaluga, by holding Maloyaroslavets, and to wait till the enemy's intentions further declared themselves. "The Emperor desires to assemble to-day all the baggage of the army and to see what the enemy is going to do; it will be sufficient to take up a position in Maloyaroslavets, to have two or three bridges thrown across the river and to hold the place in force."[2]

On the morning of the 24th, at 5 o'clock, the Russian corps arrived near Maloyaroslavets from Aristovo; it had received direct orders from Kutusov to continue its march and to occupy the former place. The two French battalions, which had alone held the place up to now, were driven from it, nor was Delzons, crossing over from the other bank of the Lusha, able to recapture the town. But at 10.30 the heads of Eugène's remaining columns came up, and about noon Broussier joined in the fight, and the possession of Maloyaroslavets was furiously contested, it being repeatedly taken and retaken. Meanwhile the main armies on either side were approaching the battle-field, and their leading columns arrived at about the same time, 1 p m., in its immediate neighbourhood. The Emperor, who had left Borovsk at 9 o'clock, was just having breakfast by the roadside some five miles from that town, when the roar of cannon in the direction of Maloyaroslavets became audible. He at once hurried forward and arrived there between noon and 1 o'clock, and took his position by

---

[1] C. N. Berthier to Junot. Fominskiya, 23rd October, 5 a.m.
[2] C. N. Berthier to Eugène. Borovsk, 24th October, 3.30 a.m.

the road, where the heights slope down to the Lusha valley. Davout and the Guards, as they came up, were placed in reserve to the right and left of the road. On the other bank of the river the approaching columns of the Russian army were plainly visible. The first of their troops immediately entered Maloyaroslavets to support its exhausted defenders, and Eugène also ordered his last troops, the divisions of Pino and Lecchi, to join in the struggle for its possession. He succeeded in becoming master of it, but all further advance from the little town was frustrated by the Russians. A final attempt on the part of Kutusov to recapture the place, towards evening, failed. The Emperor had also ordered the divisions of Gérard and Compans to cross the Lusha in support of Eugène and to take up positions about 5 o'clock on the right and left of Maloyaroslavets. Thus when the artillery fire died out, about 11 p.m., the town remained in the hands of the French, and with it the possibility of crossing the Lusha. Kutusov's whole army had come up in the course of the day and bivouacked within sight of Maloyaroslavets.

The Emperor, accompanied by his Guards, established his headquarters at Gorodnia, slightly to the rear. At 5 a.m. on the following day an orderly-officer, left during the night with the outposts, reported to him that the Russians were still in position and that some cavalry were to be heard moving in the direction of Medinj. The Emperor summoned Murat, Bessières and Lobau, showed them the map and said: "It seems the enemy is remaining stationary and we shall have a battle. Is it to the advantage of the army, in the position in which we are, to fight a battle or to avoid it?"[1] The opinions of the generals, thus questioned, was, that under the circumstances a retreat was more advisable. Lobau was for retreating to Moshaïsk, the other two

[1] Gourgaud N. et la Grande Armée en Russie, ou Examen critique de l'ouvrage de M. de Cte. Ph. de Ségur, 329.

straight to Smolensk. The Emperor listened to their opinions, but decided, before taking a definite resolution, first to inspect the enemy's formation with his own eyes. He rode forward; a sudden attack of some Cossacks on his staff was repulsed in time by his escort, and he spent the greater part of the day in reconnoitring the enemy's positions. But this does not seem to have led him to take any decided course, he on the contrary still hoped the Russians would see cause for retreating themselves. Where were the times of Arcola, the days of the young General Bonaparte, who never waited until the enemy decided of his own accord to yield, but forced him by his boldness and resolution to do so? His actions were now constantly paralyzed by the feeling, so foreign to his nature, that he had to economize his men. This could not fail to have an upsetting influence upon him who at the close of his career said of himself: "I have never considered men, and have always treated them as they deserve to be treated."[1] Kutusov had, however, already resolved to fall back upon Kaluga and was making preparations for this movement. Nevertheless, the Emperor's indecision must appear strange considering the situation. At night he returned to Gorodnia.

The next morning he again mounted his horse, to ride to Maloyaroslavets and resume his reconnaissance of the enemy. He took the Guards with him. On the edge of the heights he ordered a camp-fire to be lit, and while he was waiting the welcome news came in about 9 o'clock, that the enemy had evacuated his position and retreated. Kutusov had indeed fallen back about 5 a.m., and left only a rearguard in front of Maloyaroslavets. The Emperor in his turn now resolved to retire upon Borovsk, to begin from there his definite retreat by Moshaïsk and Viasma to Smolensk.

It is said that in this resolution he yielded to the

[1] Cte. de Waldbourg-Truchsess, Nouvelle relation de l'itinéraire de N. de Fontainebleau à l'île d'Elbe, 35.

unanimous opinions of his subordinate officers and that his own wish was to attack the Russians. Whether this plan was the best, or even desirable, may for the present remain undecided ; for in our study of the general's mind the origin of the action is the most important fact. And here we must mention, that undoubtedly the generals unanimously voting for the retreat furnished the final reason for the resolve, but that on the other hand the Emperor himself was already half inclined to do so. His inactivity during the 25th is evidence of this. There is no doubt that had the subordinate leaders been eager to fight, or with an army sure of victory, the general would on this occasion have delivered an attack, but this very fact proves the great change which had taken place in his mind. It is characteristic of genius to buoy up others and carry them along with it, and it never shows itself greater than when impending misfortunes bid fair to crush ordinary men. In contrast with Maloyaroslavets we call to mind the lofty spirit of Frederick after Kolin and after Hochkirch, when the King was fighting not to subjugate the world, but to preserve the existence of his kingdom; the unwavering soul of Hannibal after Zama, nay, even the headstrong obstinacy of Charles XII. at Bender, of General Bonaparte at Arcola, or after the first battle of Aboukir, or after Acre. These examples form the condemnation of Napoleon, belittled, enervated and rendered callous by an excess of despotic power.

But to return to the domain of pure strategy, let us consider the operations from the 19th October, the day of the departure from Moscow. The first movement, the massing of the army on the road to Kaluga, was only the natural consequence of Kutusov's sudden offensive against Murat ; the army had to be quickly prepared to meet him. But when Kutusov failed to advance further, the question arose, whether the French were to march against him or to start at once upon their retreat, which would in any case, sooner or later, be inevitable. All opinions will probably agree that the advance was the correct move. It was possible at any rate to get as far as the Pachra; thence the road would still always remain open for the march to the right towards Smolensk. Moreover if Kutusov came out from Tarutino, a good opportunity might arise to strike a blow at him. The Pachra was crossed; but Kutusov remained stationary, and now assuredly it was best with the army, weakened and possessing but little internal solidity, not to advance to the attack of Tarutino, which would undoubtedly entail heavy loss, as Borodino had shown, losses which the army ought only to incur if a decided success could confidently be expected. But this hope was negatived by the experience gained at Borodino.

Therefore the French turned aside to the road from Moscow to Borovsk and Kaluga, a perfectly correct strategical movement. If the Emperor succeeded in deceiving Kutusov, he might reach Kaluga and undertake from there the retreat to Smolensk through an untouched country by Yuchnov and Yelnya. If not quite successful, still, if he managed at Maloyaroslavets to reach the crossing of the Lusha before the enemy, the road through Medinj to Viasma would be open. Finally, if this plan also failed, he would certainly have to fall back upon Moshaïsk by Borovsk and Vereya, but this would be no worse than if he had started along this road at once from Moscow or later from Vatutinki, north of the Pachra. Consequently the Emperor determined to march to the right to Nary Fominskiya and then through Borovsk. At first Kutusov was deceived, but afterwards he started in time for the respective vanguards to meet at Maloyaroslavets. Here, however, the position and the crossing over the Lusha after all remained in the hands of the French. The Emperor and Kutusov both arrived there in person, and now three possibilities presented themselves to the former, viz. to prosecute by main force his original plan, i.e. to gain Kaluga, or at least the

The Beresina

road through Medinj by attacking Kutusov; or to look upon that plan as having failed, and to fall back at once by Borovsk; or lastly, to remain stationary and wait to see what Kutusov would do.

Perhaps neither of these resolutions was to be absolutely rejected, though we cannot, properly speaking, call that which was actually taken, a resolution, for it was rather a putting off of a resolution, and for this reason we must consider it as contrary to the Emperor's nature, and therefore a deterioration from his former mental excellence. But when that possibility opened up before him and Kutusov fell back, leaving the road to Medinj free, we cannot but wonder at the course taken by the Emperor. He neither followed Kutusov, to see whether he would give up Kaluga, nor did he take advantage of the road to Medinj. No! Just when he was able to reap the reward of his manœuvre, he retreated to Borovsk, a course he could have taken on the 24th, saving forty-eight hours and avoiding a loss of 5000 men in battle. This retreat led him at Moshaïsk back again to the road by which he had advanced, and therewith he lost every possible advantage which his march upon Kaluga round Kutusov's left flank might have offered. For he could, as early as the 21st, have marched from Fominskiya[1] through Moshaïsk to Smolensk on the road by which he had previously come.

In consequence of his resolve to retreat, the Emperor (91) issued the following orders:—Davout was to follow Kutusov with two of his divisions as a corps of observation, while leaving two as a rearguard at Maloyaroslavets and one at Gorodnia; the 1st and 3rd cavalry corps were placed under his command; he would thus form the rearguard and follow the main army at 9 or 10 p.m. towards Borovsk. Eugène was to start at 2 p.m. and march to within a short distance of Borovsk. These arrangements having been made at noon at Gorodnia, the Emperor returned to Borovsk and sent out orders from there, that Poniatowski was to advance to Yegorievskoyay. Ney, who

[1] Nary Fominskiya

reached Borovsk during the evening of this day, was to march to Vereya, and Mortier to fall back from this place to Moshaïsk; the two divisions of the Young Guard, under Claparède and Roguet, were to return to Mortier's corps. With the latter's arrival in Moshaïsk Junot was to fall back upon Viasma. Victor was instructed to send to Dorogobush whatever troops he might already have set in motion towards Yelnya, in accordance with his original orders.

With this began the complete and unconditional retreat of the French army, which in its ultimate stages was to have such fatal and decisive consequences. But on the 26th not only the Emperor, but his opponent also, as we know, began a retrograde movement. Kutusov, leaving a rearguard behind in front of Maloyaroslavets in the position which his army had occupied, conducted the latter back to Gontsharovo, and in the evening, whilst Davout was evacuating Maloyaroslavets and retreating towards Borovsk, the Russian rearguard also abandoned its position and fell back to Afonassova. The Emperor himself reached Vereya on the 27th and met Mortier there, while the army marched in the directions indicated the day before and continued its retiring movement on the following day. Junot, starting from Moshaïsk, reached the convent of Kolotskoyay, Mortier was slightly in advance of him; Ney, crossing the Protwa, reached Borissovo, followed by Eugène from Vereya; Davout was at Borovsk, and Poniatowski started from Yegorievskoyay to Gshatsk. The Emperor took up his headquarters in the castle of Uspenskoyay, which had been almost entirely destroyed.

In the course of the afternoon a captured Russian officer had been brought before him, who reported that Kutusov's army had started on its march to Smolensk. A message from Davout coming in during the night, dated 4 p.m. from Borovsk, announced that the French rearguard had up till then only been followed by some Cossacks, which seemed to confirm this assertion. The

Emperor therefore determined to continue the retreat as rapidly as possible with his Guards, so as to be able to oppose Kutusov, who wished to outstrip him wherever opportunity might offer. Early in the morning of the 29th he left Uspenskoyay and arrived in the evening at Gshatsk after a short stay at Kolotskoyay, where the great hospital for the men wounded of the 7th September had been established, and where he gave orders to pack as many as possible of them on the baggage waggons of the army. He had driven in his carriage, and thus or on foot did he proceed along almost the whole line of retreat. The Guards and Junot also reached Gshatsk, Ney fell back to Kolotskoyay, Eugène to Uspenskoyay, Davout reached Moshaïsk. Thus the entire French army had assembled on the high road from Moscow to Smolensk, and no further manœuvring was to be attempted; nothing remained but the uninterrupted progress of the retreat, one corps behind the other toiling along the high road, with increasingly severe privations and losses, and fast-growing want of coherence.

Kutusov had received news on the 27th of the retreat of the French, and had immediately assumed it would be in the direction of Medinj, a proof that the Emperor could very easily have taken that road. The Russian army, however, did not start until the evening, and marched in its turn towards Medinj, arriving at Polotnianyay Zavodi. The advance guard had in the morning, upon hearing that Maloyaroslavets had been evacuated, returned there from Afonassova. It now executed a flank march to gain the road to Medinj, and reached Tshornoloknia, and the next day, whilst the army remained stationary, Adamovskoyay. On the 29th Kutusov arrived in Adamovskoyay, his advance guard being ordered forward as far as Yegorievskoyay on the road to Moshaïsk, as the direction of the French march was now known.

At 5 p.m. on the 30th the Emperor took up his quarters for the night in a solitary farmhouse near Velitshevo, and on the 31st, at 4 p.m., reached Viasma. The Guards and Junot marched through this town and took up a position beyond it; Ney reached Velitshevo; Poniatowski and Eugene were at Gshatsk, and Davout at Gridnyeva.

(89) At Viasma the Emperor had found waiting for him despatches from Paris up to the 14th October, as well as numerous reports as to the state of affairs in his rear and on his flanks. Maret's letters from Vilna were of as recent date as the 26th, there were reports from Victor up to the 24th, and finally letters from Saint-Cyr up to the 19th or 20th. The work of attending to all these and answering them kept the Emperor in Viasma the whole of the 1st November as well as the forenoon of the 2nd, and he left this town only at noon on the latter day.

From Maret's reports he learned that Schwarzenberg, after having, as we know already, taken up a position at Brest—Litovsk behind the Muchavyes, had evacuated the same during the night of the 10th October, when Tshitshagov's army, marching up from Liuboml through Sburash, appeared before it. He had retreated to Drogitshin, where he crossed the Bug on the 15th. Tshitshagov, who remained stationary at Brest—Litovsk, had consequently an open road in front of him to march towards the Beresina, and threaten the French line of retreat.

Nor could the news from Victor have been very reassuring. The latter had, as we know already, arrived at Smolensk, to serve as a general reserve, and had there received the Emperor's instructions as to his further movements. In these it was mentioned that news had come in that the Russian army of Moldavia had crossed the Dnieper, and if it marched to join Kutusov at Kaluga, Victor was to move up through Yelnya to reinforce the main army. But it might also join Tormassov, and as Wittgenstein likewise had been strongly reinforced, there was danger on both sides of the lines of communication. Therefore Victor was to keep a good look-out in both

The Beresina

directions and post his troops from Smolensk to Orsha "in such a manner that the Duke of Belluno will form the general reserve ready to march either to the support of Prince Schwarzenberg and cover Minsk, or to aid Marshal St.-Cyr and cover Vilna, or to Moscow to reinforce the Grand Army."[1]

Victor had, therefore, left 15,000 men to garrison Smolensk and stationed the rest at Orsha, Sienno and Babinovitshi. Here he received news of the resumption of the Russian offensive against St.-Cyr. Wittgenstein had advanced for this purpose on the 15th October, and forced his opponent towards Polotsk, attacked him there on the 18th and threw him back into the town. As at the same time Steinheil approached along the left bank of the Dwina from Disna, having crossed this river near Druya, and his vanguard had arrived at the Ushatsh, St.-Cyr retreated during the night of the 19th behind the Dwina, evacuating Polotsk. On the 20th Wittgenstein occupied Polotsk, whilst St.-Cyr's troops lay opposite the town on the other bank of the Dwina. A force sent out against Steinheil on the Ushatsh, surprised and destroyed this general's advance guard and compelled him to fall back to Disna. St.-Cyr determined to fall back behind the Ulla as soon as the Russians attempted to cross the Dwina. Upon learning of these movements, Victor started with all his troops, except the garrison of Smolensk, and marched to Tshashniki to the support of St.-Cyr.

Such was the information which reached the Emperor at Viasma as to the state of affairs on the Dwina, the Bug and his line of retreat. At Polotsk and at Brest—Litovsk stood the enemy's flank corps; the danger to the communications of the French army was great and urgent, but the Emperor could lend no help. He was reduced to the hope that Victor would have recaptured Polotsk and driven Wittgenstein back; but he enjoined him to send as speedy news as possible of all that happened in rear of

[1] C. N. To Berthier. Moscow, 6th October.

the army. "The Emperor's orders are, General, that you should send an officer of your staff to Marshal St.-Cyr and to the Duke of Belluno to inform them that the army being to-day, the 1st November, at Viasma, will on the 3rd be at Dorogobush; that we await news from them most impatiently; you are to keep me informed of all the direct or indirect news that you can gather about the movements of the Duke of Belluno, General Saint-Cyr and Prince Schwarzenberg."[1]

This being his knowledge of the situation, the Emperor left Viasma at noon on the 2nd November and arrived in the evening in Semlevo, where he took up his quarters for the night in a church. He had the Guards with him; Junot was a little in advance, Eugène and Poniatowski were at Fiodoroivskoyay, Davout immediately behind them, and Ney had on the preceding day reached Viasma. This marshal now received orders to form the rearguard, he was therefore to remain at Viasma until all the other corps had marched through, and was then to follow. All the marches were from now to be performed in square, in order not to offer to the Cossacks, as formerly to the Mamalukes in Egypt, any openings for breaking the ranks by surprise; "it is most important to change our manner of marching in the face of an enemy who possesses such large numbers of Cossacks. We must march as we marched in Egypt, the baggage in the centre, well closed up, in as many ranks as the road permits; a half battalion in front, another in rear, some battalions in file on the flanks, so that if a halt is made, fire can be opened in all directions."[2]

(91) Kutusov had on the 30th continued his march to Moshaïsk, and had reached Kremenskoyay; his advance guard taking the direction towards Kolotskoyay. But a corps of Cossacks sent out in front, which had reached Yelnya, near Borodino, reported Kolotskoyay to be already

---

[1] C. N. Berthier to Charpentier. Viasma, 1st November.
[2] C. N. Berthier to Eugène. Viasma, 2nd November, noon.

occupied by the enemy, whereupon the vanguard turned to the left towards Gubino, to anticipate the enemy at Gshatsk. Kutusov himself resolved to take with his main army the direction of Viasma, and we therefore find him, on the 31st October, at Spass-Kusovy, whilst his advance guard, marching along between him and the main line of the French retreat, reached Krasnoyay. The corps of Cossacks came up with the French rearguard under Davout, near Kolotskoyay, and remained on its heels during the whole day until it reached its goal for that day's march, Gridnyeva. The next day Kutusov reached Silenki, his advance guard as far as Tatarykino, close to Zarevo-Saimishtshe, where it came in touch with Eugène, who was just passing through that town, and the corps of Cossacks that was following Davout reached Gshatsk.

On the 2nd November we find Kutusov at Dubrovno, his advance guard at Spaskoyay, and the corps of Cossacks, pursuing Davout closely, reached Fiodorovskoyay almost at the same time as the latter. We see thus, that only the Emperor himself, with the Guards and Junot, was sufficiently in advance to be safe from being cut off by the Russians. Ney at Viasma had the Russian main army twenty miles off on his flank, while the rest of the army, Eugène, Poniatowski and Davout (still ten miles behind at Fiodorovskoyay), closely pursued by the corps of Cossacks and followed on the flank by the enemy's advance guard, would assuredly no longer be able to pass through Viasma in time, if the Russian main army advanced thither on the morning of the 3rd November. A determined advance of Kutusov upon Viasma was bound to separate all these corps from the Emperor and probably annihilate them. The situation was threatening enough. Would not the Emperor mount his horse on the 3rd, the first thing in the morning, hasten towards the larger portion of his army, see to things with his own eyes, take the command personally, and do all that could be done, in order to escape from this ominous situation? (90)

The Emperor left Semlevo in the forenoon and arrived about 3 p.m. at Slavkovo with the Guards; Junot reached Dorogobush. Meanwhile the Russian advance guard had pushed forward towards the high road, and its cavalry arrived at Maximovo, where it met with Davout's leading columns coming from Fiodorovskoyay. Eugène and Poniatowski had already started for Viasma. At the same time the corps of Cossacks pressed upon Davout's rear, and the latter saw himself in an awkward position. He was, however, supported by Poniatowski, and by Delzon's and Broussier's divisions of Eugène's corps, which had immediately faced about and marched up from Viasma; and when about 10 o'clock the infantry of the Russian advance guard came up, Davout had already marched off towards Viasma in rear of Eugène. The latter had executed a flank movement to the right and met the attack of the infantry of the Russian advance guard, which forced him back to Miessoyedova. No one was in supreme command, and the Emperor was absent; the leaders therefore held a council of war and decided to retire.

Towards 2 p.m. the retreat began by Eugène and Poniatowski passing through Viasma, fighting continuously. Davout followed them, but was unable, owing to the pressure of the closely pursuing Russians, to maintain his tactical formation. Ney remained in position near Viasma until the other corps had passed through this town, when he left it, taking command of the rearguard. Kutusov only reached Bykova on that day. Meanwhile the Emperor had employed the day at Slavkovo in attending to various arrangements connected with organization; he did not exhibit any anxiety for his various corps at Viasma, but expressed the opinion that they should quietly continue their march and not immediately form up at every appearance of the enemy's troops. "Cousin, write to the Duke of Elchingen, to order the army, immediately on his taking the command

THE BERESINA 207

of the rearguard, to continue its march with all possible speed, for we are wasting the remainder of the fine weather without marching. The Prince of Eckmühl is keeping back the Viceroy and Prince Poniatowski for every petty attack of the Cossacks."[1] Had Kutusov been a Suvarov, he would not have let his day's work come to an end at Bykova, but would have used his best efforts to immediately follow the cavalry, which he had in the morning at 5 o'clock sent forward to Viasma. He would then have reached this place in the afternoon and attacked Ney; a performance in no way more extraordinary than that of Vandamme, Lannes and St. Sulpice on the 22nd April, 1809, the march from Landshut to Eckmühl, and the subsequent victorious engagement. I emphasize this fact here, because it serves to show how a final and complete downfall is always the outcome of a long series of disasters, and not the result of any combination of fatal circumstances on one unlucky day. He who takes into consideration only the day of Leipzig or that of Belle-Alliance, might be led to suppose that the Emperor of course did commit errors and therefore rightly succumbed, but that after all it was unlucky for him to have had to deal, just on the days when he made such mistakes, with able and skilful opponents, who profited by them and brought about his utter downfall. The question has two sides for the military student. True, good luck is certainly a factor, but we know that it favours the bold, and this should tend to make a general form his resolutions rapidly. We must also remember that she gives her hand permanently only to him who grasps it firmly. The carelessness of the Emperor, sitting quietly in his study at Slavkova, was not punished here as it deserved to be. If we see in the future again and again how the Emperor's energy and resolution were no longer equal to the require ments of the moment, we must no longer ascribe it to

[1] C. N. To Berthier.

fortune, if at last such oft-repeated errors were fully appreciated and turned to the best advantage by his opponents, to the utter ruin of his army. If the destruction of his army had ensued on the first day the Emperor showed a want of energy, we might call it a case of sheer ill-luck, but if we recall Ratisbon, Vitebsk, Smolensk, Borodino, Maloyaroslavets, and note moreover Bautzen, Dresden, Düben, and more instances than can be fully enumerated here, we shall have to acknowledge that Leipzig and Belle-Alliance were not only in a historical, but also in a military sense, a just retribution.

Early in the morning of the 4th the Emperor received the first news of the preceding day's events at Viasma, yet without any details. Thinking it necessary to check this adventurous spirit in the enemy, he conceived therefore the plan of assembling his army in a position between Slavkovo and Dorogobush, in a sort of ambush, from which to fall upon the enemy as they approached. He remained accordingly with the Guards at Slavkovo during the day, and Junot remained stationary at Dorogobush. Eugène, Poniatowski and Davout got very near to Semlevo, but their troops were already becoming markedly disorganized. "The royal Italian Guards were almost the only corps that still marched along in good order; all the rest seemed discouraged and overwhelmed by fatigue. There were an enormous number of stragglers, most of them unarmed."[1] "The roads were without exaggeration covered by 4000 men of various regiments of the Grand Army, who could not be induced to march together."[2] On this day the first snow fell, a premonitory sign of the Russian winter, which had long been looked forward to with dread.

Ney had taken up his position with the rearguard on the right bank of the Viasma and marched to within a short distance of Semlevo, falling back slowly before the

[1] Fézensac, Souvenirs, mil. 286.
[2] Ney to Berthier. In bivouac near Semlevo, 4th November, 5 p.m.

eagerly pursuing corps of Cossacks. The Emperor, however, gave up his plan of an ambush even before any orders to that effect had been sent to the various leaders; indeed it could hardly have had any important result. On the 5th November, at 8 a.m., he left Slavkovo, and proceeded to Dorogobush. On the side of the enemy Kutusov had meanwhile remained stationary at Bykova on the 4th, while his advance guard had followed the Cossack corps along the high road. These movements of the Cossacks and the advance guard were continued along the great road on the 5th, whilst Kutusov, marching on one side of it, reached Krasnaya. The French army was assembled around Dorogobush, with Ney a little in the rear. On the next day the headquarters were removed to Michailovka, and here the Emperor again received important news, both from Paris and from his left wing, under Victor.

The news from Paris was full of the conspiracy of Malet,[2] which, though in itself a piece of folly, was yet, in its short and peculiar course, evidence of the fact that this world-wide empire of Napoleon stood after all on feet of clay, that it rested entirely upon the life of one man, and that, on the mere rumour of his death, it seemed a matter of course to everybody that there was an end for good of the Napoleonic episode. The Emperor's exclamation, "And Napoleon II., did no one think of him?"[1] gives the measure of the significance of the attempt of the 23rd October. No; no one thought of his son; every one only gave vent to that great sigh of relief, which the Emperor himself said would after his death be the sole judgment the world would pass on him. From this day probably the thought never left him, that his presence was indispensable in Paris to keep up his tottering power. In any case he could no longer preserve his army, as every day showed more conclusively. He therefore looked upon leaving the army to itself as more and more justified;

[1] Fain, Manuscrit de 1812, ii. 224.

[2] An unsuccessful attempt to assume power in Paris by spreading a rumor of Napoleon's death.

and indeed it was so, if we consider the situation as a whole.

What the Emperor heard from Victor was also of an alarming nature. He knew the latter had left Smolensk to effect a junction with St.-Cyr. On the 29th October he had at Tshashniki joined the II. Corps, which had fallen back to this place from Polotsk, through Lepel. The VI. Corps, about 1800 strong, making a détour, had retreated to Glubokoyay, and taken up its position there. Wittgenstein, in conjunction with Steinheil, had followed the French, who fell back by Ushatsh and Lepel, and arrived on the 30th in front of Tshashniki. The next day he proceeded to attack the French there, captured Tshashniki and then forced them back behind the Lukomlia. Here Victor held the bridge at Smoliantsi until evening and fell back during the early morning hours of the 1st November in the direction of Sienno. Wittgenstein did not follow. On receiving Victor's report of these events, dated from Sienno, i.e. only thirty miles distant from his own road of retreat, the Emperor wrote to him: "His Majesty's orders are that you concentrate your six divisions, and attack the enemy without delay, drive him back over the Dwina and recapture Polotsk. This manœuvre is of the utmost importance. In a few days your line of communications may be inundated by Cossacks; the army and the Emperor will be at Smolensk to-morrow, but they will be very fatigued by a march of 120 hours without a halt. Take the offensive, the safety of the army depends on it, delay is fatal. The cavalry of the army is dismounted; the cold has killed all the horses. You must march forward, this is the command of the Emperor, and indeed that of dire necessity."[1]

It is in vain that we wish the Emperor's confidants, or rather, to avoid this word as not applicable to his case, that his nearest followers had given us an opportunity of

[1] C. N. To Berthier. Michailovka, 7th November.

seeing what was in his mind at this time. Their memoirs prove they were unable to do so. Ordinarily talkative to the verge of recklessness, indiscreet in the hour of success, communicating the pictures of his imagination to his hearers careless of consequences, he now, in the days of adversity, became secretive. "He was pale, but his face was tranquil, nor was there anything in his features which betrayed his mental sufferings."[1] He was in no way superior to the ordinary mortal of whom it is said, that he "becomes silent in his pain," and was unable to rise to that divine gift of spiritual freedom which permitted a Frederick to "express what he suffered." Of course he could not deny the ruin which was being enacted before the very eyes of his followers, but he would not allow any one, himself least of all, to acknowledge its reality, or still less its causes. Only this single cry for military assistance, addressed to Victor, broke from the Emperor's deep, obstinate silence, throwing a light, like a flash of lightning, upon his state of mind. But though the imminent danger forced from him in this one instance an acknowledgment of it, he yet could not conquer himself sufficiently to inform the more distant corps, while it was yet time, of the serious nature of his position. He preferred to commit the grave military error of leaving both Macdonald and Schwarzenberg in ignorance of the actual state of affairs.

The further retreat to Smolensk offered day by day the (91) same picture of the ever-increasing dissolution of the retreating French army, a dissolution hastened by the cold of winter which now set in. Moreover the Russians followed continually, making repeated small attacks. To describe the monotony of each day's march would be objectless. What the army suffered we will allow it itself to relate: "For some days past the greater part of the regiments have been living only on the flesh of horses and dogs, the latter of which are often met with in the burnt-

[1] Constant, Mém. v. 112.

down villages along the road or near it."¹ "All those who left the road in order to seek for food, fell into the hands of the enemy, whose pursuit was becoming more and more keen. The severity of the cold moreover increased our confusion and our sufferings. . . . After we had laid the whole country waste, we saw ourselves compelled to destroy each other; to such extremes had we been driven."² The cold, added to the pangs of hunger, completed the gradual dissolution of the French army. The roads were covered with soldiers, who threw away their arms and marched along, each by himself or in small groups. No bivouac was left without the loss of a great number of men, the victims of cold and hunger."³ "The roads were strewn with men and horses, whom hardships or hunger had killed. The men passed by, averting their eyes, and as to the horses, they were a welcome booty for our famished soldiers."⁴ "Indeed great strength of mind was necessary, to endure the sight of this misery daily, without becoming mad, or at least sick at heart."⁵

During the forenoon of the 9th the Emperor, who had passed the night in Bredichino, arrived in Smolensk, on foot, as did his whole retinue. The horses, their shoes not being roughed, were unable to walk on the thin ice of the road; there were twenty degrees of frost. During the next few days the entire army assembled in and around Smolensk, Junot and the Guards arrived there on the 9th, the V. Corps took up a position on the 10th on the road from there to Mstislavl, on the 12th Davout came up, and on the 13th the two last corps, Ney's and Eugène's, reached Smolensk. Eugène had left the high road on the 6th at Dorogobush and turned aside towards Duchovshtshina, closely pursued by the Cossacks, and having reached the Vop on the 9th, he saw himself in

---

[1] v. Lossberg, Briefe in die Heimath, 5th November, 243.
[2] Fézensac, Souvenirs milit. 290.
[3] v. Guretzky-Cornitz, Geschichte, &c., 103.
[4] Constant, Mém. v. 112.
[5] v. Lossberg, Briefe, 9th November, 248.

THE BERESINA 213

the most awkward position, his efforts to construct a bridge having failed. During the crossing of this river, covered with ice floes on that and the next day, the dissolution of the troops made rapid progress owing to the constant attacks of the Cossacks, and on his arrival on the right bank Eugène saw his force diminished to some 6000 men fit for fighting, having left sixty guns on the left bank in possession of the enemy. The whole French army which reached Smolensk numbered 50,000 men. "The march through this town afforded a sad spectacle both as regards the present and the future. We saw an army on the brink of complete dissolution."[1] Before turning to see what the Emperor thought at Smolensk, we may mention that Kutusov, having marched through Gavrukovo, Byely Cholm, Yelnya, Baltutino and Lapkovo, stood now, on the 13th November, at Shtshelkanovo on the road from Smolensk to Mstislavl, and that his vanguard, having first followed the French along the high road, had turned aside from it to the left on the 8th, and, marching through Kaskova, Alexeyevo, Lyachovo Svertshkovo, was on the 13th at Tshervonnoyay, in front of the French army. On the high road a weak force of cavalry was following the retreating French.

The Emperor's position, as we see, was dangerous, no less so than it had been at Viasma. Being at Smolensk with Kutusov just twenty-four miles to the south of him, rendered it most probable that the latter, if he manœuvred in any way rapidly and resolutely, would reach Krasni, Orsha, or some other point along the direct line of Napoleon's retreat in time to fall upon the flank of the fearfully disorganized French army during its march. Now, what did the Emperor think of this position? On his arrival at Smolensk, his first and most pressing care was to learn how affairs stood with Victor. Scarcely had he arrived, than he again sent orders to him to march without delay against Wittgenstein, to recapture Polotsk

[1] v. Lossberg, Briefe, 10th November, 249.

and drive him back behind the Dwina. In the meantime, Victor, far from attacking, had fallen back upon Tshereya, where he arrived on the 6th November. Here the Emperor's urgent request to reassume the offensive reached him. Wittgenstein had remained stationary at Tshashniki, and a force he sent out had captured Vitebsk on the 7th. On the 9th Victor reported this state of affairs to the Emperor; the officer entrusted with this message reached Smolensk on the 11th, and Napoleon replied at once: " His Majesty is about to turn with a portion of the army to Orsha; but this movement can only be executed slowly; it is all the more urgent that you should attack Wittgenstein." [1] But the just apprehension which he had exhibited so urgently in his former orders, seemed now lessened. The Emperor pretended that at the worst, namely, if Victor could not defeat Wittgenstein, he would only be forced to give up the line of the Dwina, which he otherwise would have held, and to go into winter quarters further to the rear. As to Kutusov, he represented him as having the intention of marching against Vitebsk, in order to join Wittgenstein; in connection with which Chambray rightly observes, that it was doubtful whether the Emperor was himself utterly ignorant of the situation, or believed it to be to his advantage to deceive Victor. In any case neither the one nor the other assumption was in accordance with the danger of his situation.

(89)   From the other wing also reports came in, which also were of ominous import. Schwarzenberg, who had retreated behind the Bug in the middle of October, had taken up a position at Vengrov. Tshitshagov gave his troops a rest in the neighbourhood of Brest-Litovsk, and occupied Prushany. A partial advance of the Russians across the Bug was repulsed by Schwarzenberg. Thus they remained inactive, until Tshitshagov resolved, towards the end of the month, to leave one corps in position facing Schwar-

[1] C. N. Berthier to Victor. Smolensk, 11th November.

zenberg and to start with the rest for Minsk. He therefore left 25,000 men with General Sacken, who remained near Brest Litovsk, demonstrating to keep Schwarzenberg employed. Tshitshagov himself left Tshernovtshitsy on the 28th October with 38,000 men and was on the 6th November in the neighbourhood of Slonim. Schwarzenberg, now reinforced by some 14,000 men of the division Durutte from Germany, observed the enemy's movements. He crossed the Bug on the 29th and 30th October near Drogitshin and proceeded to Semiatitshi, whence he advanced further towards Volkovisk, arriving on the 6th November in the neighbourhood of Svitshlotsh. Sacken had in the meantime marched to Drogitshin in the hope of attacking Schwarzenberg, before the latter had completely crossed; but soon saw he had been outstripped. He now also started towards Volkovisk, following in his opponent's tracks, and was on the 6th November in the neighbourhood of Orlya.

The Emperor was, on his arrival at Moscow, suffering from "strategical consumption," to make use of Clausewitz's witticism, and the numbers with which he reached Smolensk are evidence of the rapid progress which this complaint had now made. But Wittgenstein at Tshashniki and Tshitshagov at Slonim, only 200 miles distant from each other, seemed in no way inclined to await the fatal issue of this illness, but were ready to inflict a sudden and violent end on their opponent by throttling his strategical throat. The more terrible his situation, the more eagerly we inquire into the Emperor's views of it, into his moral condition, and the more disappointed we are when we get no reply to our inquiries. Was he deceived as to the mortal nature of his strategical illness, or did he wilfully shut his eyes to it? We know not, only this we are able to ascertain, that neither his letters nor any communications on the part of those near him reveal the fact that he recognized the whole extent of his danger.

(91) On the 14th November Napoleon left Smolensk at 8.30 a.m.; Junot and the V. Corps had preceded him on the 12th, followed by Claparède the next day; he was himself accompanied by the rest of the Guards. Davout remained behind at Smolensk, where Eugène and Ney had arrived in the evening of the 13th. The Emperor left orders that Eugène was to start on the 15th and Davout on the 16th; Ney also on the 16th, or if the enemy did not appear in any dangerous numbers, on the 17th, forming the rearguard, after having blown up the walls of the town. Should the rearguard be attacked, Davout was to support it. Kutusov advanced but slowly in the direction of Krasni. On the 14th he was at Yurova, with his vanguard at Sadoroshye. Some skirmishers attempted to harass Krasni, where the heads of the French army had arrived, but were repulsed. The Emperor spent the night in Koritnia. We thus see that the situation of Viasma was again repeated. Kutusov stood within twenty miles of the French flank, superior both in numbers and *moral*. Any determined attack by the Russians on Krasni must have had decisive results, all the more that, according to the Emperor's orders, mentioned above, the French army had extended into a column covering four days' march, the rear of which only left Smolensk on the 16th.

On the morning of the 15th the Emperor started with the Guards on his march to Krasni. There were now forty degrees of frost. The Russian advance guard had likewise advanced towards the high road and reached it at Rshavka, just as the Guards were passing through this place. It did not, however, attack, but contented itself with a cannonade, so that the Emperor succeeded in passing almost unmolested, and reached Krasni in the evening. At this time it was that, having his attention drawn to some cannon-shot which struck the road close to where he was, he remarked with indifference: "Bah! for twenty years now bullets and balls have been flying

The Beresina

around our legs."[1] During his whole career as a general, the Emperor showed that complete indifference to personal danger which is a necessary quality, especially when directing a battle. Only after his first abdication, when travelling through the South of France, then seething with royalist enthusiasm, on his way to Elba, his shattered nerves succumbed, and an ingenuous eyewitness communicates to us strange details about the timid precautions which the Emperor took, in the face of the personal danger threatening him from the populace.

Eugène had left Smolensk and arrived in Lubnia, Davout was still near Smolensk, Ney held this town, and Junot and the Poles were a little beyond Krasni. Kutusov had remained stationary on the 15th at Yurova, The Emperor, having reached Krasni, began to consider the proximity of the Russian advanced troops dangerous. He therefore ordered Roguet's division of the Guards to drive it off during the night. But he could no longer shut his eyes to the fact that all the columns in his rear were in a most unsafe position on account of Kutusov's proximity, and he therefore remained at Krasni on the 16th with the Guards, waiting for the approach of his troops from Smolensk and acting as their rallying-point. Kutusov now arrived before Krasni, and advanced as far as Novoselki. He did not, however, venture to attack the Emperor and his Guards, but remained inactive. The Russian advance guard had approached closer to the French and stood at Ni-Kulina, where about 3 p.m. Eugène encountered it. He was not, however, able, with his much weakened forces, to force his way along the road, and turned aside at the approach of darkness to the right by Fomina, and succeeded in reaching Krasni during the night. Ney was still holding Smolensk, whilst Davout had left this town and reached Koritnia. Junot and the Poles remained at the head of the retreat, and had reached the neighbourhood of Liady.

[1] Bausset, Mém. ii. 159.

The Emperor's halt at Krasni may appear very rash in face of Kutusov's superior numbers, ready to deal him the decisive blow, still we must say that as a general he was right. Of course, if Kutusov attacked resolutely with his whole force, it would have been hardly possible to expect a favourable result. The situation had become such that no absolute escape was any longer possible; but if the Emperor evaded attack, if he marched away to Orsha, he was certain to lose two-thirds of his army, and Kutusov, encouraged by this success, would be sure to take up subsequently a position at Krasni, blocking the road. What he did not dare to do against the Emperor himself he would undoubtedly have risked against Eugène, Davout, and Ney, coming up one by one. But the Emperor knew very well the value of his own name, so often crowned with victory, and of the reputation of his Guards, and trusting to these, he remained boldly, or if you like, rashly, stationary at Krasni, and the result was that he really rendered Eugène's and Davout's coming up possible. However dangerous the resolution was, it was the only one which afforded any chance whatever of escape, but the fact that he in such dire straits still chose the right course, in spite of its appearance of recklessness, and avoided the course which apparently was the wiser, excites our admiration. On the 17th he made the logic of his conduct still more evident. As the Russian advance guard still blocked the road at Ni-Kulina to the French corps in the rear, the Emperor determined to break through on the morning of the 17th, so as to compel Kutusov to call his vanguard to him for the expected battle. But if this obstinacy, this self-confidence, this reckoning on the enemy's mistakes demand our admiration here, how could we condemn the same qualities when they led to his staying too long in Moscow?

There is a difference. He had reached Moscow too weak to carry out his military aims there if the enemy still resisted; this disproportion between his means and the

The Beresina

task before him he ought to have recognized, and (who knows?) perhaps he did recognize it in his inmost soul. But if he started upon what was alone the correct course to save him in a military sense, namely, an immediate retreat to the Dnieper, he was as a matter of fact beaten in a political sense, and this he could not afford to be, he still hoped for political success, therefore he remained obstinately stationary at Moscow. It was, therefore, a mistake in a military sense, which the insane plans of the statesman had forced the general to commit. At Krasni there was nothing further to be considered but the thought of what was correct in a military sense, the political aim of the campaign had long ago entirely failed; but military safety was only possible if he succeeded in holding Krasni for thirty-six hours. Therefore it had to be risked, and it was, and we must admire the soldier's obstinate stand at Krasni as much as we must blame it at Moscow, where it can only be explained by pointing out the political motives.

In this case it was successful. When the Emperor led out his Guards along the road to Smolensk and took up a position on it, holding Krasni itself only with Claparède's division, the Russian vanguard received orders to fall back towards the army, so as to leave the road open to Davout, and only to follow him after he had passed it. while the main army formed up facing Napoleon. Davout, recognizing the danger of his position, had started at 3 a.m. again and joined the Emperor during the forenoon. The latter, having, at 5 a.m., made a forward movement against Uvarova and seized the village, now resolved to retire, for the Russian superior numbers, extending to the left beyond Krasni, already nearly surrounded the weak French forces. Ney must be left to his fate. What a moment this must have been! The Emperor standing on the ice-covered road, in his Polish cap of marten fur, his green velvet-lined fur coat with gold braid, leaning on a stick cut from a birch tree, holding by the mere force of his reputation, with 15,000 men, now reinforced by Davout's 10,000, the enemy's 80,000 men in check!

Kutusov had ordered his main body to take up a position to the west of Krasni on the road to Orsha, so as to cut the French off from every line of retreat. But when he heard that Napoleon himself with the bulk of his army was still at Krasni, he halted his troops and decided to let the Emperor pass through, and after he had passed, to seize the enemy's road of retreat, so as to cut off Davout. When therefore the Emperor began his retreat and marched through Krasni, he met on the other side of this town only the body of skirmishers whom we have mentioned above as present there. These fell back, and in the evening Napoleon arrived at Liady, whither Eugène had preceded him. Davout was, it is true, closely pressed by the Russian advance guard, and the rearmost of his divisions, Friederichs', suffered very considerable loss, when it evacuated Krasni at 2 o'clock in the afternoon. Still in the evening he also reached Liady. Junot and the Poles stood some distance beyond it. Kutusov collected his troops at Dobraya, and his advance guard had taken up a position near Uvarova.

Ney, who had evacuated Smolensk at 2 a.m. on the 17th, marched on this day with his 6000 men as far as Koritnia, followed and hindered by some 7000 stragglers, who swarmed, unarmed, round him. Of his dangerous position, owing to the presence of the enemy's whole army at Krasni on his road of retreat, he was ignorant. Thus he encountered unexpectedly, about 3 p.m. on the following day, the whole Russian advance guard, which had been still further reinforced by Kutusov. The losses, which his leading division sustained, soon proved to him that it was impossible to break through. He therefore resolved to turn aside to the right of the road, march to the Dnieper, cross that river and try to reach Orsha by marching along its right bank. He passed through Danilovka, reached the river near Shirokorenyay, crossed it during the night, and was on the morning of the 19th at Gussinoyay on the right bank of the Dnieper, having, however, lost one half of his numbers. But along this bank the Russian corps of Cossacks had advanced from Smolensk and was now near at hand. Amid incessant fighting and continuous losses, Ney pushed forward on this and the following day along the Dnieper and reached Yakubova in the evening of the 20th. At 9 p.m., after having sent two officers to Orsha to inform the Emperor, whom he supposed to be there, of his approach, he resumed his march, reached the road from Vitebsk to Orsha, and soon after midnight met with some of Eugène's troops, who had been sent out to meet him. But Ney now stood only at the head of some 800 men, his corps no longer existed as such.

During this time the French army had continued its retreat along the high road, and on this day, the 21st, we find Junot and the V. Corps at Tolotshin; both, however, no longer existed as corps, since the strength of the former did not exceed 200 men capable of bearing arms, the latter only 500. The Emperor's headquarters were at the château of Kamionka; the Guards stood at Kochanovo; Eugène and Davout had evacuated Orsha and approached within five miles of Kochanovo. Kutusov was at Lanitsi, his vanguard at Gorianyay. Here we must pause to relate what the Emperor had heard during these days, as to how things were going in his rear, what orders he had issued, and what measures he had taken.

We saw him arriving in Liady on the evening of the 17th; there he ordered Berthier to write to Junot at 8 o'clock, to regulate the commissariat and establish himself firmly in Orsha; allowing him to understand that the army would arrest its retreat behind the Dnieper. On the 18th he left Liadi in the morning, being obliged himself to walk on foot, and arrived at Dubrovna. Here various items of news reached him. He learnt that Davout, having been attacked during yesterday's march, had suffered heavy losses, and that his corps was seriously disorganized. From Victor he received a report that he had started from Tshereya in consequence of the Emperor's urgent commands, and had marched *viâ* Lukomlia towards Smoliantsi with the IX. and II. Corps, the latter now again under Oudinot's command. His attempt to attack Wittgenstein's position near Tshasniki on the 14th had however convinced him that it was too strong for him, and he had therefore returned to Tshereya again. Still worse was the news from the Emperor's right wing. It was to the effect that Tshitshagov had occupied Minsk on the 16th, and that the garrison of this town and the division of Dombrovski, which had marched up to its support,—the same division which, as we know, was in August left behind at Mohilev as a cover for Minsk,—had thereupon began their retreat to Borissov. The Emperor, on receiving these reports, dictated two letters to Berthier, the one for Oudinot, the other for Dombrovski, in which both were ordered to come up to Borissov. To secure immediately the passage of the Beresina was now the only course possible, since all attempts had failed to keep away the two Russian Corps of Wittgenstein and Tshitshagov, who were marching on the French line of retreat.

At 3 a.m. on the 19th the Emperor explained his views as to the situation of affairs in a fresh letter to Berthier. Victor was to come up somewhat closer and cover Oudinot's march. He was to lead Wittgenstein, if possible, to the belief that the Emperor intended to march against him, "a pretty natural manœuvre," though the Emperor's real intention was to go to Minsk, and therefore Victor would very likely be ordered up to Beresino.[1] Early in the morning of this day, the Emperor left Dubrovna, and received at the same time the news that Ney had found it impossible to force his way

---

[1] This is the Beresino which lies 50 miles to the north of Borissov on the Beresina; a town of the same name is situated on the same river, 33 miles to the south of Borissov.

along the road, and had moved northward towards the Dnieper. In the afternoon the headquarters reached the Jesuit convent at Orsha. From here Berthier again wrote to Victor, informing him that it was supposed Oudinot would start on the 20th, or at the latest on the 21st, and be at Borissov on the 24th, and that he, Victor, was to take up a position at Tshereya on the 21st, "as the army will not arrive in Borissov before the 25th or the 26th, you must be prepared to be there on the 25th or the 26th, so as to take charge of the rearguard, which his Majesty intends to confide to you."

At noon on the 20th Orsha was evacuated, no news having as yet come in from Ney. But just as the Emperor, after his arrival in Baranj, was dining, an orderly officer, left behind by him at Orsha, arrived with the news of Ney's arrival at that town. The Emperor felt relieved from one great source of apprehension. Though Ney had rejoined the army with such very reduced numbers, yet the fact that he had not been entirely cut off, nor fallen into the hands of the Russians, served to conceal after all in some measure from the latter the dissolution of the III. Corps. In the evening he wrote as follows: "My fears about Marshal Ney are removed. He has rejoined us. I have resolved to set my whole army, even the Duke of Reggio and the Duke of Belluno, in motion towards Borissov and thence to Minsk. What I am especially anxious about is food."[1] A letter to Berthier also, dated 3 a.m. on the 21st, mentions the plan of a march to Minsk. Having started from Baranj on the 21st, the Emperor reached Kochanovo in the evening and established his headquarters in the castle of Kamionka, near that little town. We see thus, that his immediate and only intention was to reach Borissov, and that he ordered up his troops from all sides, to cross the Beresina there. This done, he intended to march to Minsk. Borissov therefore was now the decisive point; should this place fall into the enemy's hands

[1] C. N. To Maret.

before the Emperor could reach it, his complete destruction appeared inevitable. This was just what did happen. Let us once more examine the actual state of affairs, as they had shaped themselves up to the 21st November, before we proceed to contemplate the final development of matters during the remainder of that month. The number of combatants available was: Junot, 200 men, and the Poles 500 men at Tolotshin; the Emperor with the Guards, 4800 men, and the remainder of the cavalry, 1600 men, to the east of and close to Kochanovo; Dombrowski, with 4000 men, had reached Borissov, and had there united with the garrisons of Minsk and Borissov, 1500 men. But on the 21st, Tshitshagov's vanguard came up with Dombrowski, and forced him, after a hard and obstinate resistance, to evacuate Borissov and fall back upon Bobr with 1500 men. Here Oudinot had arrived on the same day with 8000 men, and the garrison left by Dombrowski at Mohilev, 1200 men, marched there also; Victor, 11,000 men, stood at Tshereya. On the Russian side we find Kutusov with 50,000 men at Lanitsi, and his advance guard, 15,000 men, at Gorianyay; Wittgenstein with 30,000 men at Tshashniki; Tshitshagov with 34,000 men at Borissov; Sacken with 25,000 faced Schwarzenberg with 35,000 men. The former had advanced against his opponent, so as to contain him, but had been repulsed. He now retreated to Brest-Litovsk, and stood on the 21st at Shereshovo, whilst Schwarzenberg, who had followed him, stood near Radetshko.

The Emperor had not been long in Kamionka before he began to feel uneasy about Borissov. "If the enemy has seized the bridge-head and burnt the bridge down, thus preventing our crossing, it will be a great misfortune for us; we shall then have to look for other points of crossing, and in case this proves difficult, we shall have to be prepared to march to Lepel."[1] Certainly

---

[1] C. N. Berthier to Oudinot. Headquarters near Kochanovo, 22nd November, 2.30 a.m.

without the bridge of Borissov the passage would be extremely difficult, for the weather had entirely changed. The cold, which had been decreasing since the 14th, had given place to a thaw on the 19th; rain had fallen, the road was a swamp, the Beresina open and covered with drifting ice. The ominous news that Borissov had actually fallen into the enemy's hands reached the Emperor not far from Tolotshin, whither he was marching on the 22nd. The thought may now have come to him which Segur embodies in the following words: "He felt, that nothing was left him but to sacrifice the army, bit by bit, and save the head at the expense of the limbs."[1] How could he hope that any one would see France again, except perhaps himself?

Having arrived at Tolotshin, he sent a despatch to Oudinot, who had already begun his march from Bobr to Borissov, either to recapture the bridge of Borissov, or, if it was destroyed, to occupy another point of crossing, above or below it, near Sembin or Beresino.[2] A further consideration of the situation and a study of the map decided him not to leave the choice of the point of crossing any longer to Oudinot. He now fixed definitely upon the village of Viesselovo, where there was a ford, and at 1 a.m. on the 23rd the order was sent to Oudinot to construct bridges there, and to throw up earthworks for their protection. Soon afterwards the Emperor left Tolotshin and proceeded, accompanied by his Guards, to Bobr, where he arrived about 3 o'clock in the afternoon.

Oudinot, now as we know joined by Dombrovski, had on the 22nd marched as far as Loshnitsa, and advanced on this day[3] to the Beresina in compliance with the Emperor's orders. He met the Russian advance guard, which was on the march to Bobr, and defeated it. Its flight threw the rest of the Russian army into

(92)

---

[1] N. et la Grand Armée en Russie, II. 179.
[2] Here the Southern Beresino is meant.
[3] 23rd November.

complete confusion. Tshitshagov, suspecting an attack from the whole forces of the Emperor, ordered the bridge of Borissov to be destroyed in all haste. Oudinot occupied the town. Victor reached Doknitsi, Wittgenstein, following him and keeping in close touch with him by means of his advanced troops, arrived at Tshereya. Kutusov reached Morosovo, his advance guard crossing the Dnieper at Kopiss. Schwarzenberg's and Sacken's operations, viz. the pursuit of the latter by the former, had no immediate effect on the events on the Beresina; we may therefore neglect them for the present.

At Bobr the Emperor received, during the night, Oudinot's report of his capture of Borissov and the demolition of the bridge there by the Russians, as well as a report that a brigade of cavalry, which, leaving Wrede at Glubokoyay, had been trying to come up with the army, had succeeded in crossing the Beresina by a ford at Studienka, also that Oudinot was now fixing upon this spot as suitable for the construction of his bridge. Early on the 24th the Emperor therefore sent to him Generals Chasseloup and Eblé with whatever he had available in the way of pontoon-train and sappers, as well as tools and materials. Then he formed one corps from the garrison of Mohilev, the Poles and the remains of Ney's division, and placed it under Ney's command, with orders to make a stand at Bobr until Davout and Eugène should also have come up. He himself left Bobr at 10 o'clock, and moved his headquarters to Loshnitsa.(24th November.)

On this same day Oudinot sent out parties to reconnoitre the ford of Studienka, as well as the passages at Stachov and Ucholodi, and at 5.30 a.m. he reported to Berthier that his choice of one of these three points would depend on these observations, and that meanwhile he intended to make feigned preparations at all three places; also that he had 20,000 men in front of him. At 1 p.m. he reported further: "I have decided on Studienka, where I purpose to cross during tomorrow

THE BERESINA

night, and to-morrow I shall order feints to be made early in the morning at Ucholodi and Stachov."[1] Soon after this, however, Oudinot received a report from General Aubry, whom he had sent out to Studienka, which described the local conditions there as decidedly less favourable, and at 4.45 p.m. the marshal sent a third message to Berthier with a copy of this report enclosed, and added that he would now await the Emperor's definite orders. This message reached Loshnitsa at midnight. 24th-25th November.

The Emperor was somewhat disappointed, for he had from the former reports hoped to be able to cross that night; he immediately, at 1 a.m., wrote to Oudinot and informed him that Mortier was going to advance to Borissov to his support with two divisions of the Guards, and admonished him: "If you have not crossed during this night, it is very urgent that you should cross to-day."[2] At 5 o'clock an order was sent to Victor in which he was earnestly enjoined to keep between Wittgenstein and the French army. "You have hitherto not done so, so that General Steinheil[4] has already joined Tormassov's army, thus delaying our operation of crossing the Beresina, which it is most important that we should execute with all possible speed, considering the position in which we are."[3] Victor was now ordered to move up to Kostritsa, and to attack whatever forces might oppose him. Eugène and Davout were to come up to Loshnitsa and Natsha. Three hours later the Emperor left Loshnitsa. At 2 p.m., not far from Borissov, a message from Victor reached him, announcing that this marshal was moving up to Loshnitsa. Thus the approach to Studienka, the point of crossing chosen for the French army, was left open to Wittgenstein. The Emperor did not fail to recognize how very much worse his situation had again

(93)

---
[1] C. N. To Berthier, Borissov, 24th November.
[2] C. N. To Berthier, Loshnitsa, 25th November.
[3] C. N. Berthier to Victor, Loshnitsa, 25th November.
[4] Napoleon was in error with respect to General Steinheil.

become through this, but there was no remedy for it now. He sent word to Victor that he disapproved of his not having attacked his opponent, and having taken the direction to Loshnitsa, but enjoined him now at least to hold Ratutishi, so that the Russians might not penetrate between the columns of the army, marching along the road to Borissov. Shortly before 3 o'clock the Emperor arrived at Borissov, threw himself upon his camp-bed, and slept until 11 o'clock. (25 November.)

On the same day at 5 a.m. Chasseloup and Eblé had reached Borissov, had made a few feigned preparations at this place, and then, at noon, proceeded to Studienka. Arriving there at 5 o'clock, they found, however, scarcely any of the preparations ordered begun, and whilst Oudinot's corps, which was to cover the construction of the bridge, was marching up towards evening, the engineers began to prepare the materials for the bridge. The position of the two armies was now as follows: The Emperor had left Borissov at 11 o'clock, and established his headquarters at Stari-Borissov; the Guards were at Borissov, Oudinot at Studienka, Ney between Loshnitsa and Nyemanitsa, Eugène at Natsha, Davout between this latter place and Krupki, and Victor at Ratutishi. On the side of the Russians Kutusov was still at Kopiss on the Dnieper, whilst his advance guard had reached Tolotshin; Wittgenstein had advanced to Basan; Tshitshagov, deceived by the feigned manœuvres at Borissov and Ucholodi, and suspecting that the crossing would be attempted below the former town, had deployed towards his right, and was now in position at Sabashevitshi and Usha, observing Borissov with his advance guard, whilst only one division had remained at Brili, opposite Studienka.

Thus at the most dangerous moment, when the passage was to begin, the spot chosen for it above Borissov was almost entirely free from the enemy's troops; how could any one have been justified in expecting such favourable

The Beresina

conditions, and who can still venture to say that the destruction of Napoleon's army in Russia was altogether due to an accumulation of bad luck? His victories had not been due to good luck, nor should we attempt to explain away his destruction by the words, "bad luck."

At 5 a.m. on the 26th the Emperor left Stari-Borissov and proceeded to Studienka; the Guards also, who had started during the night, were on the march thither. In the meantime the materials had been prepared there, and at 8 a.m. the work of constructing the bridge was started, under the protection of Oudinot's troops. Since the night of the 23rd, however, the frost had begun again, and the banks of the river therefore, just at this place very marshy, could be crossed with ease, and the river also was in several places frozen over; but at the point chosen for the bridge it was still open, and ice-floes were floating down it, the ice having only begun to form at the banks.

At 1 p.m. the right bridge of the two which were to be (94) constructed, the one destined for the infantry and cavalry only, was finished, and Oudinot started crossing at once. The other bridge, built more solidly for the artillery and baggage waggons, was not ready until 4 o'clock. Oudinot, having arrived on the other bank, succeeded, in spite of the resistance offered, in forcing the hostile division posted there, to fall back upon Stachov, and held his ground in front of it. At the same time Sembin was occupied, and thus the road was open for the continuation of the retreat. The Guards and Ney now reached Studienka. Victor arrived at Borissov, having left the division of Partouneaux behind at Loshnitsa, where Davout also arrived in the evening, Partouneaux now acting as rear guard. Eugène advanced to Nyemanitsa. As to the Russians, Tshitshagov, as already mentioned, was at Sabashevitshi and Stachov; Wittgenstein reached Kostritsa; Kutusov crossed the

Dnieper and arrived at Starosselyay, with his advance guard at Moliavka.

The Emperor spent the night in a house at Studienka. During the night the waggons were to cross continually to the other bank, but the bridge, constructed in an imperfect manner under the pressing circumstances, broke down twice; first at 8 p.m., and then, being repaired by 11 o'clock, it broke again three hours later, so that it could not be used again before 6 o'clock in the morning. The bridge destined for the troops alone had served during the night for the passage of Ney's corps. At 4 a.m. Victor arrived at Studienka and took up a position covering the bridges; Partouneaux came up to Borissov. At 1 p.m. the Emperor himself crossed on horseback, followed by the Guards, whilst Eugène's and Davout's troops, who arrived in the course of the day, also crossed during the night of the 27th. The Emperor established his headquarters at Sanivki.

On this day, the 27th, Wittgenstein had started from Kostritsa and marched to Stari-Borissov, where he learnt that one of Victor's divisions had not yet left Borissov. He therefore resolved to block its road to Studienka, and for this purpose took up a position at Stari-Borissov. Partouneaux, having started from Borissov in the evening, thus encountered such superior numbers that he was soon surrounded and compelled to lay down his arms. Tshitshagov, fully enlightened on the morning of the 27th as to the real point of crossing of the French army, had in his turn also moved up towards Borissov, repaired the bridge there, and had thus resumed communications with Wittgenstein. Both now resolved to attack the next day simultaneously on the two banks of the Beresina.

At 8 a.m. on the 28th, therefore, Tshitshagov attacked Oudinot and Ney, and two hours later Victor found himself attacked by Wittgenstein. On both banks of the Beresina, however, the French troops were able to stand their ground. During this fighting the bridges were continuously being crossed by the stragglers, streaming up without arms and in disorderly masses, and forming a block on the river-bank. " Hitherto these military and non-military masses, which no longer belonged to any particular divisions of the army, and followed two side roads parallel to the main road, had of their own accord fallen into a certain order of marching, which no one dared to leave; but on the heights above Studienka, at the point where the valley opened out wide before their sight, the instinct of escape awoke in these men, who now retained a merely mechanical existence. They spread out at once on both sides, at the sight of the river, confident of finding here the long-looked-for bridges, and tried thus to reach them more quickly than their companions to their right or left; but on their arrival at the river, which on account of the floes of ice and both banks being strongly covered with ice, just beginning to form, could not be crossed anywhere else, there remained no other course to them but to return to the order of march adopted by common consent up to now; and this naturally had the consequence, that in many cases might became right."[1]

At 9 o'clock in the evening Victor also began to cross, and at 1 o'clock the last regular body of troops had got across, only a few thousand stragglers were still on the left bank. On the 29th November, at 8.30 a.m., Eblé set fire to the bridges over the Beresina, and one hour later they were destroyed. "There ended the career of the Grand Army, which had made Europe tremble; it ceased to exist in a military sense; its only safety now lay in headlong flight."[2] The army, as far as we can still call it an army, marched this day through Sembin. During the next three days the number of those capable of fighting fell to 8800 men. The Emperor left Sanivki at

---

[1] V. Lossberg, Briefe, &c. Thorn, 7th January, 1813. 283.
[2] de Chambray, Hist. de l'expedition de Russie, III. 71.

6 a.m. in a carriage and reached Kamenj during the night.

(89)   From the moment at which he had led his army to the right bank of the Beresina, he indulged in no further illusions as to what must happen. "The army is numerous, but terribly disorganized. A fortnight will be necessary to rally it round the flag, and where are we to get a fortnight? The cold and privations have dissolved the army. We shall reach Vilna, but shall we be able to hold out there? Yes, if we can make a stand for a week there, but if we are attacked during the first week, it is doubtful, whether we shall be able to remain there. Provisions, provisions, provisions; the want of food will cause these insubordinate masses to commit the most horrible excesses against the town. Perhaps the army will not be able to concentrate again until after crossing the Niemen. In this situation of affairs it is possible that I may consider my presence in Paris necessary for France, for my empire, nay, for the army itself."[1]

He acted in accordance with this conviction. On the evening of the 5th December he arrived at Smorgonj, and after having taken some food, he wrote with his own hand the 29th bulletin, dating it the 3rd December from Molodetshno. He then called his marshals together, assumed the most ingenuous air during the evening meal, and asked Eugene to read the bulletin aloud to them. Having finally handed over the command of the remains of his army to Murat, he entered his carriage about 11 o'clock, accompanied by Caulaincourt, with Rustan on the box, and drove away at full speed in the direction of Vilna. On the 18th December, at 11.30 in the evening, he arrived in the Tuileries.

We have nothing further to add. In the course of our reflections we have already expressed the conviction,

---

[1] C. N. To Maret, Sanivki, right bank of the Beresina near Sembin, 29th November.

The Beresina

that the issue of the campaign of 1812 must necessarily have been what it was, with such a general and such an army. It must be acknowledged indeed, that the general here only reaped the reward for that utter contempt for the future, which he always exhibited both in the government of his people and the training of his troops.

CHAPTER VII.

1813.

UP TO THE ARMISTICE.

(95) WHEN the Emperor, on his departure from Smorgonj, handed over the chief command to Murat, the disorganized rabble, for the most part unarmed, into which the troops had dissolved could no longer be called an army. After crossing the Beresina operations were no longer military. The cold, which reached 20 degrees (Reaumur) on the 3rd December, and increased during the following days, finished the work of ruin. "The cold, still 23 degrees (it is even said that it fell to 25 degrees), had made everybody indifferent to what happened; the greater part had their hands or feet frozen."[1] On the 8th December Murat reached Vilna with the remains of the Guard and a few thousand stragglers. Ney, with the divisions of Loison, scarcely 400 men, and Wrede, about 2000 men, formed the rearguard, but was soon forced back upon Vilna by Tshitshagov, who had taken up the pursuit. Under these circumstances there was no possibility whatever of obeying the orders which the Emperor, probably for form's sake only, had left with Murat, viz. "to assemble the army at Vilna, hold that town, and go into winter quarters."[2]

On the 10th Murat started again from Vilna and reached Kovno during the night of the 11th. Ney followed with 1500 men. From Kovno Berthier reported as follows: "I must not conceal from your Majesty that the whole army

---

[1] C. N. Berthier to N. Kovno, 12th December.
[2] C. N. Instructions, Smorgonj, 5th December.

is entirely broken up, even your Guard, which numbers scarcely 400 to 500 men. The generals and officers have lost all they possessed, and almost all have some parts of their bodies frozen. The streets are strewn with corpses; the houses are filled with them. The army forms only one short column, which starts in the morning and reaches the next place without the semblance of order."[1] Nor was it possible to obey the Emperor's second instruction, viz. to make a stand on the Niemen; and in ever-increasing disorder the helpless mass dragged itself along the Gumbinnen road. "I will not detail to your Majesty the saddening instances of looting, insubordination and loss of cohesion; everything has reached its climax."[2] On the 19th December Murat reached Königsberg, his army consisting of 400 men of the Old Guard and not quite 600 men of the Guard cavalry, followed by a few thousand stragglers. Tshitshagov's pursuit ceased on the Niemen, the frontier of Prussia.

But if this latter circumstance seemed to promise a chance of being able to remain at Königsberg, a piece of news soon arrived which put an end to this hope. We know that Macdonald's operations round Riga had come to a standstill. He was there inactive, as it were, in winter quarters, when he received, on the 18th December, at Stalgen his headquarters, a letter from Berthier dated from Vilna on the 9th, which gave him the first hint about the great events that had happened. For it ordered him to fall back upon Tilsit. He started upon his retreat and reached Tilsit on the 28th; but Yorck, the leader of the Prussian contingent, who was better informed, from private sources, as to the real nature of Napoleon's situation, concluded an arrangement with the Russians, which neutralized his corps for the time being. The news of the convention of Tauroggen

[1] C. N. Berthier to N. Kovno, 12th December.
[2] C. N. Berthier to N. Wirballen, 16th December.

reached Murat on the 1st January, 1813, at Königsberg. He saw at once that, deprived of the aid of the Prussians, he could not maintain so advanced a post. He therefore fell back upon Elbing, and then to Posen, where he arrived on the 16th January, and, handing the command of the army over to Eugène, departed for Naples.

Thus in the middle of January the line of the Vistula was abandoned; Danzig alone remaining in the hands of the French. About the same time, on the part of the Russians, Tshitshagov reached Marienburg, Wittgenstein Elbing, whilst Kutusov was advancing slowly from Vilna *viâ* Suvalki towards Plock. At Posen, Eugène received the Emperor's first plans for the reconstruction of the army. A vanguard was to be formed at Posen under Ney, for which purpose the divisions of Grenier, coming up from Italy, and the division of Lagrange, 10,000 men of the XI. Corps, were to be utilized. This latter corps had remained behind under Augereau to garrison Prussia, but had afterwards been called upon to send forward reinforcements, and consisted now only of one division under Lagrange. Protected by this vanguard, four new corps were to be created, the I. II. III. IV., at Stettin, Küstrin, Spandau and Glogau respectively; and the Emperor calculated that by the month of June he would have four divisions ready in Stettin and two in each of the other three fortresses. In addition, for the reorganization of the Grand Army three groups were to be formed from the forces left behind in France and from the freshly raised levies; viz. a Corps of Observation on the Elbe at Magdeburg, a Corps of Observation of Italy at Verona, and the First Corps of Observation of the Rhine at Frankfort on the Main. A second Corps of Observation of the Rhine would later on be formed at Magdeburg, whilst the first three corps were to advance and reach the Oder by the 1st May. Towards the end of June the Emperor reckoned upon having altogether 300,000 men at his disposal.

UP TO THE ARMISTICE 237

Indeed he considered his situation in no way desperate. He advised Ney not to evacuate Warsaw, reckoning upon Schwarzenberg, and believing that the Russians would bring only cavalry against Eugène. Even on the 26th January he says: "According to all the indications I can gather, I have no doubt but that you will be able to hold out in Posen;"[1] a view which no longer showed the clearness of judgment with which he formerly estimated facts, but was a sign of that falsifying and self-deceiving process which had taken such fast hold of his mind. He looked upon the relief of Danzig as a first success, and referred to some 50,000 men, whom he supposed to have been employed in the investment of that place. Of course he was not in earnest, the number being mentioned merely to encourage Eugene.

The facts, however, did not correspond with the Emperor's views. The Russians did advance into Prussia; slowly it is true, and in inconsiderable force; but the country showed itself more and more hostile to the French; and now Schwarzenberg deprived them of the expected support of their right wing, even as Yorck had already robbed them of their left wing. On the 7th December the Austrian auxiliary Corps which he commanded, and which lay at Slonim, had proceeded together with Reynier's Corps, *viâ* Bialostok, to Pultusk, where the two corps had taken up a position. Here he came to an arrangement with the Russians, and there was a brief armistice. With the commencement of February, however, Schwarzenberg set out for Krakau, having concluded a truce for his own Corps, whilst Reynier fell back upon Kalish.

Thus Eugène thought himself on the 12th February compelled to leave Posen with the 14,000 men he had collected there, and retreat to Frankfort-on-the-Oder, where he arrived on the 18th. The Emperor was altogether dissatisfied with this movement, which, as it

[1] C. N. To Eugène, Fontainebleau.

was made direct on Berlin, offered no obstacle to the continued advance of the enemy. He explained to Eugène that this object could only have been attained by a position on the enemy's flank; inasmuch as such a position, at a naturally strong point, would have been a constant menace to their line of operations, and would have forced them to reckon with it. Indeed he showed his step-son on the map the point which would have fulfilled that condition. "An experienced general, who would have taken up a camp in front of Küstrin, &c." [1]

"If . . . instead of falling back to Frankfort, you had concentrated in front of Küstrin, the enemy would have hesitated to throw any forces over to the left bank. You would have gained twenty days at least." [2]

But as it was, only two days passed before Eugène considered the position of Frankfort also no longer tenable, and on the 22nd he fell back upon Berlin. From here also, after one attempt to show front, which he quickly renounced, he continued his retreat, until, on the 6th March, he ultimately reached Wittenberg, and determined to make a stand upon the Elbe.

At this moment the French forces were stationed as follows:—Eugène had his headquarters at Leipzig; Reynier, with 12,000 men lay at Dresden and Meissen; Davout, with 10,000 men (the newly-created I. Corps) at Dresden; Grenier, 19,000 men at Wittenberg; Victor, 8000 men (the newly-created II. Corps) at Bernburg; Lauriston, 20,000 men (the Corps of Observation of the Elbe) at Magdeburg; and finally, 6000 men under Vandamme held Bremen.

The Emperor beheld this hasty retreat with undisguised dissatisfaction. "We must at last begin to wage war. . . . Our military operations are an object of scorn to our allies in Vienna, as well as to our enemies in London and St. Petersburg, because our army regularly runs away a

[1] C. N. Trianon, 9th March.   [2] C. N. Trianon, 15th March.

UP TO THE ARMISTICE

week before the enemy's infantry arrives, at the mere approach of some light troops, or even the rumour of it." But his interference, when he wrote on the 5th March to Eugène, "Sum total: Remain in Berlin as long as you can," an order which he repeated the next day, came too late to stop Eugène; and thus nothing remained for him but to read his subordinate a lecture. On the 9th March he wrote as follows: "I cannot imagine what forced you to leave Berlin. If you had taken up a position in front of Berlin, . . . the enemy would necessarily have thought you were going to fight a battle. In that case he would not have crossed the Oder before having assembled some 60,000 to 80,000 men, . . . but he was far from being able to do this. . . . The Russians . . . cannot possibly have at present at their disposal an army equal to yours; they are becoming weaker, you stronger." This admonition was all the more necessary, as the Emperor was well aware of the fact that, "generally speaking, instinct leads us to consider the enemy whom we see, as more numerous than he really is."[1] Then he proceeded to mention in detail all the disadvantages which the retreat to Wittenberg entailed, reminding Eugène that he had some time before recommended him to fall back on Magdeburg. His idea was to hold the Lower Elbe and thus to cover Holland. "The 32nd Military Division and Westphalia are the principal objects of importance, for on these Holland depends; they can only be maintained by an offensive position in front of Magdeburg."[2] "I know well that Dresden is a point of paramount importance, but this is a thing we cannot avoid. Should the enemy march upon Dresden with his main army, and at the same time advance upon Hanover with another body of troops, it stands to reason that you cannot possibly defend Dresden. If forced to choose between the defence of the Lower and that of the Upper Elbe, I should prefer to

[1] C. N. To Eugène, Trianon, 11th March.
[2] C. N. To Clarke, Schönbrunn, 10th October, 1809.

defend the Lower;"[1] indeed this tract of country was so important in his eyes, that he added: "I should prefer to see the enemy at Leipzig, Erfurt and Gotha, rather than in Hanover and Bremen."[2]

In addition, he pointed out to Eugène that if he wished to protect Dresden directly, he would be forced to denude other more important points, and he therefore wished to see him take an offensive position in front of Magdeburg; "this will be the surest way to assist Dresden;"[3] and he further admonished him: "You should not try to find out whether the enemy is about to move or not. . . . You must in fact take up a position, which will render you independent of the enemy, and which you can occupy, whatever he may do; one from which you can command his movements, by forcing him to move against you, so as to invest you; but this an offensive position alone can effect."[4] "If there is a fine position anywhere, it is that in front of Magdeburg, where you can continuously threaten to attack the enemy, and whence you can actually attack him if he does not appear in too great force." In his earnest solicitude to see the desired position near Magdeburg occupied for the safeguarding of the line of the Lower Elbe, the Emperor even addressed one of the corps-leaders direct, and wrote thus to Lauriston: "It is my desire that you assemble your four divisions one hour's march in front of Magdeburg. You must cover yourself by a few lunettes and publish in all directions the fact that you are going to resume the offensive."[5] There is nothing more instructive than this series of letters, in which the Emperor, map in hand, lectures on strategical defence.

The sanitary condition of his army filled him with anxiety. He was well aware that he would need all

---

[1] C. N. To Eugène, Trianon, 17th March, 4 p.m.
[2] C. N. To Eugène, Trianon, 15th March.
[3] C. N. To Eugène, Trianon, 18th March.
[4] C. N. To Eugène, Trianon, 9th March.
[5] C. N. Trianon, 14th March.

the men, capable of bearing arms, to be successful; and he therefore sent out careful instructions as to the caution to be exercised in the choice of camping stations. "Above all, choose a very healthy soil. Consult the medical men and the natives on this point. Do not permit any exceptions. If you are close to marshes or inundated meadows, you may say what you like, but you are in an unhealthy spot, and you must go higher up. You will understand that in such places I should lose my whole army in one spring month. I wish you to consult your own common sense and the natives, rather than the doctors;"[1] and his principle in this respect was: "It is better to fight the most sanguinary battle, than to encamp the troops in an unhealthy spot."[2]

At the same time the Emperor began to consider the resumption of the general offensive, as soon as he should have placed his masses in readiness under the protection of the line of the Elbe. His plan was to cross the Elbe at Havelberg, lead the whole army to Stettin, thus gaining the line of the Oder before the enemy by outstripping and surprising him, and then to advance in full force to the relief of Danzig. "Since it must be the first aim of the French army to move with all speed to the assistance of Danzig, it would, if we suppose the army of the Elbe to be assembled at Magdeburg, Havelberg and Wittenberg, and the army of the Main at Würzburg, Erfurt and Leipzig, be the natural course to take—and easily concealed from the enemy—to advance with the whole army of the Elbe and the army of the Main behind it, *viâ* Havelberg, to Stettin. It will probably be my purpose to advance, covered by the Thuringer Wald and the Elbe, *viâ* Havelberg, reach Stettin by forced marches with 300,000 men, and continue to march as far as Danzig, which town we could reach in a fortnight; we shall have relieved that town by the 20th day

[1] C. N. To Eugène, Paris, 28th March.
[2] C. N. To Davout, St. Cloud, 16th August, 1811.

after the army crosses the Elbe; we shall be masters of Marienburg and the island of Nogat, and hold all the bridges over the Lower Vistula. So much for the plan of the offensive."[1] He thus emphasized the great importance of Havelberg, and he regretted that there was no fortress there and that it was not like Magdeburg, " but there is no help for it."[2]

This was the Emperor's great plan, which need not fear comparison with his best, either in point of boldness or of brilliancy. It was bold, for he proposed to advance on the extended line from Stettin to Danzig with his left wing along the sea, exposing his right to a flank-attack. It was brilliant, for he had well calculated that, safeguarded by the Thuringer Wald and the Elbe, he would be able to accomplish his concentration towards Havelberg by surprise, so that the enemy would have neither time nor opportunity to execute the apprehended flank-attack; and that even if such an attack were made, he would be superior to the enemy not only in numbers, but more especially in energy, unity, and strategical experience, and that he would certainly succeed in relieving the large garrison of Danzig, and gaining the important base of the Lower Vistula. But even more than the actual advantage of such a success, he valued the moral effect, which his reappearance on the Vistula would produce throughout Europe; and rightly so, for "in war the prestige and moral effect are more than half the battle."[3]

On the 21st March Eugène at last took up the position so urgently emphasized by the Emperor, and assembled Victor, Grenier, and Lauriston in front of Magdeburg. The enemy was at that moment disposed as follows: Wittgenstein, 13,000 Russians, and Yorck, 20,000 Prussians, were at Berlin with advanced bodies

[1] C. N. To Davout, St. Cloud, 16th August, 1811.
[2] C. N. Notes for the Viceroy of Italy. Trianon, 11th March.
[3] C. N. To Clarke. Schönbrun, 10th October, 1809.

UP TO THE ARMISTICE 243

along the Lower Elbe; Bülow, 12,000 Prussians, and Borstell, 5000 Prussians, were marching up from the Oder. The other forces of the Prussians and Russians were as yet further to the rear, the former under Blücher in Silesia, the latter, the main army under Kutusov as commander-in-chief, at Kalish. Scarcely had Eugène assumed the offensive attitude recommended by the Emperor, than its effect became evident. Wittgenstein, who held the chief command over Yorck, Bülow and Borstell, had advanced to Rosslau, in order to open communications with Blücher, who was on the march towards Saxony. But as Eugène now threatened Berlin, he at once turned against the latter; and on the 5th April (96) succeeded in forcing back his advanced posts at all points, and compelled Eugène to withdraw behind the Elbe and to destroy the bridge. Eugène now formed front against the Upper Saale, with his left wing resting on the Lower Saale and his right on the Harz mountains.

One consequence of the plan decided upon by the (95) Emperor, namely, placing the central point of his defence on the Lower Elbe, and remaining undisputed master of that country, was the abandonment of Dresden. Hamburg had been evacuated by its French garrison on the 12th March, and Davout was now fixed upon by the Emperor to recapture that town, so that he might have a *point d'appui* for the protection of the left wing of his army. "You will station the Prince of Eckmühl with his sixteen battalions to the left of Sich; he will be very useful there. He knows Hamburg and is known there, and his proximity to this town will be of advantage."[1] "This marshal will be well suited, on account of his local knowledge, to restore order and make an example."[2] In consequence Davout blew up one pier of the Elbe bridge at Dresden on the 19th March, and then started for Lüneburg. On the 26th Dresden

[1] C. N. To Eugène. Trianon, 15th March.
[2] C. N. To Eugène. Trianon, 18th March.

was entirely evacuated by the French, the suburb of Neustadt having been abandoned on the 22nd; and the next day the town was occupied by a detachment of Russians, who preceded the main army.

(96) The Emperor left St. Cloud on the 15th April at 4 a.m., and arrived at 2 a.m. on the 17th in Mayence. He found his army at that moment in the following formation: Davout, 30,000 men, was on the march to Lüneburg; Eugène, 70,000 men, stood on the Saale; the First Corps of Observation of the Rhine, under Ney, 50,000 men, was marching towards Erfurt; the Second Corps of Observation of the Rhine, under Marmont, 27,000 men, was on the march towards Eisenach; and the Corps of Observation of Italy under Bertrand, 40,000 men, on the march to Bamburg. The Guard, 18,000 men, was at Mayence. All these figures, however, are exaggerated and were by no means fully reached at that time. The sum total of all his forces between the Elbe and the Rhine, or on the march from Italy through Bavaria, was probably somewhat below 200,000 men. With these forces at his disposal the Emperor now formed his army into the following corps:

The Emperor.
Chief of the Staff: Berthier.
Guard: Mortier.
I. Corps: Davout.
III. Corps: Ney.
IV. Corps: Bertrand.
V. Corps: Lauriston.
VI. Corps: Marmont.
VII. Corps[1]: Reynier.
XI. Corps: Macdonald.
XII. Corps: Oudinot.

---

[1] The VII. Corps consisted for the present only of one division, 4000 strong; as soon as it reached the Elbe it was once more to absorb the troops of Saxony.

The II. Corps, Victor, was still in process of formation, and did not take the field until a little later.

Poniatowski, in Gallicia, counted as the VIII. Corps.

Augereau was busy in Bavaria with the formation of the IX. Corps.

Finally the garrison of Danzig under Rapp was reckoned as the X. Corps.

UP TO THE ARMISTICE

At 8 p.m. on the 24th the Emperor left Mayence, "he arrived at Erfurt on the 25th April and already appeared very uneasy."[1] His knowledge of the enemy's positions was very scanty, for he suffered considerably from his want of cavalry, for this arm is not so easily formed on the spur of the moment. And he had always most earnestly insisted upon his cavalry being and remaining in constant touch with the enemy. "A colonel of Chasseurs or Hussars, who goes to sleep, instead of spending the night in bivouac and remaining in constant communication with his piquets deserves to be shot."[2] His present cavalry was indeed far from being equal to this task, and he therefore remained in ignorance of the enemy's measures. "I do not yet know properly what they (the enemy) are going to do; they have nothing but light cavalry in front of the Viceroy, they have nothing but light cavalry in front of Erfurt; we have not learnt that they have any infantry nearer than Leipzig."[3] "I should be able to finish matters very quickly if I had 15,000 more cavalry, but I am rather weak in this arm;"[4] and eye-witnesses of the campaign confirm this. "Never, in any campaign, has the want which a dearth of cavalry creates been more painfully felt than in this."[5] "The infantry, fatigued by the past days' work, had to march against the enemy's horsemen; for the scanty cavalry was quite insufficient, and as it consisted for the greater part only of regiments of the Guard, it was always kept in reserve. How strikingly the saying has been proved true in this campaign that newly recruited troops can be easily made into infantry soldiers, but not into cavalry."[6]

To the very end of his life, after his extensive experience of offensive as well as defensive warfare, the Emperor laid

[1] O. v. Odeleben, Napoleon's Feldzug in Sachsen im 1813. 32.
[2] C. N. To Berthier. Paris, 2nd January, 1812.
[3] C. N. To the King of Wurtemberg. Mayence, 18th April.
[4] C. N. To the King of Wurtemberg. Mayence, 24th April.
[5] Berthezène, Souvenirs mil.
[6] O. v. O. Napoleon's Feldzug, etc. 50.

emphasis upon the value of cavalry in conducting a really decisive campaign. "General Lloyd asks, What is the use of much cavalry? I on my side ask, How is it possible to carry on anything but a defensive war, covering oneself by entrenchments and natural obstacles, if one has not a cavalry fairly equal in strength to that of the enemy? if if you lose a battle, your army is lost. . . . An army superior in cavalry will always have the advantage of being able to cover its movements, of being well informed as to the enemy's movements and giving battle only when it chooses. Its defeats will have few evil consequences, and its successes will be decisive." The whole campaign of the Allies, Lützen, Bautzen and the retreat to Silesia will furnish proofs of this. And in order that the cavalry may be independent in all situations which may arise, he declared that a long-range rifle is indispensable for it. "It is universally conceded that the Cuirassiers have difficulty in using their carbines; but on the other hand it seems absurd, that 3000 or 4000 brave men should be exposed to being surprised in their cantonments or stopped in their marches by a couple of light companies. . . . I cannot reconcile myself to seeing 3000 men, picked troops, liable to be overwhelmed by any partizan leader during a popular rising or in a surprise by light troops, or to be arrested on their march by a few good sharpshooters behind a brook or a house; it seems absurd to me. It is my wish that every man should have a musket; even if it be only a very short carbine, carried in the manner most convenient to the Cuirassiers, it is all the same to me. . . . Place therefore some proposal before me, so that these 3000 men may not have to depend on infantry to protect them in cantonments, and that they may be able to clear their way if any infantry, inferior to them in numbers, attack them. . . . As to the Lancers, see whether we could not manage to arm them with a carbine in addition to their lances; and should this be impossible, at least one-third of each troop ought to be armed with carbines."[1] We thus see that the Emperor had learnt what experience in war has taught us.

It had been the Emperor's plan at first, when he became aware of the enemy's advance into Saxony, "to refuse my right wing and to allow the enemy to push forward towards Bayreuth, that is, to execute the converse manœuvre, which I executed in the campaign of Jena, so that, if the enemy advance to Bayreuth, I may be able to reach Dresden before them and cut them off from Prussia."[2] This reference to Jena fully shows us not only how he recognized the existence and justification of certain methods of conducting strategical operations, and the possibility of adjusting them so as to suit different situations, but it comprises the wisdom of those teachers who have tried to elucidate the nature of these methods, their value or worthlessness, their strength or weakness.

But when the Emperor noticed that that expected forward movement of the enemy did not take place, but that they remained stationary in Saxony, he decided as follows: "My first object is to throw the enemy upon the right bank of the Saale, then upon the right bank of the Mulde, and lastly even upon the right bank of the Elbe."[3] For this purpose he intended to direct his forward movement on Leipzig. "I think, our first point will be to get to Leipzig. The Viceroy might advance viâ Merseburg."[4] But, as had always been the case with him, the first thing he looked to was the concentration of his masses, before approaching the enemy closely. "At this moment my first object is to unite with the Viceroy."[5] "The

---

[1] Oeuvres xxxi. 508, 509. Notes sur l'introduction à l'histoire de la guerre, etc., par Lloyd.
[2] C. N. To Clark. St. Cloud, 12th November, 1811.
[3] C. N. To Bertrand. St. Cloud, 12th April.
[4] C. N. To the King of Würtemberg. Mayence, 24th April.
[5] C. N. To Ney. Erfurt, 28th April, 3.30 a.m.

main object at this moment is concentration;"[1] and in order to succeed in this safely and unnoticed by the enemy, "all my movements will be executed behind the Saale as behind a curtain."[2] From behind that curtain he purposed breaking out with superior numbers, in order either to force his opponents, whom he fairly correctly estimated at 60,000 to 70,000 men, to the South off their lines of communications with Berlin, or to encounter Wittgenstein still unsupported, for "as Wittgenstein is inclined to be daring, we may, if we attack him with large numbers, inflict great losses upon him."[3]

On the day of the Emperor's arrival in Erfurt, his army stood at the following points: Eugène (with Lauriston, Macdonald and Reynier) on the Lower Saale; Ney in front of Weimar, holding the defile of Kösen; the Guard at Erfurt; Marmont at Gotha; Bertrand at Saalfeld and Oudinot at Coburg. The enemy's positions were as follows: Wittgenstein lay with 22,000 men between the Lower Mulde and Saale; Blücher, 23,000, was at Altenburg; the vanguard of the main army, 11,000 men, at Chemnitz; this latter itself, now under Tormassov, 18,000 men, at Dresden; and lastly 10,000 men under Winzingerode at Lützen. From the above-mentioned places the French army advanced during the next few days towards the Saale, Eugène taking the direction of Merseburg, and the Emperor with the remaining corps that of Weissenfels.

We cannot but admire the iron energy of the man and his high gifts as an organizer, when we see him a few months after the tremendous ruin of a whole army in Russia, standing again on the Elbe with so large a force. But no human energy could give to these newly-formed regiments the value of those of 1805 and 1806. No one indeed in the army indulged in any such opinion, and all were carefully mindful of

[1] C. N. To Ney. Erfurt, 26th April.
[2] C. N. To Ney. Erfurt, 27th April, 8 a.m.
[3] C. N. To Ney. Erfurt, 28th April, 3.30 a.m.

UP TO THE ARMISTICE

Napoleon's admonition, "We must act cautiously and not endanger inferior troops, nor be foolish enough, as some are, to think that to be a man is to be a soldier. Troops such as you have" (the words are addressed to Clarke in 1809 in connection with the Walcheren expedition) "are just the kind which need most entrenchments, earthworks, and artillery. . . . The more inferior the quality of a body of troops the more artillery it requires. There are some army corps with which I should require only one-third of the artillery which I need for other corps."[1] For this reason the Emperor tried to create everywhere the belief that he was well provided with this arm, and indeed took care to be well equipped in this respect, so that on the resumption of hostilities after the truce he again had 1300 guns at his disposal. After Lützen and Bautzen we hear him say, "It is the artillery of my Guard which generally decides my battles, for, as I have it always at hand I can bring it to bear, wherever it becomes necessary."[2] And after the end of the campaign he wrote, "Great battles are won by artillery."[3]

But noticing that the spirit of enterprise in his subordinate leaders was much depressed by the consciousness of being at the head of troops upon whom they could not depend, he admonished them thus: "Do not be afraid of trusting your troops in actual fighting."[4] Moreover, we shall see himself acting and fighting from the very beginning, with this army, just as if he had the old one still under him. It is characteristic of genius not to be dependent for success on the worth of the material at command, but, on the contrary, to handle the material available in such a manner that to gain victory becomes possible.

[1] C. N. Schonbrunn, 18th August.
[2] C. N. To Clarke. Neumarkt, 2nd June.
[3] C. N. To Eugène. St. Cloud, 20th November, 1813.
[4] C. N. To Bertrand. Liegnitz, 6th June.

More ominous, however, was the fact that the officers also were not equal to their task, for "it is the officers and non-commissioned officers who are the backbone of any body of men."[1] The Emperor's complaints about "these incapable officers, who make the soldiers laugh," and about "these young men who have just left college, and know nothing," show how deeply the general felt the want, though of course as a statesman he ought to have confessed that it was he himself who, by his never-ceasing wars, had consumed all the capable officers, and that it was high time now to pause.

It is true that in the higher posts we still see those names which the Emperor's campaigns had rendered famous throughout the world, and there was therefore no want of experience in administration and in war; but we have noted already how the influences of time and luxury and the growth of Napoleon's power had begun to make themselves felt in these men, and their effects were now fully apparent. It had been even too late when, in 1811, the Emperor wrote these grand words: "The honour of a general consists in obeying, in keeping those under his orders in the way of duty, in enforcing a strict discipline, devoting himself exclusively to the interests of the state and the sovereign, and forgetting entirely his own private interests."[2] But here we read the contrary: "It was almost the exclusive occupation of the superior and inferior officers, when they were left to themselves, to satisfy their physical wants. All that the Emperor's proximity could effect was at the most to induce the troops to attend punctually to their ordinary duties. As to confidence in the leaders, or the necessary good understanding between these and the men, it was for the most part non-existent."[3]

(97a) On the 28th April the Emperor's advanced columns

[1] C. N. To Decrès. Posen, 15th December, 1806.
[2] C. N. To Berthier. St. Cloud, 8th June.
[3] O. v. O., etc., 193.

reached the Saale, and the next day the masses of his own and Eugène's army arrived respectively at Weissenfels and Merseburg; thus the junction planned had been accomplished. The advance was now continued in the direction of Leipzig; and on the 1st May the Emperor and the Guard reached Lützen, driving Winzingerode thence. Ney arrived at Kaja, Marmont was in the Pass of Rippach, Bertrand at Poserna, Oudinot at Naumburg, Eugène and Lauriston at Markranstädt, Macdonald a little behind the latter, and Reynier still at Merseburg. On the part of the enemy also some concentration had been effected, of which, however, the Emperor was unaware. Thus the corps of Wittgenstein, Blücher, and Winzingerode stood now at Zwenkau and Rötha, between the Elster and the Pleisse. Tormassov was at Lobstädt, and the vanguard of the main army had been sent forward to Altenburg to cover the left flank. The chief command had been entrusted to Wittgenstein, and he determined to cross the Elster on the following day and to fall upon the right flank of the French, whilst one division, 5000 men, was posted at Lindenau, in front of Leipzig, so as to occupy and divert the enemy's attention. The Elster and the Flossgraben were, therefore, crossed early in the morning of the 2nd May, and about 11 o'clock the Prusso-Russian army stood between Werben and Domsen, with Tormassov at Pegau in reserve. The former vanguard of the main army left Altenburg for Zeitz.

The Emperor "did not expect to be attacked on that day, at least not in the direction whence the attack came,"[1] for "he was not acquainted with the real position of the enemy, and had not expected them to take the offensive so soon."[2] Still he had been informed so far as to be aware of some movements for the purpose of concentration at Zwenkau, and he knew that Wittgenstein had been entrusted with the supreme command. He did not, however, intend for the present to change his

[1] O. v. O., 52.   [2] Marmont Mém. v. 15.

direction towards Leipzig, for, though the enemy were in position higher up on the Elster, yet the masses advancing upon Leipzig would be able to attack them in the most favourable direction, since they would engage their strategical flank. He therefore ordered Lauriston at 4 a.m. to march direct to Leipzig; Macdonald was to follow to Markranstädt in support, but was at the same time to keep an eye upon Zwenkau; and in addition he ordered Ney to reconnoitre in that direction as well as towards Pegau. Marmont was to push forward to Pegau, and Bertrand to Taucha. The Emperor himself intended to accompany Lauriston.

He was on the road to Leipzig, when at 9 a.m. Lauriston began an engagement with the enemy's division posted in front of Leipzig; and its obstinate resistance confirmed the Emperor for the present in his view that the greater part of the hostile army was still there, and that he had probably its right wing in front of him. For his own flank he feared but little, and had therefore called up Marshal Ney in person to the road to Leipzig. "At 11 a.m. Napoleon had passed the Gustavus Adolphus monument. Prince Eugène had joined him. At his side was the Prince of the Moscova, who had ridden up to receive personally the Emperor's orders for the rest of the day. They advanced, and already perceived the fusillade of General Lauriston's advanced guard among the first houses of Leipzig. The Emperor, impatient to know whether the resistance was serious, had dismounted and directed his telescope upon the town. He could distinguish the roofs covered by inhabitants, spectators of the fighting. At the moment when he noticed that no hostile forces showed themselves on this side of the town, a terrible cannonade became audible on our right wing, almost in our rear, in the direction of the place where the Prince of Moscova's troops had spent the night."[1]

"Napoleon remained calm, but watched for a few minutes

[1] Fain, Manuscrit de, 1813, i. 348.

the distant smoke and thunder, and immediately changed his plan."[1] Eugène was to advance with Macdonald's corps from Markranstädt against the enemy's right, whilst Lauriston continued to keep in play his present opponents in front of Leipzig. Marmont was to join in the battle from the right, and Bertrand was to advance from Poserna against the enemy's left and rear. The Emperor himself hastened at a gallop towards Lützen, where he intended to lead the Guard forward in the centre and to use them as a reserve.

Wittgenstein's attack had met in the first place Ney's corps, which was in possession of Gross and Klein Görschen, Kaja, Rahna and Starsiedel, and to which that marshal, hurrying on in front of the Emperor, returned. A violent struggle began around these villages, which were again and again captured and lost, but as yet remained definitely in the hands of neither combatant. To the right of Ney, Marmont marched up soon after noon and occupied Starsiedel; Bertrand also appeared about 4 p.m., and in order to meet this threatening flank attack, Wittgenstein needed all the Russian troops still at his disposal, so that he was unable to support the Prussians, who had, with heavy losses, taken Gross and Klein Görschen, Rahna, and finally Kaja also. Their attack upon Starsiedel, however, which was the key of the French line, was unsuccessful, and the Russian troops also were unable to hold Eisdorf, the *point d'appui* of the French left.

The Emperor, who felt how great, nay perhaps decisive, (97b) the impression would be which, after the events of 1812, the issue of this first battle would create in Europe, had exposed himself so persistently to the fire, encouraging and inspiring his young troops, that Marmont said: "On this day he probably ran the greatest personal risks of his whole career."[2] He had up to now looked with considerable apprehension upon the fight for the

[1] O. v. O., 53. [2] Mémoires, v. 26.

villages in his centre; "an ill-concealed embarrassment became visible among his retinue when the fire approached closer and closer, and Kaja, the critical point, was wavering in the balance."[1] Then, about 5 o'clock, when Kaja was lost, "he judged that the decisive moment, which determines victory or defeat in a battle, had come;"[2] and he ordered his reserve, the Guard, to deliver the decisive attack on Kaja, sending to their support one of Marmont's divisions. At the same time he commanded Drouet to establish a battery of 60 guns at Starsiedel, in order to clear the way, as usual, for breaking the enemy's line. Kaja was recaptured, and the Prussians fell back along the whole line. It is true that a Russian division came up from the reserve to their support, and succeeded for a moment in restoring the battle; but at 7 p.m. Macdonald's corps broke out from Eisdorf on the flank of the Allies, and the Russian reserve, hurrying up, was only able to afford the retreating army a rest between Gross Görschen and the Flossgraben. At Leipzig Lauriston had continued his advance, and at 2 p.m. the town was evacuated.

(98) The Emperor returned to Lützen on horseback at nightfall, arriving about 10 o'clock. His elation at his victory was mingled with the consciousness of how necessary this success had been to him in his situation; and he called Lützen an "unexpected victory, and one which materially changed the situation of affairs."[3] The Allies had during the night before the 3rd May fallen back behind the Flossgraben; there was no doubt now of their further retreat behind the Elbe, and this was executed in two columns through Dresden and Meissen. The Emperor followed them on roads towards Wurzen, Colditz and Rochlitz, feeling again most deeply his want of cavalry. He reached Dresden on the 8th, the allies

---

[1] O. v. O., 60.
[2] C. N. Bulletin of the Grand Army, Lützen, 2nd May.
[3] C. N. To Cambacérès. Hainau, 7th June.

evacuating the left bank of the Elbe and destroying the bridges in and near Dresden, viz. a floating bridge, a pontoon bridge, and a wooden one, which had been temporarily constructed to fill the gap in the stone bridge blown up in part by Davout on the 19th of March; they still held, however, the suburb of Neustadt.

Before the Emperor entered the town itself, he personally reconnoitred the Elbe, ordered the floating bridge, which was not yet half burnt, to be drawn in to the left bank, the fire to be extinguished, and the bridge to be restored at once, in order that he might have the means of crossing the river without delay, near the Schusterhäusern. He assembled near Dresden during the next few days the Guard, Bertrand, Marmont, Macdonald and Oudinot, whilst Lauriston was at Meissen. Ney had for the present remained in Leipzig, as his losses at Lützen had been very heavy; he was to march later to Torgau, in order to be able to push forward thence to Berlin; for this purpose Reynier also, coming up from Halle, as well as the new corps of Victor formed at Bernburg, and a division under Sebastiani, 12,000 men, coming from Lüneburg, were placed under his command. At the same time Ney's appearance at Torgau was to induce the enemy not to dispute the passage of the Elbe at Dresden too obstinately, for the Emperor said: "I do not know whether I shall be able to cross at Dresden; I fear I shall meet with difficulties in our passage there; for I have pontoniers, but no pontoons; they will not arrive for a fortnight. If I have no boats and the enemy defends the crossing seriously and exposes Dresden to the chances of war, I shall be forced to march to Torgau, but your presence at Torgau with your army-corps should make an impression upon the enemy, and induce him to renounce the plan of defending the Elbe."[1]

At first the Allies appeared to have every intention of disputing the crossing of the French; at any rate

[1] To Ney. Colditz, 6th May.

they established some forty guns at Uebigau on the 9th May, and directed a strong fire upon the point of crossing. But the Emperor ordered Drouet to place about sixty guns in position, and towards the end of the day the enemy withdrew, and during the night the Neustadt was also evacuated. Nevertheless, the local circumstances proved so little favourable to the construction of bridges, that the Emperor, now through the evacuation of the Neustadt in possession of the partially demolished stone bridge, preferred to restore the latter. The work continued the whole day of the 10th and the whole night, repeatedly urged on by his personal presence; and at 10 a.m. on the 11th of May the two arches which had been blown up were replaced by seven wooden piers, and Macdonald began to cross at the head of the army. On the next day, whilst the Emperor himself with the Guard and Oudinot remained in Dresden, he pushed his corps forward in the form of a fan, to facilitate the reconnaissance of the country; thus Bertrand was ordered to Königsbrück, Marmont to Kamenz, Macdonald to Bishofswerda, from which latter town he drove the Russians. Ney and Lauriston united at Torgau, the latter having also been placed under Ney's command, as well as Reynier, who had re-assumed command of the Saxons, 8000 men; Victor and Sebastiani were between Bernburg and Köthen with orders to march to Wittenberg.

The Prusso-Russian army had, after the evacuation of the line of the Elbe, fallen back behind the Spree; and had taken up a position on its right bank near Bautzen, where they decided to await attack. The Emperor had at first been very much in doubt as to the enemy's movements. He was inclined to think the Russians would retreat to Breslau, and the Prussians, on the other hand, to Berlin. Not until the night of the 13th did he receive definite news that the enemy had not separated, but had fallen back to

Bautzen. He was of opinion, however, that they would make no stand there, but continue the retreat to Breslau. But on the morning of the 17th he was informed that the Allies were ready for battle at Bautzen; and early on the 18th he sent orders to Ney to come up there, in order to fall on the enemy's right flank during the attack which he meditated. As the point on the battle-field which he was to aim at, he designated Dresha, in the rear of the Allies. Ney had already had his attention drawn to the fact that the enemy seemed to be preparing for battle at Bautzen, and consequently in his advance towards Berlin on the 17th he had made a slight change of direction, Lauriston marching from Dobrilugk to Senftenberg, Ney's own corps from Luckau to Kalau, and Reynier from Dahme to Luckau. On the 19th the above-mentioned orders from the Emperor reached the marshal at Hoyerswerda, whilst Lauriston arrived at Weissig and Reynier at Kalau. The remainder of his army the Emperor assembled behind Bautzen, on the left bank of the Spree.

At noon on the 18th he left Dresden and went to (99a) Harthan, whence he started early the next day, moving his headquarters to Klein Förstgen, not far from Bautzen. He reconnoitred the enemy's position personally, accompanied only by a small escort, from a rocky eminence near Stiebitz, and afterwards from a height above Salzförstgen, then from the Hill of Schmochtitz, and finally from the windmill of Lohsau. At 7 p.m. he returned to Little Förstgen. During the afternoon the sound of cannon had been audible from the direction of Königswartha; this sound increased towards evening, and at eight o'clock the Emperor mounted his horse again and rode to Klein Welkau, listening to the firing. Only when it ceased at midnight did he return to his headquarters.

The cause of the firing had been the fact that the (98) Allies, informed the day before that the corps of Lauriston was approaching by Seuftenberg, had sent out a Prusso-Russian corps under Barclay on the 19th, to meet it. The Russians met at Königswartha a division sent thither by Bertrand, which was to open communication with Ney. Observing no caution on the march, it was surprised and entirely routed. At Weissig the Prussians encountered the corps of Lauriston, and were engaged with it during the whole day. At nightfall Barclay returned to Bautzen.

(99a) In the evening of the 19th the Emperor's army was in the following order: on the right stood Oudinot as far as the Spree; Macdonald occupied the two sides of the Dresden road in front of Bautzen; to his left, opposite Nimmschütz, was Marmont; further to the left, towards Jeschütz, Bertrand, and at Förstgen stood the Guard,
(98) as a reserve. Of Ney's column, the leading division, Lauriston, was at Weissig, Ney himself at Maukendorf, and Reynier at Kalau. On the morning of the 20th
(99a) May, at 9 o'clock, the Emperor rode out to the Hill of Schmochtitz, to direct the battle. The enemy's army stood in front of him in the following positions: the vanguard had occupied Bautzen; the main body of the Russian army stood on the line from Klein Jenkowitz to Baschütz; to the right of it the Prussian corps Yorck; and at Burk the Prussian corps Kleist. Blücher was stationed between Kreckwitz and Pliskowitz, and finally Barclay formed the right wing at Gleina. The reserve was at Klein Baschütz

About noon the Emperor opened the attack. Macdonald advanced in the centre against Bautzen; here he found the stone bridge across the Spree intact and crossed; Marmont and Bertrand constructed four bridges and crossed the river likewise; and thus at 3 p.m. the French troops had gained a footing on the right bank, and directed their attacks against Bautzen. The town, after repeated attempts, was taken by a division of Marmont's corps at about 6 o'clock, and its defenders fell back upon a well-entrenched position, selected beforehand as their second line of defence. Kleist, who had held his position on the heights of Burk during the whole day against Marmont's attacks, fell back to his second line of defence between 8 and 9 o'clock, but not until Marmont's division had left Bautzen subsequently to having captured the town and had seized the heights of Nieder Keina on Kleist's left flank. Oudinot, also, had crossed the Spree at Grubschütz. He first drove the left wing of the Allies from the heights on which it had been posted, but was in his turn driven from them at the fall of night. Ney had only exchanged some shots with Barclay's advanced posts near Klix; he was still on the left bank of the Spree, and Reynier's division of his army corps had reached Hoyerswerda. Thus nothing really decisive happened on May 20th; the Allies, forced back from the banks of the Spree, had retreated to a second position, selected and fortified by them beforehand, whilst the French had succeeded in crossing the river in the face of the enemy, and had established themselves on the right bank of the Spree.

The Emperor returned about 9 p.m. from the battlefield to his headquarters, now in Bautzen itself; there he attended to some military affairs with Berthier until about midnight, and then, having dismissed the chief of the staff, he was busy working again until 5 a.m. At that hour he mounted his horse again and rode forward towards Klein Jenkowitz. Near a defile, which affords a view of the plain of Klein Jenkowitz and Baschütz, he dismounted. The main blow of the day could only be delivered by Ney, therefore any serious attempt at victory in the front by the main force was inadvisable until the moment when the marshal's attack on the flank would be effectively felt. The Emperor therefore waited at this point quietly for that moment, sending at 8 a.m., when his right wing was already engaged, orders to Ney to attack. In order to make up for his lost night's rest, he slept for a few hours within range of the enemy's fire. At a later date he expressed the opinion that "such a sleep gives the leader of a very large army the important advantage of waiting quietly for the reports and joint action of all his divisions, instead of perhaps being carried away by one single occurrence, of which he may have been an eye-witness."[1]

In the meantime, Oudinot, advancing in the direction of Mehltheuer, had kept the enemy's left wing engaged since the morning in desultory fighting. The Allies now occupied the following positions: on the right wing stood Barclay between Gleina and Marschwitz; in the centre Blücher on the heights near Kreckwitz; to the left Kleist and Yorck on the line Litten—Baschütz; whilst the left wing, composed of what had been the vanguard, held the heights and woods to the south-east of Baschütz, and the reserves were posted behind this latter village. Oudinot's attack was soon supported by Macdonald's appearance. At 8 o'clock, as mentioned above, the Emperor had sent to Ney the order to attack, on a slip of paper, written in lead pencil, commanding him to be in Preititz by 11 o'clock, and to attack the enemy's right wing. The marshal, who had commenced fighting at 9 o'clock, and had forced Barclay back *viâ* Preititz to Baruth, received the Emperor's order at Preititz at 10 o'clock. As he was not expected at this latter place until an hour later, according to that order, he now established himself in the village, not pressing forward at present any further in the direction of the enemy's line of communication, viz. the road through Wurschen.

There is a system of command which absolutely precludes any attempt at disobedience or any idea of deviating from the letter of an order. This gift of authority has always characterized great leaders, and the Emperor possessed it in a very high degree. But he who adopts this system of command claims infalli-

[1] Mémorial de Ste. Hélène, ii. 410.

bility for himself and kills in his subordinates the spirit of independent action. This also was in a high degree the case with Napoleon, and it explains the fact that the greatest leaders have never had great pupils. Napoleon curtailed all strategical thought in his subordinate officers, and trained them to utter dependence on himself, since he always claimed to guide everything and be responsible for everything. This increased, it is true, his personal standing as a general; but I cannot refrain from repeating that for the lasting success of an army, and consequently the assured maintenance of a state, the training and education of a definite school of leaders, though individually they may never reach the highest summit of greatness, is of greater value than the barren appearance of one gigantic genius like Napoleon. And the events of 1813 are specially calculated to teach us how the conjoint action of many independent free agents may conquer even genius in the end, for the latter, in order to remain victorious, must never once flag—a state of perfection which has not been granted to human beings, and against which the size of modern armies, the extent of modern theatres of war, and the development of modern science especially militate.

The capture of Preititz threatened the right wing of Blücher's position to such an extent, that the latter sent assistance to that village, and Kleist also hastened up to recapture it. Thus an obstinate fight began for the possession of this hamlet, and at about 1 p.m. the Prussians succeeded in becoming masters of it. The firing was quite audible at the Emperor's standpoint, and proved to him that Ney, with the left wing, had become seriously involved in the battle. He therefore mounted his horse and proceeded to an eminence near Nieder Keina, whence he noticed how by Ney's advance the enemy's position at Kreckwitz was already seriously threatened in flank. He therefore ordered Bertrand also to advance by Nieder Gurick and Marmont by Basankwitz, so as to turn it altogether. Blücher soon became aware that he could no longer hold out under the artillery fire of Marmont and Ney on his flank; he therefore evacuated the heights of Kreckwitz, and Yorck, sent thither to his support, found them already crowned by French batteries. Thereupon the Allies decided between 3 and 4 o'clock to relinquish their positions and commenced their retreat, to the left towards Löbau, and to the right towards Weissenberg.

The Emperor urged his troops to a vigorous pursuit of the retreating enemy; but here again his want of cavalry was fatally felt, and the Allies, who after all had abandoned the battle before being entirely defeated, retained their good order. The Emperor pitched his tent in the evening near the inn of Klein Burschwitz; Ney and Lauriston reached Wurschen, Reynier went a little beyond it, and the remainder bivouacked in the positions just stormed. The next day the Emperor started at 4 a.m. in pursuit of the enemy. The latter, who had again received some reinforcements, concentrated at Görlitz; Reynier was in touch with their rearguard, and here it was that a cannon ball struck down at Napoleon's side the man who of all men stood nearest to him, namely Duroc. In consequence, an order was published the next day, reducing the Emperor's retinue and settling definitely what persons were to form his immediate entourage. All others were to remain behind the squadron of mounted grenadiers, who in their turn were to be at a distance of more than a kilometre from the Emperor; "the persons accompanying the Emperor must always move in twos or fours, never in a body."[1]

During the next few days the Allies fell back in two columns by Bunzlau and Haynau, and by Löwenberg and Goldberg. On the 23rd they retired behind the

[1] Norvins, Portefeuille de 1813, i. 440.

Neisse, and at noon on the same day the Emperor arrived in Görlitz, and his army, crossing the Neisse, halted east of the town; but the following were still in rear: Lauriston at Hochkirch, Ney at Weissenberg, Oudinot at Bautzen; Victor, however, had come up closer to the army, and was now at Rothenburg. The next day the Emperor, again aiming at Berlin, commissioned Oudinot to seize that capital and to advance thither *viâ* Hoyerswerda, Luckau and Lubben. The French army, now again joined by Ney and Lauriston, followed the Allies during the next few days towards Bunzlau and Löwenberg; the latter, however, determined now not to continue their retreat any further in a direct easterly direction, but, wheeling to the south, to march towards Schweidnitz. Their left column consequently proceeded on the 26th to Liegnitz, whilst the right remained at Goldberg; the former succeeded in surprising with its cavalry one of Lauriston's divisions, and in inflicting considerable losses upon it.

The Emperor had been at Bunzlau since the preceding day, and issued orders thence on the 26th, at 6 a.m., that Lauriston and Reynier were to pursue towards Liegnitz, and Bertrand and Macdonald towards Goldberg, Marmont, to whom the newly-formed Cavalry Division of Latour-Maubourg, 8000 men, was attached, was to operate against the enemy's left flank and to ascertain where his main body really was; he was to keep between the two principal columns. Ney's corps (the marshal himself was, however, in supreme command of Lauriston and Reynier) was kept back at Bunzlau by the Emperor, with the Guard, as a reserve. Victor, who had been told to move on Glogau to relieve that fortress, now received orders to march to Sprottau, and, if necessary, to support Oudinot's operations against Berlin. "Napoleon was extremely elated during these days. It tickled his self-love to see the enemy driven along in front of him, and to know that he would soon be in possession of a large part of Silesia, where his movements would be facilitated by a better supply of provisions."[1]

On the 28th May we find the French army stationed as follows: The Emperor with the Guard at Liegnitz, Ney with Reynier, Lauriston, and his own corps extended from Liegnitz to Neumarkt; Marmont at Jauer, Macdonald and Bertrand between this latter town and Goldberg. It was the Emperor's intention to advance with his main army to Breslau, and to pursue the Allies, of whose flank movement to Schweidnitz he was aware, only with Bertrand and Macdonald. Thus he would again, as so often before, have turned the enemy strategically; for being in possession of the line of the Oder and attacking with his main body from Breslau, possibly through Strehlen, the communications of the Allies behind Schweidnitz, he could force them back against the Eulen mountains and annihilate them. But though conception and system were the same as in 1805 and 1806, and though we may derive from them the same lessons, the *moral* of his army was no longer the same. He might possibly have been able to carry his plan through with an army like that of 1805 and 1806; but his energy, weakened by victory, by age and indulgence, was no longer equal to the task of making up by increased exertions on his own part, as the youthful Bonaparte had done in 1796, for the imperfections of his raw army to a sufficient extent to risk the last throw after the partial successes of Lützen and Bautzen. Just as after the partial success of Wagram, a truce, premature from Napoleon's point of view, was agreed upon at Znaym, so here also hostilities ceased; and again the career of the general showed that a genius may indeed gain victories even with the most imperfect instruments, but that a lasting success can only be secured by the organization of the army on a sound basis.

O. v. O., 125.

So early as the 26th the Emperor had sent Caulaincourt to begin negotiations; and on the 1st June, in the evening, the plenipotentiaries concluded an armistice for 36 hours, beginning at 2 p.m. on the 2nd June, after which, without any resumption of hostilities, a definite truce was to begin. This latter was to last until the 20th July, with six days' grace. Later on, however, it was extended until the 10th August, so that the 16th August was the actual date of the resumption of hostilities.

In the meantime, the Allied army had continued its movements, and at the beginning of the truce was on the line Nimptsch—Strehlen. The Emperor had Ney, Lauriston and Reynier in the neighbourhood of Breslau, Macdonald and Bertrand in the vicinity of Schweidnitz; his own headquarters were at Neumarkt, with the Guard. Victor, sent to Sprottau on the 26th, moved afterwards on Glogau and raised the investment. Oudinot had been at Hoyerswerda on the 27th, had there repulsed an attack of the Prussian corps operating in defence of Berlin, and had then advanced towards the capital. But at Luckau he again met with the enemy, and failed in his assault upon their position; he consequently fell back upon Uebigau on the Black Elster, where the truce arrested him. Finally, in the north, Davout and Vandamme had (95) joined forces and had advanced against Hamburg, which was occupied only by a weak and isolated corps. This corps, waiting in vain for the 25,000 Swedes, who lay at Mecklenburg under Bernadotte, to come to its support, and perceiving, on the other hand, that Denmark was preparing to second Davout's attack, evacuated Hamburg during the night of the 29th May. Thus this town also was in the Emperor's hands, when on the 9th June the news of the armistice arrived there.

From this time forward Hamburg remained uninterruptedly in possession of the French troops, in spite of all the defeats of their armies in the field, until the 25th May, 1814, when, after the Emperor's fall, the new

Government ordered the evacuation of the town. Twelve thousand men marched out; battles and sickness had cost the French 17,000 men, and 5000 men still lay in the hospitals. Davout had, in the fullest measure, put into practice the Emperor's ideas as to the defence of strong places. " It is essential, both for the commander's honour and the glory of the French arms, to prolong a defence. One must hold out until the last moment, without taking into consideration whether relief is coming or not. To surrender one day too soon is to commit a military crime. A commandant must think of nothing but his fortress, and prolong its defence, without being influenced by political reasons."[1] "Commanders of fortresses have not to trouble about politics; it is no business of theirs to take care of the safety of the empire; they are entrusted with the defence of a post, and they must defend it to the utmost, since every day added to the defence of a fortress may bring a chance of relief, or may be of the greatest use to the state, inasmuch as it prevents the enemy from disposing of his troops elsewhere. . . . In a word, a fortress must hold out until it has no longer either bread or ammunition; or until the enemy, having crossed the ditch, has gained a footing in the breach; and even then the governor is to blame if he has not thrown up works which may render the breach ineffective."[2] Resistance of this sort can result only from the greatest perseverance, steadfastness and energy, coupled with the utmost severity against the civil inhabitants of the place. And if these latter, as was the case in Hamburg, are hostile to the garrison, this severity will have to be increased and the people kept in terror, if necessary.

A country cannot be permanently ruled by terror, as is proved by the French Revolution; but a country, and still more a fortified place, easily can be, while the war lasts, and even in our modern wars, in which the

---

[1] C. N. To Berthier. Dresden, 19th June, 1813.
[2] C. N. Note on the defence of Corfu. Rambouillet, 19th May, 1811.

whole population of the country invaded by the enemy is ready to take a share, to rule by terror is indispensable. The Emperor acted therefore quite correctly in sending Davout to Hamburg; and he, as well as Vandamme and Carra Saint-Cyr, served the purposes of war in a perfectly correct manner, though their acts may individually have been unjust and arbitrary, or even rough and cruel. Every soldier will subscribe to Sporschil's criticism: "There is certainly no military power in Europe but will wish for men like Davout to command besieged fortresses. His hard measures were rendered necessary by the exigencies of war."[1]

The lines of demarcation between the two parties for the duration of the armistice ran for the French army from the Bohemian frontier in a straight line by Lähn to the Katzbach; followed this river and the Oder as far as Müllrose, descended thence to the Elbe along the Saxon frontier, and followed its course. That for the Allied armies passed from the Bohemian frontier by Landshut, followed thence the Striegan Wasser as far as Canth, from which place, excluding Breslau, it ran to the Oder and there joined the first mentioned line. There remained therefore between the two armies a small neutral zone in Silesia, five leagues broad, unoccupied.

(98)

That the truce of Poischwitz formed one of the most important turning points in Napoleon's career, the course of subsequent events has proved. Was it also, as Jomini thinks, the greatest mistake he ever committed? If we consider the matter simply from the military standpoint, it must certainly be called a mistake. By their politically correct, but in a military sense, considering the relative strength on the two sides, somewhat risky retreat behind Schweidnitz, the Allies exposed themselves to the danger of being, by the turning of their right wing by the French army from

[1] Die grosse Chronik, part i. vol. iii. 1216.

Breslau *viâ* Jordansmuhle or Strehlen, entirely surrounded or forced into the mountains; a strategical situation at least as favourable to the Emperor as any, even the best, that had ever occurred in his campaigns. And yet he concluded an armistice! The Emperor himself said: " I decided for it on two grounds; first, because of my want of cavalry, which prevented me dealing great blows, and secondly, because of the assumption of a hostile attitude on the part of Austria." [1]

We must doubt whether these two reasons fully explain this surprising act. However troublesome his want of cavalry and the uncertain condition of his army, generally speaking, may have proved, and have discounted the successes gained, compared with what might have been expected, and rightly so, with other instruments, yet one tremendous advantage remained, viz. his great superiority in numbers. The effect of masses and their correct employment had ever been the most characteristic features of the Emperor's strategy, and had won him his successes. He had known how to appear on the scene with superior numbers; and, where the relative strengths did not allow this, he had been able, by his strategy, to ensure superiority at the decisive point. Here he had the superiority already in his hands, and yet he renounced it and concluded an armistice!

His fear of Austria? The man who fought Austerlitz, when Prussia was in a position, and almost resolved, to fall upon his rear; the man who advanced into Poland and Eastern Prussia, when Austria might have played the same part; the man who, leaving the hostile continent in his rear, wanted to cross over to England; the man who continually ran every strategical risk when he could hope to gain a decisive victory in battle; this man can hardly have been forced to such a decision by such a reason. But even if the two reasons adduced by himself were really the grounds which decided him, we should still have

[1] C. N. To Clarke. Neumarkt, 2nd June.

to call these very reasons a mistake, because they showed that he now yielded to considerations, the neglect of which had hitherto been the source of his success. Hitherto his success had been due to the fact that his genius was able to overcome all material difficulties, by using his instrument, his army, recklessly, without a thought of its condition; and because he had always boldly and correctly recognized that the danger to which he might have exposed himself in any strategical position vanished when he won a great and decisive victory. If he acted differently here, he turned aside from what had made him great; he became untrue to himself, and therefore was in the wrong. We saw premonitory symptoms of this decrease of genius even at Ratisbon and at Wagram. At the opening of the campaign of 1813, and at his first appearance at Lützen, he rose to his old grandeur; but at Bautzen he once more showed signs of failure. How favourable was his position at this battle; yet Ney's entrance into the fight, which might have annihilated the enemy, only brought about their retreat. The old Napoleonic conduct of a battle was wanting, which knew so unfailingly how to give the decisive thrust. The armistice showed a yielding to circumstances; formerly it had been characteristic of his genius to make circumstances yield to him. (99b) (98)

Here again, moreover, we realize from the great example of Napoleon that human affairs are not dependent on blind good or bad luck, but on the man himself. It happened more and more frequently, that the Emperor's genius flagged at the critical moment, and the consequences were at first, incomplete victories, then half-successes, until finally, circumstances worked together in such a manner that they brought about his fall. "All great events hang by a hair. The man of ability takes advantage of everything and neglects nothing that can give him a chance of success; whilst the less able man sometimes loses everything by neglecting a single one of those chances."[1] All his actions were connected with his own individual personality and based upon it alone; so when this became weak, there was no longer anything in his army or state that could support or sustain him.

If Napoleon's strategy possessed a grandeur of conception and boldness of execution, such as I, for one, cannot find in the same degree in Frederick or the Archduke Charles, yet the conduct of these two Generals does not exhibit such a declension; they remained true to themselves and their nature, though they never fully attained to the height of Napoleon's military genius. To use a simile, they resembled steadily burning flames, which give a lasting warmth and consume their substance only so far as it can easily be replaced; whilst Napoleon's genius, like a flaring firebrand, certainly made, when in full blaze, an overwhelming impression upon the spectator, but also consumed rapidly away, and, though fitfully throwing a few bright showers of sparks as high as ever, finally sank down into extinction.

[1] C. N. To the Minister of Foreign Affairs, Passariano, 26th September, 1797.

CHAPTER VIII.

DRESDEN.

FROM the moment when the armistice was decided upon, the Emperor began, in his strategical considerations, to look upon Austria as his enemy, for he was well aware that he would never be able to consent to purchase its alliance, or its friendly mediation, or even its neutrality by any sacrifice, however small, on his part. Thus he had to take into account, that on the whole semi-circle from Mecklenburg through Brandenburg and Silesia to the frontiers of Bohemia and Saxony, hostile forces would collect against him, whose total numbers would at least be equal to his own, or possibly exceed them. In order to be able to meet them with the mass of his army at any point most important for the moment, and to do so at the right time, he must be entirely master of the chord of this great arc, viz. the Elbe. He therefore chose this stream for his base, and his first task was to render it secure. He already had full possession of its central portion, for he held the fortresses of Torgau, Wittenberg and Magdeburg. It is true he thought it would be advisable to still further increase its strength by the construction of temporary fortifications opposite the mouths of the canal of Planen and of the Havel, but as the local conditions on the left bank proved unfavourable to this plan, and as he was not allowed to cross to the right bank before the cessation of the truce, he postponed the execution of this

(100)

plan for the present. But in the beginning of July he personally inspected the fortresses along the Middle Elbe.

More important, however, was the question of rendering the Upper and Lower Elbe secure. And here two points of support had to be considered, whose possession the Emperor intended absolutely to secure to himself, viz. Dresden and Hamburg. The manner in which these two places were to be absolutely secured by the employment of the art of fortification, was to be different in each case. Dresden would never be quite deprived of the protection of an army, since the theatre of war would in any case be always in the district to the east and not far from the capital of Saxony. Hamburg, on the other hand, distant from the principal theatre of events, might easily have to depend for its defence on a proportionately small detached force.

(95)

(100) The Emperor therefore decreed that the Neustadt of Dresden was, by the erection of earthworks, to be changed into an entrenched camp, "because it may be assumed, that circumstances may compel me to defend the right bank and to station 50,000 or 60,000 men there."[1] On the left bank, on the other hand, he only wished to secure the capital against a *coup de main*, for he was convinced that, if he placed his army there in an entrenched camp, "I should only be invested and my communications with France would be lost;"[1] moreover he had no time to construct works on such a scale. What he wanted here was merely to construct a complete *enceinte*; "the sum-total of all that is necessary to prepare for the defence of the suburbs, is to provide the walls with loopholes; insure the inter-communications, so that field-pieces may be rapidly moved about within the radius of the suburbs; and close the gaps by palisades, where there are no walls, leaving six or eight openings for the use of

[1] C. N. Note on the entrenched camp of Dresden. Dresden, 5th July.

the public."[1] If after this there were time and opportunity, it would always be possible to throw up earthworks in front of the gaps left open. The Emperor thought: " When all this has been done, it is plain that Dresden may be looked upon as a fortified place ; " but added immediately, for he knew as well as any one how to estimate the value of such works in comparison with the permanent defences of real fortresses, " not, if the Elbe is surrendered, but only as long as the army remains in advance of this river."[2] The degree of defensive capacity of such works must always depend on the garrison, though the former are calculated materially to increase the former's defensive capacity.

With Hamburg the case was different. " The possession of Hamburg is of the greatest political importance, and I cannot feel reassured, as to this important point, until Hamburg can be considered a fortified place and until it is provisioned for several months and provided with all that is necessary for its defence."[3] This was the end he aimed at; and how can this end be reached? " A town like Hamburg could only be defended by a garrison of 25,000 men and an immense amount of material, and in order to run the risk of losing a garrison of 25,000 men and enormous warlike stores, we must have a place, which could be held at least two months after the opening of the first trenches. But, in order to enable the fortifications of Hamburg to hold out two months after the opening of the first trench, no less than ten years and thirty to forty million francs would be required. And yet I wish to hold Hambrg, not only against its own inhabitants and against troops of the line, but even against a siege-train. I wish not only to render the town safe against a *coup de main*, if 50,000 men appear before it, but to enable it to defend itself and force the enemy to

(95)

[1] Note on the entrenched camp of Dresden. Dresden, 5th July.
[2] C. N. Note on the defence of Dresden. Dresden, 28th June.
[3] C. N. To Davout. Dresden, 15th June.

open trenches, and to hold out fifteen to twenty days after the opening of the trenches."[1] It was therefore to be a provisional fortress. For this purpose the Emperor demanded a citadel faced with earth and provided with palisades between the river and the town, as a place of refuge for the garrison and a bridge-head; the construction of a bastioned *enceinte* and a ditch, the closing of the gorges of the bastions, the more important ones by loopholed walls, and the others by palisading; a palisaded covered way, the glacis to be cleared, bridges over the small arms of the river to the islands, two large ferries over the main stream and the arming and palisading of Hamburg. "If you take all these works as completed, and they can be finished within a few months, it will be clear, that four companies of artillery and 5500 men will be able to hold Hamburg."[1]

There is probably no better military situation in existence, to illustrate in one single example the mutual relations between an army in the field and the various forms of fortification, than this base of the Elbe chosen by Napoleon, the arrangements made for its defence, and above all, the Emperor's comments on it. Its full security on the Middle Elbe, which is permanently fortified; the possibility of holding the point of support on the Lower Elbe, where the works were executed provisionally, not for two months, but at least for two or three weeks, even against very superior forces. And finally the conviction that he would lose the field fortifications thrown up at Dresden, if the army were not present there for their defence. All this shows the clearness with which Napoleon, in all circumstances, could recognize material, actual facts, and take them into account.

(100) Thus he had rendered his base secure, and could calmly look beyond it to the countries where the die would be cast. He ordered all the roads to Silesia from Saxony, as well as the course of the Elbe and the Bohemian frontier,

[1] C. N. To Davout. Bunzlau, 7th June.

DRESDEN

to be zealously reconnoitred. He had laid down the rules for such reconnaissances: "When I ask for a reconnaissance, I do not wish people to bring me a plan of campaign. An engineer has no business to mention the enemy. His business is to reconnoitre the roads, their character, the slopes, ravines, and obstacles; to ascertain whether they are fit for waggons, but to abstain altogether from plans of campaign."[1]

The definite plan for the coming campaign was fixed by the Emperor in August. He decided upon an offensive operation with his left wing, 100,000 men, upon Berlin and against the Lower Oder; for this Davout was ordered up from Hamburg, Oudinot, to whom three army corps and one corps of cavalry were entrusted, from Lower Lusatia, and one division from Magdeburg. His right wing, formed of the main army, some 300,000 men, was for the present to remain on the defensive, and he now searched the map for the point best suited for the purpose. "I should prefer to remain at Liegnitz";[2] but he calculated that he would in that case be too distant from his base and his principal object, Dresden, and since the latter town, as we have seen, could only be protected by field fortifications, he was obliged to remain in a position to be able to hasten up to its protection. On the other hand, to divide his forces in two, place half his army at Liegnitz and half within reach of Dresden, was too much against his principles of concentration; "I certainly feel some regret at giving up Liegnitz, but, if I occupied it, it would be difficult to keep all my forces concentrated."[2]

He therefore retreated further on the road to the Elbe and stood fast at Bunzlau. This point gave him "the advantage of leaving me in a situation to prevent the enemy from passing between me and the Oder,"[2] but it still appeared rather too advanced to him, and therefore he decided to put his army in a position between Görlitz and

---

[1] C. N. Orders; Imperial camp of Schönbrun, 9th August, 1809.
[2] C. N. Directions for Ney and Marmont. Dresden, 12th August.

Bautzen, holding the camps of Königstein and Dresden, "so that I cannot be cut off from the Elbe, but shall always hold this river; I shall be able to feed the troops through Dresden, and see what the Russians and Austrians are going to do, and take advantage of circumstances . . . . . if the Austrians and Russians wish to fight a battle, we shall crush them. If we lose the battle, we shall be nearer the Elbe and be more in a position to take advantage of their stupid mistakes."[1] The next day he settled upon some further details of this position; the camp of Königstein was to be occupied by one corps, the I. Corps was to go to Bautzen, the Guards to Görlitz; the II. Corps between there and Zittau; the VIII. Corps would stand at Zittau; the XI. stood already at Löwenberg; the VI. at Bunzlau; the V. at Grünberg, and finally the III. as advanced guard between Haynau and Liegnitz.

Now, what was the enemy going to do? The Emperor enumerates the three possibilities of their offensive, assuming that 100,000 Austrians stood in Bohemia and less than 200,000 Prussians and Russians in Silesia. In this he, as a matter of fact, estimated the proportion of numbers too favourably as regards himself; the Allies were going to have at their disposal against him 320,000 men; not: "less than 300,000," on this part of the theatre of war, whilst he himself would not have the 300,000 estimated men ready on resuming hostilities. But this difference was not of great account for the plan of campaign as a whole; it only shows how very much the Emperor was already inclined to see things more as he desired them, than as they actually were. He was of opinion that the Austrians could advance either upon Dresden by Peterswalde, in which case, whilst the corps from Königstein, and afterwards that from Bautzen, defended the capital, he would have time to come up himself with the Guards and the II. Corps. Or, if they advanced *viâ* Zittau, he would also be able to meet them in time with the VIII.

[1] C. N. Directions for Ney and Marmont. Dresden, 12th August.

and the II. Corps and the Guards and subsequently with the I. Army Corps and two divisions of cavalry. Should the Prusso-Russian army take the offensive simultaneously with the Austrians, there would still remain four army corps and one body of cavalry at Bautzen, to oppose them. "The third alternative movement of the Austrians would be to advance viâ Josefstadt and to combine with the Russo-Prussian army, all breaking out together. In that case my whole army would collect at Bunzlau."[1] He therefore thought he could in any case look forward calmly to the battle, and he hoped for it, for "it seems to me, that this present campaign cannot lead to any good results, if no great battle takes place to begin with."[2]

The intention to advance was the first part of the (95) plan for the campaign of August, 1813, which took shape in the Emperor's mind. To begin with, Davout was to take up an offensive position in front of Hamburg, at the cessation of the armistice, with his corps of 30,000 men, in order to draw, by the threat of an offensive, as many of the enemy as possible on himself and away from Berlin; or if this did not happen, he was to advance on the real offensive towards the Lower Oder. "The part you have to play is a very active one. It is especially necessary that your threatening movement should be made early, so that the enemy may not be able to turn his whole forces against our corps advancing upon Berlin, and that you may not be neglected."[3] "You must therefore manœuvre in such a manner, that you harass the enemy on his right flank, and effect a junction with the Duke of Reggio's corps on its march to Berlin."[4]

Here, the principal offensive would fall to Oudinot's (100) share, who had 70,000 men assigned to him for this purpose; he was to push forward to Berlin, and the

[1] C. N. Instructions for Ney, Gouvion Saint-Cyr, Macdonald and Marmont. Dresden, 13th August, evening.
[2] C. N. Direction for Ney and Marmont. Dresden, 12th August.
[3] C. N. To Davout. Dresden, 8th August.
[4] C. N. To Davout. Dresden, 12th August.

(95) Emperor reckoned that he would reach that town by the 4th day after the resumption of hostilities. As soon as he had reached Berlin, in which movement the Emperor anticipated no particular difficulties, he was to drive the enemy behind the Oder, relieve Stettin and Küstrin and invest Spandau, an operation which the Emperor had spoken of in July, as one of the first to be undertaken. "It will be our first task to relieve Küstrin and Stettin. . . . Another operation, which will also be among our first tasks in this campaign, will be the siege of Spandau."[1]

(100) This then was Napoleon's plan for the opening of the coming campaign, the first great defensive plan he had resolved upon; and our first question will be, whether he was right in choosing the defensive. He was only right if circumstances really compelled him to it, for without being absolutely forced to it, no great leader will renounce the offensive, the more effective form of warfare. And if we wish to deny the necessity of the defensive in this case, the question immediately arises, to what point ought the offensive to have been directed. As on every theatre of war, there were three directions for it here; to the right, to the left, or straight forward; to the right against Bohemia and the Main Army, to the left against Mark Brandenburg and the North Army, and straight forward against Silesia and the Prusso-Russian army. The last two directions, implying the seeking out of the enemy at a distance, if he did not approach of his own accord, were rendered impossible by the fact, that the enemy's main army, breaking out over the Erzgebirge, would in that case seize the Emperor's base, the Elbe, and his point of support, Dresden.

But could the latter not penetrate into Bohemia, and there attack the Main Army of the Allies? Certainly in this case also, the other two armies could have advanced in his rear, reached the Elbe, and even taken Dresden,

[1] C. N. To Sorbier. Dresden, 17th July.

DRESDEN

but all these losses would have been far outweighed by a victory over the enemy's Main Army, as had been proved already in Napoleon's career. All this would have been the case, if only that victory over the Main Army could have been secured. But it was quite possible—and in the circumstances even probable—that the Main Army of the Allies would avoid giving battle, in which case the Emperor would either, if he became aware of this in time, have had to deliver a blow at hazard, which was both risky and dangerous in his present position, or, if he penetrated too far into Bohemia, he would have got into a most dangerous situation, which would undoubtedly have led up to another Leipzig.

The reason, therefore, which induced him to reject every one of the three directions in which he might have taken the offensive, was in each case his anxiety for his base. We now ask, was this anxiety really a question of the first magnitude? Had not the Emperor formerly, e.g. in 1805 and 1806, ventured to neglect this point in a measure, in the certainty that a victory would compensate for everything? Here, the proportion of numbers on the two sides exerted its influence. In itself this would not have absolutely excluded an offensive on his part, but, if we assume this to be taken by the Emperor's 350,000 men against the Allies' 430,000, and add to it the loss of their base by the former, he would have been lost. It was different in 1805 and 1806, where the Emperor ran a similar risk, but where he possessed such a superiority of numbers, that, if the enemy undertook to cut him off, they would themselves have been cut off. Here, the two circumstances, viz. the want of a suitable goal and the disproportion of numbers, worked together, to render the defensive necessary, and therefore it was the only right course to pursue.

And now, having come to this conclusion, the question arises, whether, if the defensive was in itself necessary, the form here chosen was the best under the given circumstances. This question must unhesitatingly be answered in the affirmative. The most effective form of a defence consists always in short offensive dashes against that one of the concentrically approaching enemies who is most easily reached and threatens to become the most dangerous, and, if a large river, difficult to cross, such as the Elbe, makes one's rear secure, these thrusts can be delivered most effectively from such a base. This indeed was the reason why the Emperor had been loth to extend his lines as far as Liegnitz. The enemy certainly could have turned this base of the Elbe by a very wide enveloping movement; this could not have been done on the left wing, because of Hamburg and Davout, but on the right wing the enemy could have advanced with his main army *viâ* Bayreuth. In that case the Emperor, however, would "have wished them 'bon voyage,' and allowed them to go on, sure that they would come back quicker than they went. What is of importance to me is not to be cut off from Dresden and the Elbe; I care little for being cut off from France." [1]

Lastly, the question remains to be asked, whether the offensive movement of the left French wing upon Berlin and the enemy's northern army was justified; and this also we shall have to answer in the affirmative, if there was a just proportion between the advantages to be gained and the stake involved. The advantage expected was an extension to the left of the theatre of war as far as the Lower Oder, and this advantage was all the greater, as the north-western course of the Elbe limited the Emperor's sphere of action on the left wing. This very wing being extended, with the possession of the Lower Oder, which runs nearly due north-east, and a position acquired, flanking the Saxon and Silesian theatres of war. If we consider Napoleon's position on the inner line, every extension of the theatre of war, every further extension of his enemies, was a

[1] C. N. To Saint-Cyr. Bautzen, 17th August.

weighty advantage to him. Besides, Küstrin and Stettin would be relieved, Spandau besieged, and the capture of Berlin would undoubtedly have produced a great moral effect. The stake involved consisted of 100,000 men, which would keep in play an equal number of the enemy, and, considering the personal qualities of Bernadotte, with which the Emperor was so well acquainted, he could reckon upon success. And even if the movement failed, there always remained to the French a sure retreat through Wittenberg and Magdeburg. In considering any advance into Mark Brandenburg, one is liable to be biassed in one's judgment by the later failures of Grossbeeren and Dennewitz, forgetting that these defeats could not be anticipated, and that the Emperor was, considering everything, fully justified in expecting a very different result. We can easily imagine how very favourable the situation would have been for the Emperor, if, while he held the Upper Elbe, as he did, Davout had been with 100,000 men at Küstrin, and the Prussians, who certainly would have made a stand somewhere, had been beaten, and Bernadotte, as was indeed his intention, had fallen back upon Swedish Pomerania.

On the other hand, we cannot conceal the fact that here the Emperor again betrayed his ever-increasing inclination to look at things as he wished them to be. His contempt for the forces constituting the Northern Army, whom he continued to call a rabble, did not correspond to the facts; besides he undoubtedly over-estimated the effect which a capture of Berlin would have produced. He expected results from the capture of this geographical point, which in war a victory over the enemy's active forces alone gives, and which in the circumstances of the time could only be attained by such a victory. Marmont is probably right in saying: "Passion prompted him to move as rapidly as possible against Prussia. He desired the first cannon-shots to be directed again Berlin; he wished to wreak a heavy and terrible vengeance immediately hostilities were resumed."[1]

We must entirely approve of the general plan of the second campaign of 1813, though subsequent mistakes in its execution caused it to fail; we must approve of it not only in the fact that it was defensive, but also in the nature of this defensive. " It seems to me, that to bring about a decisive and brilliant result, the best way is to keep in a close formation and allow the enemy to approach."[2] "What is quite clear is that 400,000 men, supported by a system of fortresses and with such a stream as the Elbe for their base, cannot be turned."[3]

At the moment of the resumption of hostilities the Emperor's army was disposed as follows:—

The Emperor.

Chief of the Staff: Berthier.   Headquarters: Dresden.

The Guards		58,000 men	Dresden.
I. Corps:	Vandamme	33,000 men	Ordered up from the North; on the March to Dresden; arrived there on the 17th August.
II. Corps:	Victor	25,000 men	Rothenburg
III. Corps:	Ney	40,000 men	Liegnitz.
IV. Corps:	Bertrand	21,000 men	Peitz.
V. Corps:	Lauriston	28,000 men	Goldberg.
VI. Corps:	Marmont	28,000 men	Bunzlau.
VII. Corps:	Reynier	21,000 men	Kalau.
VIII. Corps:	Poniatowski	7,000 men	Ostritz.
XI. Corps:	Macdonald	24,000 men	Löwenberg.
XII. Corps:	Oudinot	19,000 men	Baruth.
XIII. Corps:	Davout	30,000 men	Near Bergdorf in front of Hamburg.
XIV. Corps:	Gouvion St. Cyr	36,000 men	In the camp of Pirna.

---

[1] Mém. v. 139.
[2] C. N. Instructions to Ney and Marmont, 12th August.
[3] C. N. To Saint-Cyr. Bautzen, 17th August.
[4] The IX. Corps, Augereau, was forming at Würzburg. The X. Corps, Rapp, formed the garrison of Danzig.

Cavalry Reserve.[1]
Murat.

1. Corps.	Latour Maubourg:	16,000 men	Görlitz.
2. Corps.	Sebastiani:	10,000 men	Freistadt.
3. Corps.	Arrighi:	11,000 men	Dahme.
4. Corps.	Kellermann:	5,000 men	Zittau.

It must be noted, that the numbers given above are the strengths estimated on the 6th August, and not the actual strength of the 16th August, so that, to arrive at the numbers with which the Emperor, as a matter of fact, entered the campaign, some not inconsiderable deductions have to be made. In the enemy's camp, he was estimated at 350,000 men, in accordance with the total result of the reports collected, and as they were in Germany itself, these reports were likely to be true, and from other sources, we may take that number as approximately correct. If the Emperor himself frequently referred to 400,000 men, it is due to the fact, that he on the one hand liked to use round numbers in his considerations, and on the other hand, as we know, always represented his forces, before fighting, to his generals, at as high a figure as possible, though after a victory they always became considerably inferior to those of the enemy.

"The Allies stood divided into three groups. The Main Army, 230,000 men, composed of Austrians, Prussians and Russians, stood under the immediate chief-command of Schwarzenberg, who nominally had also the supreme command in this war; it was accompanied by the headquarters of the three monarchs and stood in Northern Bohemia, in the neighbourhood of Melnik. The Silesian Army, 95,000 Prussians and Russians under Blücher, had, disregarding the conditions of the armistice, advanced on the 14th August into the neutral zone, and taken up a position in front of Breslau and near Striegau. Finally, the Northern Army, Swedes, Prussians and Russians with

---

[1] The 5th Corps, L'heritier, was still in the rear, marching up. The 5th (a) Corps, Milhaud, was only just forming.

various auxiliary corps, 156,000 men under Bernadotte (from which, however, some divisions were detached on special service, investments of fortresses, etc., so that its effective numbers can only be put at 110,000 men), lay around Berlin.

On the 15th August, at 5 p.m., the Emperor left Dresden, examined the Lilienstein carefully that evening, and arrived at Bautzen about 2 a.m. on the 16th; here he also remained during the 17th; he had the Guards with him. Having received news that a large part of the Russian forces had started from Silesia to Bohemia as a reinforcement for the Main Army, he intended to mass his army behind Zittau at Eckartsberg in the space between the Elbe and the Iser mountains, and to await the main attack there. For this purpose Victor was ordered up to Zittau. On the other hand, however, he took into consideration the fact that Blücher, whom he credited with 50,000 men after the departure of the Russians, might advance, and in that case he would fall upon him. Having thus beaten the central mass of the Allies, he would, standing as he was on the inner line between their two exterior masses, advance against one of these and attack it in its turn. "The army of Bunzlau, which numbers 130,000—140,000 men, without the Guards, can be reinforced by the latter, and I can break out with 180,000 men against Blücher, Sacken and Wittgenstein, who are, as it seems, marching forward against my troops this day, and once I have annihilated or reduced these corps, the equilibrium will be destroyed, and I shall be able, according to the success of the army which is marching upon Berlin, to support this latter against Berlin, or march through Bohemia behind the army which is invading Germany."[1] In the meantime he was going to wait till he could see his way better, and sent orders to Vandamme at 9 p.m. to come up to Bautzen, intending to move him forward thence either to Zittau, or,

[1] C. N. To Saint-Cyr. Bautzen, 17th August.

DRESDEN

if the enemy should threaten Dresden on the left bank of the Elbe, to send him back again thither to Saint-Cyr's support. To this marshal he set the following tasks: "to gain time, dispute the ground and hold Dresden, keep up secure and active communication with Vandamme and the headquarters; this is what you have, for the moment, to attend to carefully."[1] In the evening of the 17th the Emperor went to Reichenbach, and on the 18th he arrived at Görlitz.

Here he obtained confirmation of the news that 40,000 Russians had started from Silesia for the main army in Bohemia, and had been on the preceding day at Böhmisch Leipa; he therefore determined to go to Zittau. "I shall possibly penetrate immediately into Bohemia, in order to fall upon the Russians and catch them on the march."[2] However, he still remained inactive, waiting to see what the enemy would do. "In this situation I am waiting to see what the enemy are going to do; and whilst my corps, concentrated at Löwenberg, Bunzlau, Zittau and Görlitz, hold the Austrian, Prussian and Russian armies in check, I am prosecuting my manœuvre upon Berlin. Up to the present we have only very conflicting reports as to the enemy's movements. It is reported that 60,000 men of the Russian and Prussian armies have gone into Bohemia, and that the Emperor Alexander arrived at Prague on the 15th. If this is the case, they will either take the offensive along the road through Zittau, the only serviceable road for their advance on the right bank, when they will be arrested by the camp of Zittau and General Vandamme's corps, as well as by the reserves from Görlitz which I can move thither in a day and a half; or they will manœuvre on the left bank of the Elbe and break out by Teplitz and Peterswalde, in order to march upon Dresden, in which case Marshal Saint-Cyr can assemble

[1] C. N. To Saint-Cyr. Bautzen, 17th August.
[2] C. N. To Vandamme. Görlitz, 18th August.

60,000 men in two days, and in four I can be there with 150,000 men; or finally the enemy will enter upon operations beyond our calculations, and will penetrate into Germany, marching either upon Munich or upon Nürnberg, in which case they will leave the whole of Bohemia open for my offensive. But if, on the other hand, the Russian army has not passed into Bohemia, or only an insignificant corps has gone thither, I shall be able to collect 200,000 men in two days against the enemy's army. You see therefore that the plan of the campaign is drawn up on a large scale."[1]

On the following day, the 19th, the Emperor left Görlitz at 7 a.m., and went personally to Zittau, to the Bohemian frontier, in order to gain some insight into the state of affairs. He pushed forward a strong reconnaissance over the ridge of the frontier mountains as far as Gabel and accompanied it in person. About midnight he returned to Zittau. He had thus gained the certainty that Schwarzenberg had been at Melnik on the 17th and at Schlan on the 18th, that he was now marching away in a westerly direction, and that the Russians were apparently following him. There was thus for the present nothing serious to be apprehended in the passes near Zittau, and no advantageous blow to be delivered against the Russians in Bohemia; he therefore returned to his resolution to fall upon Blücher. He calculated that if the Bohemian army, hearing that the Emperor himself had been at Gabel, turned towards Zittau, it could not arrive there in less than five days, and then Victor and Poniatowski would offer a strenuous resistance in the mountain passes there, and Vandamme in those of Rumburg: "the Emperor desires that you should fight to the bitter end."[2] This would at any rate give time for Napoleon to return from his forward movement towards Silesia, which he called "an episode in the operations

---

[1] C. N. To Clarke. Görlitz, 18th August.
[2] C. N. To Berthier. Zittau, 20th August.

against Bohemia,"[1] and to throw himself then upon the enemy's main army.

At 2 p.m. on the 20th he was back again in Görlitz, and said immediately: "The great thing at this moment is for us to concentrate and then march against the enemy."[2] The news coming in, gave him good reason to hope that a battle was imminent, for Blücher had been advancing against the French since the 16th, and the latter had fallen back before him, and on the evening of the 20th, Ney, Marmont, Lauriston and Macdonald were on the left bank of the Bober at Löwenberg and opposite Bunzlau, with Blücher facing them on the other bank. The Emperor was at Lauban in the evening, and issued his orders thence, to cross the Bober on the next day and to attack. Macdonald, Lauriston, the Guards, led by himself, and Latour-Maubourg assembled at Löwenberg, whither Marmont also was moved. Ney was to cross the Bober at Bunzlau and then march up through Old-Giersdorf towards the enemy's right flank. In the morning of the 21st the passage of the Bober was effected under the eyes of the Emperor, who had hastened to Löwenberg; but the enemy did not stand his ground and fell back behind the Deichsel.

In this Napoleon thought he saw evidence of the little confidence which the enemy's leaders placed in their raw troops, and of their disappointment at the fact that he himself was making forward movements, instead of withdrawing behind the Elbe. Also he thought too favourably of his situation, not recognizing the truth, that the retreat of the Silesian army was a well-considered strategical manœuvre. Formerly his appreciation of the enemy's intentions had been clearer, but now his habit of self-deception had taken too great a hold upon him, and he persuaded himself that the combination he desired had actually come to pass. But he was

(101)

---

[1] C. N. To Saint-Cyr. Löwenberg, 22nd August.
[2] C. N. To the Marshals Ney and Marmont.

forced to a painful confession; his subordinate leaders, as we pointed out before Lützen, were no longer able to cope with the situation. "The worst feature, generally speaking, of our situation, is the little confidence my generals have in themselves. Wherever I am not present, they exaggerate the enemy's strength."[1] This fact was destined to become more and more clear to him in the course of the campaign, and after receiving the news of Grossbeeren and the Katzbach, he exclaimed: "Every plan which involves my absence, represents a regular war, in which the superiority of the enemy in cavalry, in numbers, and even in generals, would lead me to absolute ruin."[2]

And his subordinate officers were themselves conscious of this; they felt the results of seventeen years of Napoleonic guidance, and one of them wrote to him, to remonstrate against the plan of campaign, which demanded that one or other of the marshals should temporarily operate independently in the Mark, as well as in Silesia: "I greatly fear that your Majesty will learn on the day when you yourself have gained a victory, and think you have gained a decisive battle, that you have lost two."[3] In fact, these leaders dreaded a free, independent command, which should be the goal of ambition of every soldier. They only knew how to obey, they no longer knew how to lead. Spain had been a severe touchstone for them, where none had stood the test, and 1813 found them even less able to act on their own initiative.

On the 22nd August the French continued to force the enemy back, and the latter retreated behind the Katzbach. The Emperor, who had ridden forward half-way to Goldberg, returned to Löwenberg in the evening, and received there at night a letter from Saint-Cyr,

[1] C. N. To Maret. Löwenberg, 23rd August.
[2] C. N. Note on the general situation of my affairs. Dresden, 30th August.
[3] From Marmont N. Bunzlau, 15th August.

dated the 22nd August, 11 p.m., in which the latter reported that the enemy's main forces were on the point of invading Saxony, and that he was becoming apprehensive as to the fate of Dresden. The Emperor immediately determined to hasten himself to the aid of this most important point. He handed over the chief command in Silesia to Macdonald with orders to force back Blücher as far as Jauer, and then to occupy a defensive position on the Bober on the line Bunzlau—Löwenberg—Hirschberg, thus blocking the road to Dresden and preventing the enemy also from marching either towards Berlin for the purpose of a junction with the North army, turning one French wing; or towards Zittau for the purpose of a junction with the Bohemian army, turning the other French wing. He assigned him Lauriston, the III. Corps, which Souham would command (for Ney accompanied the Emperor himself to Dresden), his own corps, the XI. with Gérard in command, and finally the cavalry corps of Sebastiani.

Vandamme and Victor received orders to march to Dresden, whither the Guards, Marmont and Latour Maubourg started also. The Emperor mentioned in these orders that if the enemy actually advanced to Dresden he would fight within the fortifications of that town; "if the enemy takes definitely the offensive against Dresden on the 23rd or 24th, it is my intention to let them take the initiative and to withdraw at once within the fortified camp of Dresden, where I shall fight a great battle; and as the enemy in that case will have his back to the Rhine and we ours to the Oder, I should in case of defeat return to my fortified camp."[1] Should the worst happen he intended to fall back upon the right bank, effect a junction with Macdonald again and break out from one of the fortresses on the Middle Elbe. Should he however hear, on the march, that the advance of the Bohemian army was not very determined, he would in his turn take the

[1] C. N. To Berthier. Löwenberg, 23rd August, noon.

offensive by Zittau against Prague. During that movement Macdonald was to cover his line of communication *viâ* Zittau to Bautzen, and, in case he was forced to retreat, fall back not to the base of the Elbe, but to Zittau, so that the Emperor might always be able to collect all his forces on this line of operations. After the Emperor had arrived at Prague and was again able to resume his communications with Dresden, Macdonald would be at liberty to fall back according to circumstances either to Zittau or to Dresden. This is an important lesson which the Emperor gives here, namely, that the communications of an advanced corps must always be in the direction of the main army and not on any geographical point.

(102) In the forenoon of the 23rd Napoleon was still at Löwenberg, whilst, in conformity with his orders, Macdonald's troops forced Blücher back as far as behind Jauer. In the afternoon he drove back to Görlitz, and the various corps, which he had selected for Dresden, started on their march thither. During the morning of the 24th August the Emperor remained in Görlitz, whilst his troops hastened forward in forced marches; he now considered his situation to be as follows: "It is my intention to go to Stolpen. My army will be assembled there to-morrow. I shall spend the 26th there in making preparations, so as to allow my columns time to close up. In the night of the 26th I shall order my corps to march *viâ* Königstein, and with daybreak on the 27th I shall be in position in the camp of Pirna with 100,000 men. I shall manœuvre in such a manner that the attack upon Hellendorf will begin at 7 a.m. and that by noon I shall be master of that place. Then I shall place myself across the network of roads. I shall capture Pirna; and have two bridges ready to throw across the river at Pirna if necessary.

"The enemy will have either chosen for their line of operations the road from Peterswalde to Dresden, in

DRESDEN

which case I shall be in their rear, with my whole army massed, whilst they will not be able to collect theirs under four or five days; or they will have taken the road from Kommotau to Leipzig for their line of operations; in this case they will fall back to Kommotau, Dresden will be relieved, and I being in Bohemia, nearer to Prague than the enemy, shall march thither. Marshal Saint-Cyr will at once follow the enemy as soon as the latter show signs of confusion. I shall veil this movement by covering the bank of the Elbe with 30,000 light cavalry, so that the enemy, seeing the whole bank occupied, will believe my army to be near Dresden."[1]

By simple and effective plan Napoleon intended to cut off the enemy advancing to Dresden by crossing with his own entire army at Königstein, or, if the enemy, making a detour, moved in the direction of Leipzig, he would march to Prague, thus again getting in their rear. The Emperor had judged quite correctly; Schwarzenberg's first idea, after beginning to cross the Erzgebirge on the 22nd, had been to march to Leipzig; only the day after, he determined to go direct to Dresden, and now, on the 24th August, his vanguard appeared under the walls of this town, whilst the bulk of his army was at Dippoldiswalde. Saint-Cyr's troops withdrew within the fortifications, one division, Mouton-Duvernet's, holding the camp of Königstein.

The Emperor, however, renounced after all the more effective operation of breaking out with his whole army *viâ* Königstein against the enemy's rear, and moved instead direct to Dresden, to meet the enemy frontally from the entrenchments of the town. The fact was, this place was only protected by field fortifications; the Emperor had therefore always entertained the possibility of being forced to throw his army within them to aid the defence, and thus he added to his remarks above quoted: "This is my plan; it may, however, have to be

[1] C. N. To Maret.

modified by the enemy's operations. I presume that, when I attack, Dresden will not be so seriously threatened, that it could be taken within four-and-twenty hours." Accordingly when further news reached him, that the Allies had already appeared before Dresden., he said: "If I went into Bohemia I should be at Prague in three days; but I prefer the more cautious plan, viz. to advance through Dresden, with a view of attacking in force the army coming up on that side."[1]

The Emperor therefore proceeded *viâ* Bautzen, from whence he started again at 1 a.m on the 25th, to Stolpen, and arrived there about 7 o'clock. Vandamme reached Neustadt and Stolpen on the 25th, the Guards and Latour-Maubourg were posted along the road from Bischopwerda as far as Stolpen, and Marmont and Victor a day's march behind this latter place. The Emperor still cherished hopes, that the reports from Dresden would permit him to march *viâ* Königstein against the rear of the Allies. At 9 a.m. he wrote to Saint-Cyr, entered into the details for the defence of the fortifications of Dresden and expressed the hope that he would be able to hold out a few days; but an hour later he sent orders to Vandamme, to collect all his forces in the camp of Lilienstein, and to hasten forward in person to Königstein to reconnoitre the ground. In the afternoon the Emperor received news of a defeat which Oudinot was said to have suffered on his advance to Berlin, though at first he attached no great importance to this. The most important question of the moment was, as we have seen, Dresden, and on this the direction of his own further forward movements would depend. Immediately on his arrival at Stolpen the Emperor had said: "The moment I am sure of the safety of Dresden and the success of the measures taken to put it into a proper state of defence, it is my intention to break out by König-

---

[1] C. N. To Macdonald. Görlitz, 24th August.

DRESDEN

stein."[1] But this assurance he could not yet feel. "If the three entrenchments already marked out were completed, if the barricades in the town itself were finished, and if the Pirna ditch were properly dug, I should feel more reassured as to Dresden."[2] In order to gain definite information on these points by the report of an eye-witness, the Emperor had, on the previous day, sent his orderly officer Gourgaud to Dresden, and the latter on his return at 11 p.m. described the situation there as so urgent, that the Emperor became convinced immediate aid was necessary, if the capital was to be preserved.

He therefore gave orders at 1 a.m. on the 26th for the Guards and Latour-Maubourg to start for Dresden at 4 o'clock, whilst Vandamme was to continue in the direction given him, viz. towards Pirna. Marmont and Victor were, immediately on their arrival, to follow, according to circumstances, either the former or the latter. As a matter of fact, they marched eventually to Dresden. The Emperor himself hastened forward to this town, where he arrived about 9 o'clock, examined the works of the *enceinte*, approved of them, and at 1 o'clock made a further reconnaissance of the suburb of Pirna and then went to the Royal Castle. Since 10 o'clock his troops had been entering Dresden by the stone bridge over the Elbe, the Guards leading, they having marched 90 miles in 72 hours. The rapid movements of great bodies of men alone rendered it feasible to apply the same mass of troops in rapid succession at different points, thus multiplying the forces and gaining victories. How was this accomplished? By the fact that the Emperor did not march in our modern marching columns, but on a broad front, and thus crowded together numerous forces in a short column, corps side by side with corps —corps close behind corps. At ten minutes past three

---

[1] C. N. To Murat. Stolpen, 25th August, 7.30 a.m.
[2] C. N. To Rogniat. Stolpen, 25th August.

o'clock the Emperor was informed, that the serious attack upon the town appeared to be beginning, and he proceeded on horseback to the square near the castle in front of the Elbe bridge, giving directions to his columns from this spot himself. He was extremely content, and sure of victory, saying: "Although my enemies set to work in the right way, yet they are already beginning to play their parts wrongly, and if they attack me now, it may cost them the campaign."[1]

(103) During the forenoon the Allies had, it is true, advanced on all sides, though they had not made any serious attack upon the town; but the French had been forced to withdraw altogether within the lines of their fortifications. These now consisted, in addition to the *enceinte*, which had been placed in a state of defence, of five lunettes arranged for barbette fire, and provided with palisaded ditches. At noon the Russians were at Gruhna; to the left of them the Prussians, at Strehla-Leubnitz, were already in possession of one part of the Great Garden; and, finally, on the left wing, the Austrians, who had occupied Plauen, having captured the little fort there, and driven the French from all the farms and houses in front of their fortifications, had also captured Löbtans after some severe fighting.

At 4 p.m. Schwarzenberg commenced the general attack upon the position of Dresden. On the right wing the Russians advanced between the Elbe and the road to Blasewitz and threw the French back as far as the environs of the town, which had been placed in a state of defence; but here they were exposed to a cross fire from Lunette I. and a large battery on the other bank of the Elbe and were brought to a standstill, suffering heavy loss. The Prussians had in the meantime been trying to seize the Great Garden and had succeeded in taking it after a brave resistance by its defenders. They then

---

[1] Aster: Schilderung der Kriegsereignisse in und vor Dresden vom 7. März bis 28. August 1813 : 193.

advanced against Lunette II. and the walls of the *enceinte*; twice they failed, and when, at the third attempt the Russians arrived from the right to their aid, the Emperor delivered his counter-thrust, taking the offensive. The Austrians also had commenced their attacks upon Lunettes III. and IV., at first unsuccessfully, but at last they succeeded in capturing the former, though they were arrested in their further advance by the *enceinte*. Here there was a pause in the attack until at 6 o'clock the French reserves issued forth in all directions for the counter-stroke.

From the suburb of Pirna Mortier advanced against the Russians with two divisions of the Young Guard; driving them from all the copses and farms in front of the town, which they had captured earlier in the day, and forcing them to fall back to Striesen, thither he followed them and entered the village about 8 o'clock. But it was not until after midnight, that the Russians evacuated it after an obstinate resistance. Against the Prussians one of Saint-Cyr's divisions delivered the counter-attack, and drove them, just as they were exhausting themselves in vain attacks upon the *enceinte*, with heavy loss back to Strehla. Finally against the Austrians Ney led out two divisions of the Young Guard in the direction of the little outlying fort and Lunette III. Both these points were taken by storm and the enemy then fell back to the line Zschertnitz—Räcknitz—Plauen. Between the Weisseritz and the Elbe an Austrian corps had advanced, and occupied Cotta and Schusterhäuser and then began to bombard the suburb of Friedrichstadt. From here Murat broke out at 6 o'clock with two divisions of infantry and drove the Austrians from the ground they had occupied.

The Emperor rode on the same evening through the positions of his troops and returned late in the night to the Royal Castle. He could contemplate the day with satisfaction, for, with 70,000 men he had not only repulsed the attacks of 150,000, but had actually gained a victory.

The strength of his genius had been able to atone for a minority of 80,000 men, and I know of no example in war which furnishes clearer evidence, that the numbers and *moral* of troops, important factors as these are, may be over-matched by the weight of one person of genius. We know also that the qualities of the Emperor's troops were anything but satisfactory, and Napoleon himself was well aware of this, for, a few days later, when Monthion, regretting Vandamme's annihilated corps, exclaimed: "It was one of the finest corps of the army," the Emperor answered: "Yes, with respect to numbers, but with respect to their military qualifications, they were louts, like all the rest. Now only am I beginning to feel the full extent of the losses which I sustained during the last campaign."[1] And yet this consciousness, which so often paralyzed the activity of other generals, cannot be noticed in the conduct of affairs on the 26th August. The victory here was due in the first place to the coolness with which a small force was exposed to the superior numbers of the Allies at the beginning of the action, and until the decisive moment had arrived; then, secondly, when success wavered in the balance, to the manner in which the carefully husbanded reserves were launched in a general and decisive counter-stroke.

(102) During the night Marmont and Victor arrived in Dresden, and thus supported, the Emperor could look forward calmly to the 27th. Vandamme had crossed the Elbe at Copitz, and had engaged in an artillery duel with the enemy's division which, left behind at Pirna, had been recently reinforced. On the morning of the 27th, in
(104) pouring rain, Napoleon formed his army in the following order: to the right Murat with Victor and Latour-Maubourg; in the centre Marmont, the Old Guard, and Ney with his two divisions of the Young Guard; Saint-Cyr next, and on the extreme left, Mortier. Opposite stood the Russians on the line Reick—Leubnitz; next in

[1] F. v. D. Napoleon in Dresden. II. 75.

DRESDEN

order, the Prussians between Leubnitz and Möckritz, and lastly the Austrians between Räcknitz and Plauen. The corps, which had advanced on the preceding day, and had taken up a position between the Weisseritz and the Elbe, now formed a reserve both behind the Austrian line, and also on the other side of the Weisseritz. One division was pushed forward to the Elbe itself, with the intention that its communication with the troops on the Weisseritz should be maintained by the interposition of a corps, which had remained behind during the advance, and which had on the previous day been vainly expected at Tharandt.

The Emperor noticed this gap, and after an artillery duel which began at 7 o'clock, he ordered Murat to advance at 10 o'clock. The latter took the villages of Nauslitz, Wölfnitz, and Gorbitz, thus cutting off the isolated division on the Elbe; he then penetrated as far as Rossthal and forced the troops on the left of the Weisseritz, to fall back by Döhlen and to cross the valley of Plauen. He now brought all his cavalry to bear with such force upon the isolated division on the Elbe that it was completely overwhelmed; those who were not killed being taken prisoners. In the centre and on the left wing nothing decisive took place; the Allies maintained their positions on the heights and the French did not make any determined effort to capture them. Mortier, it is true, penetrated as far as Seidnitz and captured it, but was subsequently driven back again by the Russians.

At 5 o'clock Schwarzenberg received intelligence from the corps previously stationed at Pirna, that it having been unsuccessfully engaged since the morning with Vandamme, it had been forced, owing to the latter's advance, to evacuate Pirna, and to fall back along the Peterswalde road. At the same time the commander-in-chief was informed of the unfortunate series of events taking place on his left wing, and deemed it advisable to issue orders for a general retreat, in the following order:

(105)

the right wing to fall back *viâ* Berggieshübel and Hellendorf to Peterswalde ; the Austrians *viâ* Dippoldiswalde to Altenberg and *viâ* Freiberg to Kommotau. In the evening the retreat was, however, only so far begun as to discontinue the battle.

During the engagement Napoleon scarcely stirred from his comfortable place by the watchfire. He breakfasted with Berthier, and seemed to attend to affairs "as though they were only of secondary importance."[1] When, in the afternoon, the enemy began to give way, he considered his day's work to be ended. "He sent for his horse, rain dripping from the sleeves and the body of his grey overcoat, and the brim of his hat hanging down over his neck. In such guise did Napoleon, Hero of battles, the Terror of Europe, enter the castle about 6 o'clock, at his ordinary leisurely trot, accompanied by the general staff, and amidst the acclamations of the troops crowding round him, wild with joy."[1]

If we make a careful study of Napoleon as the General and Tactician, during these last two days, we are forced to remark that, though the flame of his genius burns at times with its former steady splendour, yet frequently it flickers and glimmers but fitfully. Bautzen and Dresden stand out as isolated successes, not, as in past days, links in an endless chain of triumphs. We must point out that, on the 27th, the Emperor made but a half-hearted attack on the enemy he had virtually defeated on the 26th, and far from pursuing them hotly in person, when they evacuated their positions in the afternoon, he rode back to the castle and expressed the opinion that "the enemy was not on the retreat, but that yesterday's events should be considered only as an unsuccessful attack ; that it was doubtful, whether they would start on their retreat that night .... that everything led him to believe a great battle would take place the next day, and that the enemy's

---

[1] O. v. O. Napoleon's Feldzug, etc., 313, 314

army was very numerous."[1] This, indeed, is no longer the general, who in past days would often announce the enemy's flight, on the morning of the day on which he intended to beat them.

With the 28th the retreat of the Allies into the Erzgebirge began; the corps, which had been previously stationed at Pirna and had fought its way to Peterswalde through Vandamme's troops, was now retreating by Hellendorf; the rest of the army had reached Glashütte, Dippoldiswalde and Pretzschendorf. The French were in touch with the rearguard, but did not press it hard. Early in the day the Emperor had attached himself to Marmont's corps, which was to follow the enemy to Altenberg; whilst Mortier and Saint-Cyr, marching in the direction of Berggieshübel, would serve as a support for Vandamme, and Murat was proceeding to Freiberg. The Emperor observing that heavy masses of the enemy were crowding along the road to Maxen, gave orders that Saint-Cyr was to follow in pursuit *viâ* Dohna. These retreating masses were composed of the Russians and Prussians of the enemy's right wing, who, being ordered to take the road to Peterswalde, had gone round towards Maxen, in their fear of finding the former road blocked by Vandamme.

Napoleon rode forward to Räcknitz, watched the retreating Austrian columns, and then galloped over to the road to Pirna, taking up a position near this place, where Vandamme had been stationed the day before. The latter was now in pursuit of that corps of the enemy which had made an attack, with a view to clearing its way to Peterswalde. This attack had at first surprised him, since, at the moment, he was as yet unaware of the course of events at Dresden. He followed the corps closely, engaging it in severe rearguard fighting, as far as Berggieshübel, his vanguard meanwhile reaching Hellendorf. The Emperor watched the enemy retreat-

[1] C. N. To Berthier. Dresden, 27th August, 7 p.m.

ing in all directions into the ravines of the Erzgebirge, and at 4 p.m., finding himself in full possession of the whole road from Pirna to Berggieshübel, said to Lobau: "Well, I cannot see any more. Let the Old Guard return to Dresden, the Young Guard will remain here and bivouac."[1] Saint-Cyr had already ceased to follow Vandamme; the Guards also were halted, and could not therefore move up quickly to his support. At this very moment that general received the following orders from Napoleon :—

"One hour's journey from Pirna,
"August 28th, 1813, 4 p.m.

"The Emperor orders you to take the direction of Peterswalde with your entire army corps, the division of Corbineau,[2] the 42nd division,[3] and the brigade of the II. Corps under the command of General Prince Reuss, making altogether an increase of 18 battalions. Pirna will be occupied by the troops of the Duke of Treviso, who will arrive there this evening. The marshal has also orders to relieve your posts in the camp of Lilienstein. General Baltus will reach Pirna this evening with your battery of twelve-pounders and your park of artillery; you will send for him. The Emperor wishes you to collect all the forces at your disposal and to penetrate into Bohemia, where you will crush the Prince of Würtemberg,[4] in case he resists your invasion. The enemy, whom we have beaten, seems to have taken the direction of Annaberg.

"His Majesty thinks, you should reach their line of communication to Tetschen, Aussig and Teplitz before

---

[1] O. v. O. 318.
[2] A division of light cavalry belonging to Latour-Maubourg's corps.
[3] Mouton-Duvernet's division of Saint-Cyr's corps; it had been left behind as a garrison of the position of Pirna at this place. On the other hand the division of Teste, belonging to Vandamme's corps, had been moved to Dresden and fought there under Murat.
[4] A Russian general; he commanded the right wing of the Allies, which was retreating to Peterswalde.

the enemy, and could thus capture his waggons, field-hospitals, baggage, in fact all that usually follows an army. The Emperor orders the pontoon-bridge at Pirna to be demolished, and a similar bridge to be constructed at Tetschen."[1]

"And then, calm and cheerful, he ordered his carriage, and entering it, drove away to Dresden."[2] We therefore note, firstly, that Napoleon left the pursuit of the enemy to the individual corps-leaders, without encouraging them in person; secondly, that he relinquished the general conduct of affairs and all personal responsibility at the moment of the invasion of Bohemia by his troops, and paid little heed to the general harmony of their movements; lastly, that he directed a single isolated corps against the enemy's line of retreat; failing to allow this isolated corps the forces necessary for their support in their dangerous task, by sending part of these available forces in another direction, and by ordering the rest to remain stationary. Such a course of action is beyond military criticism, for, in such a man as Napoleon, it cannot be explained by the alleging of any erroneous or mistaken view of the situation. In seeking for any possible explanation, we can only endeavour to fathom the Emperor's mind, which may have reasoned that, since the enemy was in full flight success was certain. Fortune, in the past, had led him always to expect a favourable issue, and he now, doubtless, considered any further effort, or exertion on his own part, to be unnecessary. His fatigue, his previous hardships, the pouring rain of the 27th, and his custom of now "looking after his own comfort to such a degree that he made it his principal business," may also furnish a clue to his inertia.

Whatever may be the explanation, the strategical error was heavily punished. Whilst the Emperor remained in

[1] C. N. Berthier to Vandamme. Pelet: Des principales opérat. de la camp. de 1813. 64.
[2] O. v. O. 318.

Dresden on the 29th and 30th, working in his study, Vandamme penetrated into the plain of Kulm, and finding the Russian corps, which had retreated before him, occupying a strong position at Pristen, attacked it, but without success. On the following day, Schwarzenberg determined, on his side, to take the offensive and advance against Vandamme with his troops, of which the greater part now occupied the plain. The other French corps were in the following positions: Saint-Cyr at Reinhardsgrimma, Marmont at Falkenhayn, Murat at Lichtenberg, whilst Mortier, as already mentioned, remained stationary at Pirna. Of the Allies the Russians moved to Altenberg, the Prussians to Fürstenwalde, and the Austrians to Dux, Sayda and Gross Walthersdorf. Vandamme had taken up a position near Kulm, with his right wing resting on the Erzgebirge, and his left on the heights of Striesowitz, with the intention of holding out until the reinforcements, which he believed to be approaching, should arrive, and then to deliver his attack.

But at 8 a.m. on the 30th he was himself attacked, and at noon was forced back into the Erzgebirge, after an obstinate resistance. From this position, perceiving a column of men debouching in his rear from one of the mountainous ravines, he concluded that it was led by the anxiously-expected Mortier; but he became soon convinced, that it was the Prussians, and that nothing further remained for him, but to try and break through to the rear. Meanwhile the Prussians received continual reinforcements, the Austrians and Russians simultaneously attacked in force, and Vandamme's isolated corps was entirely dispersed, and only some fragments of it succeeding in escaping into Saxony. The other corps of the Emperor occupied the following positions: Saint-Cyr at Liebenau and Lauenstein; Marmont at Altenberg with his advanced guard at Zinnwald; Murat at Zetha. Mortier had advanced as far as Berggieshübel, but hear-

DRESDEN

ing there of Vandamme's fate, had returned immediately to Pirna. On the 31st, whilst the Allies remained in the valley of Teplitz to reorganize their troops, Mortier arrived at Hellendorf, Saint-Cyr at Dittersdorf, Marmont at Zinnwald and Murat at Sayda.

On the same day at 2 a.m. the Emperor received the news of the annihilation of his Ist Corps, and this was not the only disastrous intelligence which reached him at this time. He had already heard, on the 29th, of the defeat Macdonald had suffered on the Katzbach and of his retreat before the victorious Blücher. The Marshal, unfortunately misinterpreting the Emperor's strictly defensive instructions, had, on the 26th, resolved to take the offensive against Blücher, who was again advancing, and meeting him at the Katzbach, had been severely beaten. His army being disorganized by the vigorous pursuit of the Prussians, had been forced back on the 31st beyond the Queiss, leaving 18,000 prisoners and 103 guns in Blücher's hands. The latter stood on the right bank of the Queiss at Naumburg and opposite Lauban. In addition to these disasters, the rumour of a defeat in the Mark Brandenburg, which had reached the Emperor's ears on the 25th, was now confirmed. Oudinot had advanced irresolutely and not in accordance with Napoleon's principle: "Once your resolution is taken, you must cling to it, there are no further ifs and buts possible." His advance had failed, and one of his corps having suffered defeat at Grossbeeren on the 23rd, the Marshal led his army back to Wittenberg, and on the 31st remained at Marzahne, with the enemy's Northern Army at Trenenbrietzen. (102)

On two occasions, therefore, Napoleon's plans had fallen short of success owing to the fault of his subordinates, and on the third and most important occasion, he, himself, had failed to grasp the danger of the situation. The defensive which he wished to maintain from his position on the inner line, by offensive movements against his enemies, taking advantage of them while as yet separated from each other, had now been rendered extremely difficult by their close approach; already the strategical advantage of being on interior lines threatened to change in the disadvantage of being tactically surrounded. Under these difficult conditions, how was Napoleon effectively to carry out his proposed operations?

CHAPTER IX.

LEIPZIG.

IN answer to this question, we possess a most valuable (106) document, viz. "Notes on the general situation of my affairs," dictated by Napoleon at Dresden on the 30th August. Therein we read as follows :—

"I take my Silesian army to be assembled behind the Bober ; it would not even be a disadvantage, if it went behind the Queiss.

"If I ordered Prince Poniatowski to join the army of Berlin, the line of advance from Zittau would no longer be guarded. However he might reach Kalan within four days; in that case it would be indispensable for the Silesian army to make its base at Görlitz or even in front of Bautzen. As soon as one corps only holds Hoyerswerda, my operation against Berlin will be safe.

"If I renounced my operation against Bohemia, in order to take Berlin and provision Stettin and Küstrin, Marshal Saint-Cyr and General Vandamme could take position with the left wing on the Elbe; the Duke of Ragusa would form its centre and the Duke of Belluno the right wing ; the King of Naples could command these four corps and station himself at Dresden, with Latour-Maubourg; this would be a fine army. It would be possible for it to cover itself by a few entrenchments within some well-known positions. This army would be a menace to the enemy ; it would not have to run any risks and could retreat to Dresden, whilst I came up from Luckau.

"The Silesian army could rest upon Naumburg with its left wing at Weissenberg, and occupy Bautzen and Hoyerswerda.

"Both my armies would then act on the defensive, covering Dresden on both banks, whilst I operated against Berlin and moved the theatre of war to the Lower Oder."

Then he examined the plan of an advance to Prague with his main body, but came to the conclusion that the advance to Berlin was preferable, and therefore his final remarks are:—

"I. The Prague Project: I should have to go there in person and employ the II., VI., XIV., and I. Corps with the cavalry of Latour-Maubourg; the Prince of Eckmühl would take up his position before Hamburg; the three corps under Oudinot at Wittenberg and Magdeburg; the Silesian army at Bautzen. In this situation I should be on the defensive and leave the offensive to the enemy; I should threaten nothing; it would be absurd to pretend that I should threaten Vienna; the enemy could mask the Silesian army, break out by Zittau, attack me in Prague; or, while masking the Silesian army, he could send some forces to the Lower Elbe, and proceed to the Weser, whilst I should be at Prague, and there would be nothing left me but to return in haste to the Rhine. The general in command at Bautzen would not admit that the enemy in front had been weakened, and my army at Hamburg and Magdeburg would be entirely beyond my reach.

"II. Project: In this the I. Corps, the XIV., the II., the VI. and Latour-Maubourg would remain quietly around Dresden without fear of the Cossacks; Augereau's corps would move up *viâ* Bamberg and Hof; the Silesian army would be on the Queiss and the Bober and at Bautzen; I should feel no anxiety about my communications, my two armies from Hamburg and Reggio would be at Berlin and Stettin."

We were at a loss for a reason why the Emperor left the army on the 28th at Pirna and withdrew to his study, and the result of his mental labour while thus secluded still remains an enigma. We saw that on the 28th (as far as his personal leadership was concerned), he renounced the invasion of Bohemia with a view to encountering the enemy's main army, and on the 30th his strategical judgment also decided against it. This is a most peculiar moment in Napoleon's military career. Hitherto we have repeatedly had occasion to refer to a certain diminution of the Emperor's energy, both mental and physical, and a lack of vigour in the execution of his plans, and have had sometimes to recognize that he was personally unequal to the demands of the moment, yet we have never failed to admire the entire theoretical correctness of his strategy. Now we cannot but question the latter.

Hitherto, the guiding principle of the Napoleonic strategy had always been to render all secondary resistance useless and ineffective by a blow against the enemy's main body. But, now, Napoleon neglects the main army, at the very moment when, owing to its being composed of troops of three allied powers and owing to the presence of the three allied monarchs in its camp, any blow dealt at it might have broken the bond which united their common interests. Yet he permits an operation of secondary importance (which, as such, when considering the plan of campaign immediately after the armistice, we allowed to have its justification) to take the place of the main operation. The reasons he gives for this determination are so untenable, so lacking in conviction, that they form a striking contrast to the pitiless logic which formerly met with our unconditional approval. He maintains, in speaking of his "Prague Project," "that it would force him on the defensive, that he would not be threatening anything, and that it was absurd to say he would be threatening Vienna." Certainly, the

Emperor would not be threatening Vienna, but he would be threatening the main army, against which he would march in a direct manner, and would thus act on the offensive. His armies in Silesia and in the Mark would be on the defensive, but this would not have been a disadvantage, for in the other plan preferred by himself, of an advance against Berlin, his other two armies, that of Silesia and that at Dresden, would also be on the defensive, and to this he raises no objection.

The most characteristic feature in the whole plan of campaign is this, that the Emperor now refers only to geographical points, and no longer to the attack or defeat of this or that hostile army; this is no longer Napoleonic strategy. In 1809, he first committed the practical mistake of no longer making the absolute annihilation of the enemy the aim of the war, and brought the war to a close without having attained that aim. Immediately afterwards we heard him depreciate the theoretical importance of a battle, and we then came to the logical conclusion, that such conduct and such assertions might be justifiable in a Frederick or an Archduke Charles, but indicated in a Napoleon a declension from his former standard, so here also he commits the practical mistake of relinquishing his operation against Schwarzenberg's main army, just when he had succeeded in coming in touch with it, and again gives utterance to a theoretical assertion, renouncing his aim of making the subjugation of the enemy the object of the campaign. Such an assertion, referring to Berlin, Vienna and Prague, like the plan at his departure for Velikye Luki in 1812, of threatening St. Petersburg, might have had some justification in the time of Frederick; such a threatening or seizing of strategical points had, in those days, a direct influence upon the enemy's armies and consequently was a factor in attaining the object of the war. But the Emperor's plans should have had a different basis; he ought to have built his plan of campaign not upon reaching Prague, nor upon taking post at Berlin and Stettin, but upon fighting a great battle either with the army of Schwarzenberg, or with that of Blücher, or with that of Bernadotte. But the execution of his plan had for the present to be postponed; circumstances compelled the Emperor to turn his attention to what lay nearest and to renounce an advance upon Berlin conducted by himself in person. It was impossible for him to embark upon this unless he could be certain that, with the four corps allotted to him, Murat could hold Schwarzenberg in check for at least a fortnight, and that Macdonald could hold out at Görlitz. The former idea, however, was rendered extremely doubtful by Vandamme's defeat, and the fulfilment of the latter was very uncertain. On the 1st September Napoleon wrote: "The Duke of Tarentum is at Görlitz this day. If he continues his retreat, it will be necessary for me to march, in order to put things straight again there; I must not let him retreat beyond Bautzen."[1] For the present, therefore, he was forced to withdraw Marmont, Mortier and the cavalry of Latour Maubourg closer to Dresden, "because I may need my reserves at any moment,"[2] while Saint-Cyr and Victor received orders to station themselves at Pirna and Freiberg. Ney was sent to Wittenberg on the same day, in order eventually to take over the chief command of Oudinot's army.

On the 2nd, news was received that Oudinot's army had fallen back as far as Wittenberg. The Emperor then ordered Ney to be written to, urging him to advance resolutely to Berlin, and informing him that "all the troops here are being set in motion to advance to Hoyerswerda, where the Emperor will establish his headquarters on the 4th;"[3] and he would then resume communication with him *via* Luckau. The initial orders

[1] C. N. To Murat. Dresden.
[2] C. N. To Berthier. Dresden, 1st September.
[3] C. N. To Berthier. Dresden, 2nd September.

were then given for the advance to Hoyerswerda. On that day Marmont was at Dippoldiswalde, Mortier at Pirna, Saint-Cyr at Dittersdorf and Victor at Freiberg. The remnants of the I. Corps, hitherto part of Victor's corps, and now joined to the division of Teste, were collected at Berggieshübel, and the corps, thus reformed, came under the command of Lobau. But the next day the Emperor's intentions were somewhat altered by Macdonald's reports as to the condition of his army, which showed that he was in want of immediate support. "His Majesty must order this army to move so that he may be in personal contact with it, reorganize it thoroughly and restore its *moral*. . . . If this army were exposed to a reverse at this moment, it would be completely dissolved."[1] The Emperor, therefore, now sent his Guards, Marmont and Latour-Maubourg to Bautzen direct; Dresden was occupied by Lobau, to whom the 5th cavalry-corps, L'Héritier, 2500 men, which had just arrived, was attached; Saint-Cyr and Victor remained in their positions at Pirna and Freiberg.

Napoleon himself left Dresden towards evening, and spent the night at Harthau. He had urged Macdonald to keep his army, wherever he might be, in very close formation, saying, "I desire to be able to ride in half an hour along the whole front of the army."[2] He hoped to be able to deal a severe blow against Blücher, and such a success, added to that of Dresden, would have enabled him to turn his position on interior lines to good account; he would have reached the aim of his defensive, and could then, should Dresden be threatened anew, reach that town in good time. "The enemy may manœuvre against Dresden either on the left or on the right bank. If they manœuvre on the left bank, it will be a mere repetition of what has already happened. . . . As I shall in any case be able to be in Dresden within two or three days, it will be

---

[1] C. N. Macdonald to Berthier. Nostiz, 2nd September.
[2] C. N. To Macdonald. Dresden, 3rd September.

altogether a repetition of what occurred before, only that I shall be nearer this time."

If the enemy manœuvred on the right bank, he himself would be able to act in two ways: (1) along the road from Zittau; in this case he would effect a junction with the Silesian army in rear, without this affecting Dresden at all: (2) *viâ* Neustadt, in order to go to Weissig, between Dresden and the Lilienstein, cutting off the road from Dresden to Bautzen. In this case Marshal Saint-Cyr would have to occupy the camp of Lilienstein and the entrenchments of Hohenstein with the greater portion of his corps, whilst the Count of Lobau as well as the Duke of Belluno would occupy the heights of Weissig, "where there are some very fine positions, and this would give me time to effect a junction with them and after having defeated the Silesian army, to beat the great army of Bohemia again."[1]

On the morning of the 4th September the Emperor left Harthau and rode forward to Bautzen. On his way, his anger was passionately aroused by the sight of numerous bands of stragglers scattered along the road, thus showing clearly what had happened to Macdonald's army. "On seeing the first of these bands issuing from the wood, he urged his horse on to a gallop, and spurred along by the side of the road. Suddenly a little dog appeared and began to bark at his horse. This made him so angry, that he drew his pistol, and wished to shoot the dog. But his pistol missed fire and he hurled it from him in a passion."[2] Immediately afterwards he broke out into passionate reproaches against Sebastiani, whose work with the cavalry had fallen short of his expectations; indeed, he went so far in his anger that Caulaincourt considered it advisable to keep all those who had been present as far away as possible. In this gloomy state of mind Napoleon arrived at Hochkirch. Here he

[1] C. N. To Berthier. Dresden, 3rd September.
[2] O. v. O. 222.

met the advanced guard of the enemy's army, but the superior numbers of the French stopped them and forced them back towards evening. Blücher formed a correct judgment of the situation, and as he knew that the Emperor had come up with reinforcements, decided to fall back for the next few days.

(107a) The Emperor passed the night in the vicarage of Hochkirch. "When Napoleon started from Hochkirch early on the morning of the 5th September, he rode across the fields to the hill of Wohlau and at once examined the Russo-Prussian position of the preceding day."[1] His army followed the retreating enemy, who crossed the Neisse on that day, and the French reached that river and Görlitz. The events of this day convinced the Emperor that Blücher was purposely avoiding the battle his antagonist hoped for, and that he must not risk being enticed further into Silesia and away from Dresden by him. Having advanced in person as far as Reichenbach, he returned on the evening of the 5th with the Guards and Marmont to Bautzen.

He now conceived the plan of making a rapid advance in the direction of the Mark of Brandenburg, and if the occasion offered, joining hands with Ney. He, therefore, on the morning of the 6th, ordered Marmont and Latour-Maubourg to start on their march to Hoyerswerda. But immediately afterwards he found it necessary to countermand these orders.

For some time past news had reached him of a fresh threatening movement upon Dresden on the part of the enemy's army in Bohemia, and now these reports became so definite that he decided to return thither. Latour-Maubourg therefore received orders to start with all possible haste on the road back to Dresden; Marmont was to take up a position at Kamenz, in order, if necessary, to be moved thither also. Blücher on this day fell back behind the Queiss, followed by Macdonald,

[1] O. v. O. 325.

though not hard pressed by the latter. In the evening the Emperor arrived in Dresden.

In the meantime Schwarzenberg had at first remained stationary in the Teplitz valley, having received contradictory reports as to the Emperor's movements. On the 5th September he sent one corps forward to Hellendorf to reconnoitre, and on the 6th, having learnt definitely of the Emperor's advance against Blücher, he sent 60,000 Austrians across the Elbe; with these he intended personally to attack Napoleon in flank through Rumburg. He had given the command of the remainder of his army to Barclay, and the latter moved his advanced guard forward into the mountain passes; they appeared near Cotta and Neuntmannsdorf. But the following day the French advanced, and the Emperor himself accompanied the heads of his columns. "About noon on the 8th Napoleon rode forward quite slowly, as if on a reconnaissance, along the Pirna road towards the so-called Tavern of Luga. The enemy held the heights of Gross Sedlitz and the little town of Dohna."[1] Driven thence by the Guards, they fell back to Zuschendorf and Zehista. The Emperor took up his quarters for the night in Dohna.

On the whole he knew nothing further about his opponents, except that they "held exits from Bohemia,"[2] though some reconnaissances towards Chemnitz, Freiberg and Dippoldiswalde had shown him that he need be under no apprehensions at present regarding his communications in the direction of Leipzig. He therefore sent orders to Victor to come up closer to Dresden. With respect to his extreme left he presumed that Ney "must have advanced on the 6th from Jüterbog to Dahme;"[4] although "there are some confused rumours of an engagement which is said to have taken place," but "no details have as yet come in."[2] However, details reached him on the same evening in

[1] O. v. O. 328.
[2] C. N. To Berthier. Dresden, 8th September, 3 a.m.

Dohna concerning the defeat at Dennewitz. The Austrian division, which had been sent forward, had halted at Aussig, and as Schwarzenberg had received news on the 7th, of the Emperor's return to Dresden, it was called in again.

The Emperor now determined to throw the troops, which had advanced, back over the Erzgebirge, and to gain an insight into the enemy's measures and intentions by penetrating as far as the openings in the Teplitz valley. He consequently gave orders for a concentration of Victor, Lobau and the Guards at Dohna and pushed forward with these forces; the enemy retreating everywhere before him. In the evening he was with the Guards in Liebstadt, Victor at Altenberg, Lobau at Berggieshübel, and Saint-Cyr at Breitenau.

But it was not part of the Emperor's plan to make any serious invasion into Bohemia, and he wrote to Berthier, on the same day to arrest Marmont, who had been recalled to Dresden, on the right bank of the Elbe. On the morning of the 10th the situation, as a whole, was as follows: Macdonald was in front of Bautzen, Marmont on the Elbe opposite Dresden, Ney was collecting his corps at Torgau, L'Héritier stood at Grossenhayn, and finally, one division, 8000 to 10,000 men, under General Margaron, covered the Emperor's rear at Leipzig. "In this situation of affairs, my army being much concentrated, I am going to-day to the high mountains, which command Teplitz, so as to gain definite news about the enemy." [1]

He therefore ordered his corps to advance towards Peterswalde and Ebersdorf. He went himself to the latter place through Breitenau, and at 11 o'clock reached the summit of the Geyersberg, which affords a wide view. Here he was forced to confess that it would be impossible to enter the valley in the face of the army standing ready there, especially considering that the roads were now become impassable on account of the repeated retreats of

[1] C. N. To Maret. Liebstadt, 10th September, 8 a.m.

the Allies. "It went against the grain for Napoleon to renounce his intentions. For a long time he contemplated the enemy's position and the beautiful landscape of the Teplitz valley, wrapped in a grey mist. He sent General Drouot down for some distance to examine the road, but this officer soon returned with the disappointing report that the road was altogether impassable. . . . Very much annoyed, Napoleon finally left his point of observation. The greater portion of his troops—all his Guards —received orders to face about immediately and to encamp in this bleak district, now entirely devastated and without any food. The whole position, including all the arrangements, seemed to present great difficulties to him. The Emperor wished, at first, to remain in Ebersdorf, and then in Fürstenwalde; finally he went back as far as Breitenau. He could hardly find any shelter in this poor village, which was almost destroyed. The horse-dung had first to be removed from the pastor's house, before quarters could be prepared for him and Berthier."[1] Mortier, who had, somewhat against the Emperor's intentions, conducted the entire Young Guard back as far as Pirna, received orders to hold himself ready for a march to Bautzen; a proof that all idea of an advance into Bohemia, had it ever been thought of, had now been given up.

The 11th September brought no material alteration in the mutual positions. The Emperor on this day went to the Peterswalde road *viâ* Oelsa, and having reached the height of Nollendorf towards evening, he watched the enemy's cavalry being forced back by Lobau. Then he took up his quarters in the parsonage of Peterswalde. But on the 12th he began to conduct his troops back again to Saxony: he himself reached Dresden with the Old Guard; Mortier with the Young Guard was at Cotta, Lobau at Nollendorf—Peterswalde; Saint-Cyr at Borne —Fürstenwalde; Victor in the neighbourhood of Sayda

[1] O. v. O. 333.

and Marienburg; Marmont, having only just arrived on the Elbe, was directed to go to Grossenhayn on the 13th, in order to cover the arrival of a large convoy of flour, which was proceeding from Torgau to Dresden. Murat was also sent thither with Latour-Maubourg, L'Héritier likewise being placed under his command. "The arrival of this convoy is of the greatest importance to ensure supplies in our central depôt, Dresden."[1] The Allies did not begin any forward movement on the 12th; but on the next day they determined, that Barclay should hold the mountain passes with the right wing and keep the enemy engaged, whilst Schwarzenberg should advance to the left against the Emperor's communications. Accordingly on the 14th, one corps, sent forward by Barclay on the Nollendorf road, forced Lobau back as far as Berggieshübel.

The Emperor quickly perceived that this was not a serious offensive movement by the whole hostile army; he therefore left Dresden at 7 a.m. on the 15th and drove as far as Mügeln, from whence he proceeded to Pirna, and there ordered a bridge to be constructed for communication with Macdonald. In the meantime he had led the Guards forward, and in conjunction with these Lobau forced the enemy back again beyond Nollendorf. The Emperor spent that night in Pirna. On the 16th September he went to Nollendorf, but was unable, on account of the fog and bad weather to gain any clear view; he therefore remained the night in Peterswalde, and resolved to gain intelligence the next day by a bold move forward into the valley, for he judged rightly, that, "it is of importance to the enemy, to keep possession of the roads by which he has advanced, so as to be sure, that I do not take the offensive, whilst he is beginning operations."[2]

Schwarzenberg concentrated his troops at Külm during the night of the 16th, as soon as he became aware of the

[1] C. N. To Berthier. Dresden, 12th September.
[2] C. N. To Berthier. Pirna, 16th September, 8 a.m.

advance of the French, and abandoned his movement to the left against Napoleon's communications. When, therefore, on the morning of the 17th, the Emperor, who had betaken himself to the chapel of Nollendorf, commenced the attack, he found the enemy fully prepared; and the latter soon tried to cut off the French troops, which had penetrated into the valley, by turning them *via* Kninitz, and they were forced to retreat again to the mountains. During the engagement the Emperor had ridden down as far as Tellnitz, and had "intended at first to pass the night in the chapel of Nollendorf; but as the place was too inhospitable and unpleasant, and as moreover his whole retinue was still in the wretched village of Peterswalde, he resolved, late in the evening, to return there."[1]

On the 18th he again rode forward at noon towards the valley, halting first at Kninitz, from whence at various heights the hostile army became clearly visible to him, and said, turning to Berthier: "All I see are about two corps of 60,000 men. They will need a whole day to join forces and attack."[2] On that day only a few skirmishes occurred, for Schwarzenberg was determined to act merely on the defensive, but the Emperor recognized that he was unable at present to push forward from the Erzgebirge and he therefore returned to Pirna. The situation was now as follows: Marmont and Murat were at Grossenhayn; Macdonald having fallen back before Blücher (who, immediately on the Emperor's departure, had advanced again), was on a level with Fischbach; Victor, Saint-Cyr and Lobau were covering the passes into the Erzgebirge at Freiberg, Borne and Berggieshübel.

At the present moment neither side showed any wish to arrive at any great tactical decision by taking the offensive with the main mass. Napoleon wrote on the 16th, that he wanted to throw the enemy back into the plain, and that

(10%)

[1] O. v. O. 341.   [2] O. v. O. 193.

possibly he might go to Stolpen. But Schwarzenberg, on the evening of the 18th, thought that the movements of the French portended a general offensive into Bohemia, and therefore concentrated all his forces to prevent this. The Emperor, divining his intentions, said: "I cannot believe, that the enemy is going to attack in earnest; if he is getting ready, it is merely because he expects to be attacked."[1] As to his own intentions, he said, "I shall be content with this game of moving hither and thither, and wait for an opportunity."[2] He intended to station himself on the northern side of the Erzgebirge and only to move to meet the enemy, if the latter assumed the offensive with his whole army; "but I shall not allow him to tempt me to any such movement simply by sending forward troops, or light divisions, as has just been the case."[3]

It is not just to reproach a general for a mere change of purpose. War, by its ever-varying nature, demands that a leader should adapt himself and his plans to the pressure of circumstances, however variable, and he merits our highest praise by acting with decision and rapidity in the face of discouraging and unexpected changes. Napoleon, in the campaign of 1796, when placed in a similar position, changed his resolutions according to the requirements of each day, and made it apparent that a general should possess sufficient mental versatility, not to confine himself to one plan only. To the man of ordinary ability, the thoughtful evolution of a definite course of action requires such mental effort, that he clings tenaciously to his scheme and dreads any alterations in his projects.

When perusing the Emperor's writings of the year 1813, I cannot help feeling that the attitude revealed in them differs entirely from that shown in similar circumstances

---

[1] C. N. To Lobau. Peterswalde, 18th September, noon.
[2] C. N. To Saint Gyr. Peterswalde, 18th September.
[3] C. N. To Berthier. Peterswalde, 18th September, 5 p.m.

in 1796, and I am reluctantly convinced against my will that there are undoubted evidences of indecision and hesitation, not of a quick adaptation to changing circumstances, in his intentions, as he first turned off towards Berlin, then towards Bohemia, and then again towards Silesia. I think facts justify my view. And what did the Emperor gain during this period? One might of course say that he gained the object of his operations, that he forced the enemy back into Bohemia, without venturing upon a battle; that he crowned the mountain passes of the Erzgebirge, and lay in ambush behind them, waiting for Schwarzenberg to come and attack him; a course of action which he spoke of as "the best thing that could happen."[1] But meanwhile, time had been lost, and Blücher had taken advantage of this to come to dangerously close quarters. On the other hand, Schwarzenberg also may be said to have attained his object. His daring advances to Pirna had called Napoleon back from Silesia and relieved Blücher, and then, when the Emperor appeared in a threatening attitude at the mouth of the passes of the Erzgebirge, Schwarzenberg stood his ground. Still he had been unable to carry out all his projects, since his two offensive movements, one to the right to Rumburg, the other to the left to Leipzig, failed at the very outset on account of the French advance through the passes of the Erzgebirge.

Properly speaking, the final result was negative, for the operations on both sides neutralized each other in their results, and the decision was postponed. Our judgment as to Napoleon's conduct must therefore depend on the question whether he gained time or lost time. Generally speaking, the postponement of a decision must be/put down as a gain for the defensive; indeed, pure defence, e.g. the defence of a fortress, demands nothing else. Now the Emperor was on the defensive. But this general rule is after all only right,

[1] C. N. To Lobau. Peterswalde, 18th September, noon.

when such a postponement does not place the enemy in a position to force a decision upon us later on under circumstances much less advantageous to us. Who would venture to say now, that Frederick was wrong, when he made his advance in 1756 which led up to such a dangerous decision, and one which should have been postponed, since Austria and Russia had determined not to begin the war until the spring of 1757? After the great king's death, one of his fellow-workers at that time expressed this opinion in the Berlin Academy, and the spirit to which it gave birth soon bore the fruit we know of. Whoever stands with inferior forces between two stronger opponents can do nothing better than strike at them boldly as soon as possible, while they are yet separated. If he gives them time to think, to bring harmony into their plans, and to join their forces, he will assuredly be crushed by their superior forces united. It is just in such situations that one must make up for weakness in numbers by rapidity of movement, as indeed Napoleon did brilliantly in 1796 during those last days of July and first days of August; a course I then admired, failing to understand why a great critic should condemn him on that very account. In summing up the results of this period, we must consider the postponement of a decision by the Emperor as a loss of time and for this reason—a mistake.

Two additional circumstances justify this judgment, inasmuch as they show that to stay in his position was far more disadvantageous to the Emperor than to his opponents. For although the Emperor expected to be reinforced by Augereau, to whom he had sent orders on the 17th to lead up his 16,000 men as quickly as possible to Jena, yet on the other hand 50,000 Russians under Bennigsen were on the march from Breslau to join the Allies. Secondly, the difficulty of obtaining supplies in Saxony, now an entirely exhausted area, was so increasingly serious, that Napoleon a few days after the events just described, could not help exclaiming: "The army is no longer fed; it would be mere self-deception to look upon it in any other light."[1] A convincing evidence of their distress were the measures we saw him take to secure the flour-transport expected from Torgau. When, before this, had he ever sent a corps of infantry and two cavalry corps forward on such an errand? And the enemy were well aware of this source of weakness, and partly based their calculations upon it.

The Emperor now saw that something must be done to force Blücher back again, for he had approached so close to the central position of the French army, that the whole strategical edifice was shaken. Napoleon therefore moved Mortier on the 19th of September forward to Lohmen, but no determined advance to Bautzen was made, either on that day or on the next, owing to a cause which, like so many other things, was a new factor in the Napoleonic strategy: the weather was too bad for the Emperor. "Yesterday and last night have been so horrible, that there was no possibility of making any movement."[2] We again see the same strange want of energy in the Emperor: "Why hurry? we have time enough; what cannot be done to-day will be done to-morrow." "Cousin! Write to the King of Naples, the Duke of Ragusa, the Duke of Tarentum and Prince Poniatowski, that the wretched weather to-day renders every movement out of the question, and that, if the weather is no better to-morrow, we cannot be ready to move until the day after."[3] But in war, more than in many other circumstances, it is true that—

"The moment we let slip to-day
No eternity can restore."

In 1805 the Emperor's way of thinking was very different.

[1] C. N. To Daru. Harthau, 23rd September, 4 a.m.
[2] C. N. To Marmont. Pirna, 20th September, 4 a.m.
[3] C. N. To Berthier. Pirna, 20th September.

He then wrote: "It is raining heavily, but that will not delay the forced marches of the Grand Army."[1]

And whilst he thus lost day after day, he had immediately afterwards to confess that in his present position, time was of the greatest importance. "In a war based on combinations like this, days are of great importance."[2] But in another place he said: "The great business of the moment seems to be to save our arms and cartridges as much as possible."[3] The fact is, that that equilibrium between insight and promptitude, which he himself pointed out as most desirable in a general, was no longer present, and we thus understand why irresolution, with wavering, inconsequent, illogical action, and therefore failure, were the result.

On the 21st September he conceived the idea of collecting all the forces around Dresden and giving his troops a rest. Accordingly he entrusted Saint-Cyr with the covering of the Elbe from Pillnitz as far as Königstein, and placed Lobau and Lauriston for this purpose under his command, making altogether 40,000 to 50,000 men, according to his calculations. Mortier was to return to Pirna, Murat and Marmont to Meissen. Ney was to cover the Elbe from Magdeburg to Torgau. However, the various reports which came in as to Blücher's movements, some of which pointed to a march to the right and others to a march to the left, induced the Emperor to give orders at 2 a.m. on the 22nd, to Macdonald, to advance steadily on that day, until he learnt, by the resistance offered, where the main forces of the enemy lay; although his hopes to force a decisive battle had become very slight; "this would be very advantageous for us, but seems to lie outside their calculations."[4]

Napoleon himself drove about noon to Fischbach,

---

[1] Bulletin of the Grand Army. Zusmarshausen, 10th October.
[2] C. N. To Macdonald. Dresden, 22nd September, 10 a.m.
[3] C. N. To Marmont. Pirna, 20th September, 4 a.m.
[4] C. N. To Marmont. Pirna, 20th September, 4 a.m.

LEIPZIG 323

where he mounted his horse and rode forward viâ Schmiedefeld. Blücher's advanced posts were driven in by the corps of Souham and Gérard, pushing forward by Harthau; Bischofswerda also was captured and Lauriston advanced to Neustadt. The Emperor spent the night in Harthau. The next day the French corps continued their forward movements in the same directions and Blücher fell back upon Förstgen. The Emperor had "passed the whole forenoon of the 23rd in Harta, a prey to irresolution."[1] During the night a message from Ney, dated "Düben, the 22nd, 4 p.m.," had reached him, announcing that the enemy had completed a bridge over the Elbe at the junction of the Elster, on the 20th, and that therefore they could cross at any moment. At 4 p.m. he once more rode to Lauriston's troops and watched the retreating enemy; then he went back again to Harthau.

He now decided to give up the right bank of the Elbe entirely, bringing Macdonald over to the left bank; where he would hold himself in readiness to move across the stream, as soon as the enemy advanced against him. "It is my intention to have a bridge at Königstein, one at Pirna, one at Pillnitz, three at Dresden and one at Meissen, and to allow my forces to go over to the left bank, so as to allow them to rest. All these bridges will be defended by strong bridge-heads, and all the issues from the Dresdener Wald will be held in force: in this position I shall watch the enemy closely, and if they engage in any offensive operation, I shall fall upon them, so that they cannot evade a battle."[2] He had decided, therefore, upon a pure defensive, as he had done formerly behind the Passarge; the same resolution, the same form, and yet how great the difference! Then, the decision had been arrived at voluntarily and was carried out immediately, in spite of an inferior enemy in full retreat; now

[1] O. v. O. 346.
[2] C. N. To Murat. Harthau, 23rd September.

the same resolution had been forced upon the Emperor as the only feasible way of escape after long irresolution and hesitation by a superior enemy, who, in accordance with a definite plan, was avoiding a decisive blow. Then, the resolve to act on the defensive had not been absolutely necessary; it was taken because it was the best course in the circumstances; now, it was most unwise, and was evidence of the fact that the Emperor was in the awkward position of having his proceedings dictated to him by the enemy.

(107c) On the 24th, therefore, the retrograde movement began; Mortier marched to Dresden, where Souham and Lauriston were to arrive on the 26th; Poniatowski also fell back by Fischbach, so as to cross the Elbe; Macdonald was to cover this movement, by taking up with his own corps and Sebastiani's a position at Weissig; Marmont and Latour-Maubourg were to proceed to Meissen; L'Héritier remained at Grossenhayn in an attitude of observation. The Emperor, who had ridden forward almost to Bischofswerda, returned to Dresden during the night.

In consequence of this resolve to fall back entirely behind the Elbe, Marmont and Latour-Maubourg were, during the next few days, moved further back from Meissen to Wurzen, whilst the Old Guard and two divisions of the Young Guard, Macdonald, Souham and Sebastiani lay in and around Dresden. Mortier, with two divisions of the Young Guard, was, like Lauriston, facing Pillnitz; Saint-Cyr and Lobau at Borne and Berggieshübel, with Victor on their right, covered the roads from Bohemia. Finally Poniatowski was sent back to Waldheim *viâ* Nossen, since the Emperor no longer felt any anxiety about the western issues from the Erzgebirge.

Let us once more cast a brief glance at Ney's army, so as to take in the whole situation. The Marshal had, after Dennewitz, fallen back as far as Torgau, where he

LEIPZIG

collected his troops again on the 8th September; he then withdrew behind the Elbe and took up a position at Düben. On the 19th the XII. Corps was broken up by the Emperor's orders and distributed amongst the other two corps; Oudinot proceeded to Dresden, and on the 25th took over the command of two divisions of the Young Guard. In the meantime the enemy had slowly approached the Elbe and thrown bridges across at Acken, Rosslau and Elster; upon this Ney sent Bertrand to Wartenburg, and the latter took this village on the 24th. The enemy thereupon, during the night of the 25th, destroyed the bridge at Elster. Ney advanced against Rosslau, but could not seize the bridge-head there, so he placed Reynier in position at Oranienbaum and Wörlitz, and Bertrand at Kemberg, his lines extending to the right as far as Wartenburg.

The Emperor's anxiety as to the western passes of the Erzgebirge and the possibility of Schwarzenberg attacking there, was increased, when, on the 28th, the cavalry division of Lefèbvre-Desnoëttes, which had been sent forward to clear the rear of the army of the hostile partisan leaders and light troops, who were becoming bolder and more enterprising, was compelled to evacuate Altenburg, where it had been stationed. The French troops were continually being pushed back further and further. Marmont withdrew to Leipzig, leaving Latour-Maubourg at Wurzen, Lauriston to Nossen, Poniatowski to Frohburg, and Victor to Chemnitz; the latter was joined by L'Héritier, whose place at Meissen was taken by Souham.

On the 1st October the Emperor became aware of the fact that Schwarzenberg was actually operating towards the left. "All reports agree that the enemy is making a movement along the road from Kommotau to Marienberg."[1] As to Blücher, the Emperor noticed

---

[1] C. N. To Macdonald. Dresden, 1st October.

that he too was also moving towards the right. "It seems that the corps of Langeron, Sacken and Blücher have all executed a movement towards Elsterwerda and Grossenhayn."[1] In this he only discerned the intention of an attack from the north, upon his position at Dresden, on account of the more favourable lie of the ground. "It is possible that this is done in order to attack our fortified camp from the side of the plain along the roads from Berlin and from Meissen. As they thus avoid the forest, this, as a matter of fact, is the most vulnerable point."[2] Blücher, however, had undertaken a much larger and more effective manœuvre, and a truly Napoleonic operation, when he marched on the 26th September with 70,000 men to the right viâ Königsbrück and Kamenz, in order to cross the Elbe somewhere near Elster. And only when this operation had entirely succeeded, when Blücher had crossed the Elbe and beaten Bertrand at Wartenburg, did the Emperor become apprehensive as to the disappearance of that general. On the 4th October he wrote to Macdonald: "I attach great importance to knowing definitely what has become of Langeron, Sacken, and Yorck. I desire you therefore to order a reconnaissance of 7000 to 8000 men, infantry, cavalry, and artillery, towards Grossenhayn (for Sacken has been in that neighbourhood), as well as other reconnaissances in other directions, so that you may learn with certainty what has become of the enemy's Silesian army."[3]

During these days it became very evident how much the Emperor had changed, how he had become in everything the very opposite of General Bonaparte, and how no insight, no genius is sufficient in war if it is not combined with resolution and mental energy. We need only to quote himself as a witness, and his own words condemn him. In 1806 he had addressed the Prussian army

[1] C. N. To Macdonald. Dresden, 2nd October.
[2] Ibid.
[3] C. N. Dresden.

with just scorn: "While you deliberate, the French army marches." Now he, himself, at Dresden, sat deliberating, considering this plan and that, while the enemy disappeared from before Dresden and moved on his flanks. Formerly, he prosecuted his plan steadfastly; he watched the enemy's movements in order to make use of them and altered his own accordingly, and, on the whole, his strategical idea, once conceived, was kept before him and carried out. Now, he seemed always to wait until some measure of the enemy forced him to a partial counter-move, just as Mack had done at Ulm. Furthermore, we must confess that at this time the Emperor's military insight showed distinct deterioration, for how otherwise can it be explained that he, who in the past had accomplished the march to the right to Piacenza, and also the march to Rossassna with such success, could now be so deceived by the equally important march of Blücher to Elster, that the battle of Wartenburg alone showed him his error! Up to now he had been sitting at Dresden, to use the ignoble, but not inapt simile, like a spider in its web, ready to pounce upon the first who should touch his strategical threads, but now, when Blücher and Schwarzenberg turned aside to the right and left, this web lost its importance, and although the Emperor remained in it obstinately and yet irresolutely, the force of circumstances compelled him at last to recognize the danger of his being surrounded and crushed in his own web, and he was forced to come out of it.

If we examine the state of affairs as it stood shortly (107d) before he took this enforced resolution, we find, on the 4th October, the Emperor himself with the Guards, Lobau, Saint-Cyr, Macdonald and Sebastiani in and around Dresden, Souham at Meissen, and Marmont and Latour-Maubourg at Taucha. Augereau, who had come up with his 16,000 men, including the cavalry corps of Milhaud, stood at Jena. The task of watching Schwarzenberg had been entrusted on the 2nd October to a detached force under Murat, and which on the 4th was disposed as follows:—Poniatowski at Altenburg, Victor and L'Héritier at Flöha and Freiberg, and Lauriston at Mittweida. Ney's corps were at Bitterfeld and Düben. The Emperor had altogether 220,000 men in Saxony. On the other side Blücher stood on that day with 64,000 men at Kemberg, after having on the previous day beaten Bertrand's corps at Wartenberg and forced the passage of the Elbe. Bernadotte stood with 80,000 men at Acken and Rosslau, partly on the left bank of the Elbe. Schwarzenberg had on the 27th of September begun his march to the left with 170,000 men, and now occupied Marienberg, Annaberg, Schwarzenberg and Kommotau. In his rear Bennigsen had reached Teplitz with 50,000 men.

During the night of the 4th October the Emperor received the report of the defeat Bertrand had suffered, but without any details. He, at once, at 2 a.m., ordered Marmont with Latour-Maubourg and Souham who was to join them from Meissen, to march to Ney and place themselves under the latter's orders; he was then to drive the enemy back again over the Elbe and seize their bridges. Oudinot was sent forward to Meissen to take Souham's place. Then, in his study the Emperor examined in detail the strategical position, as well as the measures to be taken: his views are shown in various documents which he dictated:[1]

FIRST NOTE. POSITIONS OF THE ENEMY.

"It seems certain that the enemy's Silesian army has

[1] I take these interesting notes from "Norvin's Portefeuille de 1813," ii. 366, although they are not found in the "Correspondance"; for they are a true picture of the state of affairs at the time and of the Emperor's views; the only thing which may throw some doubts upon their authenticity is the fact that the corps are indicated by numbers, whilst in the notes for his own use the Emperor used almost invariably the names of the corps leaders. In four places the numbers are evidently wrong, and I have therefore put 6th instead of 2nd, 2nd instead of 3rd, 14th instead of 15th, and 5th instead of 15th. These places are marked by asterisks (*).

gone to Wittenberg, and that the large army from Teplitz is making a movement to the left.

"The Silesian army cannot be estimated at less than 60,000 men with the corps of Yorck, Blücher and Langeron.

"The army of Berlin, composed of the Swedish corps, one Russian corps and the corps of Bülow and Tauentzien, cannot be inferior in strength to the Silesian.

"There should therefore be an army of 120,000 men on the Lower Elbe; however, it remains to be seen whether it has not detached some forces towards Hamburg.

"The army of Teplitz, composed of the Austrians, one Prussian corps and one Russian corps, cannot be estimated at less than 120,000 men.

"The plan of the Allies would therefore seem to be, to let two large armies march one to the right and one to the left, so as to force the Emperor to quit Dresden."

SECOND NOTE. POSITIONS OF THE FRENCH ARMY.

"The 4th and the 7th Corps, under the command of the Prince of the Moskova, are on the Lower Elbe.

"The Duke of Ragusa with the 1st Cavalry Corps and the 3rd Infantry Corps is in the neighbourhood of Eilenburg and Torgau. These two armies form together a force of 80,000 men, which cover the left wing.

"The 1st, 14th, 2nd, 5th and 8th Corps form a force of 70,000 men, which cover the right wing.

"Finally the 11th, the Guards and the 2nd Cavalry Corps, a force of 60,000 men, are in the centre."

THIRD NOTE. WHAT IS TO BE DONE?

"This evening it will be known whether the whole Silesian army or only a part of it has marched to Wittenberg.

"According to the one or the other assumption, we might resume the offensive on the right bank and march with the Guards and the 11th Corps to Torgau, effect there a junction with the 6th * and 3rd, and thus move with an army of 100,000 men from Torgau along the right bank against the enemy's bridges.

"All the corps which cover the right wing would fall back upon Dresden before the enemy, as soon as they became aware of that movement, and evacuate Dresden, if it were necessary, so as to march to Torgau."

Another Plan.

"This plan would consist in leading all the forces to Leipzig, giving up Dresden altogether.

"For this purpose the 11th Corps, the Guards and the 2nd Cavalry Corps would begin their march to Wurzen; the 2nd * and 5th Corps would march to Colditz, and the 1st and 14th to Dresden.

"After having thus sacrificed the magazines, the fortifications and field hospitals, we should endeavour to beat the enemy's right wing, and if successful, return to Dresden.

"If unsuccessful in defeating the enemy's right wing, because it had retreated too far, we should evidently be forced to occupy the line of the Saale."

Third Plan.

"To reinforce the left wing of the 11th corps, and in this position await events."

Other Notes on the Situation of the Army.

"It is impossible to go into winter quarters in Dresden without having fought a battle.

"Two courses are open to us:

"First:—To preserve Dresden and try to fight a battle so as to return thither, when we shall find everything in the same condition, if we win that battle.

"Secondly:—To leave Dresden altogether, try to fight a battle, and if we win it, to return to Dresden, driving the

LEIPZIG 331

Austrian army into Bohemia. We should in this case only go to Dresden temporarily, for even if we had won the battle, the Elbe would not be available during the winter, and we should have but little chance of an offensive movement towards Bohemia; Dresden could therefore no longer be the centre of our operations. It would be much more advantageous to be at Leipzig or Magdeburg."

MOVEMENTS UNDER THE FIRST PLAN.

"If we wished to preserve Dresden, we should have to act as follows:—
"Hand over the safeguarding of Dresden to the 1st and 14th * Corps.

"Leave the 2nd, 5th and 8th Corps as corps of observation at Chemnitz and Freiberg, and march with the 6th, 4th, 7th, 11th and the Guards, to fight a battle."

MOVEMENTS UNDER THE SECOND PLAN.

"We should have to station by the day after to-morrow the 2nd, 5th and 8th Corps (the latter at Altenburg and no longer at Dresden) so as to occupy Chemnitz, but in such a manner, as though we came from Leipzig; the 1st and 14th would have to be set in motion for Dresden in order to follow the movement, or the 1st and 14th Corps would have to be ordered up, so as to be stationed likewise on the Nossen road, about in a line with Waldheim, with its rear towards Leipzig."

DIFFERENCE BETWEEN THE TWO PLANS.

"As I should, in the first plan, be obliged to leave the 2nd and 5th Corps in a position with their backs to Dresden, the enemy could, if he marched to Altenburg, anticipate them. He would in that case reach Leipzig so quickly, that this town would immediately see itself threatened, and the troops, left behind in Dresden, would, by the least error, be exposed to the danger of being driven from Dresden instead of evacuating that town.

"In the second plan, in which two armies would immediately be formed and at once stationed in their natural order, we should be enabled to preserve our central position, and to march either to the right or the left.

"Should the Emperor leave Dresden, the 1st and 14th Corps, and the 2nd and 5th* would be in a false position, and could not operate in harmony with each other and might see themselves cut off.

"In the first plan, these corps being left behind to preserve Dresden, His Majesty would have to remain in or near Dresden. In this case many possibilities on the left wing would be lost; it would even be doubtful whether it were advisable to fight a battle, if His Majesty is not present in person. If we lost it, the situation would become such, that we should have to fall back from the Elbe to the Saale."

The next day the Emperor had made his choice. He resolved to turn in person with the main body of his army against the enemy, who had crossed the Elbe, and hoped there to be able to fight a battle. The Old Guard, Mortier, Macdonald and Sebastiani were to march to Meissen, whither the Emperor himself intended to proceed; Murat was to relinquish the connection with Dresden, kept up until now, and station himself between Schwarzenberg and Leipzig; Saint-Cyr and Lobau were to evacuate their positions in the Erzgebirge and withdraw their forces to Dresden. The former, who arrived in this city during the afternoon, had an interview with the Emperor, who explained to him his plan of action; viz.: he desired Saint-Cyr with the I. and XIV. Corps to defend Dresden, whilst he himself was fighting against Bernadotte or Blücher. "His manner of speaking was so hurried and violent; his resolution seemed to me so fixed, that I did not think of venturing upon any remarks on any one of the points about which he had been speaking."[1] For the rest, however, he was calm and cheerful, and soon leaving his present situation, he criticized Soult's operations in Spain against Wellington, which had just then been very unsuccessful. His remarks were so apposite and stated with so much clearness, that they excited the admiration of his listeners.

At midnight, he again sent for Saint-Cyr and informed him that he would also take the two corps in question with him on his offensive operations, and his reasons for this determination were irrefutable : " I shall certainly fight a battle; if I win, I shall regret not having all my forces at hand, and if I lose, you, if left behind here, would not have been of any service to me in the battle and would be irrevocably lost. For the rest, what is the use of Dresden to-day ? It can no longer be the corner-stone of the operations of the army, which would be unable to exist there any longer, considering the entire exhaustion of the surrounding country. . . . In Dresden there are 12,000 sick, who are sure to die, because they are the remnants of the 60,000 who have entered the hospitals since the beginning of the campaign. Add to this that the season is advancing, and that the Elbe, once it is frozen over, no longer affords a good position. I shall take up a new position, in which to spend the winter ; I shall keep my right wing back, resting it upon Erfurt, and extend my centre along the Saale, which affords a good position in all seasons, because the heights on its left bank always lend themselves admirably to a defence. I shall rest my left wing on Magdeburg, and this town will be of much more importance than Dresden. . . . Dresden is too near to Bohemia ; as soon as I make the slightest movement away from the environs of this town in order to approach that country, the enemy's armies would immediately retreat to it, since they have only a short distance to go, and I have

[1] Gouvion Saint-Cyr, Mém. iv. 184.

not got the means to cut them off, by moving on their rear. Finally I shall, by the more distant position which I am about to occupy, form a 'blind alley'; you understand what I mean."[1] From this fine strategical exposition it will be seen that he had at last become aware of the great danger to which his extremely protracted stay in Dresden had exposed him.

At 1 a.m. on the 7th October the following note, dictated by him, gave a definite form to the whole plan of offence :—

Note on the Movements of the Different Army Corps.

"(1.) In the course of the 7th a forced march will be made to Wurzen. I can establish my headquarters there with the cavalry of Sebastiani, with that of the Guards and the corps of Oudinot at a distance of four hours' march from Wurzen, so that I could be in Leipzig by the morning of the 8th, if this became absolutely necessary.

"(2.) The III. Infantry Corps will probably be at Wurzen, since the Duke of Ragusa has set it in motion towards the Mulde.

"(3.) General Lauriston will be able to take up a position at Rochlitz, having only to march for three hours; the Duke of Belluno may go to Mittweida, starting somewhat late; both will be in touch with Prince Poniatowski, who is at Frohburg. By to-morrow they can be at Frohburg and thus arrest the heads of the enemy's army.

"Marshal Saint-Cyr may this day, the 7th, lead the I. and XIV. Corps back to Dresden, occupy Meissen on the 8th, and begin his movements; evacuate Dresden on the 7th, and start on his full march to Wurzen.

"The result of these operations will be, that I shall be in a position to act as I like. From Wurzen I shall be able to march to Torgau, or against the enemy, by marching

[1] Gouvi on Saint-Cyr, Mém. iv. 185.

out from Wittenberg, or I can lead my whole army back to Leipzig and fight a pitched battle, or retreat behind the Saale.

" Details : The King of Naples would go to Mittweida, screening his movement; he would not evacuate Flöha until the night of the 7th. The enemy would not know until the morning of the 8th that the road from Chemnitz to Dresden was clear.

" General Lauriston would reach Rochlitz and quit Mittweida only after the heads of the II. Corps had arrived there.

" On the 8th the II. Corps would go to Rochlitz, and would remain in observation from Rochlitz to Frohburg, occupying Colditz, in order to keep in touch with the army. It would remain there until further orders, unless the enemy attacked it in force, in which case it would approach Leipzig, without allowing itself to be forced away from the Mulde.

" On the 8th the army under my personal command would be at Wurzen.

" On the 10th Marshal Saint-Cyr's Corps would be at Wurzen."

In this simple and practical outline of operations, we again, for a time, recognize the general who has so often excited our admiration by similar plans. His central position at Dresden having become untenable, he would therefore occupy another one on the Mulde at Wurzen, from whence he could fall upon any forces crossing the Elbe, attack them vigorously and throw them back over that river; after which he could safely effect a junction with Murat, in order to fight the decisive battle against Schwarzenberg.

The second possibility he was considering, viz., that of concentrating his army upon Leipzig, was certainly not particularly favourable, for then, the enemy, advancing concentrically, would be fully at liberty to bring up all their forces and crush him. If such an idea occurred to him it was, probably, only in order to enumerate all the possibilities which his march away from Dresden offered, or possibly, because he reckoned upon his absolute superiority in directing battles, a superiority hitherto always indisputable. "His great mental superiority gave him such confidence that he considered himself strong enough to defeat his enemies, whatever system of warfare they might adopt." [1]

Finally the third plan, that of withdrawing behind the Saale, was certainly the most cautious and the wisest. That point he could always reach in safety, however much the enemy hastened; there he could be reinforced, whilst the enemy would be compelled to leave some troops behind during their advance: on the Saale he would find a new and excellent line of defence, and might begin a new phase of his defensive plan, after having concluded that on the Elbe. Still, in the Emperor's situation, it was perhaps impossible for him to carry out such a wise and cautious plan. He, the successful soldier on a throne, could not, though in a military sense it were better, retreat with impunity, give up countries he had once occupied, and retire to his own frontiers. Besides, it would have been a great encouragement to the Allies, who always felt a certain dread of a pitched battle, and had tried to gain everything by marches and counter marches, if the whole of Saxony now fell into their hands without any battle, as the successful issue of their strategical manœuvres. For this reason, the continued march to Düben, which the Emperor actually was about to execute, was probably the best course for him to pursue under existing circumstances.

According to this plan the marching orders were now issued. "The Emperor himself worked without intermission until the morning of the 7th October, then took a bath and started after 6 o'clock." [2] He proceeded *viâ* Wilsdruf to Meissen, and arrived, after a short stay in this

[1] Berthezène, Souvenirs mil.   [2] O. v. O. 357.

town, at the castle of Seerhausen, in the afternoon. He was now aware that the whole Silesian army had crossed the Elbe at Wartenburg, and was all the more eager for a battle. Nevertheless, the idea came to him at Meissen of still holding Dresden, and he sent orders from there to the Corps Saint-Cyr and Lobau to remain there.

We are not in a position to explain or account for this sudden determination in the Emperor's mind. It was undoubtedly a mistake in generalship; not one of those which here and there are committed in a weak moment by the most able generals, and which only prove that even the most able cannot escape having their weak moments; but it was, at the most decisive juncture, a complete departure from those great principles which had laid the foundation of his successes. He holds a secondary point, Dresden, whilst the great question was now to gain a decisive victory. Dresden would after such a victory have, as a matter of course, fallen again into his hands; but the loss of the two corps, which he left behind there, was destined to be felt bitterly by him on that battle-field of Leipzig, where not only the fate of Dresden, of Saxony, of Germany, nay, of the whole of Europe was to be decided.

There was scarcely one principle that he emphasized more frequently or more strongly than this : " I still hold to my opinion, that whenever one wishes to fight a battle, . . . one should not divide, but concentrate all one's forces and bring overwhelming masses into play; all the troops left behind run the risk of being beaten singly or being forced to abandon their positions."[1] " All the enemy's troops which engage in distant manœuvres will be out of reach on the battle-field."[2] Even in the most insignificant circumstances this principle must hold good : " Even when divisions are about to fight, every single man must be mustered."[3]

[1] C. N. To Berthier. Paris, 6th December, 1811.
[2] C. N. To Saint-Cyr. Bantzen, 17th August, 1813.
[3] C. N. To Davout. Schönbrunn, 15th November, 1805.

And the very night before, he had explained to Saint-Cyr so clearly, so convincingly, why he was obliged to take these two corps with him. In this clinging to Dresden we see not so much the mistake of a general, as the obstinacy of a ruler, who will not admit that he can be compelled to relinquish anything, and who, not without reason, is alarmed for the continuance of his rule, based only upon force, so soon as he gives any indication that this force has diminished. This same general, who in 1796 gave up without any regret the siege of Mantua, in order to gain a tangible military success, now saw himself forced by the want of stability in the state of things which he had himself created, to sacrifice an actual military advantage to the semblance of keeping up his dominion. The man who, above all, always recognized facts, had now to sacrifice facts to appearances, and thus he was at variance with himself; he had become his own enemy, and his military mistakes were only the external signs of inward disturbance.

On the 7th October we therefore find: Souham at Torgau, Latour-Maubourg along the Elbe as far as Torgau, the Old Guard, Oudinot, Mortier, Macdonald and Sebastiani at Meissen or beyond this town, Marmont at Taucha and Ney at Bennewitz on the Mulde. Blücher and Bernadotte, who knew but little about the French, stood, on that day, the former around Düben, the latter on the line Köthen—Jessnitz, with the corps of Tauentzien in his rear at Dessau. On the 8th, the Emperor stood with the mass of his troops collected around Wurzen; Bertrand at Schilda forming his right wing, and Marmont with Latour-Maubourg at Taucha his left wing. Ney with the corps of Reynier was near Eilenburg and Wurzen. The Emperor presumed Blücher to be with 60,000 men at Düben, and was going to attack him there by starting all his corps at 6 a.m. on the 9th and marching concentrically towards that town. Therefore on the morning of the 9th the entire French army was on the march forward, whilst Blücher was marching away to the right, in order to post himself behind the Saale in accordance with an agreement with Bernadotte. By the forward movement of the French, one of Blücher's corps, which had stood at Mockrehna, was in danger of being cut off, was only able to avoid the dangerous point, Düben, by a night march and reached Raguhn at 10 a.m.; the two other corps reached Jessnitz Mühlbeck and advanced to Zörbig on the 10th. Bernadotte had remained stationary.

On the 9th the Emperor had arrived at Eilenburg with the Guards; Souham was at Priestäblich, Reynier at Düben; Bertrand and Macdonald advanced to Auenhain and Mockrehna, and the rest of the army stood between Eilenburg and Wurzen. On the 10th the Emperor moved his troops forward to the Elbe; Macdonald advanced to Wittenberg, Bertrand to Schmiedeberg, Ney to Gräfenhaynchen, Reynier, *viâ* Schköna to Kemberg, and Sebastiani to Trebitz. The Emperor himself drove to Düben, where he arrived during the first hours of the afternoon, in a bad temper, and established his headquarters in the little castle there. He had the Guards and Latour-Maubourg with him.

He was annoyed to see the same game played again before him, which previously on the fields of Silesia had forced him to march fruitlessly hither and thither and had placed a decisive victory out of his reach. What could he do? He knew already that Schwarzenberg's army was on the march to Leipzig, and that Murat would not long be able to block its way. It appeared to him, and we believe, justly, that Blücher and Bernadotte were on the point of falling back again behind the Elbe, since they had not stood their ground before him; he wanted to follow them, and in case they wished to defend the passage of that river, find there at last the opportunity for the battle so eagerly longed for. He also intended, either after that battle or without fighting one, to cross the Elbe and take his line of operations on its right bank from Dresden to Magdeburg. Murat, whose force he estimated at 62,000 men, was to try to hold out at Leipzig, but to avoid any general battle against superior forces. Should the enemy develop any such strength, he was to fall back *via* Eilenburg and Düben to Torgau and Wittenberg, in order to cross the Elbe.

Thus the Emperor would have deprived Schwarzenberg of the object of his operations, viz. Murat's army; he would have seriously damaged Blücher's and Bernadotte's armies, and, by a rapid movement, placed the Elbe between the two hostile masses. For this purpose, his corps had been moved forward *via* Schmiedberg, Trebitz and Kemberg to Wittenberg, and *via* Gräfenhaynchen, against the other bridges of the enemy, as soon as he became aware that his opponents were falling back before him. This plan was as well-conceived as any one of his plans had ever been, but the Emperor's position was so dangerous, that only quick execution, restless activity and stern persistence could grasp the situation and discover a chance of escape.

But on the same evening he again changed his mind. He now considered the plan of sending 20,000 men to Leipzig, perhaps even of concentrating his entire army on this town, and began to carry out this idea by ordering Marmont, who had already started on the march to Düben, to remain on the other side of the Mulde. But on the 11th he once more altered his views and continued his forward movement to Wittenberg. Reynier was to cross the Elbe at that point, Bertrand with Sebastiani was to proceed to Wartenburg, in order to see to the demolition of the bridges there; and Macdonald, and later, the Guards, were to follow them. Marmont was to cross the Mulde at Düben; Ney was to remain at Gräfenhaynchen and reconnoitre in every direction, for, although the Emperor suspected the enemy's main body to be around Dessau, he became now aware of the possibility of their retreat over the Saale.

This, as a matter of fact, was the resolution taken in the enemy's camp. Blücher moved to Halle and Loebejün; Bernadotte remained at Rothenburg, having left Tauentzien behind at Dessau to cover the bridges of Rosslau and Acken, and Tauentzien, threatened by the advance of the French to Wittenberg, with being cut off from Berlin, fell back behind the Elbe and took up a position on its right bank at Rosslau. On the same day Reynier had crossed the Elbe at Wittenberg and driven back to Coswig a hostile division which had been stationed in front of that fortress as a corps of observation. Macdonald followed Reynier, Bertrand reached Wartenburg, and Latour-Maubourg Kemberg.

The chief characteristic of the Emperor's proceedings during these days in Düben is his irresolution. "I saw the Emperor at this time, waiting for news from the Elbe, sitting quite idle on a sofa in his room in front of the large table, on which lay a sheet of white paper which he covered with large Gothic characters, such as may be seen on birthday cards. His geographer, d'Albe, and another assistant sat as idly in the corners of the room, waiting, at their ease, for his orders."[1] Marmont, who having arrived with despatches on the evening of the 11th of October, and having had an interview that night lasting five hours, until breakfast, which was taken at 6 a.m. on the 12th, and during which the whole military situation was minutely gone through, also came to the conclusion that: "One fails to recognize the old Napoleon again during this campaign."[2] He no longer travelled daily, ten leagues, as formerly, on horseback, in order to superintend everything and conduct everything, "he remains almost constantly shut up in his room, to which his bed and his maps have been conveyed,"[3] and instead of issuing his orders, he now consulted those about him.

During this same night of the 11th the Emperor heard

[1] O. v. O. 363.   [2] Mém. v. 271.
[3] Fain, Manuscrit de 1813, ii. 372.

of the enemy's march to Halle. At first he wanted to persist in allowing Reynier to march to Rosslau along the right bank, whilst Ney was to advance thither *viâ* Dessau, but at 9.30 he gave definite orders for all his corps to march back to Leipzig, "for it is my intention to fight a battle there with all my forces."[1] This resolution he set down in the following note:[2]

"I am giving orders to Ney to proceed to Düben. Ney will not receive this order before 2 p.m.; his troops will start upon their march at 3 o'clock; they cannot cross the bridge of Düben before the morning of the 13th (the Guards will have crossed it by that time); he can without difficulty be at Taucha on the evening of the 13th.

"Since Latour-Maubourg is at Kemberg, there will be no difficulty there either.

"The Duke of Tarentum will not receive the order until 3 o'clock; should he have crossed over the Elbe bridge, he will need the whole night to recross: he will not reach Düben until the morning of the 13th, and will start on his march to Taucha in the course of the 14th.

"General Reynier, who is on the march to Rosslau, will only be able to reach Wittenberg this night; he can be at Taucha by the 15th and march *viâ* Eilenburg.

"The same is the case with General Sebastiani.

"As to the Dukes of Treviso and of Reggio and the Reserves of the Guards, they will all cross the bridge of Düben to-day and reach Taucha early to-morrow morning.

———

"The king is this day, the 12th, at Cröbern; he will be to-morrow, the 13th, at Leipzig and Taucha, where I shall have arrived to-morrow with Curial,[3] the Old and the Young Guards, and the Duke of Ragusa, altogether

[1] C. N. To Berthier. Düben, 12th October.
[2] C. N. Notes on the concentration of the various army-corps at Taucha. Düben, 12th October, 10 a.m.
[3] In command of one division of the Old Guards.

nearly 40,000 men, which with the King's 50,000 men will make close upon 90,000 men.

"These 90,000 men will in the course of the next day, the 13th, on which the enemy will not yet be in a position to attack, be reinforced by Ney, Bertrand, and Latour-Maubourg.

"On the 15th our whole army will be concentrated.

"To-morrow, the 13th, the enemy will reach Cröbern. They will hear that the Grand Army has arrived. They will spend the 14th in massing their troops. I have therefore the 13th and 14th in which to mass mine. I go further and say, even if my whole army were at Düben, it could not arrive any earlier, unless it had five or six points of crossing."

He then recapitulated these movements, and made a calculation of the numbers of men, and came finally to the conclusion: "Thus I shall have in first line, nearly 120,000 men; second line, 70,000 men; total about 190,000 men."

Up to this time the Emperor was still under the impression that the troops which Reynier had met on the right bank of the Elbe, viz. the corps of Tauentzien, composed the whole of Bernadotte's army, and that Blücher stood alone behind the Saale. Thus he spoke of being rid of 40,000 to 50,000 enemies, and that the decisive battle would take place without them. But he felt great anxiety about Murat's situation, and at 4 p.m. sent an officer to him to investigate the state of affairs. For the rest he still continued his forward movement towards the Elbe, although he had really, as we have seen, resolved upon his departure for Leipzig; Marmont alone was on the march towards this town. Reynier therefore advanced further on the right bank towards Rosslau, and Tauentzien, who, observing Ney on the other hand, also advancing rapidly *viâ* Dessau, destroyed the bridge and retreated by a night march to Zerbst. Bernadotte had remained stationary. Blücher was concentrating around Halle and occupied Merseburg, from whence he resumed communications with Schwarzenberg, entirely in the rear of the French. The latter had, during this whole time, continued his forward movement, slowly, it is true, but uninterruptedly; Murat had in the same manner retreated before him, and was now, on the 12th, in position in front of Wachau, having his right wing, Poniatowski, on the P.eisse near Cröbern; his centre, Victor, at Güldengossa, and his left wing, Lauriston, extended beyond Störmthal; Marmont moved to Stötteritz, as a reserve. Schwarzenberg was in touch with the French line.

It cannot be open to any doubt, that, as matters stood on the 12th October, the Emperor had no longer any choice but to depart for Leipzig; this was the punishment for his irresolution. To have carried out now that bold operation beyond the Elbe, would have meant only a blind sally into air; there were no longer any forces there, and Murat, left to face thrice his numbers unsupported, would then have been lost. But the departure for Leipzig was, in itself, only a manœuvre dictated by despair; were the whole French army there, it would have greatly superior forces opposed to it, for nothing could now prevent the enemy advancing thither with their entire forces, and the tactical position there, as Marmont said very appositely, "at the bottom of a funnel,"[1] must lead to annihilation, should the battle be lost. Strategically the Emperor was already lost. Blücher and Schwarzenberg stood ominously near his only lines of communication with their main forces, and had already effected communication with each other in his rear.

If we take the most unfavourable positions in modern warfare, Ulm, Jena, Sedan, we shall find none worse than this. Even on the 11th it might still have been feasible to change the fortune of war, if the Emperor had either made a forced march to Grimma and, uniting with Murat,

[1] Mém. v. 273.

LEIPZIG

had fallen upon Schwarzenberg, or if he had rapidly called in Murat and executed his plan of crossing to the right bank of the Elbe. He adopted no general resolution, but acting as Mack, Brunswick, had done in the past, and as MacMahon was to do in the future, he pushed individual corps forward, intending to arrive at a decision, if he should be able by this means to obtain definite news of the enemy. This rarely succeeds in war, and as a matter of fact he did not stir from the spot. Formerly he had always advanced rapidly against the enemy's most vulnerable point, sure that the latter would then be forced to meet him with his main body ; now, while he hesitated to act and always sought full information first, Bernadotte disappeared, Blücher evaded him ; and, in spite of the corps, he pushed forward as far as and even beyond the Elbe, in spite of a four days' stay at Düben, the Emperor was entirely mistaken regarding Bernadotte, and lost time that could not be regained at the most decisive moment of the campaign.

At noon on the 13th the final departure of Napoleon for Leipzig began. But he was now aware that Bernadotte was at Bernburg and that therefore he was still out of his reach. He had learnt besides, that on the 8th October, Bavaria had renounced its allegiance and had joined his enemies, though this news probably had no influence upon his determination. He believed at this time, that the decisive battle would not take place till the 15th or 16th October, therefore such a distant event would certainly not modify any of his immediate measures ; what he said about this in his bulletin of the 15th October, was subsequently invented, in order to account for his defective strategy. Murat had, on this day, the 13th, fallen back as far as the heights of Wachau, and the next day repulsed a strong attack of the enemy, which the latter had undertaken for the purpose of a reconnaissance. Blücher was still at Halle and Bernadotte at Cöthen. (109)

The Emperor's army was now in full advance upon

Leipzig. Bertrand reached Eutritzsch during the night, Latour-Maubourg got as far as the neighbourhood of Radefeld, Macdonald to Gross and Klein Wölkau, Souham arrived beyond Düben; the Young Guard was at Widderitzsch; Marmont stood in position at Lindenthal; Reynier only was still in the rear, occupied in crossing back to the left bank of the Elbe. The Emperor left Düben at 7 a.m. and arrived in Leipzig at noon; he rode round the town and took up a position in the open field, to the south of the road to Wurzen, from whence he heard and saw the artillery fire of Murat, who was actively engaged; he followed the course of the combat and established his headquarters in the evening at an hotel in the village of Reudnitz.

Early on the morning of the 15th Murat came to see the Emperor and report on the fighting of the preceding day. About 10 o'clock he mounted his horse and rode forward with the latter to Liebertwolkwitz, ordered a camp fire to be lighted on the height to the west of this village, and issued his orders for the march of the corps, as they arrived, to take up their settled positions. We find the French army in the following order on that day: Lauriston at Liebertwolkwitz, Victor at Wachau, Poniatowski at Markkleeberg and Dösen, with one flank extending along the Pleisse by Dölitz as far as Connewitz; at Dösen the Polish cavalry corps of Kellermann, and Latour-Maubourg's cavalry at Zweinaundorf. At Holzhausen the cavalry were under Pajol, having come up with Augereau, and the latter himself with his own corps was at Zuckelhausen. The whole of the Guards were posted as a general reserve, at Reudnitz and Crottendorf. To the north of Leipzig Bertrand was at Eutritzsch and Marmont at Lindenthal. Of Souham's corps, two divisions advanced as far as Mockau, the third being still in the rear on the road from Düben. Lindenau, important as being the only road of retreat, had been occupied by two battalions under General Margaron.

Macdonald was at Taucha, and Sebastiani in full march towards this place, and finally Reynier had just reached Düben.

In the afternoon the Emperor again mounted his horse and proceeded first to Poniatowski on the extreme right wing of his formation, where he minutely examined the Pleisse and the points of crossing there. Then he rode along the whole front of his army, visited the cavalry at Holzhausen and Zweinaundorf, and returned finally to Reudnitz. He concluded from the reports received up to now, that Bernadotte stood at Merseburg ; as to Blücher, he did not expect him by the road from Halle, but by that from Weissenfels, and as to Schwarzenberg's army, he believed it to be collected, generally speaking, along the line Naunhof—Cröbern. As a matter of fact, however, Blücher had after all advanced along the road from Halle and stood at Schkenditz—Kursdorf and at Gross Kugel. Bernadotte was on the line Wettin—Petersberg—Zörbig and at Oppin. Schwarzenberg's right wing stood on the line Pommsen—Güldengossa—Cröbern—Mägdeborn, and his left wing at Lützen and Markranstädt, with the reserves at Audigast.

Thus, if the battle commenced on the 16th, the Emperor could bring 170,000 men into action, Reynier alone, with 14,000 men would not be able to be present on that day. The Allies could dispose of about 200,000 ; Bernadotte, with his 60,000 men, would not be able to appear in time, neither would Bennigsen, nor an Austrian corps, 65,000 strong, which had been left behind in front of Dresden, at Waldheim and Penig. On the battle-field itself, therefore, the Emperor would be only slightly inferior to the enemy, although the latter possessed, on the whole, such a marked superiority of numbers. This proves that Napoleon, having finally resolved to lead his army to Leipzig, had been much quicker than his antagonists in doing so, and had moved all his forces simultaneously. It is true that, as we have seen, he had committed the mistake of leaving Saint-Cyr and Lobau behind at Dresden, so that altogether 30,000 men would be absent. But the Allies did not advance either quickly enough or in sufficiently close formation towards Leipzig, and were therefore hardly superior to the Emperor in point of numbers on the first day of the battle. On the other hand, they realized the gravity of the situation, and ordered up the 65,000 men who had been left behind at Dresden; they would thus concentrate all the forces on the field of Leipzig, and obtain a decided superiority in numbers over the French.

On the morning of the 16th October the Emperor sent orders to Ney, who was in chief-command of all the forces north of the Parthe, to send Marmont's corps to Liebertwolkwitz; then he proceeded to that village and arrived about 9 o'clock on the Galgenberg, whilst the heads of the Guards reached Liebertwolkwitz. Immediately afterwards the Allies commenced the attack. The fighting on this day may be divided into three distinct groups; at Wachau Schwarzenberg's main forces attacked the Emperor himself; at Lindenau Bertrand defended himself against the Austrian corps of Gyulai, and to the north of the Elster Blücher directed his attack against Marmont. The latter had just set out in accordance with the Emperor's orders, which we have just named, when Blücher advanced against him; at 11 o'clock he saw himself forced to give up his intention and show front.

In the meantime Ney had, about 10 o'clock, despatched Bertrand in Marmont's place to Liebertwolkwitz; but Bertrand now turned to Lindenau at the urgent request of Arrighi, who had been entrusted with the defence of the town of Leipzig, and determined to hold this defile, the sole road of retreat, with his 15,000 men. Here he was soon attacked by a corps of 22,000 men, which first tore Leutzsch from his grasp, penetrated about 1 o'clock into Plagwitz, and about 2 o'clock even reached the southern outskirts of Lindenau. But an urgent order from the

Emperor enjoined Bertrand to hold Lindenau under any circumstances, and by putting forth all his strength, he succeeded in forcing the enemy back again through Plagwitz.

Turning to Marmont, we see that he had taken up his position on the line Möckern—Entzitzsch, and at noon a Polish division, numbering 28,000 men, came up on his right and occupied Gross and Klein Widderitzsch. The enemy, advancing, captured with little trouble the advanced posts of Freyroda, Radefeld and Lindenthal about 1 o'clock; but after this, the resistance of the French became more stubborn in Möckern, and only after heavy fighting and very severe losses the corps of Yorck was able at 5 o'clock, to establish itself definitely in this last-named village. Marmont fell back upon Gohlis and Entzitzsch. To the right of him Gross and Klein Widderitzsch also had been lost, but had afterwards been recaptured by the division of Souham's corps, which had, up to then, been behind on the road from Düben and which now arrived. Souham's other two divisions, of 12,000 men, which Marmont had expected would reinforce him, had been sent to the Emperor by Ney through Schönfeld, since, as we have seen, neither Marmont nor Bertrand had been able to execute the Emperor's orders. But the latter, having now more accurate information of the danger which threatened Marmont, sent them back again to this general; but they did not arrive in time to take their part in the fighting.

At the most important point of the battle-field the Allies advanced in the following manner: Schwarzenberg, with 30,000 men between the Elster and the Pleisse, turned towards Connewitz; on the right of the Pleisse Barclay was in chief command of 64,000 men on the line Cröbern—Güldengossa—Gross Pösna, with 20,000 men as a reserve in his rear at Rotha. The Emperor was able to oppose 115,000 men to these forces. At first some obstinate fighting took place for the possession of Markkleeberg, Wachau and Liebertwolkwitz; the Emperor had even to fall back temporarily in person towards the sheep-farm of Meusdorf, but between 11 and 12 o'clock he noticed, that the favourable moment had come to deliver his counter stroke, for the hostile attacks were wanting in unity and he had now all his corps well in hand. This, (110) then, was the situation: Poniatowski was still in possession of Markkleeberg and defending Connewitz and the Pleisse against Schwarzenberg; only the castle of Dölitz had been lost, and Augereau had arrived to his support at Dösen. Victor was defending Wachau, Lauriston Liebertwolkwitz; Mortier and Oudinot were behind this village, the Old Guard on the Galgenberg, and Macdonald had reached Holzhausen. The Emperor had given orders to Drouot to plant a tremendous battery of 150 guns between Wachau and Liebertwolkwitz.

It was now his intention to pierce the centre of the Allies at Güldengossa, mainly by a grand charge of his entire cavalry, which, with the sole exception of Sebastiani, who was on the left wing, marching towards Little Pössna, was now collected under Murat behind the centre of the French line of battle. After that he intended to turn the right wing of the enemy entirely by advancing *viâ* Seiffertshayn and the University Copse. A general forward movement of the French now took place. Macdonald captured the Colmberg and advanced towards Seiffertshayn, Mortier between the Colmberg and Liebertwolkwitz, Victor, reinforced by Oudinot attacked the sheep-farm of Anenhayn, and Augereau marched by Markkleeberg towards Crostewitz.

It was indeed a critical moment for the Allies, and, had the Emperor's plan been entirely successful, he would have owed his success to two circumstances. First, he was fighting here, at the most decisive point of the whole theatre of war, with 115,000 men against 114,000, although he was, in point of fact, operating with 214,000 only, against 325,000, a fact which proves his strategical genius.

LEIPZIG

Secondly, that he knew how to detect with unerring glance, in the middle of the battle, the moment and the point, where the decisive blow had to be delivered, while his opponents confined 30,000 men in an aimless manner between the Elster and the Pleisse, allowing them to waste their efforts against the easily defended ravine of Connewitz; a fact which proves Napoleon's tactical skill. Once more he showed the two great qualities of a true general in all their old lustre, but too late to avert his fate.

Victor, about 2 o'clock, took the sheep-farm of Anenhayn by storm, and Oudinot turned towards Cröbern; Mortier and Macdonald likewise forced the enemy to fall back, Güldengossa alone, where his reserves became engaged, resisted Lauriston's attacks. Then at 3 o'clock the Emperor threw his cavalry from Wachau on to the Allies' centre; namely, Latour-Maubourg, Kellermann and a part of Pajol's regiments, all under the command of Murat. They advanced straight to Güldengossa, and penetrated beyond this village, but then their strength was exhausted. And while Napoleon had played all his cards and his troops were already wearied, fresh forces joined the Allies' line of battle about 4 o'clock. These were the Austrian reserves, which, at the urgent request of the Emperor Alexander, Schwarzenberg had sent to this, the most important point of the battle-field. Thus the southern portion of Markkleeberg was again wrested from the French, though Augereau held the northern portion, and though an advance of the Austrians by the castle of Dölitz failed. Victor was compelled, after an obstinate resistance, to give up the sheep-farm of Anenhayn about 5 o'clock and fell back to Wachau; accompanied by Oudinot; and at the same time Macdonald again found himself forced to evacuate Seiffertshayn.

The actual result of this day was, therefore, that neither side had definitely gained an inch of ground, and this sealed the Emperor's fate, for, only a very decisive victory on this day, when the relative numbers were still fairly equal, could have saved him. Such a victory he had failed to gain, and in a military sense there was now only one thing to be done, namely, to retreat at once. But in that case Napoleon as a Monarch was lost, and the interests of the sovereign had precedence over, though they were at variance with, those of the General Napoleon.

The Emperor ordered his tents to be pitched for the night in a dried-up pond, not far from the old brick shed. " Napoleon was very uneasy during that night; Nansouty and other generals were summoned to his bedside."[1] He had recourse again to his old device—negotiations; he sent the Austrian general Meerveldt, who had been made prisoner at Dölitz, to the headquarters of the Allies, but now, as after Moscow, he met with no success. On the morning of the 17th, a rainy Sunday, Murat appeared before the Emperor. " Both were exceedingly grave and thoughtful, and Napoleon deeply buried in thought, walking alone up and down on the embankments between the old ponds, for half an hour."[2] Afterwards the Emperor did not quit his tent again, but towards evening he was no longer able to resist the pressure of circumstances; he could not but be aware that at any rate he must move his army closer into Leipzig, to prepare for the retreat, which had to be organized, though its execution might be temporarily postponed.

At 2 a.m. on the 18th October his troops stood under arms again. He himself entered his carriage and drove to Reudnitz, where he woke up Ney and conversed with him until 5 o'clock; then he went to Leipzig, took Bertrand, who had spent the night in that town, with him, and drove to Lindenau. " He inspected the bridge and the ground about it, where, two days before, the attack upon Bertrand's corps had taken place, and took the opportunity to give this general orders to march to

[1] O. v. O. 382.   [2] O. v. O. 385.

Weissenfels. First on horseback, and then again in his carriage, he returned through the suburbs on the same road to Stötteritz. It was now about 8 o'clock. The Guards had arrived at Stötteritz. The Emperor breakfasted at one of the farms there, but the thunder of the artillery, beginning in all directions, a few minutes later, aroused the whole headquarters." [1]

(111)

His army now took up the following positions: Poniatowski defended the Pleisse at Dölitz and Connewitz; Augereau's corps extended its lines from Dösen as far as the ponds of Lössing; Victor held Probsthayda, to the west of which village Drouot had established his guns. Behind Augereau stood Kellermann's cavalry; to the left was Oudinot, and behind Victor the cavalry corps of Bordesoult[2] and Pajol. All these formed the right wing under Murat's chief command. On the left wing stood Macdonald on the line Zuckelhausen—Holzhausen; on his left rear the cavalry of Sebastiana, and in the second line Lauriston. As a general reserve the Old Guard was at Thonberg. Here, on the hill to the south-west of this little village, near a tobacco mill, the Emperor had taken up his station. Mortier had been sent to Lindenau, in order to take Bertrand's place there, Bertrand being sent elsewhere. On the northern side of the battlefield of Leipzig, Marmont stood at Schönfeld; the Polish division, mentioned already, was near the farm of Pfaffendorf, Reynier was at Paunsdorf, holding Taucha, and Souham stood at Leipzig in reserve. The cavalry corps of Arrighi had been distributed between all these army corps.

The enemy's attack was to be delivered as follows: Bernadotte, reinforced by 30,000 men from Blücher's army to a strength of 90,000, was to cross the Parthe at Taucha, and advance against Leipzig; Blücher, now only commanding 25,000 men, was to attack Leipzig from his position at Gohlis, which he had taken up on the 17th. Schwarzenberg had formed his army into three columns;

[2] O. v. O. 387.   *Vice* Latour-Maubourg, wounded.

50,000 men were to advance along the right bank of the Pleisse towards Connewitz, 60,000 men under Barclay towards Probsthayda along the roads *viâ* Wachau and Liebertwolkwitz, and 65,000 men under Bennigsen towards Zuckelhausen and Holzhausen from Seiffertshayn. Finally, towards Lindenau, the attack was to be renewed once more by the Austrian corps of Gyulai, 20,000 men, which had been already engaged there on the 16th.

It will thus be seen that the Emperor was strategically and tactically entirely on the defensive and surrounded by enormously superior numbers, and that these superior numbers, attacking him simultaneously on all sides, must necessarily crush him. The retreat, which the Monarch had refused to begin voluntarily on the 17th, the defeated General would be compelled to begin on the 19th. The complete want of bridges over the Elster was not the fault of the Monarch's position. The whole mass had to march over Lindenau; this is an indication how far the General's carelessness as to all the necessary details had gone. Certainly the Emperor's staff ought of their own initiative to have taken these precautionary measures. When speaking of Asparn I already have laid stress upon the importance of a thoroughly educated staff in view of the size and general development of modern armies, but the staff can never quite take the place of the commander, and the latter will always have to be responsible for the general conduct of affairs; posterity will not exonerate him, when, if beaten, he attempts to lay the blame on his staff.

At 7 a.m. the Allies began the battle. Let us follow the progress of the separate columns of attack. The one which advanced on the right bank of the Pleisse met with an obstinate resistance in Dölitz and Dösen, and succeeded only after protracted fighting in taking these two villages and then Lössing also. Connewitz, however, remained in the hands of the French. Barclay had little difficulty in forcing his opponent back by Liebertwolkwitz. He found Wachau already evacuated, captured the sheep farm of Meusdorf about 10 o'clock, and then turned towards Probsthayda; at 2 o'clock he began his first attack upon this village. But here Victor could not be dislodged, and supported by Lauriston, repulsed all assaults. Bennigsen captured Zuckelhausen, and, after an obstinate resistance, Holzhausen also. Thereupon Napoleon himself rode forward towards Probsthayda, in order to inspire his hard-pressed centre to continued resistance by his own presence. Then he returned to his post on the heights. Bennigsen now tried unsuccessfully to capture Stötteritz also; he then extended more and more to the right towards the road of Wurzen, in order to come in touch with Bernadotte; he thus captured Baalsdorf and Zweinaundorf, and having thereby gained touch with Bernadotte, he took, with the assistance of the latter's left wing, the villages of Mölkau and Paunsdorf about 3 o'clock. Bernadotte had arrived in front of Taucha about noon, and there met with an obstinate resistance, but finally captured the village by turning it. Ney withdrew his right wing and took up a position on the line Schönfeld—Sellerhausen—Stuntz. At this time, soon after 3 o'clock, the Emperor visited Ney for a short time, in order to see how matters stood with him; for some ominous reports had reached him about Ney's position, but he soon returned to his former station, as he no longer had any troops in hand to send to Ney's assistance. In the Emperor's centre Probsthayda and Stötteritz remained in the hands of the French until evening, but at all the other points they were forced back close to the outskirts of the town of Leipzig; Marmont by Blücher, and Ney by Bernadotte and Bennigsen. Bertrand, who, as we know, was marching to Weissenfels, met the Austrian corps, which was advancing towards Lindenau, but he forced it back as far as Knauthayn and reached Lützen, his advanced guard indeed getting as far as Weissenfels.

At 4 p.m. the French army recognized the impossibility of any further resistance, and the victory of the Allies was decided. The Emperor, who, at the approach of darkness, ordered a watchfire to be lighted at his station, gave the order to retreat, then slumbered on a wooden footstool which had been procured, a sign not so much of physical fatigue as of nervous exhaustion, which showed itself now that the battle was decided. However after a quarter of an hour he started up again wide awake. "Until after 8 o'clock the Emperor remained at his camp-fire; at first his quarters were to be provided in a building near the Thonberg, but as all the houses in the neighbourhood had been very much soiled by the wounded, he could find no shelter there, and therefore rode to the Ross-platz and established himself in the Hotel de Prusse." [1]

The German campaign was lost, and, as had happened in the same month only a year before, nothing remained to be done but to retreat; Germany had to be evacuated, even as Russia was then. But the campaign of Germany had been lost in a different manner from that of Russia. It is true, in Russia, Napoleon had also been guilty of grave military errors, but our general impression had been more that the Emperor's instrument, the army, was not equal, as regards its organization, to the carrying out of the Emperor's plans; that the burden laid on it was too heavy, and that, having reached Moscow, it was incapable, even under the best guidance, of executing Napoleon's scheme of conquest to its full extent. But in Germany, on the other hand, the Emperor had ample means at his disposal for his immediate object, viz., to repulse the enemy's attacks successfully; and it was only the most glaring military errors, and the temporary paralysis of his military genius, that allowed him to be overwhelmed by the enemy, and caused his final crushing defeat at Leipzig. It is important to lay stress on the fact that it was not his genius that had, as a whole,

[1] O. v O. 399.

deteriorated, for some individual actions in the campaign of 1813 are equal to the greatest of his former deeds, but that it was the want of stability in his genius that led to his reverses. It was not because the mental gifts of the young general of 1796 were greater, that victory then followed his steps, but because his energy, which never then relaxed, enabled his genius to prove itself equal to the difficult tasks it had to accomplish.

Again, we note with interest that frequently the very same qualities which formerly formed the greatest factors in his successes now became, by their excess, factors in his defeats. For example, it had always been in his favour that, contrary to the practice of most generals, he put little faith in the reports about the large forces of the enemy, and always reduced these in his own judgment to more moderate and more correct estimates. But now when his subordinate officers reported to him that the enemy had appeared in superior numbers, he contemptuously ignored their statements. He ignored the fact that the exaggerated reports of the numbers of the skirmishing corps of Tschernyschew, Thielman and Platov, were only evidences of the actual impression made by those attempts upon the French army, and that reality formed the basis for all such exaggerations. In the same manner he had in 1812, wilfully, in the face of facts, called Tormassov's army "a hastily collected rabble of third battalions, recruits without any capacity of resistance, and at the most, fit for police work."[1]

It is well for us now to examine the question which arose when we were considering the plan of 1812, namely; whether, with such large forces as we find in 1812 and 1813, Napoleon's plan of operations along one line are still indisputably the best, or whether, in such cases, an advance along several lines of operations, converging concentrically towards the decisive battlefield, is not more likely to lead to success.

[1] C. N. To Berthier. Glubokoyay, 22nd July.

In the first place, we must not forget, that this second plan does greatly facilitate the safety of all questions of commissariat, and that this matter becomes increasingly important as the number of combatants increase; "10,000 men can live anywhere, even in the desert,"[1] said Napoleon, and this is quite correct, but 200,000 require careful preparations, and 400,000, kept together on one line of operations, present almost invincible difficulties, especially in a country either little cultivated or in one already exhausted. Thus Smitt, speaking of 1812, says very appositely, with respect to interior lines of operations: "In most cases it is undoubtedly more advantageous to keep to them, but cases may also occur where exterior lines have their advantages; for example, in this very war; the Russians would have been lost if they had used interior, and Napoleon exterior lines of operations, because he would, with his enormous superiority of numbers, have cut them off from their resources and have crushed them. . . . He would have had the following advantages on his side: (1) he would have cut them off from the resources of their country and used these for himself; (2) his army, in that case consisting of 200,000 men on each side, would not have worn itself away by its own unwieldy size, but could have moved with greater ease, and each part would still have been separately strong enough to meet the Russians, in whatever direction they turned, with superior numbers; (3) he would have had the country open in his rear and consequently could have drawn all his supplies with safety from it."[2]

On the other hand, of course, there is the advantage, and one assuredly not to be estimated lightly, of being able to manœuvre with the entire mass along one line of operations, whether interior or exterior, thus allowing complete harmony in the conduct of affairs; rendering the commander-in-chief independent of any possibly

---

[1] C. N. To Clarke. Fontainebleau, 5th November, 1807.
[2] "Zur näheren Aufklärung über den Krieg. 1812." 37.

divergent views or inferior capacity in his subordinate officers; affording an assurance that whenever the battle has to be fought the whole mass will be present; an assurance which is certainly not afforded in the same measure by a concentric approach along various lines. For the latter method is attended by the danger of the enemy concentrating all his strength against one of the armies. What we have to investigate is, whether, on the one hand, these advantages, and on the other this disadvantage, exist in the same proportion in armies of greatly increased numerical strength.

Here we are able to adduce an authority of especial weight, namely, that of the inventor of the expression: "operation on interior lines," Jomini himself, who, certainly, did not look with very favourable eyes upon concentric operations. With that clearness of military conception which distinguished him, he adds the following words to his disquisition on "interior lines": "However, the experiences of these two celebrated campaigns (1813 and 1814) have given rise to a strategical problem, which would be difficult of solution by assertions based upon mere theories, namely, whether the system of central masses does, or does not, lose its advantages, if the masses employed are too large"; and then he continued, " It seems indubitable to me that a mass of 100,000 men, occupying a central position against three separate armies, each of 30,000 to 35,000 men, would be more calculated to overwhelm them one after the other, than a mass of 400,000 combatants would, if pitted against three armies of, say, 135,000 men each; and this for several weighty reasons:

" (1) Because with an army of 130,000 to 140,000 combatants one can easily resist a superior force, considering the difficulty of finding convenient ground and the necessary time required to bring such large forces into play on the day of battle.

" (2) Because, even if driven from the battlefield one

possesses still, at least, 100,000 men to secure a good retreat, without incurring too great losses, while awaiting connection with one of the other two minor armies.

"(3) Because a central mass of 400,000 men requires such quantities of provisions, ammunition and materials of all kinds, that it has much less power of movement and of transferring its action from one portion of the field of operations to another; without reckoning the impossibility of drawing sufficient provisions from the country which is always of too little extent to feed such a mass.

"(4) Finally it seems certain that the two separate portions of the army, which the central mass would have to oppose to the two exterior lines of the enemy, even if they had merely to keep them in check, would in any case have to be of a strength of 80,000 to 90,000 men; so that, if the army of observation committed the stupid mistake of engaging in any serious fighting, it might suffer defeat, the consequences of which would be so damaging, that they would far outweigh any advantages gained by the main body."[1]

If we weigh the above reasons, we shall, it is true, have to confess, that for very large armies the dangers of advancing along separate lines of operations are much fewer, and this is still more the case in our days, when the telegraph almost removes one of the dangers which were formerly present, namely, the want of concerted action in the various operations.

But, on the other hand, we cannot fail to be convinced that with the growth of armies, the advantages claimed for a single line of operations have diminished. In 1812, when Napoleon succeeded, by placing his army in echelon, in keeping it together as one connected whole, and even retaining in his hands the possibility of a personal conduct of the corps of Eugene and Jerôme, who were to meet the enemy later on, we see, as a matter of

[1] Précis de l'art de la guerre, 145.

fact, that Jerôme manœuvred independently, and in a manner which did not coincide with the great plan. And even if we admit, that, where the army covered so little ground as in 1812, the Emperor might, by greater personal activity, have been able to nullify this disadvantage, had he not remained inactive at Vilna, yet this is not always the case. It is true, that General Bonaparte was at Montenotte on the 12th April, at Millesimo on the 13th, and at Dego on the 14th, but the Emperor Napoleon could not have fought at Grossbeeren on the 23rd August, on the Katzbach on the 26th and on the same day at Dresden. It was the numerical growth of the armies, which so extended the theatre of war, that, for any one man to direct all the movements of the troops, became an impossibility, not only on the outer but even on the inner line of operations, and rendered the advantage of a greater number of no avail.

The case seems scarcely any better, with respect to the undivided employment of the whole mass on the day of battle. Certainly we see, that at Leipzig, Napoleon, fighting on the interior tactical line, was as much compelled to allow Ney and Bertrand to do their fighting independently of him, as Blücher and Gyulai were forced to do on the part of the Allies, who were approaching on separate lines ; even the Emperor could no longer control the whole of the large battlefield single-handed. Various weighty reasons may be quoted to show that the idea of strategical separation in the advance of an army should no longer be rejected, though Napoleon rejected it both in theory and practice, and these reasons, if we consider the size of modern armies, apply alike to the commissariat and the leading of masses of troops.

Of course it is impossible accurately to fix the numbers to which this applies, for that must always depend on the special circumstances of the case; still, it seems that about 200,000 men is the limit for the full advantage of operations on one line, and 400,000 the number at which the advantages of the two methods of operations are very evenly balanced, and where on the nature of the armies and of the theatre of war will depend the question which of the two methods affords the greater certainty of success. The use of interior lines may possibly be advisable even in very large armies, for, the fact that Napoleon failed with it in 1812 and 1813, was due mainly to his errors in execution. Thus, in 1866, an undivided advance on the Prussian side might still have been admissible, as is implied by the words of the account given by the General Staff: " Nothing would have been more desirable than for the whole combined forces to advance in one body. . . . The difficulties as to supplies, which arise in the massing of a quarter of a million of men, could have been overcome if an immediate advance had been contemplated."[1] In 1870, on the other hand, where the forces were at first massed in one body, and then separated, immediately the advance began, and all questions as to the mode of operating and as to the commissariat, were provided for, we have a model for the conduct of a campaign with the huge armies of our own time.

In conclusion, we may mention here that a modern army, resolving upon strategical separation, must undoubtedly possess certain qualities, in order to derive all the advantages possible from such a separation, and to avoid all the dangers inherent in it. The principal qualities for this purpose are probably: an eagerness for the offensive, the independence and proper training of all the superior officers in time of peace, the highest capacity for manœuvring and marching on the part of the troops; a careful arrangement of all matters of transport and the utmost utilization of all the means of communication furnished by modern science.

During the night of the 18th October the whole French

---

[1] The campaign of 1866 in Germany. Edited by the Military History Section of the Great General Staff.

army fell back upon Leipzig and in the morning of the 19th its departure began by Lindenau, the only passage open for this purpose. At 9 o'clock the Emperor also mounted his horse. " From the moment that the Emperor mounted his horse and was on the point of leaving Leipzig altogether, the most evident gloom was noticeable on his face. Wholly absorbed, with a blank look that might mean mere vacancy, he rode first towards the inner Rannstädt gate, diagonally across the market-place, and when it was seen that everything was blocked up there on account of the enormous crowding of soldiers and carriages, he took his way round inside the town, past the two gates blocked up long ago, and past the church of St. Thomas, towards the Petersthor. Here the Emperor inquired for a moment where he was, and then rode back again towards his quarters on the Rossplatz, or rather along the avenue as far as the neighbourhood of the municipal school."[1] " He turned back once more, passed by the Petersthor, and rode round the town to the Rannstädt-Steinweg. He was scarcely able to pass through the indescribable crush of all arms of his troops."[2] " Napoleon followed quite calmly the main stream of his flying troops, along the high road, as far as beyond Lindenau. Here he halted, and appointed different officers, who were to indicate to the fugitives arriving in disorder, the points where their corps were to collect."[3] Here, not far from the bridge over the Elster, General Chateau met at this time " a man in a peculiar dress and with only a small retinue; he was whistling the air of ' Malbrook s'en va-t-en guerre,' although he was deeply lost in thought; Chateau thought it was a burgher and was on the point of approaching him to ask a question. . . . It was the Emperor, who, with his usual phlegm, seemed to be perfectly callous to the scenes of destruction which surrounded him."[4]

(112)

[1] O. v. O. 401. [2] O. v. O. 402. [3] O. v. O. 403.
[4] Jomini, Précis pol. et mil. des Camp. de 1812 à 1815, ii. 207.

All order among the troops in Leipzig disappeared under the close pursuit of the Allies, who now advanced towards the town from all sides and penetrated into the suburbs. As at the Beresina, everyone thought only of crossing the Elster as quickly as possible, but when some of the enemy's shot fell close to the bridge, this was, owing to the mistake of a subaltern, blown up about 2 p.m.; whereby the remnants of Lauriston, Reynier and Poniatowski's corps had their retreat cut off and only a few stragglers were able to escape. At about the same time the Allies ordered an assault upon Leipzig, and the town was captured. They remained there with the exception of Yorck's corps, which had been sent forward in pursuit on the evening before, and stood now at Halle and Merseburg.

The Emperor had first dismounted at the mill of Lindenau; towards noon he proceeded to Markranstädt, his army being distributed around this place and extending as far as Weissenfels, whither Bertrand, as we know, had preceded it; at 11 o'clock the Emperor heard that he had occupied the place. Oudinot's corps, near Lindenau, formed the rearguard. On the 20th Napoleon continued his retreat to Freiburg. He himself started in a carriage at 3 a.m., accompanied by the Old Guard, and was only able to make slow progress, forcing a passage through the flying masses. He adopted, at this time, the same sphinx-like attitude that he had shown when disaster fell upon him in Russia, and his staff, watching their silent, unapproachable leader, whispered, " Look at him; thus he appeared when he left Russia."[1] He took up his quarters for the night in a little house in the vineyards near Weissenfels, whilst his army crossed the Saale at this same town and Bertrand reached Freiburg. Of the Allies Blücher reached Lützen, Yorck, in front of him, Frankleben and Reicherstwerben and Schwarzenberg

[1] O. v. O. 410.

somewhere on the line Naumburg—Zeitz, occupying the bridge at Kösen. This last point keenly excited the Emperor's apprehensions, and certainly, if the enemy broke through there in considerable force, the flying army must have been in the most awkward situation. " It is important that no one should be allowed to advance against us over the bridge of Kösen."[1] On the 21st, therefore, Bertrand occupied, by the Emperor's orders, the heights of Neu-Kösen, and under his protection the 80,000 to 90,000 combatants, who still composed the French army, passed through Freiburg over the Unstrut and reached Eckartsberga, only slightly harassed by Yorck's weak force, which had advanced as far as Freiburg. The Emperor having started between 3 and 4 a.m., had spent some time near Freiburg, endeavouring to bring order into the disorganized masses; at the crossing of the Unstrut about 3 p.m. he himself crossed this river and immediately afterwards the enemy appeared in sight of it. After having personally attended to the measures for holding the bridge, the Emperor went in the night to Eckartsberga. Schwarzenberg stood with his right wing still at Naumburg and by the bridge of Kösen and with his left at Eisenberg; Blücher threw a bridge across at Weissenfels and pushed some forces rapidly forward towards Freiburg.

The next day the Emperor did not start from his quarters until late, at 8.30, and leaving a rearguard at Eckartsberga, he conducted his troops to Buttelstädt and fixed on Ollendorf as his own quarters for the night; but as some Cossacks showed themselves near the road thither, and appeared to be watching him, he started, after having taken a hasty meal in that village, at midnight and arrived in Erfurt at 2.30 a.m., on the 23rd October. Blücher had reached Freiburg on the 22nd and had there effected a junction with Yorck again, but

[1] C. N. To Berthier. Weissenfels, 20th October, 6 p.m.

the difficulties of restoring the bridges over the Unstrut forced him to make a detour viâ Langensalza to Eisenach, in order to turn the Emperor's left flank, as he anticipated the French would stop at Erfurt and show front. Schwarzenberg reached the line Neu-Kösen—Jena.

But the condition of the French army did not permit the Emperor to think of facing about in this way, and even if the *moral* of his army had been far better, this course would have become altogether impossible, since, in consequence of the treaty of Nied on the 8th October, the Bavarian army under Wrede, 56,000 men, which had gone over to the side of the enemy, was moving against the French line of retreat. Therefore the French army continued its retreat viâ Gotha to Eisenach, where the Emperor arrived on the 26th. Blücher had followed in a parallel line by Sömmerda—Teunstädt—Langensalza, without being as yet able to reach him; Schwarzenberg, who was convinced that he would find the Emperor at Erfurt, ready to make a stand, advanced cautiously and with massed forces, and on the 26th had arrived to the south of Erfurt, and was watching this town.

The Emperor had turned the Thüringer Wald at Eisenach and entered now upon the direct South-West road leading towards Mainz, by Vach—Fulda—Schlüchtern. Blücher, who at first started in pursuit of him, soon received orders to march viâ Giessen and Wetzlar; for Schwarzenberg had already relinquished all hope of overtaking the Emperor, and only wished now that Blücher should reach Coblentz before him, in case he should find himself compelled to turn towards this place while avoiding Wrede; he himself moved slowly through the Thüringer Wald towards Frankfurt.

Thus as a matter of fact Wrede was the only obstacle in the way of the Emperor's retreat, and those knowing Napoleon and his military procedure, could predict with certainty that he would not avoid any obstacle, but would clear it out of his path. Wrede, who had not advanced sufficiently quickly or in close enough order, was, on the 29th October, in position at Hanau, with only 40,000 men, having the woods of Lamboi and Bulau in front of him and an advanced guard at Rückingen.

The Emperor reached Langenselbold at 7 p.m., and Macdonald also arrived there during the night with the remnants of the V. and XI. Corps; Victor and Augereau were in the direction of Gelnhausen, Marmont at Saalmünster, where Bertrand also arrived during the night; Oudinot and Mortier were still in the rear at Steinau and Flieden. On the 25th October the Emperor, at Gotha, had as yet no definite knowledge of Wrede's plans, but received the necessary information while advancing during the next few days, and then realized that he must force his way through his enemy, and prepared to do so ; he removed his trains from his present line of march towards Coblentz.

Thus on the 30th October at 8 a.m. Macdonald advancing, met with Wrede's advanced guard, and drove them into the forest in their rear. But when he pushed forward through this forest, he discovered the enemy in position, and saw himself arrested by the strong artillery they brought up; his repeated attempts to force his way on proved unsuccessful. In view of this situation the Emperor received Drouot's report, that it would be possible to place the artillery in a strong position on the flank of the enemy's left wing; he assented to the proposal, and whilst he ordered Macdonald and Victor to keep the enemy's right wing engaged and collected his entire cavalry in the centre and along the main road, Drouot established a battery of 50 guns as proposed. The fire of this battery was so galling, that Wrede sent his cavalry against it about 3 p.m., in order to rid himself of it, but the French cavalry, standing ready in the centre, drove them back, and Drouot's artillery immediately advanced into a second closer position. About an hour later the same attack was repeated with the same want of success, and about 5 o'clock the French began to advance along the whole line. The enemy, who had suffered heavily, was no longer able to hold out, and when the French followed up their success, the whole of the enemy's line of battle was broken; their left wing was thrown back into the town of Hanau, whilst the rest of their army fell back over the bridge of Lamboi and the Kinzig, and though the bridges over the river remained in Wrede's hands for the night, he found himself compelled to evacuate Hanau, which was bombarded.

By his determination, therefore, Napoleon had succeeded in freeing himself, even when in full retreat, and in a most disastrous position, as he had also done a year before at Krasny on the 17th November. On this latter occasion, the mere show of a determination to fight, had scared the enemy; now this determination, firmly carried out, had compelled the enemy to yield. Notwithstanding the hesitation and the grave mistakes of Napoleon which led up to the defeat of Leipzig, he again compels our admiration at Hanau, by the renewed manifestation of two of his greatest qualities, his boldness of resolution and his firmness of execution. We are confirmed in our opinion that the waning of his star was due less to the absolute deterioration of his genius, than to his vacillation. And the fact, that his mind could no longer maintain its former high level was owing to the loss of empire over himself, though he aimed at and almost attained an empire over his fellow-men.

On the day after the battle of Hanau, the Emperor left Marmont behind with the III., IV. and VI. Corps to hold Wrede in check, whilst he himself retreated further through Frankfurt to Mainz. At 3 p.m. Marmont also followed, leaving Bertrand to cover the rear; the latter, sharply attacked, held out until 7 o'clock, when he set fire to the suburbs and the bridge and left also.

On the morning of the 2nd November the Emperor arrived at Mainz; at 10 p.m. on the 7th he left this town, and 48 hours later was back in the palace of St. Cloud.

CHAPTER X.

THE CAMPAIGN IN FRANCE.

(113a) AT Mainz the Emperor had already settled upon his first measures for the evacuation of the right bank of the Rhine, now become necessary, and had decided upon the positions of his army along this river. He divided its course into three parts: the Lower Course from Holland up to Coblentz; the Middle Course from Coblentz to Bingen, and the Upper Course from Bingen to Switzerland. Along the first, he gave the chief command to Macdonald, with Cologne as his headquarters; the latter was to collect here the two divisions of his corps and Sebastiani's three cavalry divisions. Marmont was entrusted with the defence of the part from Coblentz to Bingen; he was to establish himself in Mainz, where he had his own corps, consisting of two divisions (after the III. had been incorporated in it) as well as Milhaud's three cavalry divisions; the V. Corps (one division) was sent to Coblentz, with the three divisions of Arrighi's cavalry; at Worms stood the one division of the II. Corps; at Kreuznach the four divisions of the I. Cavalry Corps, and finally, as a rearguard, Bertrand's corps, raised to four divisions, and at present on the right bank of the Rhine at Kastel. The Upper Course of the Rhine was placed under Victor's command, who did not however for the present receive any troops from the field-army, and had only the available garrisons and the new levies under his command.

This first distribution of the forces was partly intended

to cover, in a wide formation, the new conscriptions and the massing of the new levies along the whole country; and was mainly due to the endeavour to keep up the pretence of defending, in a military sense, the old frontier of France, rather than doing what would have been correct strategically, but which would have entailed the evacuation of some nominally French territory. We saw something resembling this in the Emperor's strategy on the occasion of his holding on to Dresden; and here again we notice that he, the man of stern facts, was untrue to himself in thinking so much of appearances. How he mocked his enemies in bygone days when they felt unable temporarily to give up things, which appeared to be important, but which after all, were immaterial, instead of concentrating their whole strength at the decisive point! And now he himself frittered his forces away; he tried still to gain successes in Italy and in the Pyrenees, and attempted to carry on a campaign in Belgium, though no events there could in any way have had any decisive influence upon his fate and that of France, as to which matters would be definitely decided in the plains of Champagne or Picardy. "Thus, in spite of the urgent danger, Napoleon kept up the pretence of showing front in all directions; and, at a moment, when a thousand motives should have led him to think first of defending his own capital, he left his best troops at places of secondary importance, where the greatest success could not possibly have any influence upon the results of the main campaign."[1]

Scarcely had the Emperor arrived in Paris, after having thus temporarily secured the line of the Rhine and settled the chief commands there, than he occupied himself with his second project, viz. the conscriptions for the formation of a new great army. He reckoned upon 150,000 men from the current conscription, and 125,000 men from

[1] Koch, Mém. pour servir à l'histoire de la Campagne de 1814, i. 181..

those exempted during the years 1804 to 1807. Of these he intended to assign 40,000 men to the Italian army and 25,000 to the army of the Pyrenees; whilst the first reinforcements furnished by this process were to be sent to the troops left behind on the Rhine, so that the II. Corps would be increased to three divisions, the V. Corps to two divisions, the VI. Corps to four divisions, while the I. Corps would be re-established with three divisions. Moreover, anticipating the year 1815, 200,000 men were to be levied, with which, for the present, reserve armies would be formed; namely 30,000 men at Turin, 30,000 men at Bordeaux, 80,000 men at Metz and 40,000 men at Antwerp.

The third object, which now claimed the Emperor's attention, was the coming military operations. On the 16th November, he said, dwelling on this point: "It seems that our movements must be directed towards Holland, and that the enemy's intentions tend in that direction;"[1] and a few days later: "It is probable, that the enemy will not attempt to cross the Rhine ... if the enemy does cross the Rhine, he will cross the Lower Rhine."[2] As a matter of fact, his most eager opponent, Blücher, intended to do so with his headquarters, and only on account of the conflicting interests due to the peculiar composition of the allied army, was this intention relinquished.

The more however the Emperor recognized, that his most vulnerable points were the lines of approach from Liège and Brussels, both on account of their directness and because they would compel him to separate from his forces employed in the South, in Spain and Italy, the more we have to blame him for sending new forces to the South. Here again, the Monarch with his unlimited aims, became the enemy of the experienced General. General Bonaparte would never have troubled about any side issues, but would have massed all his forces for the

[1] C. N. To Marmont, St. Cloud.
[2] C. N. To Marmont, St. Cloud, 20th November.

decision. The Emperor Napoleon could not lower himself so far, as to betray to *his* people of Italy, to *his* departments of the mouths of the Scheldt and the Rhine, that he was no longer able to hold or protect them.

But he soon noticed, that, after the passage of the Rhine had taken place, it was the plan of the Allies, not to attack from the direction of Belgium, but to advance with one army from Switzerland and with another from the Middle Rhine. He therefore altered the distribution of his forces so far as to station Marmont at Colmar with one division of the II. Corps, the VI. Corps and the I. and V. Cavalry Corps ; Victor with the other two divisions of the II. Corps was to remain at Strasburg ; Mortier at Langres, Ney at Epinal and Augereau at Lyon were to collect troops. Macdonald was still left with the Coblentz corps and the I. Corps reconstituted under Maison, on the Lower Rhine, although the decisive point was now unmistakably moved to the Upper Marne.

Then the Emperor considered the situation as a whole. He saw that Bülow was advancing with 20,000 men towards Belgium, but thought that, being forced to send some detachments to Gorkum, Bergen-op-Zoom and Breda, he would be reduced to 12,000 or 15,000 men, whom Antwerp would hold in check.

Blücher was advancing towards Metz with 60,000 men, but would have to leave 30,000 men before Mainz, Luxemburg, Saarlouis and Diedenhofen.

Schwarzenberg, advancing from Bâle with 100,000 men, would have to leave 50,000 men in Switzerland, before Besançon, the fortresses on the Rhine and Belfort ; he therefore came to the conclusion, that if Blücher and Schwarzenberg effected a junction, they would be able to march upon Paris with only 80,000 men : " This operation would therefore be a piece of madness, still we must consider it."[1]

[1] C. N. Note on the present position of France. Paris, January, 1814.

On the other hand, he reckoned, that Maison would cover Belgium with 15,000 men, and Macdonald with 10,000 men would march against Blücher's right flank. Marmont (15,000 men), Victor (12,000 men) and Mortier (12,000 men) would fall back before the enemy to Paris, where meanwhile 80,000 men would have collected. Orders to this effect were despatched to the Marshals.

The arbitrary nature of these assumptions is self-evident; not only did he, as we shall soon see, underestimate the enemy's forces, but even, if we allow the correctness of the figures given above, some considerable deductions must be made in the numbers which he presumed would have to be left in the rear. We should thus arrive at a result which would by no means justify the Emperor in characterizing the operation as a "piece of madness." The deterioration of his military gifts through voluntary self-deception is clearly evident here, and we have been able to follow its progress hitherto very distinctly. In the beginning of 1812, the most correct and brilliant conception of the plan of campaign failed only on account of the general insufficiency of the forces, and the occasional relaxation of the Emperor's personal energy. But after Moscow we find him elaborating a plan, which disregarded the actual facts, though in its execution he still took these facts into consideration, and relinquished the plan. Again in 1813 he showed more and more clearly in what he actually did, that he underrated his enemy, and disregarded facts, and now he developed such indifference as to the actual proportions of numbers and the probable actions of the enemy, that the results could only compare with those that are due to a want of military insight in an incapable general or to the listless inertia of a leader deficient in resolution.

The development of events soon showed that affairs were very different and the situation very dangerous. The Allies began their general advance across the

THE CAMPAIGN IN FRANCE 375

Rhine much earlier than the Emperor expected, viz. during the first days of January, 1814. Bülow had entered Holland with 30,000 men, and was for the present, certainly outside the decisive operations against the Emperor, but Blücher, leaving 28,000 in front of Mainz, crossed the Saar with 47,000 men on the 9th and 10th of January, and Schwarzenberg, having crossed the Rhine at Bâle with 209,000 men, was on the march to Langres. In the face of this advance with immensely superior numbers the Emperor's weak corps had to fall back, without any serious resistance, so as to concentrate to the rear.

The situation at the beginning of the year was as follows: Maison was with 16,000 men at Antwerp; Macdonald, XI. Corps, 8000 men, with the V. Corps, 4000 men, the II. Cavalry Corps, Excelmans, 2000 men, and the III. Cavalry Corps, Arrighi, 2000 men, was at Coblentz and Cologne; Morand, IV. Corps, 13,000 men, formed the garrison of Mainz; Victor, II. Corps, 12,000 men, with the V. Cavalry Corps, Milhaud, 5000 men, stood at Baccarat, having retreated behind the Vosges; Marmont, VI. Corps, 14,000 men, with the I. Cavalry Corps, Doumerc, 3000 men, at Dürkheim. Behind these Ney had collected 8000 men at Nancy, Mortier 8000 men at Langres, and Augereau 1600 men at Lyons. From the rear another 21,000 men were on the march forward. On the 15th August, 1813, the Emperor had opened the campaign in Germany with 350,000 men, of these 56,000 men only recrossed the Rhine; on the 15th December he had again 103,000 men; typhus carried off more than 60,000 men during this month, thus, in spite of all the reinforcements—about 125,000 men in round numbers— he had now only reached a strength of 117,600 men, reckoning all the troops still on the march forward.

Victor now fell back before the Allies to Nancy, where he effected a junction with Ney on the 13th January. On the preceding day Mortier, who had at first been sent away to defend Holland, arrived at Langres, having received orders to return. Marmont retreated to Metz, where he was on the 11th. Macdonald had, to begin with, fallen back upon Maestricht, and marched from there on the 14th towards Chalons-sur-Marne; the first fighting, which had to be done without him, revealed the mistake the Emperor had made when he departed from the Napoleonic principle of massing all his forces towards the decisive point. The entire army was now concentrated in the rear towards Chalons-sur-Marne. The Emperor looked upon all this fairly calmly; he gave orders now and then to offer some resistance, and blamed his officers when this had not been done, but he was not very much in earnest, for he himself, as we have seen, had already determined to fall back gradually upon Paris, since circumstances compelled him to do so.

(113b) The Allies continued their advance, Blücher leaving 19,000 men in front of the fortresses on the Moselle, and then taking the direction of Arcis-sur-Marne. Schwarzenberg collected his troops in front of Langres, to attack Mortier there, but before he could do this the latter had marched away. The French corps now concentrated further to the rear towards Vitry-le-Français. In the meantime the Emperor had resolved not to continue his retreat as far as the walls of his capital, but to assume the offensive, in spite of the great inferiority of his forces, by advancing into the midst of the disunited corps of the enemy and trusting to the superiority of his genius; "on the 26th I shall resume the offensive and spread disorder among the enemies' columns."[1] He calculated that Victor and Ney were at St. Dizier; Gerard with 12,000 men of the reinforcements, which were marching up, at Brienne; Mortier at Bar-sur-Aube; "I shall collect all these forces and throw myself upon the first hostile corps within my reach."[2]

[1] C. N. To Berthier. Paris, 23rd January.
[2] C. N. To Belliard. Paris, 23rd January.

Before he left the capital he cast a rapid glance over the military situation, and said : " I assume the army to be at Chalons, Vitry and Bar-sur-Aube. The enemy do not appear to be threatening from the direction of Soissons and the Ardennes.

" In the direction of the Northern fortresses they are not yet in possession of Belgium.

" The enemy's whole movements tend towards Langres, St. Dizier and Dijon.

" The enemy's movement *viâ* St. Dizier and Langres is held in check by the army ; that *viâ* Dijon is not held in check at all." [1]

After commenting upon the defensive measures in this latter direction he added : " I do not expect that more than a few scouting cavalry divisions will be able to advance along this road." [1]

At 3 a.m. on the 25th the Emperor left Paris and reached Chalons-sur-Marne at 5 a.m. on the 26th. He found Marmont, Ney and Victor at Vitry-le-Français, Mortier at Vendeuvre, Gerard on the march up, and Macdonald at Mezières. When the Emperor joined the army, his resolution was fixed ; he intended to attack the very next day, and at 9.45 the order was issued, that the whole army, forming one column, was to be in readiness on the road from Vitry to St. Dizier ; the foremost corps, Victor, as close as possible to St. Dizier, behind him Marmont, and lastly Ney. In the afternoon the Emperor went to Vitry, thinking he had Blücher with about 25,000 men in front of him at St. Dizier, and believing Schwarzenberg to be behind Bar-sur-Aube. This latter general certainly lay near this town, with some portions of his troops at Neufchateau and Chatillon-sur-Seine ; but Blücher was at Dommartin, and only a weak rear-guard had been left behind in St. Dizier, to await the corps of 19,000 men, which, being now relieved in front of the Moselle fortresses, was on the march hither.

[1] C. N. Directions to Joseph. Paris, 24th January.

When therefore the Emperor advanced to St. Dizier on the 27th, he drove the enemy thence without any difficulty and heard that Blücher had departed for Brienne. He therefore determined on the 28th to follow him; "if he makes a stand, it is possible something may occur to-morrow at Brienne."[1] He consequently collected his whole army on this day around Montierender, leaving only Marmont in St. Dizier, whilst his opponent, who had reached Brienne on the preceding day, remained stationary there. Schwarzenberg moved slowly forward towards Troyes, whither Mortier had fallen back. The Emperor did not know accurately what forces had marched away in the direction of Brienne, what part of them had already gone behind the Aube, and what portion he really had in front of him.

(113c) On the 29th he therefore ordered Victor forward to Maizières to reconnoitre, and moved Marmont up to Vassey; he thought his own appearance in front of the Pass of Bar-sur-Aube would arrest the enemy's advance to Troyes, and hoped at the same time to be able to attack a column which was reported to be on the march from Joinville to Bar. He sent orders to Mortier to march up to Arcis-sur-Aube, toward the right wing of his army. But this order was intercepted by the enemy, and thus Blücher became aware of the Emperor's approach, and decided to make a stand at Brienne.

About 1 o'clock the Emperor's cavalry met the enemy's advanced guard at Maizières; it penetrated then as far as Brienne, and when the infantry had come up, the town itself was attacked by a turning movement, as evening was coming on; the fighting continued with great zest until midnight, when Blücher evacuated Brienne and fell back upon Trannes. The Emperor, who had spent the night at Perthes, on the morning of the 30th began his movement against the position of Trannes; he opened his artillery fire and recognized that Blücher was making

[1] C. N. To Clarke. St. Dizier, 28th January.

The Campaign in France

a stand there, but as the day was nearly ended he renounced the attack, though Gerard had now joined him.

On that day the Emperor stood with Gerard, Ney and Victor on the line Dienville—La Rothière—Chaumesnil, holding the bridge at Lesmont; his headquarters were at Brienne. Marmont was at Montierender, and Mortier received fresh orders to move up. As for the enemy, Schwarzenberg lay with his main army at Bar-sur-Aube, and two corps at Joinville; Blücher's corps, coming up from the Moselle fortresses, under Yorck, had arrived in St. Dizier, driving Marmont's rear-guard from that town. The reports which the Emperor received as to the enemy, induced him to suspect Schwarzenberg was on the march towards Auxerre, and he remained stationary in the hope of still forcing Blücher to a battle here, while as yet isolated. Indeed he did not wish to fall back, for fear of influencing his position unfavourably in view of the political negotiations just begun.

The danger which he thus ran in the face of the concentric advance of the two portions of the enemy's army is evident, still we cannot here accuse the Emperor of having committed a definite mistake. The real reason why this inner position was so unfavourable for him was owing to his relative inferiority of numbers; in view of this he ought not to have taken the offensive at all, for it was clear that any advance against the centre of the enemy's line must, sooner or later, have led to a very critical position. But he was forced chiefly by his position, to take the offensive, for he, the successful soldier, could not fall back upon Paris and subsequently to the South, which, in a purely military sense, would have been the best course. He was therefore compelled to push forward; he did so resolutely and successfully, and now, when the situation became ominous, he held out boldly; all this we must, in a military sense, praise, though we may see that the logical development of his career had here, at La Rothière, changed the bold general into a reckless gambler.

Napoleon once said that " in war nothing succeeds except it be based on calculation ;"[1] but another saying is also true: " Genius has its intuition, mere talent can only calculate."[2] For the creation of a truly great general, an almost supernatural combination of gifts is requisite, amongst which the penetrating, divining glance of genius must be united to and stand in perfect equilibrium with a keen, logical power of calculating possibilities,

"Resolution must boldly seize upon the possible."

The fact that this equilibrium was disturbed in the Emperor's mind, that he no longer knew how to bring a cool calculation of the limits of the possible into harmony with the intuition of his genius, nay, that he, as it were, being fettered by his former deeds, could no longer rest content with a deliberate calculation of what was within his reach, all these points were in a military sense responsible for his fall. When he, on his arrival in Vitry, was asked about the reinforcements which he presumably had brought with him, he said: "I have brought none. There was not a man in Chalons."—" But with what are you going to fight?"—"We shall try our luck with what we have, perhaps fortune will favour us ;"[3] and his terrified subordinates "thought they were dreaming when they heard this announcement."[4]

On the 31st January the Emperor remained fairly stationary; Marmont advanced to Morvilliers; Mortier received orders to re-occupy Troyes, which had been evacuated; Macdonald reached Chalons. Blücher also remained quietly stationary in front of the Emperor, for now Schwarzenberg's corps were approaching and he could therefore reckon upon immediate reinforcements; his main body was still at Bar-sur-Aube; one

[1] C. N. To Joseph. St. Cloud, 6th June, 1806.
[2] Fain, Manuscrit de 1812, ii. 194.
[3] Marmont, Mém. vi. 23. [4] The same.

corps had already joined Blücher; another arrived in the course of that day, one stood at Vassy and another at Doulevant. Thus on the morning of the 1st February the Emperor was ready; he had Gerard at Dienville, Victor at La Rothière, Marmont at Morvilliers and Chaumesnil, and Ney in reserve at Brienne. Blücher, who now had under his chief command the two corps of Schwarzenberg's army, which had joined him, intended to attack him on this day.

But on the previous evening the Emperor's hopes had already been disappointed; he could no longer hope to force Blücher to give battle unsupported, and was already considering the necessity of retreating. For this purpose, indeed, the entire army stood under arms; "we shall in this position wait for news of the enemy, and all will be held in readiness to march away in the direction fixed on."[1] And when the Emperor perceived on the morning of the 1st February that Blücher made no sign of departing, he became convinced that after all Schwarzenberg must be nearer than he thought, and he intended to march behind the Aube viâ Lesmont. Ney was already starting on this march when at 1 o'clock Blücher, who had only waited for the arrival of the 12,000 men of the Russian Guards, began his attack. The Emperor now did not wish to evade the battle, indeed he probably could scarcely have done so.

The enemy began with a cannonade directed against La Rothière. Victor's cavalry threw itself upon this artillery, but could not capture it; it had to fall back before its fire, and tried next, when the enemy's infantry advanced, to attack the latter, but was itself thrown back by a counter attack of the Russian cavalry. In the meantime, as we said, the enemy's infantry had advanced against La Rothière; it penetrated this village and an obstinate fight began for its possession. On the right French wing, on the Aube, Dienville, situated on the right

[1] C. N. Berthier to Marmont. Brienne, 31st January, 9 p.m.

bank of this river, was furiously attacked between 4 and 5 o'clock, and the part of this village lying here was lost. On the left wing the village of La Giberie fell into the enemy's hands, and Marmont saw himself forced back upon Chaumesnil. And when the enemy's corps, which had reached Doulevant, advanced by Soulaines on the left flank of the French line, this latter was pierced between Morvilliers and Chaumesnil.

In the meantime Victor had, it is true, again gained some ground for the moment; for he had recaptured La Giberie, but was soon forced back again by the superior numbers of the enemy, which were developing more and more. At the same time between 4 and 5 o'clock, Marmont lost Chaumesnil; the Emperor indeed hurried thither himself, to recapture this village and to free his rear, but in vain; the place remained in the enemy's hands, and when, with darkness already coming on, the attack was continued against Morvilliers, Marmont evacuated his position and fell back. The Emperor, it is true, tried, after night had already fallen, to lead up his reserves on the roads from Chaumesnil and La Rothière, but the movement was unsuccessful; La Rothière had, after a violent combat in the village, to be given up definitely, and the Emperor ordered it to be set on fire, so as to secure his retreat. A strong cavalry attack in addition inflicted severe losses upon the retreating French. On the right wing the fighting continued into the night around Dienville, when the enemy ceased his attacks; but at midnight Gerard evacuated the village. Thus the Emperor's army was totally thrown back upon Brienne.

The victors did not pursue, and the Emperor was during the night still able to get his army in order on the road from Brienne to Lesmont and to place it in readiness for its movement to Troyes over the bridge of Lesmont, on the following day. He had left the battlefield at 8 o'clock; an hour later from the castle of Brienne, he issued his first orders for the preparations for the retreat, and at 11.30 for the actual retreat. He spent the night there, watching with great anxiety to see whether the enemy would follow up their victory by a pursuit, or not; at 4 a.m. he left Brienne. The bridge of Lesmont was at first covered by a strong force of artillery, and then by Marmont, who, stationed at Perthes, was to divert the enemy's attention; protected by these measures the French army retreated on the 2nd February, fairly unmolested, behind the Aube. Ney, retreating last, set the bridge on fire; Marmont, it is true, was attacked, but succeeded, without any great losses, in retiring behind the Voire. On the 3rd he reached Arcis-sur-Aube; the main army reached Troyes, where it joined Mortier. The Emperor, who had spent the night in Piney, also arrived there.

The army was still in a very bad condition after its defeat and the precipitate retreat, but things were much better than on the evening of the 1st February. If the enemy had then imitated Napoleon's methods of pursuit, the campaign might have ended with this battle, and, as Russia had been irrevocably lost to the conqueror on the Beresina, and Germany on the Elster, so France might have been lost to him on the Aube. An eye-witness of the disorganization of the army remarks emphatically, that it was "so great, that it reminded me of the defeats in the preceding campaign and gave rise to the fear of the greatest catastrophes." [1] But the enemy remained inactive, lost touch, hesitated, so that even at Piney, the Emperor was able to speak of fresh operations, and weigh their possibilities. "It is possible, that Blücher's army will move between the Marne and the Aube towards Vitry and Chalons. I shall operate from Troyes according to circumstances, so as to arrest the column, which, as I am assured, is moving *viâ* Sens towards Paris; or so as to return and manœuvre against Blücher and check his march." [2]

[1] Marmont, Mém. vi. 40.   [2] C. N. To Clarke, 2nd February.

The Emperor had judged quite correctly; Blücher was marching to the right of the great army towards the Marne, as had been resolved upon in the Allies' headquarters. The situation on this stream was such, that Blücher's corps under Yorck, which was operating there, had reached the Moivre on the 3rd, and stood face to face with Macdonald, who was at Chalons. On the 4th the Emperor took up a position to defend Troyes, for he could not but believe, that an enemy so much his superior would advance directly against himself; but the latter merely advanced on the two following days to the left, avoiding an immediate attack. Yorck had arrived in front of Chalons and Blücher was on the march to Fere-Champenoise. But the Emperor had already become aware of this march on the part of Blücher, and in the first morning hours of the 5th he had already resolved to march to Nogent-sur-Seine, in order to oppose his enemy near the bridge over this river. "The Emperor is hastening to Nogent-sur-Seine; he will be on a line with Mery this evening." [1] Marmont received orders to proceed thither also in full haste. "You will march as quickly as possible to Nogent-sur-Seine, in order to hold the bridge at this town, which, possibly, is already threatened by the column that passed near Arcis yesterday." [2] Marmont reached Mery-sur-Seine on the 5th.

The Emperor's first thought was to protect his capital; and as he was obliged to do this, he had to give up for the present his intention formed on the 2nd, of manœuvring, more or less on the offensive, againt Sens in the valley of the Seine, or against Blücher, although he was loth to renounce these operations. "My plans have been considerably interfered with by these arrangements, for I intended to attack Bar-sur-Seine to-morrow, in order to beat the Emperor Alexander, who seems to me to have taken wrong measures, but I sacrifice everything in order to cover

---

[1] C. N. To Berthier. Troyes, 5th February, 3 a.m.
[2] C. N. Berthier to Marmont. Troyes, 5th February, 4 a.m.

The Campaign in France

Paris."[1] In 1809 Napoleon's first problem, in face of the superior numbers arrayed against him by the enemy, had been to take up a position behind the Lech. Thanks to the enemy's mistakes he was able during the progress of operations to pass to an ever increasingly resolute offensive. On the present occasion also his first thought was the defensive, but here too, we shall notice, in proportion to the mistakes of the enemy, the Emperor gradually developed a bold and successful offensive. Once more we shall witness a sudden and brilliant recrudescence of Napoleon's military genius, reminding us of his best days, but it was to be for the last time.

It is true that the characteristic feature of great generals is to avoid the defensive and to engage by preference in offensive operations, yet this preference should never develop into rash and ill-considered actions. Was it not the very opposite of great military qualities, which induced the leader of the Austrians in 1805 to prosecute his desultory offensive movements as far as the Iller, and the leader of the Prussians to do the same as far as the Thüringer Wald, the operations in both cases being out of harmony with the means at their disposal? And was it not his genius which induced Napoleon in 1807 to plan the defensive operations on the Passarge, those on the Lech in 1809, and in 1814 those on the Seine, conscious that he would be able at the right time to resume the offensive, wherever and whenever the enemy's movements should demand or permit this to be done?

The Emperor now moved towards Nogent, where he (118d) arrived on the 7th. Mortier left Troyes with the rearguard during the night of the 6th, and Schwarzenberg took up positions on this latter day in and around this town. Macdonald, falling further back, got as far as Dormans and ordered the important bridges over the Marne at Chateau-Thierry and La Ferté-sous-Jouarre to be occupied. Yorck reached Epernay with 18,000

[1] C. N. To Joseph. Troyes, 6th February, 3 p.m.

men; Blücher's various corps, which we have now, in view of the coming considerations, to treat separately, were in the following positions: Sacken, 20,000 men, at Etoges; Olssufiev, 3700 men and the headquarters at Vertus; and two days' march to the rear of Vertus were Kleist, 8000 men, and Kapzevitsch, 7000 men, both coming up.

In the meantime the Emperor had received most ominous reports, to the effect that the enemy were at La Ferté-sous-Jouarre, nay even at Meaux; but in spite of his most embarrassing position, he did not allow his calm judgment to be clouded, and declared these reports to be "mere alarms." Nay more, his correct military insight revealed to him the possibilities of success which lay in the proposal, sent him by Marmont on the evening of the 6th. For the Marshal had been informed by the inhabitants of the country of the loose order of the enemy's advance, and this proposal was to make a dash forward with 12,000 to 15,000 men amongst the isolated hostile corps in the direction of the network of roads between Vitry and Meaux. The Emperor caught at this idea and *developed it; should this operation prove feasible, he himself would deal this blow, and seek to gain more than merely a partial success. "At this moment I am sending off 20,000 men to occupy Sezanne. I shall go there during the night, with all the forces necessary to beat and hurl back whatever we may meet on those roads. From there I shall go in all haste to the road towards Meaux." [1]

Against Schwarzenberg he thought he had an advantage of three days' marches. He therefore had ordered Marmont to march to Sezanne; he was to reconnoitre from there as to how matters stood at Montmirail and along the road from Vitry to Meaux, and if the news gained confirmed previous intelligence, the Emperor would follow with the army through Sezanne. "In this position of

[1] C. N. To Joseph. Nogent, 7th February.

THE CAMPAIGN IN FRANCE 387

affairs we must show confidence and take bold measures."[1]

Thus Marmont reached Fontaine-Denis on the 7th, whilst the Emperor was at Nogent with Ney, Victor, Gerard and Mortier. At 4 a.m. on the 8th, he received news from Marmont, to the effect, that on the 6th some large bodies of cavalry, but no infantry, had passed through Sezanne, and at that moment some 7000 to 8000 men were still there, and that some artillery firing was said to have been heard in the neighbourhood of Epernay. He ordered Marmont to move as early as possible to Sezanne; Ney also started and reached Villenauxe, and Gerard St. Hilaire; Victor and Mortier, as well as the Emperor himself, remained as yet in Nogent, where the latter waited impatiently for further news, for, before he operated definitely, he wanted to be sure, on which of the three roads of advance, viâ Sezanne, viâ Montmirail or along the Marne valley, Blücher was marching, and how far, approximately, he had already advanced. The Emperor, himself, considered the middle road as the most probable and did not feel inclined to believe in his march along the valley of the Marne.

However, Marmont, who had arrived in Sezanne during the forenoon and driven some Cossacks out of this village, reported that in all probability the main body of the Silesian army was advancing by the Marne valley. The real situation on this day was as follows: Sacken was at Montmirail, Olssufiev at Etoges, Kleist and Kapzevitsch at Chalons, whilst Yorck was pursuing the retreating Macdonald as far as Dormans. The latter crossed the Marne at Chateau-Thierry and destroyed the bridge. Marmont pushed an advanced guard forward as far as St. Prix, and placed his corps in position at Chapton; from here he reported, that Sacken was evidently advancing through Montmirail.

Thereupon Napoleon resolved to throw himself upon

[1] C. N. To Joseph. Nogent, 7th February, 7 p.m.

the Silesian army, and, as soon as he had defeated it, fall back to Nogent, from which place he would begin operations to arrest Schwarzenberg's advance. About 3 p.m. on the 9th he started from Sezanne for this purpose. His arrangements and plans were now as follows: Oudinot stood with 25,000 men on the Seine and Yonne near Provins—Montereau—Sens; Victor, with 14,000, inclusive of Gerard and Milhaud, at Nogent; these were to cover Paris against Schwarzenberg. Victor was ordered to hold out as long as possible in Nogent, if directly attacked there; but if Schwarzenberg were to march to Sens without paying attention to him, he was to effect a junction with Oudinot at Montereau on the right bank of the Seine. In the meantime the Emperor with the Old Guard, 8000 men, Ney, 6000 men, Marmont, 6000 men, the cavalry of the Guards under Nansouty and the cavalry of Doumerc, 10,000 men, would operate against the Silesian army, which he estimated at 45,000 men, of whom however Macdonald would engage 5000. "The sum total of my forces is therefore 60,000 to 70,000 men of all arms, including the Engineers and Artillery. I calculate having 45,000 men of the Silesian army and 150,000 men under Schwarzenberg against me, including Bubna and the Cossacks, so that, if I gain a victory over the Silesian army and put it *hors de combat* for a few days, I shall be able to turn against Schwarzenberg with 70,000 to 80,000 men, reckoning the reinforcements, which you will send to me from Paris, and I do not think he will be able to oppose more than 110,000 to 120,000 men to me at this point. Even if I do not find myself strong enough to attack him, I shall be strong enough to keep him entirely in check for fourteen to twenty days, during which time new combinations will be made."[1] This last sentence proves, that in spite of this assumption of the offensive against Blücher, the Emperor's general intention was after all only to gain time, which must indeed be the great aim of any

[1] C. N. To Joseph. Nogent, 9th February, 2 p.m.

defensive; but he intended to make his defensive active by offensive strokes, just as he had done eighteen years before on the plains of Mantua.

At this moment when the Emperor had definitely decided upon dealing the blow he had planned, his subordinate officer, the very one from whom the first proposition for the operation had emanated, considered it incumbent upon him to abandon it. Marmont thought that the right time had gone by, that the enemy having become aware of Napoleon's intentions, would concentrate, and therefore the attempt on their flank must be given up, and the French be content with opposing them frontally at Meaux; he consequently withdrew his corps to Sezanne. The lessons of the moment are most instructive. We see a leader, having just proved himself to be possessed of a correct insight into the situation and of a resolute spirit, hesitate in the act of executing a well-conceived plan, because he feared lest the enemy should already have taken the best counter-measures, and lest it should be too late. But the Emperor did not allow himself to be disconcerted by any further considerations; he had raised his arm for the blow, and the blow must be dealt, even at the risk of striking the air or of breaking his own sword. And he who desires success must follow his example; he cannot weigh all possible contingencies, and there is nothing more foreign to the genius of a military leader than such a mood as Hamlet's, where:

> "The native hue of resolution
> Is sicklied o'er with the pale cast of thought;
> And enterprises of great pith and moment,
> . . . their currents turn awry!"

Our calculations have always to include the risks of chance, there must ever be a possibility of failure, and this uncertainty can only be successfully met by such quick resolve and such vigorous action as the Emperor displayed on this occasion. He was justified in his proud assertion, which he afterwards made at St. Helena: "I consider myself to have been probably the boldest man in warfare that ever existed."[1]

(114a) Napoleon therefore persisted in his forward move, and Marmont, falling back upon Sezanne, found Ney there already, and consequently had to advance again. In the evening the Emperor himself arrived in Sezanne with the remainder of the troops chosen for the forward movement. On the side of the enemy Sacken stood at Montmirail, Olssufiev at Champaubert, Kleist and Kapzewitsch not far from Vertus, and Yorck at Chateau-Thierry. Macdonald was at La Ferté-sous-Jouarre.

On the 10th, the French army, with Marmont in the van, started from Sezanne and advanced towards Champaubert. At Bayes Marmont met with Olssufiev's advanced guard, and attacking it about 9 o'clock, in accordance with the orders of the Emperor, who had himself come up, soon forced it to fall back on its main body at Champaubert. The latter also was attacked by a turning moment, entirely defeated and almost annihilated. On the same evening the Emperor directed Nansouty to take the road to Montmirail, and followed with the whole army at 5 a.m. in order to fall upon Sacken, who was in the same isolated position as Olssufiev had been in, when attacked. One division of Marmont's and Doumerc alone took up a position at Etoges to cover him against Blücher. Macdonald also received orders to advance resolutely on his own side.

"The Emperor was intoxicated with delight."[2] This victory over 4000 men of the enemy excited the vivid imagination which was one of his characteristics, so that he already saw the other corps of the Silesian army beaten in the same manner, and the whole of this army, "the pick of the Allies,"[3] dispersed, and himself driving

---

[1] Mémorial de Ste. Hélène, vii. 155. [2] Marmont, Mém. vi. 52.
[3] C. N. To Joseph. From the farm L'Épine-au-Bois, between Montmirail and Vieux Maisons, 11th February, 8 p.m.

Schwarzenberg behind the Rhine. At first the situation justified such hopes. Blücher withdrew on receiving news of the events at Champaubert, Kleist's and Kapzevitsch's corps, which had reached Fere-Champenoise, fell back to Bergères during the same night, whilst Sacken stood at La Ferté-sous-Jouarre, and Yorck at Chateau-Thierry. The former of these started during the night for Montmirail, at which town the Emperor's van, under Nansouty, also arrived about midnight.

When Sacken advanced against the latter on the morning of the 11th, the Emperor delayed him by a cannonade, until the bulk of his forces had come up, and then, about 2 p.m., he proceeded to the attack. He directed this mainly against Sacken's left wing, so as to prevent him reaching the road from Chateau-Thierry, whence alone help could have come to him in the person of Yorck; he therefore fell back with his own left wing in order to entice Sacken more and more towards the right. He was entirely successful. Sacken captured Le Bois-Jean and Courmont, and while he was thus occupied the Emperor took the farm of Haute-Épine by storm.

In the meantime Yorck began to come up from Chateau-Thierry, but without any heavy artillery, which had been left behind on account of the impassable roads; moreover, 5000 men had been left at Chateau-Thierry to hold the bridge there. The Emperor sent Mortier against him, and the latter drove Yorck back behind Fontenelles, whilst on the other wing Sacken's fate was sealed about the same time. Here some heavy fighting had occurred for the possession of Marchais; Sacken had, by putting forth all his strength, taken this place for the third time, but it was again wrested from him by a turning attack of the Old Guard. His retreat was now unavoidable, and he started upon it with heavy losses during the night along the road to Chateau-Thierry, accompanied by Yorck and covered by the latter's cavalry.

The Emperor spent the night in the farm of Haute-

Épine. In the morning of the 12th he started for Chateau-Thierry in pursuit of the beaten enemy. He hoped Macdonald would oppose them at the bridge over the Marne and the operation would thus become decisive. It is true this expectation was not fulfilled, though the passage of the Marne was attended with heavy loss for Sacken and Yorck in the face of the Emperor's close pursuit. He was indeed justified in saying to himself gleefully after the days of Champaubert and Montmirail: "For such great successes I have employed only very few troops."[1] In the morning of the 13th the Emperor, having passed the night in the farm-house of Lumerout, began to construct a bridge at Chateau-Thierry, as the enemy had burnt the one there. By the evening he had led his army to the right bank and Mortier with the advanced guard reached Rocourt in pursuit of the enemy who had retreated along the road to Soissons.

(114b) That very morning the Emperor had still been in doubt whether he should not be contented with the success gained and now turn against Schwarzenberg, though he did not think the latter would venture to advance to Paris, whilst Napoleon, victorious over the Silesian army, was able to attack him in the rear. "I do not believe that Prince Schwarzenberg will continue his march towards Fontainebleau, as long as we are masters of the bridge at Nogent. The Austrians are too well acquainted with my methods of manœuvring, and have too long borne the marks of them; they will undoubtedly expect me to attack their rear, as I have done here, if they leave the bridge of Nogent in our possession."[2] For the present, Macdonald, with the reinforcements which had reached him, in all 12,000 men, received orders to march to Montereau, so as to reinforce the troops there.

In the meantime Schwarzenberg, going round to the left, had taken the direction of Sens, while attacking

---

[1] C. N. To Joseph. Suburb of Chateau-Thierry, 12th February.
[2] C. N. To Joseph. Farm of Lumerout, 13th February, 10 a.m.

Nogent at the same time with two corps. The former town fell into his hands by a surprise on the 11th, and Nogent was evacuated on the 12th, by Victor, the French leaders falling back upon Montereau. Blücher had remained stationary at Bergeres on the 12th with his two corps ; on the 13th he advanced against Marmont, forcing him back as far as Fromentières. The Emperor received news of this offensive at 3 a.m. on the 14th, and recognized immediately, the opportunity now offered for a victorious blow against these last two corps of the Silesian army, before he left the latter alone and fell back to the Seine.

He set himself in motion without delay. "I hope to be in Montmirail before 7 o'clock in the morning, to attack the enemy before noon and to give them a salutary lesson."[1] Marmont fell back on this day, at first further towards Montmirail, and Blücher followed him. But at 8 o'clock Napoleon arrived at this place, and ordered Marmont immediately to show front and to assail the enemy's vanguard, which had arrived at Vauchamps. The latter, attacked about noon, was soon entirely overthrown. The Emperor, whose troops had now come up, Mortier alone having continued in pursuit of Sacken and Yorck, advanced against Blücher's main body, and, while he attacked it in front with his infantry, his cavalry, under Grouchy, proceeded to its direct rear, blocking its line of retreat between Champaubert and Etoges. Blücher was forced to break through, and did so with heavy losses; he then returned to Bergères, closely pursued by the French as far as Etoges. On this day Schwarzenberg was in possession of the Seine from Nogent as far as Montereau; Oudinot and Victor were at Nangis.

Who can contemplate these days from the 9th to the 14th of February, 1814, without yielding to the same admiration for the Emperor, now forty-four years of age, that we accorded to the general of twenty-six, during the days from the 12th to the 15th April, 1796? Here,

[1] C. N. To Marmont. Chateau-Thierry, 14th February, 3 a.m.

at Champaubert, Montmirail and Etoges we see the same quick perception of the situation, the same bold resolution, the same firm execution, as we saw at Montenotte, Milesimo and Dego. But now it was the last eruption of the dying volcano, then it had been its first sign of activity.

On the 15th as early as 4 a.m. the new orders were issued; the army was set in motion towards La Ferté-sous-Jouarre; for the Emperor thought it incumbent upon him to hasten to the immediate protection of Paris, since Schwarzenberg had gained the line of the Seine. He fixed upon Guignes as the probable place of meeting, being the junction of the roads Melun—Meaux and Paris—Nangis; should however Schwarzenberg show the least sign of hesitation or even fall back, the Emperor intended immediately to advance again *viâ* Montmirail towards Chalons-sur-Marne or Vitry and manœuvre on the right flank or in the rear of the enemy. He left Marmont behind to do the same for Blücher as Macdonald had done in August, 1813, namely, first to drive the enemy back a little more, and then, should the latter resume the offensive, to fall back from position to position *viâ* Montmirail to La Ferté. At 5 p.m. the Emperor was at Meaux. On this day Oudinot, Victor and Macdonald had taken up a position on the little river of Yerres; Schwarzenberg was within the square: Nogent—Montereau—Nangis—Provins.

(114c) On the 16th, at 3 o'clock in the afternoon, Napoleon arrived at Guignes; he collected on that day his army—Victor, Oudinot, Gerard, Macdonald, Ney, the Old Guard, and the cavalry corps of Nansouty, Milhaud, Excelmans and Kellermann (the newly formed VI. Corps)—on the line Chaumes—Guignes, with the intention of attacking on the following day. The forces, which he had led up from Montmirail, had marched about 47 miles in 36 hours. The Emperor advanced in the morning of the 17th along the road to Nangis, Schwarzenberg at the same time falling back in all directions upon the line

The Campaign in France 395

of the Seine. The advance guard of the corps, which had lain at Nangis, was too late to escape the attack and was completely defeated at Mormant. When the Emperor reached Nangis, he ordered Oudinot forward to Provins, Macdonald to Dommarie and Victor to Montereau, but the bridges over the Seine still remained in Schwarzenberg's hands. Against Schwarzenberg, therefore, the Emperor made a frontal advance, not a flank movement, as had been the case against Blücher. It was his urgent anxiety about Paris, which induced the Emperor to attack in this manner, for he wanted first of all to cover the capital in a direct way, and this same reason gives the clue to the further direction of his operations.

Napoleon had reckoned with certainty upon Victor's gaining possession of Montereau on that same day, for it was through this town that he wished to break out, to make sure that Schwarzenberg would not, while engaging him on the Seine, turn his right flank towards Fontainebleau and appear after all before Paris. The absolute security of Paris was necessarily the central object of his operations, considering the proximity of the capital and the peculiar relations which existed between it and the Emperor. But Victor had halted before reaching Montereau, and Napoleon, in his anger at the success of his manœuvre having been endangered by this halt, dismissed him from his command, and placed him at the head of two divisions of the Guards under Ney, while the II. Corps, incorporated with Gerard's troops, passed under the chief command of that general.

As a general or as a newly-crowned Emperor in 1805 and 1806, he would not have had to resort to such a punishment; his operations would not have failed through the fault of a subordinate officer; he would have commanded, urged on, would have hastened forward in person, until he was certain, that all he considered necessary for success had actually been done.

It is remarkable, as shown by his letters, how many reprimands and punishments Napoleon inflicted on his marshals and generals during this campaign. Formerly, when the vigour of his genius added to the superiority in numbers of his troops over the enemy, carried all before him, he was well satisfied with the successful issue of events, and did not trouble to remedy defects, or correct errors in judgment or execution. Now, too late, he was seeing the dire results of such negligence. Remembering, regretfully, the former youthful energy of his companions in arms, he broke out into these words: "It is no use talking of acting as you have done lately, you must put your boots on again and also your determination of '93."[1] In actual war complaints and severe punishments come too late; it is in the time of peace that we should appoint men of judgment and activity to high posts, and remove those who have lost these qualifications.

The next day the passage was effected at Montereau by Gerard under the Emperor's personal supervision. Macdonald and Oudinot arrived in front of Bray and Nogent, but the bridges over the Seine remained in Schwarzenberg's possession, who stationed his main forces behind Nogent: upon the news of the loss of Montereau, however, he decided upon a general retreat to Troyes.

Blücher, who again had collected his corps on the 16th at Chalons-sur-Marne, was directed to come up to Arcis-sur-Aube, and matters were again in the same condition as three weeks previously; undoubtedly a great triumph for Napoleon in the face of a superiority of two and a half to one.

But while we admire the return in all its old vigour of the Emperor's military activity, we cannot shut our eyes to the clear evidence that his mind had lost its power of discriminating between successes likely to have a permanent result, and that which would be merely of an

[1] C. N. To Augereau. Nogent, 21st February, 1814.

ephemeral nature. In a purely military sense, we here see him once again, as in his best days, weighing the circumstances correctly, and making use of certain data, but we see also that the military success once attained, he no longer utilizes it, in a statesmanlike manner, to secure what is still within reach, but immediately abandons all considerations of existing circumstances. After Champaubert, intoxicated by victory, he had talked of being again seen on the Vistula. Now, having barely succeeded in forcing Schwarzenberg back a little, the Emperor recalled the concessions, which he had permitted his plenipotentiary to make at the negotiations for peace at Chatillon, and a proposal for a truce being made by the Allies, he lost his head altogether, burst out into vulgar vituperation, and shut his eyes to the only possibility of bringing to a successful issue this struggle, which must necessarily lead to his ruin, on account of the unequal proportion of forces on the two sides. In this he showed himself inimical to his best interests.

In the morning of the 19th Napoleon's army crossed the Seine at Montereau, whilst Schwarzenberg started upon his retreat up the river. During the next few days the Emperor continued crossing the Seine and collecting his army at Nogent. Schwarzenberg did the same at Troyes, and Blücher arrived at Mery-sur-Soane on the 21st February. Napoleon was determined to advance against Schwarzenberg; both he and his army had regained the full consciousness of their moral superiority. But as this advance to Troyes was threatened in the flank by Blücher's position, the Emperor ordered Oudinot with 10,000 men to attack Mery on the 22nd; half of the town situated on the left bank of the Seine was captured, but the French were unable to advance beyond it in the face of the 60,000 men of the Silesian army. At the same time the Emperor's main army, 53,000 men, advanced against Troyes, but there also the enemy's 80,000 men were found drawn up in (114d) battle order, and an attack seemed inadvisable, considering the disproportion of numbers on the two sides. The Emperor had desired to establish his headquarters at Mery, but was now forced to forego this intention and spent the night at Châtres in the hut of a carrier. At this time Mortier was with 10,000 men at Soissons, being on the march to Chateau-Thierry, and Marmont with 8000 men stood at Sezanne; the latter having been told by the Emperor: " (1) to cover Paris along the roads from Chalons and Vitry; (2) to unite with the army on the Aube and at Troyes at the same time as Blücher, if the latter effects a junction with the Allied army."[1]

In this situation Schwarzenberg decided upon a retreat behind the Aube, since he had only a superiority of two to one, with which to face the Emperor in person. This was the feeling of all, Blücher excepted, who saw themselves opposed to the Emperor, and Napoleon said afterwards, with pride, at St. Helena, he had been reckoned equal to a "hundred thousand men." Both here and at Dresden, we have proof that the strength of his genius did actually counterbalance the presence of fully 100,000 men. At the same time that the resolution was arrived at that the main army should retreat, Blücher conceived the plan of going to the Marne, to effect a junction there with the corps which had come up from Belgium, and stood in the neighbourhood of Rheims and Soissons, and then to march direct to Paris.

Thus Schwarzenberg fell back on the 23rd February and stood on the 24th at Bar-sur-Aube. On the same day the Emperor entered Troyes. However the enemy did not intend to arrest their retreat at Bar, but arranged to fall back still further, to Langres. Napoleon divined both this intention and Blücher's movement, and thought of attacking the latter in the rear. For the moment he sent Ney and Victor after him, whilst Macdonald, Oudinot and Gerard followed in Schwarzen-

[1] C. N. To Berthier. Château of Surville, 20th February, 5 a.m.

berg's tracks; he himself remained at Troyes as a
reserve with the Old Guard, the cavalry of the Guards
and Excelmans watching to see what movements his
separated opponents were going to make, and against
which of them he would have first to throw the weight
of his own activity into the scale.

On the 25th only a strong rear-guard of Schwarzenberg's (115a)
army remained behind at Bar-sur-Aube, the remainder
having retreated behind the Aube; on the next day Bar
also was evacuated, and now the whole Allied army was
on the right bank of this river. Gerard and Oudinot had
followed the enemy to Bar and occupied this town,
Macdonald took the direction of Bar-sur-Seine, with
orders to push on to La Ferté-sur-Aube afterwards; on
the 26th he was on a line with Mussy. During these two
days Blücher had, in pursuance of his plan, marched
forward against Marmont towards Sezanne, had driven
him on the 25th out of this latter place and had advanced
on the 26th to La Ferté-Gaucher. Marmont had fallen
back to this latter place, whilst Mortier, having on his
march hither reached Chateau-Thierry, fell back on this
day to La Ferté-sous-Jouarre.

At 5 p.m. the Emperor received the news of Blücher's
determined advance on Sezanne and immediately urged
Ney on to operate in his rear, in order to relieve
Marmont; he was to cross the Aube at Arcis and Victor
at Anglure, whilst Arrighi was to cross the Seine at
Nogent; "the Marshal Prince of the Moskwa is directed
to give the necessary supervision to all these movements.
Let his general instructions be, that Blücher is on no
account to be permitted to gain a footing at Sezanne."[1]
But during the night further reports came in, announcing
a rapid advance on the part of Blücher and as rapid a
retreat of Marmont viâ La Ferté-Gaucher, and by the
morning of the 27th the Emperor had resolved to take
the operations in Blücher's rear into his own hands. Ney

[1] C. N. To Berthier. Troyes, 26th February, 5 p.m.

was urged on to a vigorous advance on Sezanne; Marmont, who was informed of the Emperor's approach, was to effect a junction with Mortier, and keep Blücher engaged frontally. At this time the two last-mentioned marshals had, after uniting their forces in the evening of the 26th at La Ferté-sous-Jouarre, reached Meaux by a night march.

In the forenoon, at 11 o'clock, the Emperor left Troyes. Macdonald, under whose commands Oudinot, Gerard, the cavalry corps of Milhaud and Kellermann, altogether 33,000 men, were placed, was told off to watch Schwarzenberg, and everything possible was to be done to keep the enemy under the impression that the Emperor himself was still present with these troops. "It is incumbent upon you to say that I am at Bar-sur-Aube, and to send all the messages addressed to me, to Bar-sur-Aube and Vendeuvre, for it is of the highest importance that the enemy should not doubt but that I am still between Bar-sur-Aube and Vendeuvre."[1] He hoped to settle accounts with Blücher, before Schwarzenberg could take advantage of his absence; "I hope I shall have time to finish my operations, before the enemy becomes aware of this and advances."[2] In the afternoon Napoleon was at Arcis-sur-Aube; on the following morning he hoped to reach the main road about 9 o'clock at Fere-Champenoise, and to push forward thence *via* Sezanne to La Ferté-Gaucher, whilst Marmont and Mortier on their side would keep the enemy engaged; "I shall thus be in the rear of the whole hostile army."[3] He spent the night at Herbisse in the house of a clergyman, having the Old Guard and the cavalry of the Guards with him.

On this same day Blücher had reached La Ferté-sous-Jouarre, and half his army had crossed the Marne there; Marmont and Mortier stood at Meaux; Ney was at

---

[1] C. N. To Caulaincourt. Troyes, 27th February.
[2] C. N. To Clarke. Troyes, 27th February.
[3] C. N. To Joseph. Arcis-sur-Aube, 27th February, 5 p.m.

THE CAMPAIGN IN FRANCE 401

Sezanne. The Emperor hastened on further the next day, across the country between Sezanne and La Ferté-Gaucher, and we find his forces in columns on the road from Esternay to La Ferté. Blücher intended on that day, crossing over the Ourcq, to attack Meaux, from the North, but when his vanguard reached the Therouanne, Mortier and Marmont advanced, repulsed it and forced it away from the Ourcq along the road to Soissons. Upon this Blücher evacuated the left bank of the Marne entirely and destroyed the bridge of La Ferté-sous-Jouarre.

At 2 p.m. on the 1st March the Emperor arrived at Jouarre, but the mass of his army, on account of the swampy roads, only reached this town by the middle of the night and the next morning. No news had as yet come in of Mortier and Marmont. Acting against these, Blücher had approached the Ourcq, while they remained in their positions. Napoleon had to spend the whole of the 2nd March in constructing a bridge at La Ferté, at the same time collecting his army there, sending Victor and Arrighi to Chateau-Thierry, where they were to cross the Marne. Blücher, informed of his presence, departed in all haste for Oulchy-le-Chateau; Marmont and Mortier took up a position at Mareuil.

On the next day Napoleon wanted to find out, whether it was necessary to follow Blücher again, or whether he could leave him alone and turn against Schwarzenberg; in this latter case he intended to march *via* Chateau-Thierry to Chalons, collect as many reinforcements as possible from the towns in Lorraine, and utilizing his position on interior lines, manœuvre on the rear and the right flank of the enemy's main army. Oudinot now received orders to proceed to Arcis-sur-Aube, and Macdonald to hold himself in readiness to start. This was indeed what the French ought to have done; indeed the most correct course would have been, not to have followed up Blücher, but to have harassed

VOL. II.   D d

Schwarzenberg. There, in the headquarters of the Allies, lay the key of the situation, and, if Schwarzenberg had fallen back before the Emperor, when Blücher was at Mery ready to join him, much more would he have done so now, when the Silesian army had retreated to the Marne. If the main army continued to fall back, Blücher would probably be finally compelled to desist from his advance, either of his own accord, or, as is most probable, from receiving orders to retire. Even in that case, the Emperor's ultimate safety would not have been assured, for it was the hard fate of the General, thanks to the continued mistakes of the Statesman, to be forced to wage a hopeless struggle with 90,000 men against 200,000, under the walls of his capital. His overwhelming anxiety for Paris so fettered him that it prevented him doing what would have been correct in a military sense, that is to say, to entrust its fate temporarily to the weak forces of Mortier and Marmont, leaving them to dispute the ground step by step. However, whatever the Emperor's action for the movement, the ultimate issue could no longer be anything but failure.

(115b) At 2 a.m. on the 3rd March the bridge at La Ferté-sous-Jouarre was ready and the army immediately began to cross. Blücher again avoided the threatened attack by falling back in haste; he intended to cross the Aisne on that day at Fismes, but when the news reached him that Soissons had surrendered to the two corps which had arrived from Belgium, and which had effected a junction in front of this town, he proceeded to march in that direction and crossed the Aisne there. Mortier and Marmont followed in close pursuit up the Ourcq *viâ* Oulchy, and reached Hartennes. Napoleon remained for the night at Bezu-Saint-Germain; his army had advanced as far as Rocourt, from whence, leaving the direction of Oulchy, they were to wheel, *viâ* Fere-en-Tardenois, towards Braisne and Fismes; here he hoped to come upon the enemy's flank, for he reckoned, and was justified in so doing, upon the bridge of Soissons being blocked. On the 4th, Blücher drew up his army behind Soissons, prepared to await the enemy's attack. The Emperor reached Fismes; Mortier and Marmont approached somewhat nearer to Soissons. During the night Napoleon heard of the fall of Soissons, but as he had now reached the Vesle, he decided that the operations against Blücher should be carried through. Under these circumstances he resolved to cross the Aisne at Berry-au-Bac, in order to force the enemy completely away from Rheims towards the North. The whole army therefore marched on the 5th to Berry-au-Bac; at the same time Blücher's attention was diverted from his left wing by an attack of Marmont and Mortier upon Soissons. The walls of the town repelled the attack; but by the capture of Rheims all communication with Schwarzenberg was cut off. At Berry-au-Bac, Nansouty with the advanced guard, surprised the enemy's cavalry stationed there, and captured the bridge; the Emperor himself arrived there at 4 p.m. and the army came up in the course of the day.

On the 6th the march to Laon was continued. "After this I shall march viâ Chalons to Arcis."[1] It is true, news had arrived from the Seine, which seemed to render his speedy presence there absolutely necessary. For his absence had immediately been noticed, and on the 27th February the Allies advanced again; on this same day Bar-sur-Aube was taken, and during the next few days the whole line advanced against Macdonald; on the 4th March the latter lost Troyes, on the 6th he crossed at Mery over to the right bank of the Seine and took up a position around Provins. Such was the state of affairs there, and any further advance of Schwarzenberg must necessarily call the Emperor away from the Aisne, for the very same reason which had led him in pursuit of Blücher, viz. the protection of his capital. For the present, how-

[1] C. N. To Joseph. Berry-au-Bac, 6th March, 1814, noon.

ever, he wished to take the risk of their forcing this course upon him, for he was well aware of the methods of the Allied Headquarters, and therefore he continued his march to Laon. Marmont and Mortier also were to go thither, and likewise *viâ* Berry-au-Bac, in case they should be unable to force their way through at Soissons. Blücher, noticing this latter march, had resolved to attack them in the flank *viâ* Cerny, but stood fast in the position of Craonne, when he saw the Emperor lying in wait at Corbeny. When he left Schwarzenberg unmolested on the 27th February, Napoleon had given up waging war and only devoted himself to the task of meeting the pressing need of the moment as well as possible, and his actual death-struggle began in the military sense by his crossing the Aisne; he was no longer capable of anything but convulsive movements. We must keep this fact in mind if we wish to form a correct estimate of Napoleon's state of mind at the end of this desperate struggle.

On the 7th March the Emperor advanced to the attack of the enemy's position at Craonne, where only one Russian corps of Blücher's army stood, this latter having, with the remainder of his forces, begun a great turning movement on the Emperor's rear on the road to Laon. This movement, however, was unsuccessful, and thus about 4 o'clock the Russian corps was, after an obstinate resistance, driven out with heavy loss; it fell back upon the road Soissons—Laon and during the night reached this latter town. The Emperor's army had pursued it as far as the line Filain—Ostel, the Emperor himself spending the night at the ale-house of L'Ange Gardien. Though the day brought a tactical success, yet the outlook was most gloomy, for it had cost the French even more than the enemy, who was besides superior in point of numbers; the marches and hardships, moreover, thinned the ranks of the young French soldiers most rapidly: " The Young Guard is melting away like snow. The Old Guard is keeping up. My mounted Guards also are melting away very rapidly."[1] These facts justify us in speaking of a "death-struggle."

Blücher had on this day stationed at Laon, those portions of his army which had not fought at Craonne, and on the 8th he collected his whole army there, ready to accept battle. Napoleon resolved to advance to the same place, for he did not believe, that, after the events of the last few days, the entire Silesian army intended to make a stand there. Ney, Charpentier (who had taken the place of Victor, wounded) and Mortier advanced thither along the road of Soissons, and Marmont and Arrighi along that of Berry-au-Bac. The former column met with some resistance at the narrowing of the road near Etouvelle; the latter reached Corbeny. But the Emperor ordered the Pass of Etouvelle to be taken by a night surprise under Ney. Generally speaking night enterprises and night engagements were in his opinion to be undertaken with special advantage in one's own country, and he instructed one general, that "night marches are specially advantageous, if the country is on one's side; therefore we should employ them, in order to capture hostile posts, as we can act in concert with the natives, who will inform us of the numbers of the enemy and guide us to their rear."[2]

It had really been the Emperor's plan, not to make his attack on the 9th with the corps marching along the road from Soissons, until Marmot should be in a position to engage the enemy's left wing simultaneously, on the road from Berry-au-Bac; but he was too impatient to endure delay, and so he ordered Ney at 7 o'clock to commence the attack. The latter continued his advance at first, and captured Sezmilly while Mortier took Ardon; and these villages were taken a second time, after a counter attack

---

[1] C. N. To Joseph. Chavignon, 11th March.
[2] C. N. To Berthier. La Ferté-sous-Jouarre, 2nd March, 1814, 6 p.m.

on the part of the enemy had torn them from the grasp of the French. In the meantime Napoleon, becoming more and more angry, awaited in vain news or signs of Marmont's attack; moreover, of the numerous officers sent by him to that marshal, not one reached his goal, for Blücher, taking advantage of the one-sided advance of the French, had entirely interrupted communications between the two roads, by sending out some Cossacks. Nevertheless the Emperor resumed the fight again in the afternoon, ordered the village of Clacy, which threatened his left wing, to be taken by storm, but lost Ardon and Sezmilly to his opponent, and thus his separation from Marmont became still more pronounced.

The latter had on that day been engaged in hot fighting for the possession of Athies, and had, towards evening, captured half this village, the other half remaining in the enemy's hands. But when, at the approach of darkness, he allowed his men to encamp, they were before long attacked by superior numbers, dispersed and entirely put to flight. The enemy's cavalry pursued them as far as Corbeny. The Emperor had already issued his orders for the attack on the next day, intending, though so much inferior in strength, to envelop the enemy entirely with his own two wings. At 1 a.m. he received the news of Marmont's defeat; still he did not think of immediately beginning his retreat, since this would bring the enemy's entire force upon him; but decided to remain stationary, in a threatening attitude, in accordance with his usual bold, unbending temper, as he had done once before at Krasny. Now, as then, his obstinacy proved his salvation, and this episode shows that the boldest course is the best in war, and also proves that the Emperor had no reason to ascribe his fall to the ill-will or faithlessness of fortune.

When Blücher on the morning of the 10th saw the Imperial army, ready for battle, he sent orders to the corps which were pursuing Marmont to arrest their pursuit, and thus the Emperor's determined attitude relieved the Marshal. Soon after 9 o'clock Blücher attacked Clacy, but this village was held by Charpentier, about 2 p.m. the Emperor even thought he saw indications of the enemy's departure and advanced in his turn with Ney to the attack; but this attack failed; Ney's troops were forced to fall back with heavy losses, and at 4 o'clock the Emperor could no longer conceal from himself, that a general retreat was unavoidable. He entered upon it as night fell; he himself reached Chavignon and collected his army the next day at Soissons. Marmont did the same at Fismes, whilst Blücher remained stationary at Laon.

On the 12th the relative positions on both sides remained unchanged; but, towards evening the Emperor was informed that a corps, sent out by the enemy, had captured Rheims, and he resolved to recapture this town, because he was near enough at Soissons and Fismes, to cut this connecting link between Blücher and Schwarzenberg by a quick dash. Leaving Mortier behind for the protection of Soissons, he set Ney the same evening in motion towards Fismes and instructed Marmont to march against Rheims in the early morning of the 13th. The Emperor himself, with the Old Guard, left Soissons soon after midnight. He thus attacked the 15,000 men in Rheims with 20,000; but however bold and promising this enterprise may appear on the map, or as a move on the chessboard, we must consider it as coming under the definition of what we have called "convulsive movements," that is to say, if we view it in relation to the Emperor's situation as a whole.

Having arrived before Rheims about 4 o'clock in the afternoon, the Emperor met with obstinate resistance, and the town was not evacuated until after midnight. Here he stopped for the next few days, already busy with the idea of an operation against Schwarzenberg, and only sending Marmont out to Berry-au-Bac. On the Aube and the Seine meanwhile things had remained in (115e) the condition they had been in after Macdonald's retreat beyond the latter river; this marshal was at Provins, and Schwarzenberg around Troyes. Upon the receipt of the news of Laon on the 14th March, the latter started to force Macdonald back, but renounced this intention again, after being informed of the Emperor's arrival in Rheims, and consequently the change in the relative positions was, on the 17th, only very slight; Macdonald, having fallen back from Provins, stood midway between this place and Nangis; Schwarzenberg on the Aube at Lesmont and Arcis, and along the Seine at Troyes, Mery and Nogent; his left wing, which he had moved forward into the Yonne valley, he ordered back again to Troyes.

On this day the Emperor set out from Rheims against Schwarzenberg, having ordered up Mortier to Rheims and sent Ney forward to Chalons. His opinions regarding the situation and his operations, he expressed at this time, as follows:[1]

"We have three courses open to us:

"(1) The first is to go to Arcis-sur-Aube, thirteen hours' march; we should be there to-morrow, the 18th.

"On the 19th we could cross the Aube and be, during the night of the 19th, on the road to Mery or on that to Troyes.

"It is probable that the enemy will know by the day after to-morrow, that I have spent to-morrow night at Fere-Champenoise; from that moment the diversion will have been effected; this diversion would consequently have taken place in the course of the 19th.

"The Prince of the Moskwa will be at Arcis-sur-Aube at the same time as myself. We shall cross the Aube and be at Troyes on the 20th. I have a pontoon-train and can construct my bridges, where I like.

"I believe the headquarters are at Troyes.

"This plan is the boldest, its effects are incalculable.

[1] C. N. Notes, dictated to Colonel Baron Atthalin, sub-director of the Emperor's topographical cabinet. Rheims, 17th March.

"(2) March to Sezanne and from Sezanne to Provins. "To begin with, the roads are of the worst. From there to Sezanne is a nine hours' march, from Sezanne to Provins another nine hours; altogether eighteen hours' march.

"The cavalry could be at Sezanne to-morrow, the 18th, if no hostile cavalry is met with. If so, it would be forced to await the artillery. The Prince of the Moskwa could not be there by the 19th, he would be forced to march through this place.

"From Sezanne to Meaux *viâ* Coulommiers and La Ferté-Gaucher is fifteen hours' march. Once at Sezanne, we could go to Meaux. We could reach this town in two good days' marches. There would thus be from here to Meaux, *viâ* Sezanne, twenty-four hours' march.

"We might also go there from here, by passing through Fere-Champenoise, seven hours' march; from Fere-Champenoise to Sezanne, four hours; from Sezanne to Meaux, fifteen hours.

"Thus from here to Meaux, if we went *viâ* Fere Champenoise, there would be twenty-seven hours' march instead of twenty-four, viz. three hours more.

"(3) Finally the third plan would be, to march direct to Meaux along the great road. From here to Meaux is a twenty-one hours' march. We could be there early on the 20th. We could even concentrate the army there on the 20th and attack the enemy on the 21st.

"These three plans have all something in their favour.

"The first is the boldest; it would give the enemy a great fright and might have unexpected results.

"The second has the drawback of being always on cross-roads, but it would cut off the enemy on the right bank of the Seine.

"The third is the safest, because it would lead in a straight line to Paris, but it is likewise the one, which would render the chance of a great battle quite possible, inasmuch as it would not exert any moral effect. But, if the enemy had 70,000 to 80,000 men, this battle would be a terrible risk for us, instead of our having greater possibilities, by marching to Troyes and getting into the enemy's rear, whilst the Duke of Tarentum retreats, disputing every point."

According to this reasoning the first plan was the one he adopted, and that day, the 17th, he reached Epernay. " I shall start to-morrow before daybreak, in order to march to Arcis-sur-Aube. I shall be there by noon on the day after to-morrow. From there I shall, according to circumstances, proceed to Mery or to Troyes, so as to attack the enemy in the rear."[1] "I expect great results from my movement, which is sure to occasion great disorder and great confusion in the enemy's rear and in their headquarters, if the latter are still at Troyes."[2] At the commencement of this movement, reinforcements having come up from Paris, the Emperor had 22,000 men; Mortier remained at Rheims and Soissons with 10,000 men; Marmont at Berry-au-Bac with 7000; they were again to cover Paris from Blücher.

On the 18th the Emperor reached Fere-Champenoise, from whence he drove out a corps of Cossacks; Ney was at Sommesous. Schwarzenberg, upon the news of Napoleon's approach, withdrew his left wing from the Seine to Troyes, leaving his right wing on the Aube. On the 19th the Emperor continued his advance, crossed the Aube at Plancy and occupied Mery; he himself returned personally to Plancy. Ney, advancing to Arcis, met with no resistance on his march thither and was then also moved to Plancy; Arcis itself remained until nightfall in the hands of a rearguard of the Allies, which then fell back. Schwarzenberg on this day drew back his right wing also somewhat, so that he now stood with this latter at Nogent-sur-Aube and Lesmont, and with his left at Troyes. Macdonald had pushed his troops forward in

---

[1] C. N. To Clarke. Epernay, 17th March.
[2] C. N. To Joseph. Epernay, 17th March.

echelons between Provins and Villenauxe, in order to come in touch with the Emperor, and the latter thought: "I shall march to Brienne. I shall let Troyes be, and turn in all haste towards my fortresses."[1]

Thus the Emperor was under the impression, that the enemy was falling back before him along his whole line. This, however, was not the case; Schwarzenberg had on the contrary decided to attack the Emperor, as soon as he should, according to expectations, cross the Aube. In the morning of the 20th, therefore, Napoleon advanced upon Arcis-sur-Aube, having on the left bank of the Aube the cavalry of his Guard, and on the right Ney; about 10 o'clock that town was reached, occupied and the bridge restored. Soon after noon the Emperor left Plancy and arrived in Arcis-sur-Aube about 1 o'clock; the Old Guard likewise reached this town. Ney and Sebastiani, the latter being in command of the cavalry of the Guard, now repeated to Napoleon in person, what they had already reported to him at Plancy, namely, that the enemy was evidently advancing.

The Emperor would not believe it, and on the other hand, omitted to do what the General Bonaparte would undoubtedly have done; he did not ride forward in person, in order to convince himself, but sent an officer, and the latter's report confirmed him in his belief. Immediately afterwards the enemy's right wing, advancing from Nogent-sur-Aube along the river, delivered its attack. The French cavalry, which had been moved forward, was routed and retreated in full flight towards Arcis. The Emperor himself barred the passage of the fugitives with drawn sword, and as the Old Guard came up at the same moment, Arcis was held. The fight now centred round Torcy-le-Grand, and this village was again and again captured and lost by both sides, but finally, at nightfall it remained in the hands of the French. Schwarzenberg's left-wing had, on this day, taken no part in the fighting; it

[1] C. N. To Clarke. Plancy, 20th March.

had marched in the direction of Plancy and encamped near Les Grandes Chapelles ; Macdonald, on his march to join the Emperor, being in front of it near Marcilly and Anglure.

Napoleon passed the night in Arcis, in the château of M. de la Briffe. As the Allies had, on this day, only employed a relatively small part of their forces against him, he thought it had only been a rearguard engagement and that the Allies would draw off. But Schwarzenberg had ordered his left wing up towards Arcis, and intended thus to envelop the Emperor while issuing from this town, with a semicircle composed of superior numbers. When, therefore, the latter opened the attack at about 10 o'clock, on the 21st March, with a forward move of the cavalry of his Guards, followed by Ney, these troops saw themselves at once arrested in their advance, and Napoleon became convinced that he had been mistaken, and that Schwarzenberg was in position in front of him. He immediately resolved upon a retreat behind the Aube, about noon, ordering Oudinot to cover it, by holding Arcis. The enemy, with superior numbers, pursued keenly on all sides, and inflicted most heavy losses upon Oudinot ; the latter lost Arcis soon after 6 o'clock, but the Allies were unable to cross the river. The Emperor reached Sommepuis by nightfall.

(115d) Having seen the impossibility of acting any longer on the offensive against Schwarzenberg, he fell back again upon the plan, which, as we saw, he had discussed on the preceding day, namely, to throw himself without delay within the protection of his fortresses in Lorraine, to reinforce himself there, and to operate against Schwarzenberg's lines of communications, in order to induce him, by this strategical danger, to execute a rear movement. We see that this was only a forlorn hope, as had been his advance *viâ* Arcis against Schwarzenberg ; the Emperor could no longer devise any other plans.

Thus he now intended, first of all, to make a dash on

Vitry, and to try, whether he could not capture this place by a *coup de main*. This attempt made by Ney on the 22nd, was, however, unsuccessful, and now the Emperor decided to march to St. Dizier. He spent the night in the Château du Plessis, having ordered Marmont and Mortier to join him by Chalons-sur-Marne. Macdonald and Gerard were still in the rear at Dosnon, and Oudinot was opposite Arcis-sur-Aube. On the 23rd the Emperor continued his march and reached St. Dizier, whilst Macdonald, Gerard and Oudinot arrived on the Marne in front of Vitry.

At St. Dizier Napoleon once more reviewed the situation, and reasoned thus:[1] "We can follow four plans:

"(1) Start from here at 2 a.m., be at Vitry by 8 o'clock and attack the enemy there.

"(2) Start early to-morrow and march *via* Bar-sur-Ornain to Saint-Mihiel, so as to be in possession of the bridge at Saint-Mihiel to-morrow; from that moment my communications with Verdun are safe and I shall have crossed the Meuse; I should from there proceed to Pont-à-Mousson, which would secure my communications with Metz; I should be reinforced by 12,000 men, which I could draw from these places; I should have driven the corps at Nancy, behind the Vosges, and I would fight a battle, with Metz as my base of operations.

"(3) Proceed to-morrow to Joinville and Chaumont, whence I would take up a position towards Bar-sur-Aube, and Troyes.

"(4) Go towards Brienne or Bar-sur-Aube; we should march *via* Vassy and could be very near Bar-sur-Aube by to-morrow.

"The most sensible of these plans seems to be that which would have Metz and my fortresses for its base and bring the war nearer to the frontiers. Indeed, from St. Dizier to Metz *via* Bar-sur-Ornain and Pont-à-Mousson, is a distance of twenty-nine hours by post; to Nancy the

[1] C. N. Note, dictated to the Duke of Bassano. St. Dizier, 23rd March.

distance is thirty hours on the same road, whilst along the direct road from St. Dizier to Nancy viâ Toul and Void it is only twenty-two hours."

However, contrary to this discussion, he did not choose the "most sensible" plan, but marched on the 24th viâ Vassy to Doulevant and Joinville, whilst Macdonald and Oudinot reached St. Dizier, and Gerard Perthes. The Emperor's headquarters were at Doulevant. The next day also the march was continued in the same direction; the Emperor himself remaining at Doulevant, around which place Ney and the Guards stood; Macdonald and Oudinot reached Vassy and Gerard St. Dizier. But the Emperor's hope that this march, on the lines of communication of the Allies, would have the effect of diverting their main army, was vain. On the contrary Schwarzenberg and Blücher had approached each other mutually, the former moving to Vitry and the latter to Chalons-sur-Marne and Chateau-Thierry, and now both were marching direct to Paris. Schwarzenberg, advancing by Fere-Champenoise, met with Marmont and Mortier, who were on the march towards Vitry, to join the Emperor, and threw them back to Sezanne. Thus every possibility of a junction of these troops with the Emperor was destroyed, and before the further advance of the enemy's superior numbers towards Paris, these two marshals could only fall back in the same direction.

In the meantime, only one cavalry corps of 8000 men out of the whole army of the Allies had followed in pursuit of Napoleon, and this corps arrived at Vitry on this same day, the 25th. The Emperor did not see his way quite clearly in this situation, and probably he did not wish to see what the Allies were actually doing; on the contrary, he thought that he had succeeded in his aim, that Schwarzenberg had followed him and was at present at Vitry with his army. He now therefore decided to turn in that direction and to attack him; consequently he went, on the 26th, to St. Dizier and drove the cavalry which had followed him there, out of this town. Oudinot pursued it as far as Bar-sur-Ornain. But at St. Dizier the Emperor became convinced that the enemy's main army was not in front of him, and that it must be now on its march to the copital. He made however one more attempt, the next day, to sever, by the capture of Vitry, the communications of the enemy who were marching to Paris, and thereby to obtain a base for his own advance, *viâ* Chalons, in their rear; an advance which had now become necessary. But, on his arrival in the afternoon, before Vitry, with his troops, he recognized that this town was safe against the *coup de main* he had intended; he moreover received confirmation here of the definite advance of the Allies towards Paris and of the defeat of Marmont and Mortier at Fere-Champenoise.

The emotions and vicissitudes of these last weeks had thrown his mind into such a feverish state of excitement that it no longer permitted his former calm judgment to have free play, and he was obliged to turn to his entourage and ask his officers for advice. Berthier and Ney urged him to march at once, and as quickly as possible, to Paris with his troops, so as to try to arrive there before the Allies. The Emperor accepted their advice and returned to St. Dizier for the night. On the 28th the hurried march to Troyes was continued; Napoleon himself reached Montierender, where he received a despatch from Paris announcing that royalistic tendencies were beginning to show themselves there in an ominous manner. The next day, on the bridge over the Aube at Dolancourt, he heard of the arrival of the Allies at Meaux. He immediately sent his aide-de-camp, General Dejean, to Paris, to announce his arrival, and to instruct Marmont and Mortier to try to keep Schwarzenberg away from the capital, by informing him that the Emperor had sent really acceptable proposals of peace to the Austrian Emperor. This confirms us in our opinion that the stress of the moment and the pressure of recent events had shaken the equilibrium of the Emperor's mind.

At 11 p.m. he arrived in Troyes, rested a few hours and then proceeded on his march. The Guards were able to follow him as far as Villeneuve-l'Archevêque; then he continued his road, only accompanied by the squadron of his Body-Guard. At Villeneuve-la-Guyard he left even this behind and rode with Berthier, Caulaincourt, Gourgaud, Flahault, Drouot and a few officers to Fontainebleau; from here he continued the journey to Paris in a carriage with Berthier and Caulaincourt, and reached the post-house of La Cour de France at Juvisy by 10 o'clock in the evening. He spent the night in La Cour de France, where he received the news at 4 a.m., that the negotiations for the surrender of Paris had been signed two hours before, and that the Allies would enter the capital on that very day, the 31st March.

Napoleon thereupon returned to Fontainebleau, arriving there at 6 o'clock. His spirit was most terribly shaken by the events which had occurred. "From this moment I was struck by the entire confusion of mind, which had taken the place of his usual clearness of intellect and of that correctness of judgment which was so characteristic in him."[1] During the next few days he assembled his troops around Fontainebleau, both those which had come up from Troyes, and those of Marmont and Mortier, and decided once more to move to Paris and to attack the Allies there; on the evening of the 3rd April he started upon this march.

But those who had been his companions in arms, with Berthier and Ney at their head, in addition to Lefebvre, Oudinot, Macdonald, Caulaincourt, Bertrand, and even Maret, besought him to make an end of it; and the Emperor yielded, wrote out the following document and sent it off to the allied sovereigns:

"Inasmuch as the Allied Powers have pronounced the

[1] C. N. Marmont, Mém. vi. 253.

Emperor Napoleon to be the sole obstacle to the restoration of peace in Europe, the Emperor Napoleon, faithful to his oath, herewith declares himself ready to abdicate, to renounce France and yield up even his own life for the good of the country, which is inalienable from the rights of his son, the regency of the Empress and the maintenance of the imperial laws.

"Given at Our château of Fontainebleau, the 4th April, 1814."

In the meantime, however, Marmont had entered, on his own account, into negotiations with Schwarzenberg, and Napoleon thus lost this, his last support of 50,000 men. It was at the time of this secession, that the great egotist burst out into the exclamation : " If the Emperor has despised men, as people have reproached him with doing, the world will now recognize that he had reasons which justified this contempt." [1]

His conditional abdication was rejected by the enemy, and he conceived the plan of retreating behind the Loire; he even spoke of giving up France and throwing himself into Italy. But though there might still have been a possibility of executing either of these plans, the Emperor's energy was no longer equal to any such tasks; his power of resolution found vent only in empty words, and when he saw the general disapprobation of his subordinates, when worse and worse news came in from Paris, when the senate recalled the old Royal Family, he gave to his plenipotentiary full power to convey his unconditional abdication, for himself and his house, in the following terms :

"6th April, 1814.

" Inasmuch as the Allied Powers have pronounced the Emperor Napoleon to be the sole obstacle to the restoration of peace in Europe, the Emperor Napoleon, faithful to his oath, hereby declares that he renounces for himself and his heirs, the thrones of France and Italy,

[1] C. N. To the army. Fontainebleau, 5th April.

and that there is no personal sacrifice, not even that of his own life, that he is not prepared to make for the good of France."

The negotiations were completed by the conclusion of the treaty of the 11th April, which secured to the Emperor the dominion of the island of Elba and on the same date his Act of Abdication was published. Napoleon, during these days, in which his fate was being sealed, had remained at Fontainebleau in complete retirement; his spirit had succumbed to the effects of all these disasters; indeed he seemed no longer to possess any real determination or power of will.

It may be interesting at this point, without going into detail, to touch upon the possible connection between genius and madness. Genius is, frequently and actively, accompanied by exaltation, and indeed without such exaltation it may remain dormant; but where is the line of demarcation beyond which such exaltation ceases to be combined with full power over the intellectual faculties? Charles XII. at Bendery must certainly be pronounced intellectually unsound, and yet just the same qualities which brought him to the pass of being overwhelmed by the Turks in his impotent rage, and dragged from the burning house at Bendery, were the very qualities that laid the foundation of his successes. Normal intellectual gifts, if we may speak of any normal condition in this respect, produce effects, harmonious but withal mediocre, whilst a higher mental tension, the more tense it is, always entails the danger of superexaltation, which can only be checked by the pressure of circumstances or by the exercise of one's own power of will. "Every man is ruled by his habits, but, if through the limitations of external circumstances he is forced to control himself, self-control will become a habit with him. The very opposite will be the case in a despot; an absolute will grows in strength, and, not being held in check by external influences, must at last aim at overpassing all limits." [1] Kolin seems to me to furnish an example of how external circumstances can lessen this danger; and of the effects of a man's own power of will in spite of durable successes, of the preservation of a spirit of moderation even when on a pinnacle of human greatness. Cromwell seems to me one of the greatest historical examples. But in the Emperor Napoleon the mental equilibrium had probably been really disturbed.

During the night of the 12th April he tried to commit suicide by taking poison, of which he had carried some with him ever since 1812; but the poison did not act properly; his private physician, Yvan, came in time to save him and the Emperor recovered. The next morning he signed the ratification, dated the previous day, of the treaty, which contained his abdication. On the 28th April he left France, at 11 o'clock in the evening, on board the English frigate the *Undaunted*.

[1] Goethe, Noten und Abhandlungen zum West-Oestlichen Divan. Pietro della Valle.

CHAPTER XI.

THE GENERAL'S EXIT.

(116) THE history of the origin of Napoleon's resolve to leave Elba is still to some extent wrapped in mystery. However much may have been due to the intentions of the Powers with respect to himself and to his knowledge of those intentions, as well as of the state of affairs in France, however much also to his hopes and fears, the final motive which decided his future action was his unconquerable desire of empire and thirst for activity. These two ambitions, which had always ruled and would always rule his actions, and had led to his brilliant, but transient triumphs, were now destined to bring about those great revolutions, which would lead in the future to his sinking under the burden he carried, but could no longer sustain. His action was not due to a comprehensive examination of the whole situation, but was the spontaneous outburst of a despotic nature.

At 3 p.m. on the 1st March, 1815, the brig *L'Inconstant*, with Napoleon on board, entered the Gulf of Juan, and in the evening the 900 men with him encamped on the seashore. As quickly as possible he started on his advance. The troops sent against him at once went over to his side; he met the first of these on the 7th at Laffrey, and when he saw that they were undecided, he walked up alone to the battalion of the 5th Infantry regiment which was leading.[1] His confidence won them over. On the same day he entered Grenoble, on the

[1] Hema.

THE GENERAL'S EXIT

10th Lyons, and at 9 p.m. on the 20th he stood again in the Tuileries.

Europe, still assembled in congress at Vienna, immediately and unanimously declared against its former oppressor, and thus war became the only solution of the problem. He could either await attack within the frontiers of France, or go to meet the foe in Belgium, where the nearest forces of the enemy stood. By the former course the Emperor, remaining on the defensive, would have deprived Europe of some portion of its justification in treating him as an enemy and a general disturber of the peace the moment he reappeared on the mainland of Europe, and he might also have made better use of the resources of his country. He himself calculated that he would, in that case, have had a field army of 240,000 men, instead of one of 140,000, and 60,000 men at Lyons instead of 25,000; while 116,000 newly organized troops would have been available to defend Paris and 250,000 to defend Lyons. Moreover, he would have been able, in the meantime, to have made further preparations, more particularly with regard to the fortification of Paris. But such a course presupposed the firm rooting of his power in France, and since his recent return he was doubly a usurper, and could only rely upon the army and not upon the people. "If there had been in France one only desire, that of supporting the head of the state and conquering with him, he would perhaps have done better to have awaited the enemy."[1] But even in a purely military sense, such a course would only have encouraged the latter, who hitherto had been frequently and unexpectedly struck down by his quick offensive blows. We have seen how, even in 1814, in spite of their enormous superiority of numbers, his opponents were always ready to fall back, wherever the Emperor appeared in person.

Consequently he had to take the second plan into

[1] Jomini, Précis polit. et milit. de la Camp. de 1815, 141.

consideration, which consisted "in anticipating the Allies and commencing hostilities, before they could be ready. But they could not begin operations before the 15th July, therefore he had to enter on his campaign on the 15th June, to beat the Anglo-Dutch army and the Prusso-Saxon army in Belgium, before the armies of Russia, Austria, Bavaria, Wurtemburg, etc., could reach the Rhine. By the 15th June he might assemble an army of 125,000 men in Flanders, while leaving a screen along the whole frontier and strong garrisons in all the fortresses."[1] In my opinion, thus to commence the campaign with an offensive movement was not only the best course to be taken, having regard to the temperament of the Emperor; but was altogether the best thing to do.

It is impossible to say the result which early victory would have produced in the face of an alliance of the Great Powers, the utter divergence of whose interests had been exhibited at the Congress of Vienna. And the moment was propitious for such a victory. The enemy, whom he had to meet, consisted of two armies, the one Anglo-Dutch, the other Prussian; the one under a leader of great military gifts, but cautious by nature, "always more inclined to accept a battle than to offer one;"[2] a man of method after the manner of the days of Frederick, a man moreover, who now would meet the Emperor for the first time. The other army commanded by a general of the greatest boldness, always ready to take the greatest risks, and looking upon Napoleon with a contempt which experience hitherto had in no way justified, but which this campaign was destined nevertheless to show was not without justification; the one army having for its base Brussels and the sea, the other Liège and the Rhine.

In any plan of campaign the Emperor had to take one important circumstance into consideration, he must

---

[1] Oeuvres xxxi. Camp. de 1815, 187.
[2] Charras, Hist. de la Camp. de 1815, i. 85.

be certain of holding Paris. If time could be gained to fortify Paris this would be a very important consideration. By following out the first plan the time necessary to fortify Paris was certain. But provided Napoleon could win a victory, and this contingency necessarily entered into his calculations, as otherwise the plan would be altogether impossible, time might still be gained. This consideration therefore was no absolute argument against the second plan. It was on this occasion that the Emperor enlarged upon the great importance of fortifying a capital. "A great capital is the abode of the most eminent members of the nation; all the prominent men live there; it is the focus of public opinion, the depôt of everything."[1] And he adds, as to the feasibility of fortifying the largest towns: "People will say: 'What! You propose to fortify towns with a circumference of 24,000 to 30,000 yards? You would want for this some eighty or a hundred fronts, a garrison of 50,000 to 60,000 soldiers and 800 to 1000 guns. But 60,000 soldiers are an army! Would it not be better to employ them in the open?' This is the objection usually raised against large fortresses; but it is wrong, inasmuch as it confounds a soldier with a man. Undoubtedly, for the defence of a great capital, 50,000 to 60,000 men are necessary, but not 50,000 to 60,000 soldiers. In times of reverse, and in situations of great distress, states may be short of soldiers, but they are never short of men for home defence. For 50,000 men, with 2000 to 3000 gunners among them, can defend a capital and repulse the attack of an army of 300,000 to 400,000 men, whilst 50,000 men in the open, unless they are highly disciplined soldiers and commanded by experienced officers, can be thrown into confusion by an attack by 3000 cavalry."[2] Indeed, the Emperor went so far as to say that, "considering the armies of our days, we must have large towns for depôts."[3]

---

[1] Oeuvres xxxi. Campagne de 1815, 180. [2] The same.
[3] Note, April, 1811.

Consequently the offensive plan was adopted. The force available was disposed as follows at the beginning of June:

The Emperor.
Chief of the Staff: Soult.

Guards:		21,000 men at Compiègne.
I. Corps:	d'Erlon:	20,000 men at Valenciennes.
II. Corps:	Reille:	24,000 men at Avesnes.
III. Corps:	Vandamme:	19,000 men at Rocroi.
IV. Corps:	Gerard:	16,000 men at Metz.
VI. Corps:	Lobau:	10,000 men at Laon.

Cavalry.
Grouchy.

1st Cavalry Corps:	Pajol:	3000 men	
2nd " " :	Excelmans:	3500 men	écheloned from
3rd " " :	Kellermann:	3500 men	Laon to Avesnes.
4th " " :	Milhaud:	3500 men	

Opposed to these troops was the Anglo-Dutch army under Wellington: 95,000 men (33,000 English, 37,000 Germans and 25,000 Dutch) in cantonments within the quadrilateral formed by Brussels, Nivelles, Tournay and Oudenarde; while the Prussian army, 124,000 men under Blücher, lay between Charleroi, Dinant, Liège and Namur.

As to the form of his strategical attack, Napoleon chose for this campaign, destined to be his last, the same form with which he had so brilliantly commenced the first of his campaigns, namely, the strategical piercing of the enemy's front; and the reasons which induced him to do so were the same. He was confronted by allies whose divergent interests and different bases must probably force them, if once separated, to fall back in different directions. He was inferior in numbers, in about the same proportion as in 1796, and had consequently to endeavour to separate his opponents, in order to employ his whole force against each of them in turn. But if the success of this form of attack was to be similar to that of 1796 it would be necessary for the Emperor to act with the same judgment, resolution and rapidity as the General then did. For the space within which this strategical movement had to be made was, as it had been in 1796, very limited, and should his opponents work harmoniously and resolutely, the French, advancing between them, might be surrounded and crushed. Thus here, as in 1796, the result depended on whether Napoleon's energy was superior to that of his opponents.

As a preliminary to the attack he ordered the army to concentrate on the south of the Sambre opposite Charleroi, and on the 14th June it stood there ready. (117) The Emperor left Paris at 4 a.m. on the 12th and slept on the 14th at Beaumont. He had in front of him at Charleroi, the two roads to Brussels and to Liège; the former Wellington's line of operations, the latter Blücher's; the two were connected by the road from Namur to Nivelles, and the points where this latter joined the two lines of operations mentioned were, for the former Quatre-Bras, for the latter Sombreffe. As the Emperor's plan aimed at piercing the strategical centre and separating his opponents, he had therefore to gain possession as quickly as possible of the road on which these opponents could join forces and support each other, and had therefore to seize the points Quatre-Bras and Sombreffe with all possible speed.

Accordingly the army was ordered to start at 3 a m. on the 15th; "it is the Emperor's intention to cross the Sambre before noon."[1] In the execution of this order (118) the army started on its march on the morning of the 15th in three columns; Reille, who was at the head of the left column, encountered the Prussian advanced guard, but forced it back without any special difficulty and reached Marchienne about 10 o'clock; he crossed the Sambre there, followed by d'Erlon. The middle column, Pajol, Vandamme, Lobau, the Guards, Excelmans, Kellermann and Milhaud, drove the Prussians out of Charleroi about noon, headed by Vandamme, and crossed

[1] C. N. Marching orders. Beaumont, 14th June.

the Sambre there. The right-hand column, Gerard, had been ordered to march to Chatelet, but was still on the march towards this place. Thus the Emperor had seized the points of crossing on the Sambre, and the enemy, the Prussians, who had shown themselves in front of him, had fallen back along their whole line on the Liège road towards Fleurus. On the Brussels road they were noticed to be collecting near Gosselies, and the Emperor sent Reille forward to this place.

He himself was at that moment at the junction of the two roads, to Liège and to Brussels; when, about 4.30, Marshal Ney, having received orders to meet him, arrived. This latter was now entrusted with the chief command of the left column and received the following instructions: "You will assume command of the First and Second Infantry Corps; General Reille will march with three divisions towards Gosselies; General d'Erlon is to be at Marchienne-au-Pont by nightfall this day; you will have with you the light cavalry division of Piré; I shall give you also the two regiments of Chasseurs and Lancers of my Guard, but you are not to employ them; to-morrow the reserves of heavy cavalry under Kellermann's command will join you. Go and drive the enemy back."[1] Ney immediately hastened to his destination and found Reille in possession of Gosselies and the Prussians in retreat to Fleurus. The advance along the Brussels road was continued, and about 7 o'clock he met, at Frasnes, some of Wellington's troops, which fell back upon Quatre-Bras and took up a position there. Ney ordered his column to halt at Frasnes and proceeded in the night to the Emperor's headquarters to talk matters over with him personally.

Napoleon had driven back the Prussians, who were retreating on the Liege road, as far as Fleurus; "at 8 o'clock he returned to his headquarters at Charleroi."[2]

[1] Duc d'Elchingen. Documents inédits sur la Camp. de 1815, 4.
[2] C. N. Bulletin of the army. Charleroi, 15th June, in the evening.

"The Emperor, who had been on horseback since 3 a.m., returned overwhelmed by fatigue. He threw himself on his bed to rest for a few hours."[1] This apology for his exhaustion, giving as a reason that he had been on horseback since 3 a.m., is curious, and reminds us of the opinions which were current about him at this time: "He could no longer, as formerly, conquer distractions, sleep or fatigue. His powers of attention seemed to have reached their limits."[2] "He still possesses his remarkable intelligence. In this respect he is still the same as you have known him; but there is no longer any resolution, any will, any character in him. These qualities, formerly so very prominent in him, have vanished. Nothing remains but his mind."[3]

The Emperor had as a matter of fact changed remarkably with respect to his physical energy. We saw him suffering as long ago as 1812, we saw him afterwards in 1813 yielding to considerations of bodily comfort, and now the symptoms were again apparent in a more marked degree. He was ill; during the Russian campaign I referred to the urinary disorders from which he suffered; since 1814 these were complicated by hemorrhoids, and in addition, he had during his last stay in Paris, before his departure for Elba, contracted a sexual disease. Thus all continuous physical exertion, especially riding, must necessarily have been painful and fatiguing. He had long ago forgotten how to sacrifice himself or his own comfort to his cause; and looked upon consideration for his own person as the one and only material point, to which everything had to give way. In this matter we cannot fail to compare him with Frederick, who, while suffering severely from gout, was also attacked by fever in October, 1759, and we recall the energy with which he, in spite of this, kept the chief command in his own hands.

[1] C. N. To Joseph. Charleroi, 15th June, 9 p.m.
[2] B. Constant, Mémoirs sur les Cent-Jours. ii. 4th note.
[3] Marmont, Mém. vii. 110.

To all this was due the numerous delays which ended the campaign of 1815 within four days and led to the Emperor's ruin; although in its conception it was in no way inferior to the first and most brilliant of all Napoleon's campaigns, and although the enemy's attitude again rendered it possible, as in April, 1796, to carry out the plan as previously conceived. Napoleon said later about himself during this time: "It is certain that under these circumstances I no longer had within myself the feeling of ultimate success; I no longer felt my former confidence; either because I was beginning to be past the age at which fortune usually favours men, or because in my own eyes, in my own imagination, the marvellous lustre of my career was dimmed; in any case it is certain that I felt something was wanting within me."[1]

The course which the Emperor had hitherto pursued was one of the possibilities which had been anticipated in the enemy's camp. To meet this possible contingency Blücher and Wellington had previously resolved to avail themselves of the system of roads to collect their armies, the former at Sombreffe, the other at Quatre-Bras. There they would be in close touch with each other and could join forces and employ the superior numbers at their disposal against the Emperor. Consequently Blücher drew his various corps, upon the Emperor's approach on the 15th, together in front of Sombreffe. Wellington however did nothing beyond holding his troops ready in their cantonments. The Emperor's advance *viâ* Charleroi was not sufficient to convince him of the manœuvre planned by the latter and based upon the situation of affairs; he was in fact ruled, and destined to be ruled for some time yet, by his apprehensions for the safety of his own communications, and he therefore fixed the centre of the concentration of his troops at Nivelles; that is, he changed his plan of collecting his army at Quatre-Bras, to that of concentrating it on the Brussels road, and thus actually led up to a

[1] Mémorial de Ste. Hélène, vii. 179.

separation from Blücher, and acted in exactly the same manner as he had known Beaulieu or Wurmser had acted. Thus the commencement of the campaign proved entirely in accordance with the Emperor's wishes and expectations; Blücher met his onslaught unsupported; Wellington mistaking the position of the moment, stood fast, with his army not as yet concentrated. However, it was impossible that this could last long; if the French lost the least time, it was to be expected that either Wellington would come up quickly, or that Blücher would fall back. Of the 15th June we may say that it ought to have witnessed greater events; on that day the Emperor could have reached, and ought to have reached Sombreffe and Quatre-Bras, so as to cut the best and shortest line of communication between his two opponents. Afterwards at St. Helena he hurled the most bitter reproaches at Ney, for not having on the 15th taken possession of Quatre-Bras; but Colonel Charras proved, in a most convincing manner, in his extremely interesting and profound study of this campaign, the entire injustice and absurdity of these reproaches, as well as the absence of truth in the supposition upon which they are based. Of what use indeed would such an isolated advance upon Quatre-Bras have been? Quatre-Bras *and* Sombreffe was the thing, but the Emperor had not, as we know, reached Sombreffe on the 15th. "And if we assume that the left wing of these masses of troops had been, in an isolated state, pushed forward as far as Quatre-Bras, without Sombreffe being strongly held, there was evidently great danger to the former corps in venturing forward between two large armies; for it might have seen itself attacked on all sides; from Brussels by the English, from Nivelles by the Belgians and from Sombreffe by the whole Prussian army."

"The same would have been the case with the right wing if it had advanced as far as Sombreffe on the evening of the 15th, without Quatre-Bras being held by the left wing.

It is therefore beyond doubt that these two points had to be occupied simultaneously, in order to constitute a skilful and effective manœuvre." [1]

The most essential thing for the moment was, that at the earliest hour on the 16th, the attack upon the two important cross-roads should commence. But the 16th June broke and Napoleon did not stir. Only between 8 and 9 o'clock were the orders issued, which informed his subordinate of what he had decided upon.

(119) "I have for this campaign adopted the general principle of dividing my army into two wings and a reserve." [2] The right wing, under Grouchy, consisting of Vandamme, Gerard, Pajol, Excelmans and Milhaud, was to advance *via* Sombreffe to Gembloux and thus inform the Emperor clearly as to how affairs stood with Blücher. The left wing, Ney, with d'Erlon, Reille and Kellermann, was to take up a position near Quatre-Bras and beyond it; the Emperor, with the Guards and Lobau, as a reserve, would decide according to the result of the reports, whether to support Grouchy or whether, as he anticipated, he would have to march to the support of Ney, and advance with the latter to Brussels. So little was he as yet aware of Blücher's presence on this side of Sombreffe, with almost his whole army, that he wrote to Grouchy: "If the enemy are at Sombreffe, I shall attack them. . . . All the reports I have, lead me to think that the Prussians will not be able to oppose us with more than 40,000 men." [3] Bonaparte the General would, before daybreak, have been on horseback at the most advanced outposts, would have reconnoitred personally, would have seen that Blücher was alone, and that it was of decisive importance to attack him early and to beat him before Wellington could think of coming up. Bonaparte the Emperor remained at Charleroi, did not dream of any

---

[1] Jomini to the Duke of Elchingen. Paris, 1st September, 1814.
[2] C. N. To Ney. Charleroi, 16th June.
[3] C. N. Charleroi, 16th June.

THE GENERAL'S EXIT

serious resistance, thought he had only to march forward, and gave his orders for this advance between 8 and 9 o'clock. At 11 o'clock he arrived at Fleurus, and whilst his troops were collecting there, he reconnoitred the enemy, who were in position near Saint-Amand and Ligny. Blücher had decided to accept battle here, for Wellington, who had come there in person, gave him a definite promise that he would support him.[1]

At 2 o'clock the Emperor had finished his reconnaissance, but had not as yet realized that he had almost the entire Prussian army in front of him; "the Emperor instructs me to inform you that the enemy has assembled a body of troops between Sombreffe and Brye."[2] He decided to attack, and ordered Ney to be instructed to drive back whatever forces he had in front of him, and then to come up, so as to surround this hostile corps entirely. The Emperor commenced the battle by throwing Vandamme upon Saint-Amand; this village and La Haye were torn from the Prussians after a hard struggle. Shortly afterwards Gerard also advanced towards Ligny, but after a series of attacks no great success was gained, and the possession of the village remained undecided.

Napoleon was soon forced to see that the resistance with which he met, and the forces which he had in front of him, considerably exceeded his anticipations, and that only the immediate and full assistance of Ney against the enemy's right flank could lead to a decisive victory over this "army," as he called it now, instead of a "body of troops." Consequently at 3.15 a message was sent to this marshal, enjoining him to come up at once; "You will take the direction of the heights of Brye and Saint-Amand, so as to assist in a victory which will perhaps be decisive."[3]

On the Brussels road Ney had, in accordance with the

(120)

---

[1] This is not true. Wellington's promise was conditional.—ED.
[2] C. N. Soult to Ney. In front of Fleurus, 16th June, 2 o'clock.
[3] C. N. Soult to Ney. Before Fleurus, 16th June.

despatch he received in the morning, advanced against Quatre-Bras; he found this point occupied, though Wellington had for the present only 8000 men there, the remainder of his army being on the march thither. Ney attacked at 2 o'clock and met with obstinate resistance, but soon the enemy's reinforcements began gradually to arrive, whilst he himself was deprived of the corps of d'Erlon. This latter corps received during its march to Frasnes, from an aide-de-camp, who in this, however, probably went somewhat beyond his instructions, orders to move to Saint-Amand to the Emperor's support. Consequently Ney was too weak to capture Quatre-Bras, and had, towards evening, to fall back again upon Frasnes.

In consequence of this misdirection, d'Erlon arrived about 6 o'clock within half a league of Saint-Amand, whilst the Emperor was just getting ready to break through the enemy's centre, by employing his reserves towards Ligny. In the face of the appearance of this fresh column on the flank of the combatants, and not knowing to which side it belonged, the Emperor delayed sending his last troops into action until he was informed of the real state of affairs by an officer, whom he sent to reconnoitre. Then the blow against the enemy's centre was delivered and was entirely successful; the Prussian army was beaten and fell back in disorder. D'Erlon, whom the Emperor had not ordered up to his assistance and who was recalled by Ney, had turned round and marched back to Frasnes.

(121) Thus by the evening of the 16th, in spite of various delays, the first half of the Emperor's plan was successfully accomplished. His advance by Charleroi between his allied opponents had come upon them while they were as yet separated; Wellington had allowed himself to be prevented by Ney's attack from keeping the promise he had made to Blücher; he had not sent him any help, although the forces under his command had in the course of the day grown considerably superior in numbers to

The General's Exit

those of his enemy;[1] he had not even collected all his troops on the Brussels road, still apprehensive, as he was, of the safety of his own communications, but had left a considerable number of them at Nivelles. Thus the divergence of interests and the separate bases, upon which the Emperor's plan had been formed, had, as in 1796, soon told to his advantage; the Emperor had met one opponent alone and defeated him. The other still remained in possession of the important point Quatre-Bras; but had now, after the result of Ligny, to evacuate it.

The Emperor's task was now to manœuvre in such a manner that his opponents should be kept separate, so that he could also attack his second adversary when isolated. To this end it was most important to keep the opponent, whom he had just beaten, away from the theatre of action for some time, by an immediate and vigorous pursuit, and to drive him off in a direction which would separate him still more from his ally. He could thus keep that opponent under observation, and turn with the main mass of his forces against Wellington, who would be in greater danger, owing to the fact that he had, in the meantime, driven Ney back. The tactics which Bonaparte in 1796, at the age of 26, had employed against Beaulieu and Colli, the Emperor was glad to return to now, at the age of 45, and success would be ensured if continued promptness and energy were displayed.

The Emperor had on the evening of the day of Ligny returned to Fleurus about 11 o'clock. The night passed, without any pursuit being undertaken; the morning of the 17th June dawned: the Emperor remained at Fleurus and his army on the field of battle, only one division of cavalry, under Pajol's command, was sent out on the Liège road, along which the Prussians were supposed to be retreating in utter rout. The first order, which was issued to the army between 7 and 8 o'clock, informed it that the Emperor was going

(122)

[1] This is inaccurate and misleading.—ED.

VOL. II. F f

to hold a review; Ney was ordered to attack whatever forces he found in his way, if, as was suspected, these were only a rear-guard, and to take up a position at Quatre-Bras; should he meet, however, contrary to his expectation, with any serious resistance, the Emperor would send aid. "Between 8 and 9 o'clock Napoleon left Fleurus in a carriage, in order to proceed to the battle-field. It was heavy work over the fields intersected by ditches and deep furrows, and Napoleon therefore mounted his horse.

"On his arrival at Saint-Amand he inspected all the approaches by which this place had been attacked on the previous day. Then he rode over the battle-field, spoke to the wounded, and enjoined tender care for them, praised, in passing, the regiments standing about without arms, and was greeted with loud acclamations by them; he then dismounted and conversed for a long time with General Gerard and Marshal Grouchy about the state of public opinion in Paris, about the legislative body, the Jacobins and various other topics, having no bearing on the important matters which ought to have occupied him exclusively at such a moment."[1]

Meanwhile, the forenoon had passed away, when Napoleon sent orders to Ney to attack the enemy at Quatre-Bras immediately, for he was now informed of the latter's continued presence there, contrary to his own expectation, and he promised to send him assistance. Then he entrusted Grouchy with the chief command over Vandamme, Gerard and Excelmans, and said to him: "Start in pursuit of the Prussians, complete their defeat by attacking them as soon as you come up with them, and do not lose sight of them. I shall join Ney's corps with the troops which I am taking with me. I shall march against the English and engage them, if

[1] Grouchy, Observations on the Story of the Campaign of 1815, published by General Gourgand, and refutations of some of the latter's assertions as to the battle of Waterloo.

they make a stand this side of the forest of Soignies. You will keep in communication with me along the metalled road leading to Quatre-Bras."[1] Immediately after this the Emperor addressed a note to Grouchy, in which he laid emphasis upon the fact that he must without fail ascertain whither the Prussians had retreated, and advised him to march towards Gembloux. Grouchy started upon his march at 2 o'clock.

The Emperor entered his carriage about 12.30 and drove to Ney; his troops, after Grouchy's departure, marching towards the same destination. By this time, however, the issue of the campaign was out of his hands. Blücher, against whom nothing had been attempted during the whole night of the 16th, nor during the whole forenoon of the 17th, had not remained idle; his army had encamped at Tilly during the night, had then started at early dawn, and, giving up its own communications, had marched to Wavre, from whence it could again resume touch with Wellington. As we have seen, the Emperor had lost all trace of Blücher's force, for, suspecting it to be on its natural line of retreat viâ Namur to Liège, he had neglected reconnoitring in any other direction.

This neglect brought about the failure of the second part of Napoleon's plan of keeping the superior numbers of his opponents separated and then beating them in detail, and breaking their line, although the first part had been successful on the 16th inst. Blücher could no longer be prevented, by Grouchy's much weaker forces, which had been sent too late in pursuit, from joining Wellington, and if the English general, trusting to this, engaged the Emperor, the latter would consequently have to meet the enemy's united superior forces. If, on the other hand, he avoided battle, renounced his offensive operations and limited himself to the defensive, the campaign was none the less lost, for the united and superior opponents would

[1] Grouchy, Observations, etc.

assuredly not delay advancing against him. His waste of time, his slowness of resolve and of action had brought him to this dilemma, just as his quickness of conception, his restless energy in execution, had led the youthful leader of 1796 on to such marvellous successes. The Emperor had lost his former alert attitude, and was dull and inert.

To begin with, Ney had waited quietly on the morning of the 17th, for it was advantageous to induce Wellington, as much as possible, to remain stationary and thus render it possible for Napoleon to come up on his flank. For the same reason, however, Wellington began, about 10 o'clock, his retrograde movement towards Brussels; Ney did not immediately realize this, and therefore the French only began to follow Wellington when the Emperor's orders were issued to that effect. The Emperor himself arrived about 2 o'clock and pursued the enemy closely, until the latter arrested their retreat towards evening in a good position this side of Mont-Saint-Jean. Napoleon became aware of the fact that he had a considerable portion of Wellington's forces in front of him, and as the day was already on the decline and he could no longer attack, he made a halt at Plancenoit and established his headquarters in the farmstead of Le Caillou. Grouchy had reached Gembloux on this day.

"At 1 a.m., Napoleon, his mind full of these great thoughts, went out on foot, accompanied only by his Grand Marshal."[1] He saw long lines of watch-fires before him, and concluded from this, that Wellington's whole army was present, an opinion which was confirmed by numerous reports which came in. During the night, at 2 o'clock, a report arrived from Grouchy to the effect that he had not as yet been able to ascertain with certainty whether Blücher's main body had gone towards Wavre or towards Namur. However, the Emperor felt no apprehensions whatever as to the

[1] Oeuvres xxxi. Campagne de 1815, 219.

THE GENERAL'S EXIT 437

possibility of the former movement, he only saw Wellington before him, isolated, a sure prey. As a matter of fact, however, Wellington awaited the attack in his position of Mont-Saint-Jean, because Blücher had promised to come without fail to his assistance. In spite of all that had come and gone, the English general had not been able entirely to dismiss his fear of having his communications threatened from the right, and had therefore left 17,000 men at Hal.

At 8 o'clock Napoleon mounted his horse, and having once more reconnoitred and ascertained to his delight, that the enemy was really making a stand, he issued his orders for the attack. In the first line, on the left, Reille was to advance, and on the right, d'Erlon, both under Ney's chief command; in the second line, on the left, Kellermann, to the right of him Lobau, and then Milhaud; in the third line the Guards. After the massing was completed, Reille would form his right wing at Belle-Alliance on the Brussels road, d'Erlon his left wing at the same place, whilst the flanks would be, respectively, on the Nivelles road and near the château of Fichermont. At 11 o'clock, while the army was massing, the Emperor issued an order, that: "at about 1 p.m., at the moment when the Emperor gives Marshal Ney the order to do so, the attack will begin, by taking possession of the village of Mont-Saint-Jean, where the roads intersect."[1] The combined heavy artillery of d'Erlon, Reille and Lobau were to prepare the attack, which d'Erlon was then to deliver, supported by Reille. It was therefore by an onslaught on Wellington's left wing, that the battle would commence, which was correct and in accordance with the whole plan of campaign, depending as it did on the separation of the two wings of Napoleon's opponents. The thought never occurred to the Emperor, that Blücher could possibly assist in the battle or that he had any intention of doing so. In the

(123)

[1] C. N. Orders to corps commanders, 18th June.

morning a fresh report had come in from Grouchy, which however did not throw any further light upon the movements of the Prussians; the Marshal announced in it, that he himself was marching towards Sart-lez-Walhain. In the meantime, however, the Emperor had been informed that a fairly considerable hostile column had taken the direction of Wavre, and he therefore sent orders to Grouchy, about 10 o'clock, to march also towards this place.

Napoleon rode along the ranks of his army and then took up his position not far from the farmhouse of Rosom, on the right of the road. At 11.30 the struggle began. Reille advanced against the château of Goumont, engaging the enemy's right wing, but the massive building remained in the enemy's hands. Whilst the fight raged here, and the Emperor was watching the battle-field, he discovered about 1 o'clock a body of troops approaching from Chapelle-Saint-Lambert, and when he sent an aide to find out what it was, he was informed that this was a corps of Blücher's army, viz. the one which had not fought at Ligny, and that the rest of the Prussian army had been at Wavre during the morning. He at once ordered Lobau to show front against this hostile column, and sent word also to Grouchy to march so as to take this corps in rear.

In spite, however, of this evident danger, he meant to continue the battle against Wellington, and put the thought obstinately aside that he might be threatened in his flank and rear by an overwhelming attack of almost the entire Prussian army; only he decided to direct his main attack not so much against the left wing of the Anglo-Dutch army, as against its centre. Consequently d'Erlon advanced against La Haye-Sainte, and there began as fierce and sanguinary a struggle for the possession of this farm as was still in progress for the château of Goumont, without the French being able to capture either the one or the other; Papelotte, La Haye and Smohain

The General's Exit

also, the supporting points of the English left wing, were attacked, though less vigorously, and remained as yet in Wellington's hands. It was now 4 o'clock.

Along the whole line efforts were now redoubled to gain possession of the points mentioned: Milhaud's cavalry in particular charged the centre to the left of La Haye-Sainte, followed by the cavalry of the Guards; they indeed penetrated the English first line, but were then driven back down the slope by the enemy's cavalry. The Emperor ordered them again to the attack, and sent Kellermann to their support, and the enemy's line began to waver ominously; if at this juncture strong infantry reserves had followed up the attack immediately, it might have been definitely successful, but he could not decide to risk the only infantry still at his disposal, that of the Guards. Thus the French cavalry had to fall back again, unfit, after such efforts, for any further fighting. In the meantime d'Erlon's infantry had succeeded by a desperate effort in forcing the exhausted and weakened defenders of La Haye-Sainte and Papelotte, to evacuate these places. This was at 6 o'clock. (124)

But if the French general had thus gained an advantage against the English line, his position was, on the other hand, most ominously endangered by the presence of Bülow's corps, which was now beginning to interfere actively. This corps had found the hollow way at Lasne unoccupied, and had therefore been able to cross the Lasne brook without any delay, whereupon it deployed in the wood of Paris. At 5 o'clock it was there engaged with Lobau, and soon forced him back to Plancenoit, and the Emperor, seeing his line of retreat seriously threatened, was compelled to send a part of the Young Guard to his support. A struggle now began for the possession of Plancenoit; the defenders lost this village twice, and only when a further reinforcement from the Old Guard came up was it recaptured a little before 7 o'clock. At this moment Napoleon determined to deliver (125) a decisive assault upon the centre of Wellington's line with his last reserves, about 5000 men of the Guards, and to wrest victory from the hands of fate by his obstinacy. The general had long ago relinquished that calm calculation of possibilities, which is not only compatible with the greatest boldness, but which alone justifies it; his plans had become more and more arbitrary and incomplete; he himself bestowed less and less care upon their preparation and execution. His method of carrying on war had, in its blind confidence that Fortune would favour all his desires, become more and more like a game of chance, and when the means at his disposal became increasingly slender, he was unwilling to accept any partial success, but still insisted upon grasping all. He was no longer a general, but a mere gambler, rattling the dice-box for the last time and staking his last 5000 men.

The stroke delivered by the Guards along the Brussels road to the left, broke through the enemy's ranks as far as their last line, but here its strength was at an end and they had to fall back.[1] It was 8 o'clock. Already ruin stared the French right wing in the face. Simultaneously with the centre attack of the Guards, Reille and d'Erlon also had advanced; the latter had now taken possession of Smohain and La Haye, when, about 7.30, a fresh Prussian corps appeared on the battle-field, threw itself at once upon d'Erlon's right wing and drove it back; Smohain, Papelotte and La Haye were regained. Taking advantage of this, Wellington, feeling himself relieved, ordered a general advance of his whole line. Plancenoit only remained in French hands, but not for long. At the same time that the Prussian corps charged d'Erlon, another corps from Blücher's army had come up to reinforce the one which had arrived first, and at 8.30 Plancenoit was stormed; the French army was completely defeated; their line of retreat, the road from Brussels to Charleroi, was reached by the

[1] This is quite wrong, the French penetrated nothing.—ED.

The General's Exit

Prussians, and the Emperor's army became an entire wreck. Gneisenau himself led the pursuit which continued during the whole night, and it was not till daybreak, when he had only a few squadrons still with him, and having reached the inn called "The Emperor," that Gneisenau gave up the pursuit.

Napoleon had, when the defeat became imminent, made a few desperate personal efforts to arrest the flight already beginning, but all in vain, and at 9 o'clock he left the battle-field, riding across country to Genappe; at 5 a.m. he arrived in Charleroi, and in the suburb of Marcinelle, entered a carriage with Bertrand, and after a short halt in Philippeville reached Laon in the evening of the 19th. Twenty-four hours later he left this town, and at 4 a.m. on the 21st of June he entered Paris. "He seemed collapsed from fatigue and physical pain; his chest was painful, his breathing laboured."[1]

His empire owed its birth to military success, but he had failed, as time advanced and need arose, to furnish it with adequate support; he had remained a military leader only, and had not become a statesman, so that, with the overthrow of the general, the empire also was doomed. And now, having become incapable of any resolution through complete mental and physical exhaustion, vacillating helplessly between a personal renunciation of his crown and violent measures for its maintenance, he lost the only chance which still might have remained to him. Urgent necessity alone, and the threat that otherwise the Chamber of Deputies would pronounce his deposition, could compel him to pen a renunciation. In the afternoon of the 22nd he formulated his abdication in the following document:—

"DECLARATION TO THE FRENCH NATION.

"Frenchmen, in commencing this war for the maintenance of our national independence, I reckoned upon

[1] Fleury de Chaboulon, Mém. ii. 210.

the unanimity of all your efforts and opinions, and upon the co-operation of all the authorities of the nation; I had some grounds to hope for success, and I defied all the declarations of the Powers against myself.

"Circumstances seem changed.

"I offer myself as a victim to the hatred of the enemies of France, in the hope that they are honest in their declarations and that I alone, personally, shall suffer.

"My political existence is at an end, and I proclaim my son Emperor of the French under the title of Napoleon II.

"The present ministers will provisionally constitute the State Council. In my solicitude for my son I call upon the Chambers to organize the regency without delay by a decree.

"Let all unite for the Public Welfare, so that the Nation may remain independent.

"Given at the Palace of the Elysée, the 22nd June, 1815."

On the 29th June the Emperor started on his journey to Rochefort, and arrived there on the 3rd July. On the 15th July, soon after 6 a.m., he stepped on board the *Bellerophon;* "And the captive giant was handed over by the Earth to the guardianship of the Ocean."[1]

We have hitherto followed the Emperor step by step in his military career, and we will now halt, in order that, from a distance, we may place him in the right perspective, and obtain a clear impression of him. We find, first, that the foundation of his strength lay in his clear perception of actual facts, in his practical intelligence, of which Carlyle said: "The man had a sure, instinctive, ineradicable perception of actualities, and based himself upon facts, as long as he had any basis at all."[2] In

[1] V. Hugo, Deux Iles.
[2] On Heroes, Hero-worship and the Heroic in History, 219.

the time of his strength and his successes, he said of himself, that "he was of all men the greatest slave of a pitiless master, of the calculation of events and the consideration of the real meaning of hard facts."[1]

But with this practical intelligence there was combined the wide-reaching, prophetic glance of a boundless power of imagination. We saw that this quality is necessary to a military leader if he is to rise to the highest flights; and yet in this very quality lies the germ of the reason why the greatest military geniuses are not destined to achieve permanent results. "Napoleon, although living entirely in a world of ideas, never actually realized that there was such a world, and refused to believe in its actual existence, while all the time zealously striving to realize it."[2] In the same way as Napoleon's practical intelligence led him to overrate the importance of the numerical element, as opposed to the moral element in war, so his power of imagination degenerated into wilful self-deception. This latter predominated more and more as his dreams were fulfilled, and as his power and empire rose higher and higher, he thought at last that nothing was impossible to him. "You say, 'It is impossible;' there is no such word in French."[3] "Even in trivial things, when perhaps some course was represented as impracticable, it seemed ridiculous to him that any one should say, 'I cannot ... etc.,' and he never abandoned his own idea until the impossibility became absolutely evident. So much had good fortune spoilt him."[4]

Thus the former "slave of hard facts" was transformed by the over-luxuriance of his imagination into the most insolent and absolute despot; and the fact that he deceived not merely others, but himself also, became the source of his failures. "He became an apostate

[1] C. N. To the King of Würtemberg. Mayence, 30th September, 1806.
[2] Goethe, Ethics, 4th part.
[3] C. N. To Lemarois, Dresden, 9th July, 1813.
[4] O. v. O. N.'s campaign in Saxony, in the year 1813, 45.

from his old belief in facts, and began to believe in
things which had no reality."[1] Events were to be as he
wished them to be; and if they were not so, he declared
the hard fact to be simply untrue, thinking such a declaration sufficient to attain what was impossible and to undo
what had been done. It is a proof of an absolutely
deranged mind, that he presented to the eye-witnesses and
participators in the great disaster of 1812, only one month
after they had left Russia, the following description:
"The reports which reach me from all sides, confirm
the opinion that the Russians on the Beresina considered
themselves as lost, and that Victor would have beaten
them, had it not been for the unfortunate affair with
Partonneaux, just as we beat the admiral; that Kutusov's
corps was entirely annihilated, and that he never dreamt
of marching to Vilna, but remained at Minsk."[2]

We may here remark, that the great men of the Latin
or Slav races frequently combine, with their great
qualities, a certain charlatanism, which is foreign to the
great men of the Teutonic race. Neither Gustavus
Adolphus, nor Frederick the Great, nor the Archduke
Charles gave evidence of this, nor even Wallenstein or
Charles XII. But Napoleon could not avoid tricking
out his successes, real and great though they were, with a
few tinsel additions; they were not only to be brilliant, but
they were also to appear so. Proofs of this may be found
in all his bulletins; and of his proclamations he said
himself: "There was a touch of charlatanism in them,
though of the highest order."[3]

We must allow, however, that this to a certain extent
is quite true; indeed Napoleon himself said, "impressions are more than half the battle." Is there a man who
has not in his own life often experienced the truth, that
awkward or silent merit is outweighed by pretensions

---

[1] Carlyle, On Heroes, etc., 221.
[2] C. N. To Eugène. Fontainebleau, 26th January, 1813.
[3] Mémorial de Ste. Hél. iii. 110.

which are only calculated to attract notice, so that what at first was mere pretension becomes ultimately tangible success ? We have only to quote, as an example, Clausewitz's opinion of Kutusov: "Thus the frivolity and charlatanism of this clever old rascal turned out, as a matter of fact, to be of greater use than all Barklay's straightforward dealing could possibly have been."[1]

The men of 'the Latin or Slav races act thus, not only because they therein follow the inner promptings of their own nature, but above all because they meet the demand of their people ; and the fact that they feel themselves thoroughly in harmony with them, and fulfil their expectations in this respect also, is of the greatest assistance to them. Gambetta and Skobelew are good instances. We must never forget that success is the first and only thing for a military leader; and whenever history undertakes to judge a man merely as a general, it must judge of his qualities from this point of view alone. We shall thus understand why merit, which knows not how to cut a brilliant figure or make a brave show, is less successful, and therefore actually inferior, compared with that which knows how to advertise itself, even by means of charlatanism. Of what avail was it, I will not say, to Moreau, but to Moreau's country, that he waited modestly, until he was sought out, whilst his rival pushed him on one side and placed himself at the head of affairs, by employing all possible means, both those of pretence and those of reality ?

And in the same way as we note in intellectual Napoleon the rare combination of cool reason and glowing imagination, so we note in him as a soldier a peculiar combination of two qualities which are but rarely granted to the same leader. Military history, indeed, shows us, on the one hand, leaders of troops who, gifted with great power over the minds of their subordinates, are in their proper sphere as actual leaders and organizers of

[1] The Campaign of 1812 in Russia, 117.

battles at the head of their men, but who are wanting in the abstract power of combining strategical movements on a map. On the other hand, it shows us individuals who possess this gift of strategical combinations in an eminent degree, who can form within themselves a wonderfully clear picture of the largest dimensions, but who become confused by actual contact with the troops themselves. Thus Delbruck quotes Brandt's criticism of Clausewitz: "On the battle-field he would have been quite out of place. He lacked the art of carrying the troops along with him. This was not merely due to bashfulness or embarrassment, but to a want of the habit of command. If one saw him among the troops, one noticed in him a certain want of ease, which disappeared as soon as he left them."[1] A Blücher, on the other hand, and a Suvorov, are brilliant examples of the former quality; and inasmuch as in warfare strength of character outweighs clearness of insight, it is not a matter of surprise that their fame is greater. We know that Gneisenau possessed the second of these two qualities, but had no opportunity to prove his possession of the first; whilst the opposite was the case with Skobelev. Still with both these men we have grounds for assuming that they did possess the other quality which is needed to make a true general. In the case of Lee, however, it seems that he was endowed more with the power of strategical combinations than with power over human nature. Stonewall Jackson and Stuart were evidently in this point his superiors, and his complements.

But in Napoleon we see also both these qualities combined in the highest degree. Few men like him could carry away the common soldier by the charm of their personality. He knew how to inspire his masses with a devotion that defied death. "His appearance electrified the troops. Although the major portion of

[1] Zeitschrift für preussische Geschichte und Landeskunde. March and April, 1878, 227.

THE GENERAL'S EXIT 447

Ney's corps consisted only of quite young conscripts, who probably were this day for the first time under fire, yet rarely did any wounded pass him without crying out: Vive l'Empereur! Even the mutilated, who would in a few hours be the prey of death, paid him this homage." [1] He himself was moved by the sight of this emotion, of which he was the cause, and his own enthusiasm was kindled by this eagerness for battle, which he kindled in others. "Whenever his senses were affected by the sight of a large mass of troops, he always experienced a vivid impression, which reacted upon his resolution." [2]

His superiority in the seclusion of his study, in his labours with compass and map, was no less great; and in this consists his importance in the study of the art of war. He is not merely the great practical man of action, whose deeds are full of instruction for us; he is also the great master of theory, whose words teach us. Many of his letters are actually treatises, which might find a place in any theoretical work on strategy; and we find the expressions: base, line of operations, front of operations, lines of communications, etc., as frequently in Napoleon's letters as in Jomini's treatise on the art of war. Thus, for example: in 1806, his letter to his brother Louis, which contained the development of his plan of campaign; in 1808 his memoranda to Joseph, in 1813 his notes on the situation after Dresden and before Leipzig, and then again his letters to Dejean, about the value of fortresses and on operations in connection with fortresses. It is because the great principles of strategy were so plainly illustrated by his deeds, and because he acknowledged and emphasized their existence in his own words, that the history of Napoleon's wars are so instructive to us. "All the plans of Napoleon's fourteen campaigns are in harmony with the true principles of war; his wars were bold, but methodical." [3] This severe regularity in his whole conception and practice

[2] O. v. O. 54. Marmont, Mém. iii. 227.
[3] Oeuvres xxxi. Dix-huit notes, etc., 430.

of war renders Napoleon's strategy a most instructive example for us.

Empirics are in the habit of discounting all endeavours to gain a knowledge of the true principles of war through the study of instructive treatises, by saying that war is a living entity, the parts of which cannot be learnt, and which cannot be confined to any set of rules. We readily admit that war is a living whole, and that to wage war successfully, one must master it as a whole. But just as the physician, who desires to influence the living human organism by his remedies, must begin by dissecting the parts of the dead organism and studying the principles and the composition of the individual parts, in order to recognize the vital functions of the whole, so is it with the art of war. No one has ever maintained, with respect to medical science, that theoretical study is useless, and that a physician could at once begin with practice; indeed whoever did so, would be considered a bungler; and yet as regards the art of war, people are to be found who declare theoretical study to be actually hurtful. In medical science, although every individual case of sickness has its special features, yet may be treated according to general rules, so also in the art of war, although every situation may offer something new, yet after all will fall under general rules. Finally, as only that physician is a true master of his art, who, having all the general rules entirely in his grasp, employs them not with slavish uniformity, but modifies them according to the nature of each individual case, so only that military leader will attain to perfection in the art of war, who, while fully acquainted with the domain of theory, employs its principles according to the nature of the given case. The rational employment of general principles marks the difference between the genius of the true artist and the lack of freedom of the mechanic who is dominated by rigid rules, and the bungler, who despises all rules and denies their justification.

The General's Exit

> "For art is art. Call him not artist yet,
> Who never deeply thought on art!
> To grope is useless. Knowledge sure and true
> Alone to great success can lead."

In this respect, therefore, I trust, this attempt of mine to analyze the mind of a great general, may be considered to be justified. The Emperor himself was so firmly convinced that there existed a theory of the art of war, and that it could be expressed in definite words, that once, in speaking of the difficulties of carrying on war, he said: "if some day he had the time, he would write a book, in which he would formulate its principles in such a detailed manner, that they would be capable of being understood by every soldier, so that war could be learnt, just as any other given science."[1]

But, above all, Napoleon's importance in the history of war lies in his originality. Through him the value of masses has come to be recognized as contrasted with the art of strategy in the 18th century. In old days the tactical value of a body of troops seems to have occupied, in the opinion of generals, a higher place than its numbers. It is true, even in our days, that the efficiency of troops is of great importance, and all efforts in the direction of increasing this efficiency are of the highest value; still strategy, as founded by Napoleon, is characterized by basing all its plans upon the calculation of one's own and the enemy's numbers and upon the appreciation of masses. And the employment of masses leads necessarily to the principle, that the highest aim of strategy is the destruction of the enemy Consequently in Napoleon's strategy and in that of our days, which is based upon his, the real goal of all operations is the enemy's army, and the consummation aimed at is battle. Finally, with his principle of the employment of masses, Napoleon paved the way for wars in which whole

---

[1] v. Ranke. Weltgeschichte ii. 2nd vol. 220.

nations take part, for the formation of armies based upon universal military service.

It is of great value to us, that in the case of Napoleon, circumstances permitted a great military genius to attain its utmost development. Cæsar was assassinated on the threshold of his dominion, and though we may assume that in him the general had, by that time, given place to the statesman, yet we have no actual proof of this conjecture. Alexander died young, and we may doubt whether his military genius would have been sufficient to maintain for any length of time the empire he had conquered. To Hannibal the highest sphere of action was never vouchsafed.

It is true, circumstances have an overwhelming influence. Only the end of the last century, only the France of those days, could have produced a Napoleon. In the case of Gneisenau, whatever was Napoleonic in his nature could not come to maturity on account of the pressure of external circumstances. If, in the case of Lee, we admire much that is Napoleonic in the conception and execution of his plans, we must after all acknowledge that circumstances were with him wholly different, and another and very different future was in store for the modest chief of the academy of Lexington than for the haughty prisoner of St. Helena.

Still the predominant factor of our fate lies in our own personality. "Men's passions decide their fate, they themselves are the result of their individual positions."[1] It is true, circumstances block many paths for us, which in accordance with our natures and gifts we might pursue, yet there ever remains to us a choice of many directions; we are not inevitably compelled by fate to follow one, and only one road; and even in Napoleon's career we may note many a parting of the ways, on occasions

[1] v. Ranke. Weltgeschichte ii. 2nd vol. 220.

where he had the unfettered opportunity of framing his own future.

But if we see that a military genius of the stamp of Napoleon's is undoubtedly ready, and indeed bound to be ready, to pursue Napoleonic methods, wherever circumstances do not absolutely preclude such a course. This fact shows us that, for the lasting welfare of a state, sound military institutions are even more necessary than one military leader of genius. Rome had no general worthy to vie with Hannibal, and Rome had its Cannæ, but its military institutions withstood even that crushing blow, and finally gained the victory. Napoleon had no equal as a general, yet Waterloo brought his empire to the ground, when his genius, weakened by age and sickness, had deteriorated by self-conceit, and the France of those days did not possess any military institutions capable of withstanding the catastrophe.

We recognize consequently, that Napoleon became the greatest of generals because he voluntarily renounced becoming a great monarch; indeed, wherever the highest goal is aimed at, a certain singleness of aim, a one-sided development, is inevitable; and therefore, the further we advance in our study of Napoleon as a military leader, the oftener our judgment of him can be compressed into those words of Jomini: "The French general's manœuvre might be pronounced correct, strategically speaking, the statesman's operation was only bold."[1]

Still we must note that this one-sidedness of development is of advantage only to the individual success of a man; it is of harm as far as the permanence of his work is concerned; and we understand why the state founded by the richer and more philosophic nature of Frederick enjoyed a healthier development than that founded by the Emperor Napoleon, as is described in the final paragraph of Taine's great historical work in these mournful words: "No more beautiful barracks have

[1] Précis de l'art de la guerre, 97.

ever been built up, nor any more even and ornate in appearance, or more satisfactory to shallow minds, or more acceptable to the ordinary human intellect, or more comfortable for narrow-minded egotism, or better kept, or arranged in a more cleanly and altogether better manner, or more fit to overawe the mediocre and lower sides of human nature, whilst allowing the loftier sides of human nature to be stunted and corrupted."[1] Rigid one-sidedness may be of advantage to one human being, the life of a nation needs a more supple many-sidedness.

But in this one-sidedness of direction, in order to reach the really highest goal, an energy that knows no bounds must be displayed, which knows no repose of satiety, in fact such an energy as we saw embodied in Napoleon, and which might be seen in him in the first years of his activity. Even in 1797 that saying, characteristic and true of all the highest and Cæsarean natures, was applied to him: "I know of no other goal for him except the throne or the scaffold."[2]

Although his empire itself crumbled into dust, yet his military acts remain a lofty ideal for the soldier. Whoever now enters that vaulted hall under the dome of the Invalides, and looks at that simple, dark red sarcophagus of porphyry which bears no name, but only the laurel wreath of mighty battles, will think with marvelling admiration, and, if he is a soldier, with veneration, of that unruly, quarrelsome child; of that taciturn officer, always buried in thought, rarely sociable, often insubordinate; of that excitable general, always active, bold in resolution, unwavering in execution, ambitious and passionate; of that conqueror of genius, never satisfied, always despotic; of that egotistical Emperor, disregarding the future, despising men, a fatalist, who had become incapable of any sacrifice of his own personal comfort; of

---

[1] Les Origines de la France contemporaine. La Révolution, iii. 635.
[2] Sucy to Josselin, 4th August.

that ill-tempered prisoner of St. Helena, wanting in veracity and stretching out his hands convulsively into empty air, trying to grasp the lost empire of the world; of the corpse of him who was the greatest military genius. Every soldier will appreciate the justice of his own words: "I aimed at the empire of the world; who in my place would not have done the same?"[1]

[1] B. Constant, Mémoires sur les Cent-Jours, ii. 2nd letter, 24.

THE END.

INDEX

ABENSBERG, battle of, II. 47, 50-52.
Aboukir : Turkish army landed at, I. 156 ; French advance on, I. 157 ; battle of, I. 159-160.
Achmed Pacha, I. 141, 147.
Acre, siege of, I. 146-152.
Aderklaa, II. 94.
Adige, river, I. 56, 59, 69, 89.
Aisne, river, II. 402.
Ajaccio, I. 2 ; Napoleon's attempt to seize citadel, I. 10, 11.
Albe, Bacler d', I. 282 ; II. 341.
Albeck, I. 222, 225.
Alexander, Emperor, I. 251 ; II. 173, 187-188.
Alexandria, I. 127, 158.
Alexinki, II. 160-161.
Alle, river, I. 366.
Alps : army of, I. 16-19 ; passage of, I. 172-173, 175, 178.
Altenburg, II. 325.
Alvintzy, General : advances to relieve Mantua, I. 81, 87 ; success at Caldiero, I. 88 ; attacked at Arcola, I. 89-91 ; retreat, I. 91 ; battle of Rivoli, I. 99 ; superseded by Archduke Charles, I. 103.
Anenhayn, II. 350-351.
Anglo-Dutch army (1815) : base, II. 422 ; strength, II. 424 ; concentration, II. 428-429 ; battle of Quatre Bras, II. 432-433 ; retires towards Brussels, II. 436 ; battle of Waterloo, II. 437-441.
Aosta, I. 176.
Arcis-sur-Aube, II. 400-401, 410-412.
Arcola, battle of, I. 89-91.
Ardon, II. 405.
Argenteau, General, I. 29, 31.
Armies, large, operations with, II. 357-362.
Arrighi, General, II. 348, 375.
Artillery, importance of, I. 371 ; II. 249.
Aspam, battle of, II. 72-80.

Athies, II. 406.
Aube, river, II. 377-383, 399-401, 410-412.
Aubry, General, II. 227.
Auersperg, Prince, I. 242.
Auerstädt, Duke of. *See* Davout.
Augereau, Marshal : character, I, 52 ; attack on Ceva, I. 34 ; occupies Peschiera, I. 56 ; success at Castiglione, I. 66 ; attacks Arcola, I. 89, 90 ; command in 1805, I. 206 ; command in 1806, I. 279 ; repulsed at Eylau, I. 339 ; operations at Leipzig, II. 327, 346 ; corps in 1814, II. 373, 375.
Augezd, I. 261.
Augsburg, I. 220, 229.
Austerlitz : campaign, I. 229-266 ; battle of, I. 260-261.
Austria : Imperial Military Council, II. 9.
Napoleon's campaigns in, 1797 : strength of army, I. 103 ; advance, 105 ; orders to Joubert, 106 ; generalship of Archduke Charles, 108 ; Austrian retreat, 110 ; action at Tarvis, 111 ; ' operations in Tyrol, 112 ; Klagenfurt occupied, 113 ; pursuit of Austrians, 114 ; Leoben occupied, 115 ; peace concluded, 115.
1805 : plan of campaign, I. 202-203 ; formation of army, 205-206 ; advance of Austrians, 208 ; French trooops in Germany, 209 ; Napoleon directs operations, 210-212 ; his employment of cavalry, 213-214 ; passage of the Rhine, 216 ; Austrian concentration at Ulm, 217 ; French cross the Danube, 218-219 ; Wertingen,— Elchingen, 220 ; advance on Ulm, 221 ; Albeck, 222 ; concentration against Mack, 223 ; Elchingen taken, 225 ; Ulm occupied, 226 ;

456 INDEX

Austrian surrender at Trochtelfingen, 227; Fresh base of operations, 229; troops concentrated, 230; passage of the Inn, 231; Braunau taken, 232; cautious advance of French, 233; engagement on the Traun, 234; advance on St. Pölten, 236,—on Vienna, 237; Dürrenstein, 238-239; Vienna bridge attacked, 241-242; negotiations for truce, 242; advance on Krems—rapid marching of troops, 243-244; Vienna occupied, 244; Hollabrunn, 246-247; retreat of Russians, 248; Brunn occupied, 249; French position at Pratzen, 254-256; battle of Austerlitz, 257-261; armistice refused, 262; end of hostilities, 263.
1809: disposition of French troops, II. 29-30; plan of campaign 31-33; declaration of war, 34; Austrians cross the Inn, 35; Berthier's mistakes, 36-40; Napoleon rejoins army—retrieves situation, 39-47; actions at Hausen and Offenstetten, 44-45; Austrian retreat, 47; Ratisbon surrendered, 50; Landshut, 51-52; Eggmühl, 53, 55; Napoleon's halt at Egglofsheim, 56; action at Erharding, 61; advance on Vienna, 62; Austrian retreat to Budweis, 64; actions at Efferding and Wels, 65; Ebelsberg stormed, 66-67; Linz, 70; passage of the Danube, 71; Aspern, 72-80; communication with army of Italy established, 81; formation of army, 83; battle of Raab, 84; passage of Danube, 85-88; disposition of two armies, 89-91; Wagram, 92-97; panic among French, 97; Austrian retreat, 98; armistice concluded, 100; general operations considered, 100-103.
Austrian troops, *in* 1797: position and strength, I. 27, 29; Montenotte, 31; Dego, 32; retreat, 42, 46; driven from Lodi, 47, 49; defence of Mincio, 55; retreat across Adige, 56; Würmser's army, 59; Brescia and Corona, 60; Salo and Lonato, 65; Castiglione, 66; Solferino, 68; distribution of forces, 73; Caliano, 76; Bassano, 77; retreat, 78; advance under Alvintzy, 81;

successes under Davidovich, 82-83; Caldiero, 87-88; Arcola, 89-90; attack on Rivoli, 92; Davidovich defeated, 93; attack Verona and La Corona, 95; battle of Rivoli, 96-99; La Favorita, 100; Mantua surrendered, 100; retreat into Tyrol, 102; Archduke Charles appointed to command, 103; continued retreat, 107, 110; engagements at Tarvis, 111-112; Klausen, and Mühlbach, 113; pursued by French, 114; evacuate Leoben, 115.
1800: besiege Genoa, I. 171, 175; hold Fort Bard, 176; position, 180; repulsed at Romano, 182; defeated by Suchet, 185; advance, 186; Casteggio, 187; Montebello, 189; Marengo, 191-194.
1812: strength, II. 109; advance against Gorodetshna, 138-139; retreat from Moscow, 202; cross the Bug, 214-215; strength, 224; conclude alliance with Russians, 237.
1813: position, II. 283; operations at Dresden, 294-301, 313; Nollendorf, 316-317; strength, 328; battle of Leipzig, 347-356; pursue French, 364.
1814: advance across Rhine, II. 375, 376; join Blucher, 381; operations on Seine, 385; Sens and Nogent, 393; retreat to Aube, 398; renewed advance, 403; Arcis, 411-412; advance on Paris, 414, 416.
See also above, under Austria.
Avicio, river, I. 112.
Avignon, I. 11.

BAALSDORF, II. 355.
Bagration, General: defeat at Hollabrunn, I. 246-247; Austerlitz, I. 253, 260-261; position in 1812, II. 111; retreat before French, II. 119-125, 131, 134; joins Barclay at Smolensk, II. 143.
Bajalich, General, I. 94, 95.
Baraguey d'Hilliers, General, I. 103, 206.
Barbier, Mons., II. 107.
Barclay, General: position of army in Russia, II. 110-111; retreat before French, II. 117-119, 124-128; evacuates Vitebsk, II. 131-134; joins Bagration, II. 142-157;

INDEX 457

success at Konigswartha, II. 258;
advance on Dresden, II. 313;
Leipzig, II. 349.
Bard, Fort, I. 176. 183.
Barras, and Napoleon, I. 21, 22.
Bar-sur-Aube, II. 377, 399, 403.
Bassano, battle of, I. 82.
Battle: Napoleon's eagerness to engage in, I. 120; pitched battles, I. 263-266.
Battles: Abensberg, II. 47, 50-52.
Aboukir, I. 159-160.
Arcis-sur-Aube, II. 411-412.
Arcola, I. 89-91.
Asparn, II. 72-80.
Bassano, I. 77.
Bautzen, II. 257-259
Baylen, II. 5.
Bilbao, II. 10.
Blasowitz, I. 260.
Borodino, II. 159-168.
Bosenitz, I. 260-262.
Brescia, I. 60.
Caldiero, I. 87-88.
Caliano, I. 76.
Casteggio, I. 187-188.
Castiglione, I. 66.
Cerea, I. 78.
Ceva, I. 34.
Champaubert, II. 390.
Codogno, I. 47.
Dego, I. 31-32.
Dresden, II. 292-301.
Dürrenstein, I. 238.
Ebelsberg, II. 66-67.
Eggmühl, II. 53, 55-56.
Embabeh, I. 129.
Erharding, II. 61.
Espinosa, II. 12-13.
Etoges, II. 393.
Eylau, I. 338-342.
Friedland, I. 365-370.
Gamonal, II. 12.
Gorodetshna, II. 138-139.
Grossbeeren, II. 303.
Halle, I. 304-305.
Hanau, II. 367-368.
Hassenhausen, I. 296-298.
Hausen, II. 44-45.
Heilsberg, I. 362-364.
Hollabrunn, I. 246-247.
Inkovo, II. 143.
Jena, I. 293-298.
Katzback, II. 303.
Kliastitsi, II. 139-142.
Korssum, I. 145.
La Corona, I. 60.
La Favorita, I. 100.
La Haye Sainte, II. 438, 440.

Landshut, II. 51.
Laon, II. 405-406.
La Rothiere, II. 381-382.
Leipzig, II. 346-356.
Ligny, II. 431.
Lodi, I. 47-48.
Lonato, I. 66.
Lützen, II. 253-254.
Maloyaroslavets, II. 192-195.
Marengo, I. 192-194.
Montebello, I. 187-188.
Montmirail, II. 391.
Mormant, II. 395.
Offenstetten, II. 45.
Ostrolenka, I. 344-345.
Pratzen, I. 252-260.
Preititz, II. 261.
Pultusk, I. 322-328.
Quatre-Bras, II. 432.
Raab, II. 84.
Rivoli, I. 96-99.
Saint-Amand, II. 431.
Sediman, I. 133.
Shebreket, I. 129.
Sokolnitz, I. 258-259, 261.
Solferino, I. 68.
Somo-Sierra Pass, II. 19.
Svolna, II. 142.
Taragona, II. 14.
Tellnitz, I. 258-259, 261.
Torcy-le-Grand, II. 411.
Trochtelfingen, I. 227.
Tudela, II. 14.
Vico, I. 35.
Vimiero, II. 6.
Vyankovo, II. 186.
Wagram, II. 92-97.
Wartenburg, II. 325, 327.
Waterloo, II. 437-441.
Bautzen, battle of, II. 256-259; 310-312.
Bavaria, Crown Prince of, II. 34.
Elector of, I. 208.
Bavarian army, II. 33, 366, 367-68.
Bayes, II. 390.
Baylen, battle of, II. 5.
Bayonne, II. 2, 10.
Beauharnais, Eugene—Austrian campaign: ordered to join main army, II. 65; reaches Villach, II. 71; communication with Napoleon, II. 81; instructions, II. 83-84; success at Raab, II. 84; repulsed by Archduke, II. 92; captures Deutsch-Wagram, II. 96; command in Russian campaign, II. 108, 111; advance, II. 121-159; Borodino, II. 162-166; retreat from Moscow, II. 190, 194, 199,

205, 206; crosses the Beresina, II. 230; succeeds to Murat's command, II. 236; retreats from Posen, II. 237, 239; ordered to defend Magdeburg, II. 240; attacked by Wittgenstein, II. 243.
Beaulieu, General: position of army, I. 27, 29; repulsed at Dego, I. 32; retreat, I. 42; Lodi, I. 47-48; position of forces on Mincio, I. 55; retreat across Adige, I. 56.
Beaumont, General, I. 206.
Beauvais, General, I. 137.
Belgium campaign, 1815: plan of operations, II. 421-423; formation of army, II. 424; commencement of operations, II. 425; advance on Brussels, II. 426; Ligny, Saint-Amand, II. 431; Quatre Bras, II. 432, 434; retreat of English, II. 436; Water oo, II. 437-441; flight of Napoleon, II. 441-442.
Belluno, Duke of. *See* Victor.
Belvedere, General, II. 11, 12.
Benavente, II. 26.
Bennigsen, General: position on Narev, I. 318-320; junction with Buxhöwden, 323; engagement at Pultusk, 323-324; advance against Ney, 328; battle of Eylau, 328-342; pursues French, 353; takes the offensive, 359-361; retreats to Heilsberg, 361-363; Friedland, 365-369; proposes armistice, 370; operations at Leipzig, II. 354, 355.
Beresina, river: passage of, II. 222, 225-226, 229.
Berlin, II. 263, 305-306.
Bernadotte, Marshal: character as a general, I. 271, 312; command in 1797, 103; marches on Laibach, 113; corps in 1805, 205; orders to, 215-216, 243; reprimanded, 242; Austerlitz, 260; command in 1806, 278; occupies Schleiz, 285; advance to Dornberg, 297-298; success at Halle, 304-305; reprimanded, 306; action at Mohrungen, 329; wounded, 360; corps in 1809, II. 29; evacuates Deutsch-Wigram, 92; corps broken up, 99; command in 1813, 284; position on Elbe, 328, 338; Leipzig, 347-356.
Berry-au-Bac, II. 403.
Berthier, Marshal: Chief of Staff, I. 28; given command of reserve army, I. 170, 174; his staff, I. 281-282;
indecision and lack of judgment, II. 35, 37-40; advises abdication of Napoleon, II. 415-416.
Bertrand, Marshal: sent into Germany, I. 202; capture of Vienna bridge, I. 242; corps in 1813, II. 244; II. 253; Bautzen, 258; Kreckwitz, 261; strength of corps, Starsiedel, 282; takes Wartenburg, 325; battle of Leipzig, 346; Hanau, 368; advises abdication of Emperor, 416.
Bessières, Marshal: corps in 1805, I. 205; in 1806, I. 278; operations in Spain, II. 3, 5, 10, 12; corps in 1809, II. 34; Landshut, 51-52; Asparn, 76; command in Russia, II. 108; retreat from Moscow, II. 195.
Bianchi, General, II. 109.
Bieshenkovitshi, river, II. 129, 130.
Bilbao, battle of, II. 10.
Bischolswerda, II. 323.
Bisson, General, I. 206.
Blake, General, II. 10, 11, 12-13.
Blasowitz, I. 260.
Blücher, Marshal: 1806—joins Duke of Wiemar, I. 305; retreats to Elbe, I. 307; surrender after Lubeck, I. 308; strength of forces in 1813, II. 248; evacuates Kreckwitz, 262; position of army, 283; operations on Bober, 287; Katzbach, 303; retreats into Silesia, 312; advance, 321; skirmishes at Bischofswerda, 323; crosses the Elbe, 325-326; retires to Saale, 339, 341; battle of Leipzig, 347-356; pursues French, 364; army in 1814, 373; crosses the Saar, 375, 376; evacuates Brienne, 378; reinforced by Schwarzenberg, 381; La Rothiere, 381-382; operat ons on Seine, 384; Champaubert, 390-391; Etoges, 393; advance to Mery, 397; takes Sezanne, 399; recrosses the Marne, 401; advance to Soissons, 402; Craonne, 404; Laon, 405; marches on Paris, 414; city surrendered, 416; army in 1815, II. 424; retreats from Charleroi, II. 425-426; battle of Saint-Amand, II. 431; advance, II. 435; Waterloo, II. 438-441.
Bober, river, II. 287.
Bobr, II. 224, 226.
Bohemia, Napoleon's plans for operations in, II. 285-286, 299-305, 315.

INDEX 459

Bon, General, I. 126, 129-130, 139, 142, 156.
Bonaparte: Family expelled from Corsica, I. 11.
Jerome, King of Westphalia: his incapacity, II. 120-122; resigns his command, II. 128.
Joseph, King of Spain, II. 2, 8.
Louis, I. 7, 275-276.
Lucien, I. 8, 9.
Napoleon. *See* Napoleon.
Bordesoult, General, II. 353.
Borghetto, I. 56.
Borissov, II. 223-224, 226, 228.
Boristhenes, river, II. 145.
Borja, II. 18.
Bormida, river, I. 191.
Borodino, battle of, II. 159-168.
Borovsk, II. 190, 196, 198.
Bosenitz, battle of, I. 260-261.
Bothkeim, I. 367.
Boudet, General, I. 104, 182; II. 34.
Boulogne, I. 200.
Bourcier, General, I. 206.
Braunau, I. 232.
Braunsberg, I. 353.
Breitenau, II. 315.
Brenta, river, I. 82-83.
Brescia, battle of, I. 60.
Brest-Litovsk, II. 202.
Brienne: Military Academy, I. 3.
Operations round, II. 378.
Broussier, General, II. 108, 194.
Bruey, Admiral, I. 125-126.
Brune, Marshal, I. 359.
Brunn, I. 249.
Brunswick, Duke of, I. 276.
Brussels, II. 426.
Buen-Retiro, castle, II. 19.
Bug, river, II. 202, 214-215.
Bülow, Marshal, II. 373, 375.
Burgos, II. 12, 13.
Buttafuoco, Matteo, I. 6.
Buxhöwden, General, I. 249, 317, 318, 323.

CAFFARELLI, General, I. 245; 260.
Cairo, I. 130, 139, 153.
Caldiero, battle of, I. 87-88.
Caliano, I. 76, 83.
Campaigns: 1796-97 (Italy), I. 24-122.
1798-99 (Africa), I. 125-162.
1800 (Italy), I. 165-196.
1805 (Austria), I. 202-263.
1806-6 (Prussia), I. 272-372.
1808-9 (Spain), II. 1-28.
1809 (Austria), II. 29-100.
1812 (Russia), II. 107-233.
1813 (Germany), II. 236-368.

1814 (France), II. 370-419.
1815 (Waterloo), II. 420-422.
Carteaux, General, I. 11, 12.
Casasola, I. 110.
Castaños, General, II. 11, 13-14, 18.
Casteggio, battle of, I. 187-188.
Castiglione, battle of, I. 66.
Catalonia, II. 6.
Caulaincourt, General, I. 280; II. 265, 416.
Cavalry: employment by Napoleon, I. 213-214.
Importance insisted on, II. 245-246.'
Long-range rifles for, II. 246.
Cerea, battle of, I. 78.
Cervoni, General, I. 29.
Ceva, battle of, I. 34.
Chabot, General, I. 111, 112, 113.
Chabran, General, I. 174.
Chalons-sur-Marne: II. 376-387.
Chambarthac, General, I. 174.
Champaubert, battle of, II. 390.
Charleroi, II. 425.
Charles, Archduke of Austria: appointed to chief command, I. 103; retires, I. 107, 110; rearguard defeated, I. 113; pursued by French, I. 114; evacuates Leoben, I. 115.
Campaign of 1805, I. 201, 245, 250.
Personal character, I. 109; qualities as a general, I. 108; II. 100-102; appreciation of Napoleon, I. 228.
Position of forces in 1809, II. 33; occupies Landshut, II. 39; reorganizes army after Eggmühl, II. 56-58; concentration at Cham, II. 63; Asparn, II. 72-80; repulses Eugène, II. 92.
Charpentier, General, II. 405, 407.
Charras, Colonel, II. 429.
Chasseloup, General, I. 282; II. 226, 228.
Chateau, General, and Napoleon, II. 363.
Chateau-Thierry, II. 391, 392, 401.
Chaumesnil, II. 382.
Cintra, Convention of, II. 17.
Clacy, II. 406, 407.
Claparède, General, II. 34, 66.
Closwitz, I. 294.
Coblentz, II. 370.
Codogno, battle of, I. 47.
Coehorn, General, II. 66.
Colbert, General, II. 34.
Colli, General, I. 26, 29, 33, 34, 36.
Colmar, II. 373.
Colmberg, II. 350.
Cologne, II. 370.

460 INDEX

Commissariat: Napoleon's care for, I. 27; complaints of, I. 229.
Communications, lines of: direction, II. 290.
Importance of keeping open, I. 168, 194-195.
Compans, General, II. 108.
Concentration of forces, II. 337.
Concentric operations, I. 74-75; II. 359.
Connewitz, II. 350, 353-354.
Constantine, Grand Duke, I. 260.
Convention, The, and Corsica, I. 11.
Corbineau, General, II. 300.
Cordova, II. 3.
Corsican politics, Napoleon's participation in, I. 6, 9, 11.
Corte, I. 2.
Coruña, II. 23-25.
Cospeda, I. 294.
Cosseria, castle, I. 31.
Courmont, II. 391.
Craonne, II. 404.
Cuneo, fortress of, I. 36.
Curial, General, II. 342.

DAENDELS, General, II. 109.
Dallemagne, General, I. 43, 45, 49, 58.
Dalmanhur, I. 127.
Damietta, I. 130.
Danube: crossed by French, I. 219-220; flotilla, I. 235.
Danzig: siege of, I. 345, 357-358; base at, I. 372; plans to relieve, II. 241.
Daru, Quartermaster-General, I. 281.
Davidovich, General: command, I. 73, 75; defeat at Caliano, I. 76; advance on Mantua, I. 81; attacks Vaubois, I. 82-83; occupies Rivoli, I. 92; troops routed, I. 93.
Davout, Marshal (Prince of Eckmühl and Duke of Auerstädt): his cruelty, I. 313.
Command in 1805, I. 206; orders to, I. 215; Austerlitz, I. 261; corps in 1806, I. 278; action at Hassenhausen, I. 296-298; Königsberg, I. 370; instructions in 1809, II. 29-30; command, II. 34; ordered to advance, II. 39-41, 43; success at Hausen, II. 44-45; attacks enemy, II. 50; action at Glinzendorf, II. 93-94; corps in 1812, II. 108; operations at Mohilev, II. 129, 138; takes Alexinki, II. 161; retreat from Moscow, II. 199, 205, 206, 220; crosses the Beresina, II. 230; operations against Hamburg, II. 243, 265-267, 277; strength of corps, II. 282.
Decrès and Napoleon, II. 106.
Defence: of fortresses, II. 266; of rivers, I. 355-356.
Defensive tactics, I. 69-72; II. 278-282.
Dego, battle of, I. 31-32.
Dejean, General, A.D.C., II. 415.
Delmas, General, I. 103.
Delzons, General, II. 108, 193.
Demont, General, II. 34.
Dennewitz, II. 314.
Deroy, General, I. 206; II. 34, 108.
Desaix, General: command in Egypt, I. 126; defeats Murad Bey, I. 128; given command at Cairo, I. 131; instructions, I. 132; success at Sediman, I. 133; operations in Upper Egypt, I. 155; battle of Marengo, I. 190-194; command in 1812, II. 108.
Desjardins, General, I. 206.
Despinoy, General, I. 60, 64.
Deutsch-Wagram, II. 96.
Dienville, II. 381-382.
Directory, The, and Napoleon, I. 50, 53, 58, 124.
Djezzar, I. 141, 147.
Dnieper, river, II. 220-221.
Docturov, General, I. 256, 259-261.
Dohna, II. 313.
Dölitz, castle, II. 350, 353, 354.
Dombrowski, General, II. 108, 222, 224.
Domnau, I. 365.
Dornburg, I. 297, 298.
Dorogobush, II. 209.
Doronino, II. 160-161.
Dösen, II. 350, 353-354.
Doumerc, General, II. 375.
Dresden: evacuated by French, II. 244; occupied by Napoleon, II. 255; Elbe crossed at, II. 256; fortification of Neustadt, II. 272; enemy's advance on, II. 289; battle of, II. 292-301; enemy's second advance on, II. 313; defence of bridges, II. 323; operations round, II. 327-337.
Drissa, river, II. 141.
Drouet, General, I. 260.
Drouot, General, II. 350, 367-368.
Düben, II. 338, 342.
Dugommier, General, I. 12-13.
Dugua, General, I. 127, 139, 155.
Duhesme, Marshal, II. 6, 11.
Dumas, General, I. 126.
Dumonceau, General, I. 254.

INDEX 461

Dunaburg, II. 126, 142.
Dupas, General, I. 366.
Dupont, General: command, I. 206; repulsed by Austrians, I. 222; Friedland, 369; evacuates Cordova, II. 3; defeated at Baylen, II. 5.
Duroc, General, I. 53, 280; II. 262.
Dürrenstein, battle, I. 238.
Dutch Army. *See* Anglo-Dutch Army.
Duteil, General, I. 13.
Dwina, river, II. 118, 124-125, 203.

EBELSBURG, battle, II. 66-67.
Eblé, General, II. 226, 228, 231.
Ebro, river, II. 6-7.
Eckmühl, Prince of. *See* Davout.
Efferding, II. 65.
Egglofsheim, II. 56.
Eggmühl, battle of, II. 53, 55-56.
Egypt, campaign of 1798-99: arrival of army, I. 126; Alexandria occupied, I. 127; Shebreket and Embabeh, I. 129; Cairo and Damietta occupied, I. 130; Ibrahim attacked at Salahieh, I. 130-131; French fleet destroyed, I. 132; Sediman, I. 133; severe treatment of inhabitants, I. 134-135; discontent in army, I. 136-138; disposition of forces, I. 139-140; retreat from Syria, I. 153; re-organization of army, I. 154; advance on Aboukir, I. 155-157; battle of Aboukir, I. 159-160; Napoleon leaves Egypt, I. 162.
Eisack valley, I. 112.
Eisdorf, II. 253, 254.
El Arish, I. 142.
Elba, island of, II. 419.
Elbe, river: enemy's retreat across (1813), II. 254; crossed by French, II. 256; fortification of, II. 271; operations on, II. 271-304 : French retreat across, II. 323, 338-339.
Elchingen, I. 220, 225.
Elster, bridge, II. 325.
River, II. 251, 348.
Embabeh, battle of, I. 129.
England : plan for invasion, I. 198-200.
English army in Spain : Moore's march to Astorga, II. 17; to Valderas, II. 21; retreat to Coruña, II. 23-25.
In Belgium : base, II. 422; strength, II. 424; concentration of, II. 428-429; Quatre-Bras, II. 432-433; retires towards Brussels, II. 436; Waterloo, II. 437-441.

Enns, river, I. 234, 235.
Erfurt surrendered, I. 304.
Erharding, battle of, II. 61.
Erlon, Marshal d', II. 424, 432, 437-441.
Erzgebirge, operations in, II. 300-302, 317.
Esla, river, II. 24.
Espagne, General, I. 367; II. 34.
Espinosa, battle of, II. 12-13.
Essen, General, I. 344-345.
Essling, II. 76.
Étoges, battle of, II. 393.
Etouvelle, II. 405.
Etroubles, I. 176.
Eugene. *See* Beauharnais.
Excelmans, General, II. 375, 424.
Exterior lines of communication, II. 358-362.
Eylau, battle of, I. 338-342.

FERDINAND, Archduke, I. 207, 208, 223.
Fere-Champenoise, II. 410.
Fiorella, General, I. 67, 68.
Flitschl, I. 112.
Flossgraben, river, II. 251.
Fombia, I. 46.
Fominskiya, II. 191, 192.
Fomkina, II. 160.
Fontainbleau, treaty of, II. 2.
Forchheim, I. 274.
Fortifications : Elbe, II. 271-274.
France, I. 351.
Napoleon's opinion *re*, I. 345-353; II. 423.
Fortresses, defence of, II. 266.
Fourés, Lieut., I. 335.
Foy, General, on Napoleon, I. 36.
France, campaign in (1814) : defence of Rhine, II. 370; plan of operations, II. 372-374; enemy's advance, II. 375; concentration at Chalons, II. 376; attack determined on, II. 377; Brienne taken, II. 378; La Rothiere, II. 381-382; army disorganized, II. 383; operations on Seine. II. 384; Champaubert, II. 390; Montmirail, II. 391; Étoges, II. 393; advance against Schwarzenburg, II. 394; the Seine crossed, II. 397; retreat of Austrians, II. 398; Sezanne taken by Blücher, II. 399; fall of Soisons, II. 402; and Troyes, II. 403; Craonne, II. 404; Laon, II. 405-406; Rheims taken, II. 407; advance against Austrians, II. 408-410; Arcis-sur-

Aube occupied, II. 411-412: advance on Vitry, II. 413-414; Napoleon returns to Paris, II. 415; surrender of city, II. 416; abdication of Emperor, II. 417-419.
Frontier fortifications, I. 350-351.
Francis, Emperor of Austria, I. 208, 242, 263.
Frankfort-on Main, II. 236.
Frankfort-on-Oder, II. 238.
Frederick the Great: strategy rejected by Napoleon, I. 118.
Freiburg. II. 365.
Friant, General, I. 206, 298; II. 34, 36, 108.
Friederich, General, II. 220.
Friedland, battle of, II. 365-370.
Frimont, General, II. 109.
Frisching, river, I. 366.
Funck, General, II. 108.

GALICIA, operations in, II. 5.
Gamonal, battle of, II. 12.
Gardenne, General, I. 192.
Garnier, General, I. 26.
Gasparin, Deputy, I. 12.
Gaza, I. 143.
Gazan, General, I. 206, 239.
Genoa, surrendered, I. 185.
Gérard, General, II. 289, 376, 379, 396, 424, 431.
Gerasdorf, II. 96.
Germany: Napoleon's plan of operations in 1800, I. 167-169; concentration of French army in 1805, I. 202, 209; advance across Rhine, I. 212-216; advance to Danube, I. 218.
1806 campaign: preparations and plans, I. 272-278; Prussian advance, I. 284; engagement at Saalfeld, I. 286-287; battle of Jena, I. 294-302; Erfurt surrendered, I. 304; Prussian defeat at Halle, I. 304-305; Spandau surrendered, I. 306; Blücher's retreat, I. 307; Lübeck taken, I. 308; surrender of Blücher, I. 308; seige of Magdeburg, I. 314; French advance into Poland, I. 315; battle of Eylau, I. 338-342; siege of Danzig, I. 345, 357-358; battle of Heilsberg, I. 362-364; Friedland, I. 365-370.
1813: reorganization of army after Moscow, II. 236; defence of Magdeburg ordered, II. 240; retreat behind Elbe, II. 243; advance into Saxony planned, II. 247; advance on Leipzig, II. 252; Lützen, II. 253-254; Bautzen, II. 257-259; Preititz, II. 260-261; advance on Berlin, II. 263; truce of Poischwitz, II. 265; Hamburg occupied, II. 265; defence of Elbe, II. 271 274; disposition of troops, II. 282-283; advance against Blücher, II. 287; battle of Dresden, II. 292-300; Katzbach and Grossbeeren, II. 303; advance on Berlin, II, 305-306; operations round Dresden, II. 313-323; Wartenburg, II. 325; Dresden abandoned, II. 333; advance against Blücher, II. 338-341; battle of Leipzig, II. 346-356; retreat from Leipzig, II. 363; battle at Hanau, II. 367-368.
Girard, General, II. 109.
Glinzendorf, II. 93-94.
Glogau, II. 236.
Gneisenau, General, I. 16; II. 441.
Goldbach, river, I. 259.
Gollau, I. 365.
Golymin, I. 324.
Gorbitz, II. 297.
Gorki, II. 164-165.
Görlitz, II. 262, 309.
Gorodetshna, battle of, II. 138-139.
Gorodnia, II. 195.
Görschen, II. 253.
Goumont, chateau of, II. 438.
Grandjean, General, II. 109.
Grawert, General, II. 109.
Grenier, General, II 96.
Gridnyeva, II. 160.
Grossbeeren. battle of, II. 303.
Grouchy, Marshal: Friedland, I. 366-370; battle of Wagram, II. 96; command in 1812, II. 109; Etoges, II. 393; Waterloo campaign, II. 424, 434, 438.
Grünhof, I. 397.
Gudin, General: command in 1805, I. 206; engaged at Hassenhausen, I. 298; takes Küstrin, I. 314; fight at Pultusk, I. 323-324; command in 1809, II. 34; in 1812, II. 108.
Guieu, General, I. 66, 103, 112-113.
Güldengossa, II. 351.
Gutstadt, I. 354, 371.
Gyulai, General, II. 348, 354.

HALLE, battle of, I. 304-305.
Hamburg: attack on, ordered, II. 243; captured, II. 265; defence of, II.

INDEX 463

266-267; fortifications, II. 273-274.
Hanau, battle of, II. 367-368.
Harrant, General, I. 206.
Harthau, II. 323.
Hassenhausen, battle of, I. 296-298.
Hausen, battle of, II. 44·45.
Haute-Épine, II. 391.
Hautpoul, General d', I. 206, 290.
Heilsberg, battle of, I 362-364.
Heinrichsdorf, I. 366.
Hiller, General, II. 63, 64, 66, 67.
Hochkirch, II. 311.
Hohenlohe, Prince, I. 276, 294-296, 307.
Holitsch, I. 263.
Hollabrunn, engagements at, I. 246-247; II. 99.
Holland : Blücher's advance into, II. 375; army, *see* Anglo-Dutch army.
Holzhausen, II. 355.

IBRAHIM PASHA, I. 130, 131.
Imperial Council of War, Vienna, I. 231.
Inkovo, battle of, II. 143.
Inn, river, I. 230-231.
Interior lines of operations, II. 358-362.
Invasion of England, plans, I. 198-200.
Isonzo, river, I. 110.
Isserstädt, I. 295.
Italy, 1796-97 campaign : Napoleon's plans, I. 16-18, 20 ; proclamation to troops, I. 24; disposition of army, I. 26-29; operations commenced, I. 30; Dego attacked, I. 31-32; attack on Colli, I. 34; success at Vico, I. 35; negotiations for peace, I. 36 ; difficulty of strategical conditions, I. 37; plan of operations in Lombardy, I. 41 ; advance, I. 42, 45-46 ; success at Lodi, I. 47-48 ; appointment of Kellerman—Napoleon's threat to resign, I. 50-53 ; capture of Pavia, I. 54; passage of Mincio, I. 55-56 ; Austrian retreat, I. 56 ; redistribution of forces, I. 58; siege of Mantua, I. 59; Brescia and La Corona, I. 60; retreat on Milan, I. 61 ; siege of Mantua suspended, I. 64; successes at Salo, Lonato, and Gavardo, I. 65-66 ; Austrian surrender, I. 67; Solferino, I. 68 ; fresh advance, I. 73; Roveredo occupied, I. 75; Caliano and Bassano, I. 76-77 ; enemy's advance on Mantua, I. 81 ; Davidovich's successes, I. 82-83 ; Caldiero, I. 87-88 ; Arcola, I. 89-90 ; Rivoli, I. 92, 96-98 ; La Favorita, I. 100 ; Mantua surrendered, I. 100.
1800 campaign : military situation, I. 165 ; plans, I. 167 ; differences with Moreau, I. 168; advance commenced, I. 170; Genoa surrounded, I. 171 ; passage of Alps, I. 172-178 ; defence of Fort Bard, I. 176 ; Ivrea taken, I. 178 ; position of Austrians, I. 180-181 ; success at Romano, I. 182; passage of Ticino, I. 183 ; Milan entered, I. 183; Suchet's success, I. 185; ·Genoa surrendered, I. 185; passage of Po, I. 186 ; Casteggio, I. 187-188 ; Montebello, I. 189 ; Marengo, I. 190-194 ; peace concluded, I. 194 ; general plan of operations, I. 194; 196.
Ivrea, I. 178.

JAFFA : siege, I. 143-145 ; defences destroyed, I. 153.
Jellacic, General, I. 217.
Jena, battle of, I. 294-302.
John, Archduke, I. 250 ; II. 71, 81, 84.
Jomini, General : comprehension of Napoleon's schemes, I. 276-277.
On employment of masses, II. 359.
On strategical turning movements, I. 299.
And Ney, II. 15.
Jordan, river, I. 148-149.
Josephine, Empress, I. 23, 335-336.
Jouan, Bay of, II. 420.
Jouarre, II. 401.
Joubert, General : defence of La Corona, I. 95; Rivoli, I. 96-99 ; forces in Tyrol, I. 103 ; instructions, I. 106 ; crosses the Avicio, I. 112 ; successes at Klausen and Muhlbach, I. 113.
Jourdan, Marshal, II. 8, 9.
Judenburg, negotiations at, I. 115.
Junot, General, I. 147; defeat at Vimiero, II. 6; Russia, II. 152, 200, 221, 224.

KAJA, II. 253, 254.
Kalatsha, river, II. 162-165.
Kaluga, II. 193, 198.
Kamenski, General, I. 321 ; II. 138.
Kamionka, II. 224.

464 INDEX

Kanka, I. 130.
Kapzevitsch, General, II. 386, 387.
Kastel, II. 370.
Katzbach, battle of, II. 303.
Kellerman, Marshal: and Napoleon, I. 21; appointed to joint command, I. 50, 53; Marengo, I. 193; Leipzig, II. 346; Waterloo, II. 424, 437-441.
Keraliu, M. de, I. 3.
Kienmaier, General, I. 217.
Kilmaine, General, I. 52, 54-56, 60, 64, 73.
Klagenfurt, I. 113.
Klausen Pass, I. 113.
Kleber, General, I. 126, 127, 142, 147-149, 162.
Klein, General, I. 206, 290.
Kleist, General, II. 386, 387.
Kliastitsi, battle of, II. 139-142.
Kniazewicz, General, II. 108.
Kobrin, II. 137.
Köfering, II. 55-56.
Kollowrat, General, I. 255, 259.
Kolodnia, river, II. 152.
Kolotskoyay, II. 160, 201.
Königsberg, I. 370, 372
Königstein, II. 276, 291.
Königswartha, II. 258.
Korssum, battle of, I. 145.
Kösen, II. 365.
Kovno, II. 115.
Krasni, II. 146, 216-219.
Kray, General, I. 165.
Kreckewitz, II. 262.
Kremlin, destruction of, II. 191.
Krems, I. 242-244.
Kreuzberg, I. 366.
Kreuznach, II. 370.
Kujawien, Canon von, I. 312.
Kulm, I. 239; II. 302.
Küstrin, II. 236, 314.
Kutschitten, I. 340.
Kutusov, General: Takes command of Russo-Austrian army, I. 230; retreat from Enns, I. 235; and St. Polten, I. 237; Durrenstein, I. 238; retreat from Krems, I. 244; Hollabrunn, I. 246; joins Buxhöwden, I. 249; advances, I. 253, 254; disposition of forces, I. 256; fighting on Goldbach, I. 259; Austerlitz, I. 260-261; retreat to Holitsch, I. 263; takes chief command in 1812, II. 153; Borodino, II. 159-168; retreat on Moscow, II. 169; and Podolsk, II. 172-173; marches on Maloyaroslavets, II. 192-195; retreat, II. 196; advance to Medinj, II. 201; pursuit of French, II. 204-213, 216-221; strength and position of army, II. 224, 228.

LA CORONA, battle of, I. 60, 95.
La Favorita, battle of, I. 100.
La Ferté-Gaucher, II. 399-401.
La Ferté-sous-Jouarre, II. 399-401.
Laffrey, II. 420.
La Giberie, II. 382.
Laharpe, General: character, I. 52; command in Italy, I. 26; attack on Dego, I. 31; crosses the Po, I. 46; death, I. 47.
La Haye, II. 431.
La Haye-Sainte, battle, II. 438, 440.
Lahoussaye, General, I. 367.
Lampasch, I. 366.
Lancers, armament with carbines, II. 246.
Landgrafenberg, I. 292.
Landsberg, I. 337-338.
Landshut, battle of, II. 51-52.
Langeron, General, I. 259, 261.
Langres, II. 376.
Lannes, Marshal: command in Egypt, I. 130, 139; advance into Syria, I. 142; reprimanded, I. 145; Aboukir, I. 159-160; command in 1800, I. 174; crosses the Alps, I. 176-177; success at Romano, I. 182; Casteggio, I. 187-188; Marengo, I. 192; command in 1805, I. 206; orders, I. 215; takes Braunau, I. 232; capture of Vienna bridge, I. 242; Austerlitz, I. 260-261; corps in 1806, I. 279; Saalfeld, I. 286-288; repulses Prussians, I. 294; takes Spandau, I. 306-307; Pultusk, I. 323-324; illness, I. 331; reserve corps, I. 359; Heilsberg, I. 363; Friedland, I. 365-370; defeats Palafox, II. 14-15; takes Ratisbon, II. 61; death, II. 81; dying warning to Napoleon, II. 105.
Lanusse, General, I. 159, 160.
Laon, battle of, II. 405-406.
La Pietra, I. 83.
La Romana, General, II. 11, 13.
La Rothiere, battle of, II. 381-382.
Lasalle, General, I. 307.
Lasne, river, II. 439.
Latour-Manbourg, General, I. 367; II. 109, 316, 342, 346.
Lauriston, General (A.D.C.): negotiations with Kutusov, II. 173; ordered to defend Magdeburg, II.

INDEX 465

240; attack on Leipzig, II. 252;
reverse, II. 263; strength of corps,
II. 282; instructions, II. 324,
334; Leipzig, II. 344, 346-356.
Lavden, I. 363.
Lavis, I. 76.
Le Bois-Jean, II. 391.
Lechi, General, II. 108.
Lecoq, General, II. 108.
Ledru, General, II. 108.
Lefebvre, Marshal: Command in 1806,
I. 278; siege of Danzig, I. 345,
358; defeats Blake in Spain, II.
10, 12; command in 1809, II. 30,
34; success at Offenstetten, II.
45; command in Russian campaign, II. 108; advises Napoleon
to abdicate, II. 416.
Lefebvre-Desnoëttes, General, II. 325.
Legrand, General, I. 206; II. 34, 99,
108.
Leignitz, II. 263, 275.
Leipzig: French advance on, II. 252;
occupation of, II. 254; concentration at, II. 342-343; battle of, II.
345-356; causes of defeat, II.
356-362; retreat from, II. 363-364.
Leoben, I. 115.
Leon, II. 5.
Lesmont, II. 382-383.
Lestocq, General, I. 334, 340, 353,
370.
Leutzsch, II. 348.
Levico, I. 77.
L'Heritier, General, II. 316, 325.
Liadi, II. 220.
Lichtenstein, Count, I. 260.
Liebertwolkwitz, II. 346, 348, 350.
Ligny, battle of, II. 431.
Lindenau, II. 348, 363.
Lines of communications: direction,
II. 290.
Importance of keeping open, I. 168,
194-195.
Operations on, II. 358-362.
Linz, II. 70.
Liptay, General, I. 46.
Lobau, Count of, II. 195, 310, 424, 437-441.
Lobau, the, II. 84-89.
Löbtans, II. 294.
Lodi, I. 47-48.
Lagroño, II. 3, 11.
Loison, General, I. 174, 206.
Lombardy: conquest of, I. 20, 41-42,
49; revolt in, I. 54.
Lonato, battle of, I. 65, 66.
Looting: prohibited by Napoleon, I.
VOL. II.

35; excesses in Prussia, I. 310-312;
ordered at Moscow, II. 192.
Loshnitsa, II. 227.
Lössing, II. 324.
Löwenberg, II. 287.
Lübeck, I. 308-309.
Lukomlia, river, II. 210.
Lusha, river, II. 193-195.
Lützen, battle of, II. 251-254.
Lyons, Academy, I. 6.

MACDONALD, Marshal: Battle of
Wagram, II. 96; command in
Russian campaign, II. 109; retreat
to Tilsit, II. 235; Bautzen, II.
258; strength of corps, II. 282;
command in Silesia, II. 289;
Katzbach, II. 303; troops disorganized, II. 310-311; ordered to
advance, II. 322; Leipzig, II. 346;
Hanau, II. 367-369; defence of
Rhine, II. 370, 373; strength of
corps, II. 375; operations against
Schwarzenberg, II. 395, 400, 408;
Arcis-sur-Aube, II. 410-412; advises abdication of Napoleon, II.
416.
Mack, General: Napoleon's opinion
of, I. 207; orders Austrian advance,
I. 208; concentration at Ulm, I.
217; retreats, I. 221; success at
Albeck, I. 222, 223; advance to
Heidenheim, I. 225; surrenders
Ulm, I. 226.
Macquart, General, I. 26.
Madrid: evacuation of, II. 6; advance
on, II. 8, 17-19; negotiations for
surrender, II. 19.
Magdeburg: siege of, I. 314; formation of corps at, II. 236; defence
ordered, II. 240.
Maintz, II. 370.
Maison, General, II. 373, 375.
Malet's conspiracy, II. 209.
Malher, General, I. 206.
Maloyaroslavets, battle of, II. 192-195.
Mamelukes: defeated by Desaix, I.
128; battles of Shebreket and
Embabeh, I. 129; Salahieh, I.
131; Sediman, I. 133.
Mantern, I. 237.
Mantua: siege of, I. 59, 64, 68;
Würmser's retreat to, I. 78; surrendered, I. 100.
Marchais, II. 391.
Marching: accomplished in Egypt, I.
153.
Formation of columns, II. 293.

H h

Rapidity of Napoleon's movements, I. 79-80, 244.
Marengo: campaign, I. 165-196; battle, I. 190-194; Napoleon's opinion of, I. 9.
Maret, General, II. 416.
Margaron, General, I. 206; II. 314, 346.
Markgrafneusiedl, II. 95-97.
Markkleeberg, II. 350, 351.
Marmont, Marshal (A.D.C.): on Napoleon, I. 53; II. 341. Defends Alexandria, I. 156; command in 1805, I. 205; orders, I. 215-216; command in 1813, II. 244, 248; Leipzig, II. 253; Bautzen, II. 258; Kreckwitz, II. 262; strength of corps, II. 282; operations on Elbe, II, 314, 316, 322, 324-325, 328; Leipzig, II. 346; Hanau, II. 368; defence of Rhine, II. 370, 373; strength of corps, II. 375; La Rotherie, II. 381-382; operations round Sezanne, II. 386-389; Champaubert, II. 390; Étoges, II. 393; repulses Blücher, II. 401; engagement at Laon, II. 405-406; negotiations with Schwarzenberg, II. 417.
Marne, river, II. 384, 385, 400, 401.
Marulaz, General, II. 34, 68.
Massed troops, employment of, II. 357-362, 449.
Massena, Marshal: character, I. 52, 312. Command in Italian campaign, I. 26; attack on Dego, I. 31; advance against Colli, I. 34-35, 46, 49; crosses Mincio, I. 56; reinforced, I. 58; defeated by Würmser, I. 60; Lonato, I. 65; strength of corps, I. 73; occupies Tient, I. 76; crosses Adige, I. 78; marching record, I. 79; retreats, I. 81-83; attacks Arcola, I. 90-91; orders, I. 95; Rivoli, I. 97-99; storms Casasola bridge, I. 110; engaged at Tarvis, I. 111-112; occupies Leoben, I. 115; orders, I. 169-171; besieged in Genoa, I. 175; surrenders, I. 185. Command in Prussia, I. 345: orders to, I. 357-358. Command in 1809, II. 30, 34; orders, II. 41, 42; seizes Inn bridges II. 64; engaged at Ebelsberg, II. 66-67; Aspern, II. 76-80; Wagram, II. 93-95; pursues enemy, II. 98-99.
Mathieu, M., I. 206.
Medinj, II. 201.

Meerveldt, General, II. 352.
Meissen, II. 323.
Melas, General, I. 165, 171, 175, 184-185, 190-194.
Memmingen, I. 226.
Ménard, General, I. 47, 49.
Menou, General, I. 126, 127, 139.
Mensdorf, II. 355.
Merle, General, II. 108.
Mery-sur-Soane, II. 397.
Meynier, General, I. 26.
Michelsberg, I. 226.
Miessoyedova, II. 206.
Milan: occupied, I. 49; revolt in, I. 54; fortification, I. 61.
Milhaud, General, II. 375, 424, 437.
Military Institutions, value of, I. 240-241.
Science, value of theory, II. 448.
Mincio, river, I. 55-56, 64, 68.
Minsk, II. 222.
Mobilization: modern rapidity, I. 204.
Möckern, II. 349.
Mohilev, II. 129, 138.
Mohrungen, I. 328-329.
Molitor, General, II. 34.
Mölkau, II. 355.
Moncey, Marshal, II. 3, 10, 11.
Montbrun, General, II. 19, 34, 96, 109, 127, 143.
Montebello, battle of, I. 189.
Monte Legino, I. 29.
Montenotte, I. 31.
Montereau, II. 395, 396.
Montmirail, II. 386-387; battle of, II. 391.
Mont-Saint-Jean, II. 436.
Moore, General, II. 17, 21, 23-25.
Morand, General, II, 34, 52, 108, 190, 375.
Moreau, General, and Napoleon, I. 38, 168-169, 172.
Mormant, battle of, II. 395.
Mortier, Marshal: command in 1805, I. 235-236; defeated at Dürrenstein, I. 238; Friedland, I. 365-370; command in 1812, II. 108; retreat from Moscow, II. 191, 200; Dresden, II. 295, 297, 321-322; Leipzig, II. 350, 353, 367; division in 1814, II. 375, 376; operations, II. 391, 401, 405-406.
Morvilliers, II. 382.
Moscow: campaign, II. 136-186; occupation of, II. 171; retreat from, II. 189-232.
Moskwa, Prince of, II. 399.
Mounier, General, I. 174, 192.
"Mountain," the, and Napoleon, I. 12.

Mouton-Duvernet, General, II. 291.
Mühlbach, I. 113.
Mühldorf, I. 231.
Münster, bridge, I. 218.
Murad Bey, I. 128, 133, 155.
Murat, Marshal (King of Naples):
   Syrian campaign, I. 155, 159-160;
   Marèngo campaign, I. 174, 182,
   186; (1805) sent into Germany,
   I. 202; success at Wertingen, I.
   219-220; crosses the Inn, I. 231;
   advance, I. 234, 236, 238; enters
   Vienna, I. 242; Hollabrunn, I.
   246-248; Austerlitz, I. 250, 260-
   262. Command in Prussia, I.
   279; takes Erfurt, I. 304; Spandau, I. 306-307; engagement at
   Landsberg, I. 337-338; Königsberg, I. 370; command in Spain,
   II. 3. Command in Russia, II.
   109; skirmish at Gridnyeva, II.
   160; capture of Alexinki, II. 161;
   enters Moscow, II. 171; pursues
   Russians, II. 172-173; defeated,
   II. 186; retreat from Moscow, II.
   190, 195, 200; given command of
   army, II. 232; retreats from Vilna,
   II. 234; resigns command, II.
   236. Corps in 1813, II. 283;
   Dresden. II. 295-297, 299, 316,
   322, 328, 335, 340, 342, 344;
   Leipzig, II. 345, 352
Murati, Emissary, I. 10.

NANSOUTY, General, I. 368; II. 34,
   55, 109, 390-391.
Naples, King of. *See* Murat.
Napoleon: ability to exact obedience,
   I. 52-53.
Activity, I. 65.
Ambition, I. 109, 121-122; II. 453.
Arrogance, I. 267-272.
On artillery, I. 371; II. 249.
On cavalry, II. 245-246.
Character, I. 25-26, 83-86; II. 442-
   448.
Conquests a source of weakness to
   France, I. 164.
Courage, I. 119-120, 216.
Energy, II. 321, 452.
Excitability, I. 63.
Execution of prisoners justified, I.
   144-145.
On fortification, I. 345-353; II. 423.
Generalship, II. 446-448.
Imaginative power, II. 443-444.
Immorality, I. 335-336.
Incapacity of subordinates, II. 250,
   288.

Indecision during retreat from
   Moscow, II. 197.
Intellectual qualities, II. 442-448.
Invasion of England, plan, I. 198-
   200.
Lannes' warning to, II. 105.
Leniency, I. 36.
Luck, I. 62.
Marriage with Josephine, I. 22-24.
Mental derangement, II. 416, 418-
   419.
Message to Senate, II. 107.
Military genius, I. 117-122.
Orders to Staff, I. 211.
Personal appearance, I. 25-26.
Proclaimed Emperor, I. 164.
Punishment of subordinates, II. 396.
Refusal to acknowledge danger in
   1812, II. 211, 215.
Relations with the Directory, I. 123-
   124.
Reputation and personal influence,
   I. 108.
Self-confidence, I. 43-44.
Staff, I. 281-282.
Statesmanship, I. 165; II. 451.
Strategy and tactics: Attack, I. 38-
   40; II. 11, 15-16, 91-92, 114.
Boldness of, I. 255.
Cavalry, employment of, I. 213-
   214.
Commissariat, I. 27, 229.
Communications, I. 194-195; II.
   177, 290.
Compared with modern, I. 204.
Comprehensive plans, I. 178-179.
Concealment of strength, II. 139-
   140.
Concentration of forces, I. 40;
   II. 31-32, 337.
Concentric operations, I. 74-75.
Cordon system, II. 6.
Decline of genius, II. 197-199,
   268-270, 298.
Defensive, I. 69-72, 355-356; II.
   266, 278-282.
Early development of, I. 14.
Elimination of chance, I. 119.
Errors, I. 189; II. 307-308, 318-
   320, 326-327, 356-362; re-
   cognition of, I. 84-86.
Firing strength, I. 371.
Five chief principles, I. 167-168.
Lines of operation, II. 53, 358-
   362.
Massed forces, I. 154, 161-162,
   227.
Modern, introduced by, I. 118.
Notes and plans, II. 328-332.

468 INDEX

Organization of troops, II. 178-180.
Original, II. 449.
Pitched battles, I. 263-266.
Pursuit of enemy, I. 262.
Rapid movements, I. 57, 79-80.
Reserves, employment, I. 264-265.
Rules and principles, I. 116.
Theory, mastery of, II. 447-448.
Turning movements, II. 100, 114, 145-146.
Unique qualities as leader, II. 446.
Versatility, I. 84-86.
Want of self-control, II. 191-192.
His birthplace, I. 2; enters Brienne Academy, I. 3; development of character, I. 4; career at Paris Military Academy, I. 4; first appointment, I. 5; interest in Corsican politics, I. 6; fails to gain Lyons Academy prize, I. 6; helps his brother Louis, I. 7; his desire for fame, I. 8; returns to Corsica, I. 9; attempt to capture Ajaccio citadel, I. 10; struck off regiment, I. 10; reinstated, I. 11; writes "Supper of Beaucaire," I. 12; siege of Toulon, I. 12-13; appointed to army of Italy, I. 15; fall of Robespierre—appointed to army of the West, I. 19; memorandum on army of Italy, I. 20; deprived of his appointment, I. 22; conducts fighting in Paris, I. 22.
Campaigns—1796-97 (Italy): early plans, I. 16-18, 20; takes command—proclamation to troops, I. 24; determines to take offensive, I. 27; commissariat arrangements, I. 27; strength of army, I. 29; orders combined attack, I. 30; success of operations, I. 31; attack on Piedmontese, I. 31; victory at Dego, I. 32; advance against Colli, I. 32, 33; attack on Colli, I. 34; issues orders against looting, I. 35; grants armistice, I. 36; difficulties of strategical conditions, I. 37; plans operations in Lombardy, I. 41; advance against Austrians, I. 42, 45-46; success at Lodi, I. 47-48; threatens to resign on appointment of Kellerman, I. 50; character of subordinates, I. 52; Kellerman's appointment revoked, I. 53; fresh advance against Austrians—capture of Pavia, I. 54; passage of Mincio, I. 55-56; rapidity of movements, I. 57; redistributes forces, I. 58; directs siege of Mantua, I. 59; Austrian successes at Brescia and Corona, I. 60; orders retreat on Milan, I. 61; exaggerated view of situation, I. 62; advances against Austrians, I. 64: victory at Lonato, I. 66; determines to attack Würmser, I. 67; Solferino, I. 68; defensive tactics, I. 69-72; renews advance, I. 73; Roveredo entered, I. 75; Caliano, I. 76; Bassano, I. 77; concentration against Würmser, I. 78-80; operations against Alvintzy, I. 81-83; repulsed at Caldiero, I. 88; Arcola, I. 89, 91; attack on Alvintzy, I. 90; advance against Davidovich, I. 92; victory over, I. 93; enemy attack Verona, I. 95; Rivoli, I. 96-99; La Favorita, I. 100; Mantua surrendered, I. 100.
Second campaign of 1797: Strength of army, I. 103; opens campaign, I. 104; advance commenced, I. 105; orders to Joubert, I. 106; opinion of Archduke Charles, I. 108; operations at Tarvis, I. 111-112; Klagenfurt occupied, I. 113; defeat and pursuit of Austrians, I. 113-114; Leoben occupied—conclusion of peace, I. 115; general plan of operations, I. 116-122.
1798-1799 (Egypt); arrives at Alexandria, I. 125; subordinate officers, I. 126; occupies Alexandria, I. 127; defeats Murad Bey, I. 128; Shebreket and Embabeh, I. 129; occupies Cairo and Damietta, I. 130; operations against Ibrahim, I. 130; dissatisfaction in army, I. 131; Salahieh, I. 131; fleet defeated at Aboukir, I. 132; battle of Sediman, I. 133; severity to inhabitants, I. 134-135; discontent in army, I. 136: resignation of Beauvais, I. 137; winter quarters, I. 139-140; orders advance into Syria, I. 142; El Arish and Gaza taken, I. 143; siege of Jaffa, I. 143-145; orders execution of prisoners, I. 144; siege of Acre, I. 146; operations in plains of Jordan, I. 148-149; assault on Acre repulsed, I. 150; orders retreat, I. 152; destroys Jaffa defences, I. 153; reorganization of army, I. 153-154; advance

INDEX 469

against Turks, I. 155-156; arrives at Alexandria, I. 158; victory at Aboukir, I. 159-160; returns to France, I. 161-162.

1800(Italy): military situation,I.165; plan of operations, I. 167; differences with Moreau, I. 168; orders to Massena, I. 169; advance commenced, I. 170; enemy surround Genoa, I. 171; orders invasion of Italy, I. 172; organization of reserve army, I. 174; attack on Fort Bard, I. 176-177, 183; Ivrea taken, I. 178; passage of Alps, I. 178-179; Romano and Vercelli, I. 182; passage of Ticino—Milan entered, I. 183; orders advance across Po, I. 184; success of Suchet, I. 185; fall of Genoa, I, 185; passage of Po, I. 186; Casteggio, I. 187; orders further advance, I. 188-190; Marengo, I. 191-194; concludes peace, I. 194; plan of operations considered, I. 194-196; his opinion on the campaign, I. 9.

1805 (Austria): concentration of army, I. 202; plans, I. 203; formation of army, I. 205-206; distribution of troops in Germany, I. 209; direction of operations, I. 210-211; advance, I. 212-213; employment of cavalry, I. 214; final plans, I. 215; crosses the Rhine, I. 216; advance on Ulm, I. 218; passage of Danube, I. 219; Wertingen, Elchingen, I. 220; orders, I. 221; reverse at Albeck, I. 222; concentration against Mack, I. 223; Elchingen taken, I. 225; Ulm captured, I. 226; victory at Trochtelfingen, I. 227.

(Austerlitz): base, I. 229; concentrates army, I. 230; passage of the Inn, I. 231-232; Braunau taken, I. 232; orders cautious advance, I. 233; engagement on Traun, I. 234; fresh concentration, I. 235; advance on St. Pölten, I. 236; on Vienna, I. 237; reverses at Dürrenstein, I. 238-239; attack on Vienna bridge, I. 241-242; negotiations for truce, I. 242; advance on Krems, I. 243; Vienna occupied, I. 244; Hollabrunn, I. 246-247; Brunn occupied, I. 249; disposition of forces, I. 250; position at Pratzen, I. 254-255; orders for battle, I. 257; Austerlitz, I. 259-261; refuses armistice—orders pursuit of enemy, I. 262; meeting with Emperor Francis at Saroschitz, I. 263.

1806-7 (Prussia): preparations for war, I. 272-273; plan of campaign, I. 274-277; formation of army, I. 278-279; staff, I. 280-283; his anxiety for reports, I. 285; advance to Gera, I. 288; blocks enemy's retreat to Elbe, I. 289; memorandum on general situation, I. 290-291; march on Jena, I. 291-292; orders attack, I. 293-294; battle of Jena, I. 294-296; Hassenhausen I. 297-298; orders pursuit of enemy, I. 303, 304; reproaches Bernadotte for inactivity, I. 306; moral degeneration of army, I. 308-313; refuses agreement with Prussia, I. 315; arrives in Posen, I. 317; operations against Pultusk, I. 317-320; failure of operations in Poland, I. 321-326; winter quarters, I. 326-327; censures Ney, I. 328; determines to hold Thorn, I. 329; pursuit of Russians, I. 330-338; battle of Eylau, I. 338-342; abandons Warsaw, I. 343; orders siege of Danzig, I. 345, 357, 352; defence of Passarge, I. 354; concentration at Saalfeld, I. 360-361; advance to Gutstadt, I. 362; Heilsberg, I. 363 364; Friedland, I. 365-370; orders to corps, I. 367; concludes peace, I. 370; strategical mistakes, I. 372.

1808-9 (Spain): distribution of forces, II. 3: failure of early movements, II. 3-4; instructions, II. 4-6; censures his generals, II. 7; plan to retrieve situation, II. 7-8; incapacity of commanders, II. 8-10; formation of army, II. 10; arrives at Vitoria, II. 12; plan to defeat Castaños, II. 13-16; his want of energy, II.16; advances to Aranda, II. 17; march on Madrid, II. 18; negotiations for surrender of city, II. 19; plan to defeat English, II. 20-22; march to Astorga, II. 23-24; leaves Spain, II. 25; failure of political aims, II. 25-28.

1809 (Austria): disposition of troops, II. 29-31; plans, II. 31-33; formation of army, II. 34;

instructions to Berthier misunderstood, II. 35-39; reaches Donauwörth, II. 40; orders retreat from Ratisbon, II. 41-43; determines to attack enemy, II. 47, 50; victory at Landshut, II. 51-52; his activity, II. 54-55; operations at Eggmühl, II. 55-56; halt at Egglofsheim, II. 56; orders advance to Inn, II. 60; advance on Vienna, II. 61-62, 64; leaves Ratisbon, II. 63; chooses Passau as centre of operations, II. 65; reaches Lambach, II. 65; opinion on Ebelsberg, II. 66-67; establishes headquarters at Mölk, II. 68; Vienna taken, II. 69-70; passage of Danube, II. 71-73; defeat at Asparn, II. 72-83; formaof army in June, II. 83; advice to Eugène, II. 83-84; directs crossing of the Danube, II. 84-89; formation of army in July, II. 87-88; disposition of troops before Wagram, II. 89-91; battle of Wagram, II. 92-96; panic among troops, II. 97; indecisiveness of victory, II. 98-99; concludes armistice—returns to Paris, II. 100.

1812 (Russia): formation of the army, II. 107-109; commissariat arrangements, II. 109; court at Dresden, II. 110; plan of campaign, II. 111-114; passage of the Niemen, II. 114-115; march to Vilna, II. 116; divides his army, II. 117-118; escape of Bagration, II. 119; transport difficulties, II. 121; deprives Jérôme of his command, II. 122; operations against Bagration, II. 123-126; leaves Vilna, II. 127; orders advance to Dwina, II. 128-129; arrives at Bieshenkovitshi, II. 130; advance to Vitebsk, II. 131-133; loss of men, II. 134; rests troops at Vitebsk, II. 136; orders operations against Tormassov, II. 138; orders attack on Wittgenstein, II. 139-140; Oudinot's retreat, II. 141; reverse at Svolna, II. 142; skirmish at Inkovo, II. 143; advance to Smolensk, arrives at Dnieper, II. 144; his change of front, II. 145; attack on Smolensk, II. 147-148, 150-151; passage of Dnieper, II. 151-152; preparations for battle, II. 153; impossibility of success apparent, II. 154-158; estimated strength of forces, II. 160; battle of Borodino, II. 161-168; advance towards Moscow, II. 169; organizes reserve, II. 170; occupation of Moscow, II. 171-172; negotiations with Emperor Alexander, II. 173; formation and strength of army, II. 176; length of communications, II. 177; organization of troops, II. 178-180; decides to retreat—plans, II. 181-285; defeat at Vyankovo—leaves Moscow, II. 186; failure of negotiations, II. 187-188; retreat commenced, II. 189; orders destruction of Kremlin, II. 191; battle of Maloyaroslavets, II. 192-195; retreat to Borovsk, II. 196, 199-200; position on line of retreat, II. 202-203; orders army to march in square, II. 204; pursued by Kutusov, II. 204; his inactivity at Slavkova, II. 206; receives news of Malet's conspiracy, II. 209; orders Victor to attack, II. 210; refuses to acknowledge danger of situation, II. 211; sufferings of the troops, II. 212; orders to Victor, II. 214; departure from Smolensk, II. 216-217; stand at Krasni, II. 218; passage of Dnieper, II. 220-221; plans for crossing the Beresina, II. 222; orders march on Minsk, II. 223; strength of corps, II. 224; advance to Beresina, II. 223; Borissov taken, II. 226; passage of Beresina, II. 226-231; abandons army and returns to Paris, II. 232.

1813 (Germany): plans for reorganizing army, II. 236; displeasure at retreat of army, II. 239; orders defence of Magdeburg, II. 240; plan to relieve Danzig, II. 241; orders attack on Hamburg, II. 243; arrives at Mayence—formation of army, II. 244; lack of cavalry, II. 245; plan for advance into Saxony, II. 247; disorganized state of army, II. 249-250; advance on Liepzig, II. 252; Lützen, II. 253-254; concentration at Dresden, II. 255; passage of Elbe, II. 256; Bautzen, II. 257-259; Preititz, II. 260-261; orders advance on Berlin, II. 263; position of forces, II. 264; truce of Poischwitz, II. 265, 267; defence of the Elbe, II.

271-274; plan of campaign, II. 275; position of troops, II. 276; defensive plans, II. 278-282; strength of army, II. 282-283; advance against Blücher, II. 287; defence of Dresden, II. 290; battle of Dresden, II. 292-299; orders to Vandamme, II. 300; defeat of Vandamme and Macdonald, II. 302-303; plans for advance on Berlin, II. 305-308; position of forces, II. 309-310; demoralization of Macdonald's corps, II. 311; advance against Blücher, II. 312; abandons invasion of Bohemia, II. 314-315; skirmishes round Nollendorf, II. 316-317; failure of plans, II. 318-320; concentrates army at Dresden, II. 322; retreats across Elbe, II. 323; battle of Wartenburg, II. 325; errors in judgment, II. 326-327; notes on the situation, II. 328-332; decides to abandon Dresden, II. 333; plan of operations, II. 334-336; orders defence of Dresden, II. 337; orders concentration at Leipzig, II. 342; outmanœuvred by enemy, II. 344; battle of Leipzig, II. 346-356; cause of defeat, II. 356-362; retreats, II. 363; hears of Bavarians' advance, II. 366; Hanau, II. 367-368; returns to Paris, II. 369.
1814 (France): defence of the Rhine, II. 370; plans and arrangements, II. 372-375; concentration of forces, II. 376; joins army and assumes offensive, II. 377; takes Brienne, II. 378; La Rothiere, II. 381; disorganization of army, II. 383; operations on Seine, II. 384; decides to attack enemy, II. 388; victory at Champaubert, II. 390; Montmirail, II. 391; Étoges, II. 393; advances against Schwarzenberg, II. 394; fall of Soissons, II. 402; engagements at Craonne and Laon, II. 404-406; takes Rheims, II. 407; advance against Austrians—plans, II. 408-410; Arcis-sur-Aube, II. 411-412; marches on Vitry, II. 413-414; starts for Paris, II. 415; surrender of the city, II. 416; agrees to abdicate, II. 417; departure for Elba, II. 419.
1815 (Belgium): lands in France, II. 420; alternative plans, II.

421-423; strength and formation of army, II. 424; commences operations, II. 425; advance towards Brussels, II. 426; his ill-health, II. 427; inactivity and delay, II. 428-430; attack commenced—Saint Amand and Ligny, II. 431; Quatre-Bras, II. 432, 434; pursues the English, II. 436; battle of Waterloo, II. 437-441; his return to Paris and abdication, II. 441-442.
Nassielsk, I. 320-321.
Naumburg, council of war, I. 284.
Nauslitz, II. 297.
Negroes, plan to incorporate in army, I. 154.
Neisse, river, II. 312.
Ney, Marshal: command in 1805, I. 206; defence of Danube, I. 215, 216; captures Elchingen, I. 225; bombards Ulm, I. 226. Command in 1809, II. 279; siege of Magdeburg, I. 314; censured for advance to Königsberg, I. 328; engagement at Waltersdorf, I. 334; takes Gutstadt, I. 354; retreat to Deppen, I. 359-360, 361; battle of Friedland, I. 365-370. Command in Spain, II. 10; success at Logroño, II. 11; march to Soria, II. 13; refuses to intercept Castaños, II. 14-15. Corps in Russia, II. 108; captures Krasny, II. 146; attacks Barclay, II. 152; retreat from Moscow, II. 191, 199, 204, 206; crosses Dnieper, II. 220-221; rejoins main army, II. 223; ordered to hold Bobe, II. 226; crosses Beresina, II. 230; retreat, II. 234. Corps in 1813, II. 244, 248; Lützen, II. 253; ordered to Torgau, II. 255; Bautzen, II. 258; Preititz, 260-261; strength of corps, II. 282; Dresden, II. 295; advance to Berlin, II. 309; operations on Elbe, II. 324, 328, 342; Leipzig, II. 348. Command in 1814, II. 375; operations against Schwarzenberg, II. 395; and Blücher, 405-406, 410-412; attack on Vitry, II. 413; advises abdication of Napoleon, II. 415-416; joins Emperor in 1815, II. 426; reproached by Napoleon, II. 429; action at Saint Amand, II. 431; repulsed at Quatre-Bras, II. 432, 434; battle of Waterloo, II. 437-441.

472 INDEX

Nied, Treaty of, II. 366.
Niemen, river, I. 370; II. 114-115.
Nogent-sur-Seine, II. 384-393.
Nollendorf, II. 316-317.
Numerical superiority, Napoleon's reliance on, I. 154, 227.

OCHS, General, II. 108.
Offenstetten, battle of, II. 45.
Officers: importance of efficiency, I. 51; Napoleon's complaints concerning, II. 250; incapable of independent action, II. 288.
Ollschann, I. 251.
Olssufiev, General, II. 386, 387, 390.
Operations, interior and exterior lines, 358-362.
Orsha, II. 221-223.
Osterode, I. 343-344.
Ostrolenka, battle of, I. 344-345.
Ott, General, I. 175, 187, 189, 192.
Oudinot, Marshal: command in 1805, I. 206; Friedland, I. 366-370; command in 1809, II. 29, 34; Corps in 1812, II. 108; attacks Vilkomir, II. 117; engagement at Kliastitsi, II. 139; defeat at Svolna, II. 142; attacks Polotsk, II. 175; retreat from Moscow, II. 222, 224, 225, 226, 229; Bautzen, II. 259; advance on Berlin, II. 263, 277; strength of corps, II. 282; Grossbeeren, II. 303; retreat, II. 309; new command, II. 325; Leipzig, II. 328, 334, 350. Campaign of 1814: II. 395, 327, 412; advises Napoleon to abdicate, II. 416.
Ourcq, river, II. 401.

PACHRA, river, II. 198.
Pajol, General, II. 346, 424, 425.
Palafox, General, II. 4, 11, 14-15.
Palencia, II. 3.
Paoli, Governor of Corsica, I. 11.
Papal Government and Napoleon, I. 103.
Papelotte, II. 439, 440.
Paris: street fighting, I. 122; operations for defence, II. 384-395; enemy's advance on, II. 414-415; surrendered, II. 416; treaty, II. 418.
Paris Military Academy, I. 4.
Park, General, I. 290.
Partouneaux, General, II. 109, 230.
Passarge, river, I. 341, 343-344, 353-361.
Passau, II. 65.

Paunsdorf, II. 355.
Pavia, I. 36, 54.
Peninsular War. *See* Spain.
Peschiera, I. 56, 59.
Pfaffenhofen, II. 42-44.
Phelippeaux, Picard de, I. 147.
Piacenza, I. 46, 186.
Piave, river, I. 104.
Piedmont: plan for conquest of, I. 20; position of Italian army, I. 26, 29; attacked by French, I. 31-32, 34; defeaced at Vico, I. 35.
Pillnitz bridge, II. 323.
Pino, General, II. 108.
Pirna, II. 293, 297, 299, 316, 323.
Pizzighettone, I. 49.
Plagwitz, II. 348.
Planchenoit, II. 439-440.
Planeau, II. 294, 297.
Pleisse, river, II. 346.
Po, river, I. 46, 184, 186-187.
Podolsk, II. 172-173.
Poischwitz, truce of, II. 265, 267.
Poland: campaign of 1806, I. 316-328.
Polish corps in Russian campaign, II. 108, 109.
Polotsk, II. 175, 203.
Poniatowski, Prince: command in 1812, II. 108; takes Doronino, II. 161; retreat from Moscow, II. 191, 200, 205; corps in 1813, II. 282; Leipzig, II. 324, 346.
Posen, II. 236, 237.
Posthenen, I. 366.
Praga, I. 318.
Prague, II. 306.
Pratzen, I. 254, 255; battle of, I. 259-260.
Pregel, river, I. 370.
Preititz, battle of, II. 261.
Pristen, II. 302.
Probsthayda, II. 355.
Provera, General, I. 31, 94, 99. 100.
Prschibitschewski, General, I. 256, 259, 261.
Prussia—campaign of 1806-1807: preparations and plans, I. 272-278; disposition of armies, I. 276-278; French advance, I. 279; Napoleon's staff, I. 280-283; Prussian advance, I. 284-285; Saalfeld, I. 286-287; French advance to Jena, I. 289, 293; battle of Jena, I. 294-302; Hassenhausen, I. 296-298; Erfurt surrendered, I. 304; Halle, I. 304-305; Spandau surrendered, I. 306; Prussian defeat—surrender of Hohenlohe, I. 307; surrender of Blücher, I. 308; Lübeck taken—

INDEX 473

cruelty of French, I. 308-313; siege of Magdeburg, I. 314; French advance, I. 315; Warsaw evacuated, I. 317; advance of Russians, I. 319; engagement at Nassidsk, I. 320; battle of Pultusk, I. 322-326; French winter quarters, I. 327; Russian advance, I. 328; pursued by French, I. 330-337; Eylau, I. 338-342; French concentration at Osterode, I. 343; battle of Ostrolenka, I. 344-345; siege of Danzig, I. 345, 357-358; Braunsberg evacuated, I. 353; Gutstadt taken, I. 354; Russians assume the offensive, I. 359-361; Heilsberg, I. 362-364; Friedland, I. 365-370; conclusion of peace, I. 370.
Prussian troops: *in* 1812, II. 109; alliance with Russians at Tauroggen, II. 235.
1813: Disposition, II. 242, 243, 248; driven from Lützen, II. 251; Leipzig, II. 252; battle of Lützen, II. 253-254; Königswartha, II. 258; Bautzen, II. 258-259; Pretitz, II. 260-262; truce of Poischwitz, II. 265; position in August, II. 283; advance to Bober, II. 287; Dresden, II. 294-301; Katzbach—Grossbeeren, II. 303; retreat into Silesia, II. 312; fresh advance on Dresden, II. 313, 316, 317; Wartenberg, II. 323; general advance, II. 325; strength, II. 328, 338; retreat to Saale, II. 339, 341; Leipzig, II. 347-356; pursuit of French, II. 364.
1814: advance across Rhine, II. 373, 375; Brienne, II. 378; La Rothiere, II. 381-382; operations on Seine, II. 384; Champaubert, II. 390; Montmirail, II. 391; Étoges, II. 393; advance continued, II. 397-401; Soissons taken, II. 402; Laon, II. 405; march on Paris, II. 414, 416.
1815: base, II. 422; strength, II. 424; retreat from Charleroi, II. 425-426; concentrate at Sombreffe, II. 428; Ligny—Saint Amand, II. 431; Waterloo, II. 435, 438-441.
Pully, General, II. 96.
Pultusk, battle of, I. 316, 328.
Pursuit, Napoleon's theory *re*, I. 262.

QUATRE-BRAS: held by English, II. 426; Ney blamed for not taking, II. 429; French repulsed at, II. 432; second attack, II. 434.
Queiss, river, II. 312.
Quosdanovich, General, I. 60, 65, 66, 67.

RAAB, battle of, II. 84.
Ragusa, Duke of, II. 334, 342.
Rahna, II. 253.
Rampon, Colonel, I. 30, 156.
Ratisbon: events of, II. 29, 59; surrendered by French, II. 50; retaken, II. 61; measures for holding, II. 62.
Razout, General, II. 108.
Reggio, Duke of, II. 342.
Reille, General, II. 424, 437.
Reserves, employment of, I. 264-265.
Reudnitz, II. 346-347.
Reuss, Prince, II. 300.
Rey, General, I, 93, 97, 98.
Reynier, General: Egyptian campaign, I. 126, 129, 139, 142; command in 1812, II. 108; joins Schwarzenberg, II. 137-138; attack at Gorodetshna, II. 138-139; corps in 1813, II. 282; Dresden, II. 325, 341, 342; Leipzig, II. 346-356.
Rheims, II. 403, 407.
Rhine Confederation States—forces mobilized, II. 30.
Rhine, Advance to, in 1805, II. 209; passage, II. 212; defence of, in 1814, II. 370; enemy's advance across, II. 375.
Ried, I. 233.
Riesch, General, I. 217.
Riga, siege of, II. 142.
Rivaud, General, I. 260.
Rivoli, battle of, I. 92, 96-99.
Robespierre and Napoleon, I. 12, 13, 19.
Rödingen, I. 295.
Romano, I. 182.
Rome, peace with, I. 103.
Ronco, I. 89.
Rosas, II. 20.
Rosasna, II. 144.
Roverbella, I. 59.
Roveredo, I. 75.
Rüchel, General, I. 276, 289, 296.
Rules and principles (military) recognized by Napoleon, I. 116-117.
Russbach, river, II. 96.
Russia, campaign in (1812): formation of army, II. 107-109; advance to Vistula, II. 109; commissariat arrangements, II. 110; position of

Russians, II. 110-111; Napoleon's plan of campaign, II. 111-114; passage of Niemen, II. 114-115; march on Vilna, II. 115-117; division of the army, II. 118; Russian retreat, II. 117-121; transport difficulties, II. 121-122; Jérôme's incapacity, II. 122-123; attempt to surround Bagration, II. 123-125; Barclay's retreat, II. 125-128; resignation of Jérôme, II. 128; passage of Bieshenkovitshi, II. 129, 130; advance to Vitebsk, II. 131; retreat of Russians, II. 131-132; failure of French operations, II. 133-135; reverse at Kobrin, II. 137; Reynier joins Schwarzenberg, II. 138; Gorodetshna, II. 138-139; Kliastitsi, II. 139-142; Svolna, II. 142; siege of Riga, II. 142; operations against Smolensk, II. 142-151; passage of Dnieper, II. 151-153; Barclay's stand at Usvyatye, II. 152-153; Kutasov assumes command of Russian army, II. 153; impossibility of Napoleon's success, II. 154-159; Borodino, II. 159-168; Russian retreat, II. 169; Moscow evacuated, II. 170-172; negotiations, II. 173; Tormassov reinforced by Moldavian army, II. 174; attack on Polotsk, II. 175; French retreat imperative—consideration of plans, II. 176-186; Russian success at Vyankovo, II. 186; failure of peace negotiations, II. 187-188; retreat from Moscow begun, II. 189; battle of Maloyaroslavets, II. 192-195; retreat of French, II. 196; position on lines of communication, II. 202-203; order of march changed, II. 204; pursuit by Kutusov, II. 204-209; French defeat at Tshashniki, II. 210; sufferings of army, II. 211-212; Smolensk reached, II. 213, 216-217; stand at Krasni, II. 218-219; Dnieper crossed, II. 220-221; plans for retreat across Beresina, II. 222-225; Borissov occupied, II. 226; passage of river at Studienka, II. 226-227, 229-231; command given to Murat, II. 232; retreat into Poland, II. 234-236; convention of Tauroggen, II. 235.

Russian Troops—Austrian campaign (1805): combination with Austrians, I. 201; position, I. 209; inactivity, I. 221; Kutusov takes command, I. 230; engagement on Traun, I. 234; retreat, I. 235, 237; Durrenstein, I. 238; retreat from Krems, I. 244; Hollabrunn, I. 246-247; retreat, I. 248, 249, 251; advance against French, I. 253-256, 258-259; battle of Austerlitz, I. 260-261; retreat of Holitsch, I. 263.
Prussian campaign (1806): attempt to cross frontier, I. 316; evacuate Warsaw, I. 317; engagement at Nassielsk, I. 320-321; Pultusk, I. 322-328; advance to Mohrungen, I. 328-329; pursued by French, I. 330-338; Eylau, I. 338-342; Ostrolenka, I. 344-345; takes the offensive, I. 359-361; Heilsberg, I. 361-364; Friedland, I. 365-370.
1812 campaign. *See* above, under Russia.
1813 Campaign: advance into Prussia, II. 237; disposition, II. 242-243, 248; fighting at Leipzig, II. 252; Lützen, II. 253-254; retreat, II. 256; Königswartha, II. 258; Bautzen, II. 258-269; Preititz, II. 260-261; retreat, II. 262; truce of Poischwitz, II. 261; position in August, II. 283; Dresden, II. 289, 294-301; Katzbach, II. 303; retreat into Silesia, II. 312; fresh advance on Dresden, II. 313-316; operations in Saxony, II. 317, 323, 325; strength and positions, II. 328, 338; retire to Saale, II. 339, 341; battle of Leipzig, II. 347-356; pursuit of French, II. 364.
1814 Campaign: march towards Rhine, II. 373, 379; La Rothiere, II. 381-382; operations on Seine, II. 384; defeat at Champaubert, II. 390; engagements with French, II. 391, 393; repulsed at Craonne, II. 404; march on Paris, II. 414-416.

Rustum, I. 281.
Rybka, château of, II. 154.

Saalburg, I. 285.
Saale, river, II. 248.
Saalfeld, I. 286-287, 288.
Saar, river, II. 375.
Sacile, I. 105.

INDEX 475

Sacken, General, II. 215, 224, 386-387, 391.
Sahugnet, General, I. 62, 73, 78.
Saifnitz, I. 112.
Saint-Amand, battle of, II. 431.
St. Bernard Pass, I. 172-173, 175.
Saint-Cyr, Carra, II. 34, 69.
   Gouvion : corps in Spain, II. 10, 11 ; captures Rosas, II. 20; command in 1812, II. 108; repulsed at Polotsk, II. 203; corps in 1813, II. 282; orders, II. 285; defence of Dresden, II. 291, 332-333, 334, 337.
St. Dizier, II. 377, 378, 379, 414.
St. Hilaire, General, I. 206; 339; II. 34.
St. Jean d'Angely, Regnault de, II. 106.
St. Petersburg suburb, II. 151.
St. Pölten, I. 236-237.
St. Sulpice, General, II. 34, 55.
Salahieh, I. 131.
Saliceti and Napoleon, I. 11-13.
Salo, I. 60, 65.
Salzburg, I. 233.
Sambre, river, II. 425.
San Marco, I. 98.
San Michele, I. 82.
Santander, II. 3-4.
Saragossa : siege of, II. 4, 6, 20 ; Spanish retreat to, II. 14-15.
Saroschitz, I. 263.
Sauret, General, I. 59, 60, 65, 68.
Savary, General, I. 203; 253, 331, 344-345.
Saxony : Lützen campaign, II. 247-270 ; Dresden, II. 271-304; Leipzig, II. 305-369.
Scherer and Napoleon, I. 21.
Schippenbeil, I. 365.
Schleiz, I. 285.
Schmoditten, I. 366.
Schrannau, I. 370.
Schwarzenberg, Prince : army in 1805, I. 217 ; Russian campaign, command, II. 109 ; joins Reynier, II. 138 ; attack on Tormassov, II. 138-139; retreat before Tshitshagon, II. 202 ; crosses the Bug, II. 214-215 ; strength of corps, II. 224 ; alliance with Russians at Tauroggen, II. 237.
   Position of army in 1813, II. 283 ; battle of Dresden, II. 294-301 ; defeats Vandamme, II. 302; advance on Dresden, II. 313; success of operations, II. 316-317, 319; renewed advance, II. 325,
328, 344-345 ; Leipzig, II. 347-356; pursues French, II. 364 ; marches to Rhine, II. 373, 375 ; advance on Langres, II. 376 ; joins Blücher, II. 381 ; occupies Troyes, II. 385 ; Sens and Nogent, II. 393 ; French advance against, II. 394, 397 ; operations on Aube, II. 398, 403, 408, 410 ; battle of Arcis, II. 411-412; march on Paris, II. 414, 416; negotiations with Marmont, II. 417.
Sebastiani, General, II. 255, 311, 347, 411.
Sediman, battle of, I. 133.
Sedlitz, II. 313.
Seeger, General, I. 206.
Segonzano, I. 82.
Seidnitz, II. 297.
Seiffertshayn, II. 350-351.
Seine : defence of, II. 384 ; operations on, II. 395.
Semionovskaya, II. 162-163, 164.
Senarmont, General, I. 369.
Sens, II. 393.
Separate action, qualities requisite for, II. 362.
Serpallen, I. 339, 340.
Serurier, Marshal : character, I. 52 ; command in Italy, I. 26; attack on Ceva, I. 34 ; success at Vico, I. 35 ; advance towards Mantua, I. 55, 56 ; invests Mantua, I. 60, 64 ; force in 1797, I. 103.
Sezanne, II. 386-390, 399.
Sezmilly, II. 405.
Shebreket, battle of, II. 129.
Shiwardino, II. 160, 161.
Shooting, importance of good, I. 371.
Siegenthal, General, II. 109.
Sieges : Acre, I. 146-152.
   Danzig, I. 345, 357, 358.
   Hamburg, II. 243, 265.
   Jaffa, I. 143-145.
   Magdeburg, I. 314.
   Mantua, I. 59, 64, 68-71.
   Riga, II. 142.
   Saragossa, II. 4, 6, 20.
   Toulon, I. 12-13.
Silesia, operations in, II. 288-289, 311-312.
Skaisgirren, I. 370.
Slavkova, II. 206.
Slonim, II. 137.
Smohain, II. 438, 440.
Smolensk : French march on, II. 142-150 ; evacuated, II. 151 ; French position at, II. 202-203 ; retreat from, II. 212, 216-217.

Smolianski, II. 210.
Smorgonj, II. 232.
Soissons, II. 402, 403.
Sokolnitz, battle of, I. 258-259, 261.
Solferino, battle of, I. 68.
Sombreffe, II. 428.
Somo-Sierra pass, II. 19.
Songis, General, I. 281.
Sortlack forest, I. 366.
Souham, General, II. 289, 325, 328, 346.
Soult, Marshal: command in 1805, I. 206, 215; captures Memmingen, I. 226; success at Sokolnitz, I. 261; command in Prussia, I. 278; orders, I. 285, 287, 290; Jena, I. 295; enters Eylau, I. 338; takes Laoden, I. 363; Königsberg, I. 370. Spain: success at Burgos, II. 12; plan to defeat English, II. 21-22, 24-25; appointment in 1815, II. 424.
Spain, campaign in: disposition of forces, II. 3; failure of early operations, II. 3-4; Baylen, II. 5; Madrid evacuated, II. 6; Vimiero, II. 6; retreat behind Ebro, II. 6-8; Napoleon assumes command, II. 10; position of Spanish army, II. 11; Blake defeated at Espinosa, II. 12-13; Gamoral, II. 12; La Romana takes command of Spanish, II. 13; Tudela and Tarazona, II. 13-15; movements of English army, II.; 17-18; Spanish defeat at Borja, II. 18; Napoleon marches to Madrid, II. 17-19; city surrendered, II. 20; plan to defeat English, II. 20-22; retreat of Moore, II. 23-25; failure of Napoleon's aims, II. 25-28.
Spandau, I. 306-307; II. 236.
Stadtamhof, II. 50.
Staff, Napoleon's, I. 281-282; orders, I. 211.
Starsiedel, II. 253, 254.
Steingel, General, I. 26, 52.
Steinheil, General, II. 203.
Stettin, I. 307; II. 236.
Stötteritz, II. 355.
Stradella, I. 188.
Strasburg, II. 373.
Strategy: attack, I. 38-40; II. 91-92. Communications, I. 194-195; II. 290. Concealment of strength, II. 139-140. Concentration of forces, I. 40; II. 31-32, 337. Concentric operations, I. 74-75, 116.

Cordon system, II. 6.
Decline of Napoleon's, II. 268-270.
Defensive, I. 69-72, 355-356; II. 278-282.
Elimination of chance. I. 119.
Exterior lines of operation, II. 358-362.
Five chief principles, I. 167-168.
Fortification, I. 345-353; II. 423.
Interior lines of operation, II. 53, 358-362.
Massed forces, employment, I. 154, 161-162, 227; II. 357-362, 449.
Mistakes in, I. 16-18, 20, 84-86, 189; after Dresden, II. 301, 307, 318-320, 326-327; at Leipzig, II. 356-362.
Mobilization, I. 204.
Modern, I. 118, 204, 263-264.
Neglect of details, I. 14, 179.
Penetration of enemy's centre, II. 15-16, 114.
Pitched battles, I. 263.
Pursuit, I. 262.
Rapid movements, I. 57, 77-78; II. 293.
Reserves, employment, I. 264-265.
Retreat, II. 197-199.
Rules and principles, I. 116-117, 167.
Self-confidence, value of, I. 43.
Separate action, II. 362.
Theory, II. 447-448.
Traditions, value of, I. 240-241.
Turning movements, II. 114, 145-146.
Studienka, II. 226, 229-231.
Stura valley, I. 17.
Suchet, General, I. 175, 185, 206.
"Supper of Beaucaire," I. 12.
Süssenbrunn, II. 94-96
Svolna, battle of, II. 142.
Syrian campaign: French advance, I. 142; El Arish and Gaza taken, I. 143; siege of Jaffa, I. 143-145; shooting of prisoners, I. 144; Korssum, I. 145; siege of Acre, I. 146; operations on Jordan, I. 148-149; assault on Acre, I. 150; retreat ordered, I. 152; Jaffa defences destroyed, I. 153.

TACTICS: bold, I. 255.
Decline of Napoleon's genius, II. 298.
Employment of cavalry, I. 213-214.
Firing strength, I. 370.
Tagliamento, river, I. 105-107.
Tarazona, battle of, II. 14.
Tarentum, Duke of, II. 309, 342.

INDEX 477

Tarvis, I. 111-112.
Taucha, II. 342, 355.
Tauentzien, General, II. 341, 343.
Tauroggen, Convention, II. 235.
Tellnitz, battle of, I. 258-259, 261.
Teplitz, II. 313-314.
Tharreau, General, II. 34, 108.
Theory, strategical, value of, II. 447-448.
Thonberg, II. 353.
Thorn, I. 372.
Ticino, river, I. 183.
Tilly, General, I. 206.
Tilsit, I. 370; II. 235.
Tolentino, Peace of, I. 103.
Torcy-le-Grand, battle of, II. 411.
Torgau, II. 255.
Tormassov, General, II. 125, 130, 138, 248.
Tortona, I. 36, 45.
Toulon, siege of, I. 12-13.
Trannes, II. 378.
Traun, river, I. 234; II. 66.
Trautenberg, General, II. 109.
Treaties : Cintra, II. 17.
 Fontainebleau, II. 2.
 Nied, II. 366.
 Paris, II. 418.
 Tauroggen, II. 235.
Treilhard, General, I. 206.
Trent, I. 73, 76.
Treviso, Duke of, II. 300, 342.
Trochtelfingen, battle of, I. 227.
Troïtskoye, II. 189.
Troyes, II. 384, 385, 397, 398, 403.
Tshashniki, II. 210.
Tshitshagov, General: joins Tormassov, II. 174; advance to Brest-Litovsk II. 202; to Minsk, II. 215; occupies Minsk, II. 222; strength of army, II. 224; evacuates Borissov, II. 226, 228; attacks French on Beresina, II. 230; pursues French, II. 234-235.
Tudela, battle of, II. 14.
Turkish army: lands at Aboukir, I. 156; position, I. 158; defeat at Aboukir, I. 159-160.
Turning movements, principle of, I. 168.
Tyrol : campaign of, 1797, I. 102-115 ; subjugation of abandoned, II. 82.

ULM campaign (1805), I. 201-227; capture of city, I. 226.
Unstrut, river. II. 365.
Usha, river, II. 153.
Ushatsh, river, II. 203.
Usvyatye, II. 152-153.
Uvorova, II. 219.

VALEGGIO, I. 56.
Valence, I. 5.
Valencia, II. 3.
Valladolid, II. 3.
Valmaseda, II. 11-12.
Vandamme, General : character, I. 312-313. Command in 1805, I. 206; captures Münster, I. 218; defeated at Kulm, I. 239; Austerlitz, I. 261 ; command in 1809, II. 34; repulsed at Linz, II. 70-71 ; command in Russia, II. 108; capture of Hamburg, II. 265, 257 ; strength of corps, II. 282; Dresden, II. 292, 296, 299 ; division defeated, II. 302; Waterloo campaign, II. 424, 431.
Vaubois, General, I. 58, 73, 82, 83, 92. 93.
Vauchamps, II. 393.
Vercelli, I. 182.
Verdier, General, II. 4, 108.
Vereya, II. 191-193.
Verona, I. 95; II. 236.
Vial, General, I. 127, 129, 130.
Vialannes, General, I. 206.
Viasma, II. 154, 202, 204, 205-208.
Vico, battle of, I. 35.
Victor, Marshal (Duke of Belluno): position in Italy, I. 94; retreat from Marengo, I. 192 ; battle of Friedland, I. 365-370 ; command in Spain, II. 10-11 ; operations against Blake, II. 12-13; command in Russia, II. 109 ; position at Smolensk, II. 202-203 : orders, II. 204; defeated at Tshashniki, II. 210 ; orders, II. 214, 222-223 ; moves on Loshnitsa, II. 227-228 ; crosses Beresina, II. 231 ; strength of corps in 1813, II. 282; Leipzig, II. 325, 334, 346; Hanau, II. 367-368 ; defence of Rhine, II. 370, 373, 375 ; La Rothiere, II. 381; evacuates Nogent, II. 393; dismissed from command, II. 395
Vienna : Congress (1815), II. 421.
 Imperial Council of War, I. 231.
 Napoleon's advance on, I. 237 ; attack on bridge, I. 241-242; city occupied, I. 244 ; advance on, in 1809, II. 61-62, 64 ; evacuated by Austrians, II. 69-70.
Vierzehnheiligen, I. 295-296.
Viesselovo, II. 225.
Vilna, II. 115-117, 234.
Vimiero, battle of, II. 6.
Vistula, river, II. 109.
Vitebsk, II. 214.

Vitry-le-François, II. 376, 413, 414-415.
Vives, General, II. 11.
Voltri, I. 29.
Vop, river, II. 212-213.
Vyankovo, battle of, II. 186.

WACHAU, II. 345, 348, 350, 355.
Wagram: campaign, II. 60-103; battle, II. 92-97.
Waltersdorf, I. 334.
Walther, General, I. 206.
Warsaw, I. 317.
Wartenburg, battle of, II. 325-327.
Waterloo: campaign, II. 420-442; battle of, II. 437-441.
Wavre, II. 438.
Wehlau, I. 369.
Weimar, I. 296-298.
Duke of, I. 305.
Weissenfels, II. 364-365.
Weisseritz, river, II. 295-297.
Wellington, Duke of: Vimiero, II. 6; army in 1815, II. 424; concentration of forces, II. 428; Quatre-Bras, II. 432-434; retires towards Brussels, II. 436; Waterloo, II. 437-444.
Wels, II. 65.
Wertingen, I. 220.
Westphalia, King of. *See* Jérôme Bonaparte.
Widderitzsch, II. 349.
Winzingerode, General, I. 201; II. 248.
Wittenberg, II. 340-341.

Wittgenstein, General: engagement at Kliastitsi, II. 139; defeats Oudinot, II. 142; attack at Polotsk, II. 175, 203; success at Tshashniki, II. 210; captures Vitebsk, II. 214; strength of army, II. 224; defeats Partouneaux, II. 230; advance against Eugène, II. 236-243; army in 1813, II. 248; crosses the Elster, II. 251.
Wolfnitz, II. 297.
Worms, II. 370.
Wrede, General, II. 34, 61, 63, 108, 366-368.
Würmser, General: army, I. 59; success at Corona, I. 60; advance against French, I. 65; action at Castiglione, I. 66; Solferino, I. 68; retreat into Tyrol, I. 68; distribution of force, I. 73; defeat at Bassano, I. 77; retreat to Mantua, I. 78; joined by Provera, I. 99; surrenders Mantua, I. 100.
Würtemberg, Prince of, II. 108, 300.
Würzburg, I. 273-274.
Wurzen, II. 334-335.

YORCK, General, II. 235, 349, 364, 379, 384.

ZAJONCZEK, General, II. 108.
Zehdenick, I. 307.
Zittau, II. 284-286.
Zuckelhausen, II. 355.
Zusmarshaussen, I. 220.
Zweinaundorf, II. 355.

TITLES OF NAPOLEON'S MARSHALS AND OF HIS MOST PROMINENT GENERALS AND MINISTERS.

As many of Napoleon's marshals and most prominent generals and ministers are frequently mentioned by their titles of nobility, which are less known than their proper names, the reader will find the following lists convenient for reference.

MARSHALS.

Augereau,	appointed	1804,	Duke of Castiglione.
Bernadotte,	"	1804,	Prince of Ponte Corvo. Crown Prince of Sweden, King of Sweden.
Berthier,	"	1804,	Duke of Neufchâtel, Prince of Wagram.
Brune,	"	1804,	Count Brune.
Bessières,	"	1804,	Duke of Istria.
Davout,	"	1804,	Duke of Auerstädt, Prince of Eggmühl.
Grouchy,	"	1815,	Count Grouchy.
Jourdan,	"	1804,	Count Jourdan.
Kellerman,	"	1804,	Duke of Valmy.
Lannes,	"	1804,	Duke of Montebello.
Lefebvre,	"	1804,	Duke of Danzig.
Macdonald,	"	1809,	Duke of Tarentum.
Marmont,	"	1809,	Duke of Ragusa.
Massena,	"	1804,	Duke of Rivoli, Prince of Essling.
Moncey,	"	1804,	Duke of Conegliano.
Mortier,	"	1804,	Duke of Treviso.
Murat,	"	1804,	Grand Duke of Berg, King of Naples.
Ney,	"	1804,	Duke of Elchingen, Prince of Moskwa.
Oudinot,	"	1809,	Duke of Reggio.
Perignon,	"	1804,	Count Perignon.
Poniatowski,	"	1813,	Prince of Poland.
Serrurier,	"	1804,	Count Serrurier.
Soult,	"	1804,	Duke of Dalmatia.
Saint-Cyr,	"	1812,	Marquis Gouvion-Saint-Cyr.
Suchet,	"	1811,	Duke of Albufera.
Victor,	"	1807,	Duke of Belluno.

MOST PROMINENT GENERALS AND MINISTERS.

Arrighi,	Duke of Padua.
Bonaparte, Jerome,	King of Westphalia.
Bonaparte, Joseph,	King of Naples and King of Spain.
Bonaparte, Louis,	King of Holland.
Cambacérès,	Prince of Parma.
Caulaincourt,	Duke of Vicenza.
Champagny,	Duke of Cadore.
Clarke,	Duke of Feltre.
Drouet,	Count Erlon.
Eugene, Beauharnais,	Prince of Venice and Viceroy of Italy.
Fouché,	Duke of Otranto.
Junot,	Duke of Abrantès.
Lebrun,	Duke of Piacenza.
Maret,	Duke of Bassano.
Mouton,	Count Lobau.
Reynier,	Duke of Massa.
Savary,	Duke of Rovigo.
Talleyrand,	Prince of Benevento.
Vandamme,	Count Unebourg.

www.ingramcontent.com/pod-product-compliance
Lightning Source LLC
Chambersburg PA
CBHW060027180426
43195CB00051B/2198